CHINA'S SECOND REVOLUTION

HARRY HARDING

CHINA'S SECOND REVOLUTION

Reform after Mao

A study produced in cooperation with
the Council on Foreign Relations

The Brookings Institution | Washington, D.C.

Library of Congress Cataloging-in-Publication data:

Harding, Harry
   China's second revolution: reform after Mao/Harry Harding.
   p. cm.
   Includes bibliographies and index.
   ISBN 0-8157-3462-X   ISBN 0-8157-3461-1 (pbk.)
   1. China—Economic policy—1976– 2. China—Foreign economic
relations. 3. China—Politics and government—1976– I. Title.
HC427.92.H37 1987   87-27235
338.951—dc19   CIP

9 8 7 6 5 4 3

THE BROOKINGS INSTITUTION is an independent organization devoted to nonpartisan research, education, and publication in economics, government, foreign policy, and the social sciences generally. Its principal purposes are to aid in the development of sound public policies and to promote public understanding of issues of national importance.

The Institution was founded on December 8, 1927, to merge the activities of the Institute for Government Research, founded in 1916, the Institute of Economics, founded in 1922, and the Robert Brookings Graduate School of Economics and Government, founded in 1924.

The Board of Trustees is responsible for the general administration of the Institution, while the immediate direction of the policies, program, and staff is vested in the President, assisted by an advisory committee of the officers and staff. The by-laws of the Institution state: "It is the function of the Trustees to make possible the conduct of scientific research, and publication, under the most favorable conditions, and to safeguard the independence of the research staff in the pursuit of their studies and in the publication of the results of such studies. It is not a part of their function to determine, control, or influence the conduct of particular investigations or the conclusions reached."

The President bears final responsibility for the decision to publish a manuscript as a Brookings book. In reaching his judgment on the competence, accuracy, and objectivity of each study, the President is advised by the director of the appropriate research program and weighs the views of a panel of expert outside readers who report to him in confidence on the quality of the work. Publication of a work signifies that it is deemed a competent treatment worthy of public consideration but does not imply endorsement of conclusions or recommendations.

The Institution maintains its position of neutrality on issues of public policy in order to safeguard the intellectual freedom of the staff. Hence interpretations or conclusions in Brookings publications should be understood to be solely those of the authors and should not be attributed to the Institution, to its trustees, officers, or other staff members, or to the organizations that support its research.

For Roca

THIS volume is an overview of China's "second revolution"—the sweeping political and economic reforms undertaken in the post-Mao era under the leadership of Deng Xiaoping. The reforms are unsurpassed in scope and complexity, involving nothing less than a fundamental reshaping of Chinese society. Almost every institution in the country—from stores to farms, factories to universities, and military units to Party committees—has seen tremendous changes in personnel, structure, and operation. The ways in which goods are allocated, people employed, prices determined, policies adopted, leaders selected, projects financed, students trained, and foreign trade conducted have all been redefined. These changes are not only momentous for China but may also affect the reforms being implemented elsewhere in the communist world, as well as profoundly influence China's economic relations with the West.

Since China's second revolution is still under way, it cannot be analyzed with the certainty that hindsight would provide. Indeed, the production of this book has closely paralleled the cyclical evolution of reform in post-Mao China. The project was designed during the campaign against "spiritual pollution" in the winter of 1983–84; the principal research was conducted as the Chinese announced their urban economic reforms and their Seventh Five-Year Plan in 1984–85; the first draft was prepared while leaders in Peking grappled with the serious economic problems confronting them in 1985–86; and a second draft was begun just as student protests swept China's larger cities in late 1986. Moreover, the book appears as the Thirteenth National Congress of the Chinese Communist Party is convening—a meeting that could well be a major turning point in the history of the reform program. Each twist and turn in the tortuous course of reform has underlined the inherent problems in trying to reach a balanced assessment of the accomplishments and shortcomings of a reform process that will take decades to complete.

Despite these difficulties, the importance of the post-Mao reforms warrants an effort at a comprehensive overview and analysis. The fall of 1986 marked the tenth anniversary of the death of Mao Zedong, and the summer of 1987 the tenth anniversary of the political rehabilitation of Deng Xiaoping. Given that China's second revolution is therefore more than a decade old, a mid-course assessment of the Chinese reforms is long overdue, even though the story continues to unfold.

Harry Harding, a senior fellow in the Brookings Foreign Policy Studies program, is pleased to acknowledge the generous support and assistance of many individuals and institutions. Although the book is based on a great deal of primary research, it also relies on the previous work of other scholars from the United States, Europe, Japan, and China. The author owes a debt of gratitude to all those cited in the footnotes and to many more whose influence was less direct.

Increasingly, Chinese intellectuals have been helpful and informative guides for foreigners attempting to learn more about their country. The author wishes to thank both those formally interviewed in China, and those with whom he has conducted informal discussions in the United States, for sharing their insights and knowledge of their country's program of reform. He is particularly grateful to the Chinese Academy of Social Sciences, and specifically to Zhao Fusan, for arranging a research visit to Peking, Shanghai, and Canton in April 1985. Trips to China sponsored by the National Committee on U.S.-China Relations (December 1983), the Asia Society (November 1985), and the Pacific Forum and the Committee on Scholarly Communication with the People's Republic of China (October 1986) offered further opportunities for learning about recent developments in China.

A study group sponsored by the Council on Foreign Relations in New York, and skillfully organized and conducted by Paul H. Kreisberg and Alan D. Romberg of the Council staff, was especially helpful in developing the principal themes and conclusions in this book. The members of this ongoing seminar—A. Doak Barnett, Thomas Bernstein, Sandra Burton, Luc DeWulf, Robert M. Field, Peter Geithner, William H. Gleysteen, Jr., Steven Goldstein, Arthur W. Hummel, Jr., William G. Hyland, Virginia Ann Kamsky, Albert Keidel, Paul H. Kreisberg, Fred D. Levy, Dennis Mullin, Gordon Nelson, Charles E. Neuhauser, Michel C. Oksenberg, Robert B. Oxnam, Sara Robertson, Alan D. Romberg, Robert A. Scalapino, Francis X. Stankard, Roger W. Sullivan, Richard L. Williams, and Donald S. Zagoria—provided valuable criticisms, suggestions, and data. The results of the sessions were recorded by Moira E. Coughlin, Ted Piccone, and Constance Taube.

At Brookings, the Center for Public Policy Education, in October and November 1986, sponsored a very helpful series of conferences in Peking and Shanghai on developments in China, which the author was pleased to attend. Theresa B. Walker edited the manuscript, and Andrew C. Scobell verified its factual content, as well as providing other assistance. Bruce Dickson, Stephanie Joe, and Paul

Tam assisted with the research. Wm. J. Richardson Associates prepared the index. Susan E. Nichols provided secretarial support throughout the project.

Brookings gratefully acknowledges the financial support for this book provided by the Andrew W. Mellon Foundation, the Rockefeller Brothers Fund, the John D. and Catherine T. MacArthur Foundation, and the Henry Luce Foundation.

The views expressed in the study are those of the author and should not be ascribed to any of the persons or organizations acknowledged above, or to the trustees, officers, or other staff members of the Brookings Institution.

BRUCE K. MACLAURY
President

October 1987
Washington, D.C.

CONTENTS

PART 2

The Content of Reform

PART 3

The Future of Reform

TABLES

Author's note on romanization and statistical data

In romanizing Chinese terms, I have chosen for the most part to employ China's own *pinyin* system, which has become increasingly common in the West. There are a few exceptions. For a few historical figures and events in pre-1949 China, I have adopted alternative spellings that are more familiar to American readers. The footnotes reproduce the system of romanization used by the author or publisher of the book or article cited. Finally, I have used the English names for Hong Kong, Macao, Peking, and Canton, as well as for China.

The statistical data in the book are drawn primarily from official Chinese sources. They are intended principally to illustrate major trends in China's domestic economy and in its foreign economic relations, rather than to provide precise measures of economic activity at any particular time. Chinese statistics have been supplemented, when necessary, by data prepared by the U.S. government and by foreign research institutions. The U.S. government statistics, which are based largely on data from China's trading partners rather than from China, have been used for the analysis of the composition and direction of China's foreign trade; and data compiled by American research institutions have been employed in the discussions of China's balance of payments and debt structure. In some cases, the sets of data are not completely consistent with one another, or with Chinese official statistics. Again, they should be regarded as illustrative, rather than definitive.

Translations of Chinese periodicals and news services

Published in the People's Republic of China

Banyuetan (Bimonthly talks)
Beijing ribao (Peking daily)
Beijing jingji kexue (Peking economic science)
Changjiang ribao (Yangtze river daily)
Gongren ribao (Workers' daily)
Guangming ribao (Brightness daily)
Guangzhou yanjiu (Canton research)
Guoji shangbao (International commercial news)
Hongqi (Red flag)
Jingji guanli (Economic management)
Jingji ribao (Economic daily)
Jingji yanjiu (Economic research)
Kaifang (Opening)
Liaowang (Outlook)
Lilun yuekan (Theoretical monthly)
Nanfang ribao (Southern daily)
Nongmin ribao (Peasants' daily)
Renmin ribao (People's daily)
Shijie jingji (World economy)
Shijie jingji daobao (World economic herald)
Wenhui bao (Cultural contact news)
Wenzhai bao (News digest)
Xinhua (New China news agency)
Xinhua wenzhai (New China digest)
Yangcheng wanbao (Canton evening news)
Zhongguo fazhi bao (China legal system news)
Zhongguo qingnian bao (China youth news)
Zhongguo xinwenshe (China news service)

Published in Hong Kong

Cheng ming (Contending)
Ching pao (The mirror)
Ch'i-shih nien-tai (The seventies)

Chiu-shih nien-tai (The nineties)
Hsin wan pao (New evening news)
Kuan chiao ching (Wide angle)
Ming pao (Brightness news)
Pai hsing (The common people)
Ta kung pao (Impartial daily)
Wen wei po (Cultural contact news)

CHINA'S SECOND REVOLUTION

CHAPTER 1

Overview

FOR more than ten years, the People's Republic of China has been enmeshed in an extraordinary program of economic and political reform. The changes are manifest in a host of small details that make the China of today almost unrecognizable to those who last visited the country before the death of Mao Zedong in 1976. Chinese youth now sport the T-shirts and blue jeans familiar to their counterparts elsewhere in East Asia, and some women have again begun wearing the *cheongsam*, the traditional dress with a slit skirt and a mandarin collar that was commonplace on the Chinese mainland before 1949. Disco music blares from radios and loudspeakers on Chinese streets, and television antennas mushroom from both urban apartment complexes and the homes of suburban farmers. Vendors in the bustling free markets of China's big cities sell meat, vegetables, and clothing to avid consumers. Enthusiastic audiences patronize Western films ranging from *The Turning Point* to *Rambo* and welcome the revival of traditional Chinese music, drama, and art. Throngs of foreign tourists and business executives in the nation's coastal cities stay in modern new hotels managed by Sheraton and Holiday Inn and eat in restaurants operated by Maxim's of Paris and by some of Hong Kong's most successful restaurateurs. Fleets of Japanese cars, trucks, and buses create unprecedented traffic jams in Peking and Shanghai.

The scope and pace of reform have exceeded what most observers, Chinese and foreign alike, believed possible when Mao Zedong died in 1976. Deng Xiaoping's description of China's post-Mao reform program as the "second revolution" conducted by the Chinese Communist Party has proved accurate and appropriate.[1] The concentration of political power in the hands of the Party in order to redistribute land, wealth, and property was the hallmark of the first revolution, which the Party undertook before and after its seizure of power in 1949. In contrast, the underpinning of the current reforms is liberalization: granting society more autonomy from the state, allowing political discourse and intellectual activity more freedom from doctrine, ensuring more autonomy from the Party for both government officials and economic managers, and freeing economic activity from rigid adherence to a mandatory state plan.

This book offers an overview of China's second revolution. Although some attention is paid to the competition for power and influence among Chinese leaders, the book is not intended to be a comprehensive political history of post-Mao China or an analysis of the succession to Deng Xiaoping. The focus of the book is on the reform program: its origins, content, accomplishments, implications for the international community, and prospects. I am concerned principally with the intentions of the reformers, the effectiveness of their programs, and their struggle to maintain the requisite political support to sustain the momentum of reform.

Part one, "The Origins of Reform," explains how China's second revolution was launched and sustained. Even though China faced serious economic and political problems when Mao died in 1976, the post-Mao reforms should not be seen as an inevitable consequence of China's condition at the time. Instead, the reforms have been the result of extraordinary political engineering by a coalition of reform-minded leaders led by Deng Xiaoping. That coalition used Deng's personal prestige, as well as the unresolved grievances of the Cultural Revolution (1966–76), to push Mao's immediate successor, Hua Guofeng, off the political stage and begin a massive restaffing and restructuring of the Party and state bureaucracies, leading to a large-scale program of political and economic reform.

Since then, the reform coalition has followed a strategy of starting with programs that were likely to produce dramatic increases in production and standards of living, delaying measures that would have the most disruptive impact on the economy, and launching reforms on a nationwide scale only after they have proved successful in local experiments. The reformers have skillfully identified the shortcomings of their own program and announced remedial measures to alleviate them, thus coopting and preempting the objections of potential critics. This incremental and experimental strategy has enabled the reformers to maintain remarkable political momentum during the past decade. But it also means that many of the politically controversial reform measures most essential to the success of the overall effort are yet to be implemented.

There has been no consensus, either within society or among China's leaders, about the proper pace or extent of political and economic reform. In the broadest terms, the leaders of post-Mao China fall into two groups. More conservative leaders are cautious and skeptical about dramatic departures from the planned economy, state-owned industry, and centralized political system that were the legacy of the Soviet model. Radical reformers, in contrast, entertain bolder and riskier measures that would launch China in the direction of a market economy, new forms of public ownership, and a more pluralistic political order. The tensions between these two groups, evident since the early 1980s, came to a head in the events surrounding the forced resignation of Hu Yaobang as general secretary of the Chinese Communist Party in early 1987.

Part two, "The Content of Reform," describes and evaluates the impact of the reforms on China's domestic economic system, foreign economic relations, political structure, and principal institutions. In all four areas, two sets of reform have been proposed since the second revolution was launched in the late 1970s. Both reform programs have carried China toward political and economic liberalization, but one would take China farther and faster in that direction than the other. Consequently, the more ambitious set of reforms has aroused conflict between China's radical reformers and their more cautious and skeptical colleagues.

The moderate reforms, launched between 1978 and 1984, constituted a big departure from the Maoist style of economics and politics and from the Soviet model that China had imitated in the mid-1950s. In the realm of domestic economics, the moderate reforms have expanded opportunities for private and collective ownership in both agriculture and urban services, offered greater autonomy to enterprise managers, given economic incentives to both peasants and workers, and assigned market forces a greater role in the production, circulation, and pricing of commodities. The moderate reforms have decentralized the management of foreign trade, allowed foreign investment within restricted organizational formats, and established special economic zones along the coast of southeast China to attract export-processing enterprises from abroad. Finally, in the political sphere, moderate reform has been characterized by an explicit repudiation of the principal ideological tenets of the Maoist period, greater freedom and predictability in the daily lives of ordinary Chinese citizens, greater creative latitude in scientific and academic pursuits, and greater pragmatism, institutionalization, and consultativeness in national policymaking.

In late 1984 and early 1985, a second set of reform programs, more radical than the earlier ones, began to appear on the Chinese political agenda. If fully adopted, this second package would create markets not only for consumer goods, capital equipment, and raw materials, but also for land, capital, labor, technology, and even foreign exchange. The radical reforms also envision a fundamental change in the character of state ownership in urban industry, so that state enterprises would be leased out to individual entrepreneurs or to groups of workers or would issue shares of stock and be managed by boards of directors responsible to the stockholders. The radical reforms would extend the principles and policies of the special economic zones to the rest of coastal China and to many interior provinces, encourage an accommodating attitude toward foreign investment, and develop even broader connections with foreign societies and international institutions. The radical reformers have also begun to discuss the pluralization of Chinese politics, including a reduction in the size and power of the Party and state bureaucracies, a freer and more active press, more competitive elections, and possibly even the emergence of multiple political parties. At the time of the widespread student demonstrations of late 1986, some intellectuals even called for a sweeping reappraisal of Marxism and the wholesale importation of Western values and institutions.

Despite the ambitious goals of China's radical reformers, and despite the real changes that have occurred in China since the late 1970s, much of the basic structure of late Maoist China remains intact. Although some Americans have said that the Chinese have repudiated Marx, and although the Chinese talk about the need for new ideological breakthroughs, the country still sustains an official ideology, which restricts the scope of political and economic reform. Despite the talk of a market economy and the increases in private entrepreneurship, state-owned enterprises still dominate the industrial sector, and the government exercises a powerful influence over prices, investment, and allocation. Although life is much more relaxed than it was a decade ago, China remains a single-party state that systematically suppresses fundamental dissent. Despite the rapid economic growth since 1976, especially in the cities and suburban areas, parts of rural China remain mired in grinding poverty.

Part three, "The Future of Reform," considers the likely consequences of reform, both for the rest of the world and for China itself. Chapter 9 discusses the implications of reform for the international community. China's new commitment to modernization and reform has led it to seek much greater involvement in the international order than was true in the past. Moreover, even if reform should falter, the main outlines of China's current international orientation will probably continue throughout the rest of the century and beyond.

The prospect of a successfully modernizing China, actively engaged in international affairs, has occasioned some apocalyptic scenarios from observers in both Asia and the West: an international economy inundated by a flood of cheap Chinese exports or a regional balance of power upset by a huge, modernized Chinese military. A more dispassionate assessment suggests, however, that such cataclysmic forecasts are unrealistic. The disruptiveness of the growth of the Chinese economy will be restrained by the size of China's own domestic market and by its continuing needs for advanced technology and equipment from abroad. China will retain a stake in the stability and prosperity of the international system and is more likely to react to perceived challenges to its interests than to present a lengthy list of unsatisfied demands. The vitality of the rest of Asia, and the adaptability of the regional balance of power, will also restrain China's ambitions. The rise of Chinese power, therefore, is not likely to culminate in either a systemic political crisis (like the rise of Nazi Germany and Japan in the 1930s), a sustained cold war (like the rise of the United States and the Soviet Union in the late 1940s), or acute economic competition (like the resurgence of Japan in the 1960s and 1970s).

Still, the emergence of a new major power is usually turbulent. Although China's foreign policy will probably remain flexible and realistic, it will also assume a more nationalistic tone as China's power grows. Inevitably, China's maturation as a significant economic, diplomatic, and military actor will create tensions with neighbors and trading partners over particular issues and at particular times. Managing those tensions, and preventing their escalation, will pose a challenge to both China and the rest of the Asian-Pacific region for the rest of the century.

Finally, chapter 10 considers the prospects for both sets of reform, particularly after the death of Deng Xiaoping. A cost-benefit analysis of the reform program reveals that most of the Chinese people have experienced greater prosperity, freedom, and predictability in their daily lives and that the country as a whole has benefited from faster rates of economic growth, a more stable political order, and a higher standing in the international community. But the successes reform has enjoyed should not obscure the obstacles it has encountered. The relaxation of administrative controls over the economy, especially in the absence of strict financial discipline or an effective legal system, has produced chronic budget deficits, corruption, unprofitable investments, and shortages of foreign exchange. The growing use of market forces has aroused uncertainties about inflation, unemployment, and inequality. The liberalization of political and cultural life has introduced new ideas, fashions, and fads that some Chinese find dangerous and disruptive. The restructuring of the political and economic system has challenged the position of entrenched institutions with a stake in the old order. Moreover, the reforms have also led to rising expectations that may be difficult to fulfill in the years ahead.

Chapter 10 also suggests that the high turnover in the Party and state bureaucracies since 1978, and the rise of a younger generation of better-educated officials, has narrowed the Chinese political spectrum and shifted it toward support for most of the moderate reforms. But the radical reform package is far more controversial. China's governing coalition is divided between those who are satisfied with moderate reform and those who favor more radical measures. Although the radical reformers have the backing of Deng Xiaoping, more conservative leaders may be waiting for an opportune moment to challenge key elements of the radical reform program and even some aspects of moderate reform. Nor, despite progress, can the Chinese political system yet be described as highly institutionalized. As the sudden dismissal of Hu Yaobang in January 1987 implies, it is uncertain whether China will have the ability to resolve smoothly any important disagreements among its highest-level leaders in the absence of a figure with Deng's influence and prestige.

It is likely that the process of reform will continue in the years after the death of Deng Xiaoping. There will, of course, be alternating periods of consolidation and periods of advance, as have occurred throughout the past decade. But the course of reform should continue to trace an upward spiral, as China's leaders gradually and haltingly implement the moderate reform measures on which they have already agreed, and gain greater confidence in the feasibility and desirability of some of the more radical measures.

But some possibility remains that the reforms will falter more permanently after Deng's death. China's post-Deng leaders may lack the courage and the skill to implement the difficult and unpopular measures, such as enterprise bankruptcy and price reform, on which, in the end, the success of reform depends. They may be unable to agree on the desirability of the more radical set of reforms, whose political support is only partial and tentative. They may encounter political and economic difficulties that appear to require the reimposition of administrative and ideological controls. If such a retrogression should occur, however, its extent will almost certainly be limited. A return to Maoism is implausible, as is the revival of a highly centralized economic system or a tightly controlled political order. Increasingly, the choice for China is whether it is possible to stop at moderate reform or whether it will be necessary to move toward further economic and political liberalization.

PART 1

The Origins of Reform

CHAPTER 2

The Legacy of Mao Zedong

MAO Zedong, paramount leader of China's Communist movement since the legendary Long March of 1935–36, died shortly after midnight on September 9, 1976, at the age of eighty-two. The entire nation entered a ten-day period of official mourning. Loudspeakers and radio stations broadcast somber music; flags dropped to half staff; and portraits of the chairman were draped in black crepe. Newspapers, bordered in black, carried the obituary issued by the Party Central Committee, depicting Mao as the "greatest Marxist of the contemporary era" and describing his "immortal" contributions to the "revolutionary people of the whole world." A million people attended a memorial meeting, held in Tiananmen Square in Peking on September 18. As a 500-man military band played a funeral march, all trains, ships, factories, and mines across the country were ordered to sound their whistles and sirens in salute.[1]

Popular reaction to the death of Mao was far more ambivalent than the reports of official mourning might have suggested. During a hurried trip to Canton, Shanghai, and Peking the day after Mao's death, one Western reporter found the Chinese people "subdued and pensive, rather than shocked and distraught." Some Chinese were in tears, and some were overcome with grief, but the mood was less emotional than at the death of Premier Zhou Enlai earlier that same year.[2] A few months later, after the purge of the group of leftist leaders headed by Mao's widow Jiang Qing, some Chinese were holding up five fingers when discussing the "Gang of Four," suggesting that Mao should be counted among them.

The ambivalence toward Mao's death was a reasonable reaction to the complexity of his life. Most Chinese still revered Mao for leading the Chinese Communist movement to victory against overwhelming odds in the 1930s and 1940s. He sponsored the greatest program of land reform in modern Chinese history, launched the country on the path of industrialization, ended foreign privilege in China, and presided over the development of a modest nuclear deterrent. And yet, as the years passed, Mao acted in an increasingly arbitrary manner, and the social and economic costs of his mistakes assumed apocalyptic proportions. The Great Leap Forward, Mao's great economic campaign of the late 1950s, plunged the country into depression; and the Cultural Revolution, the political movement Mao launched ten years later, produced a decade of chaos and violence. It has been estimated that as many as 20 million to 25 million people died of hunger during the Great Leap Forward and that a half million more died of persecution during the Cultural Revolution.[3]

The ambiguous legacy left by Mao Zedong provides the starting point for understanding the political and economic reforms of the post-Mao era. In 1976 China faced both an acute political crisis and chronic economic shortcomings. Politically, the nation was torn by an intense struggle for power between those who supported Mao's vision of a continuous struggle to maintain revolutionary purity and those who wanted to redirect the nation's energies in the service of economic modernization. Millions of China's urban residents— particularly younger workers and intellectuals—had been made alienated and angry by the turmoil and hypocrisy of the Cultural Revolution. Economically, China was experiencing declining rates of growth, stagnant levels of consumption, persistent inefficiency, and growing technological obsolescence. These difficulties do not fully explain why China has undertaken reforms as broad in scope and as radical in content as those adopted since 1976. A full understanding of the reforms requires attention to the strategies and tactics enabling China's reform-minded leaders to gain political dominance over more conservative forces in the years after Mao's death. But China's economic and political problems did make some adjustment of political leadership and economic policy inevitable.

An amalgam of three sets of policies, values, and structures characterized China at the time of Mao's death. The legacy of prerevolutionary China remained, despite the modification of traditional institutions by a century-long process of internal rebellion, foreign invasion, halting modernization, and intellectual ferment. Onto this Chinese heritage was grafted the Soviet model of economic development and political organization, brought to China by Soviet advisers at the behest of China's own Communist leadership during the period of close Sino-Soviet alliance in the 1950s. Finally, the values of egalitarianism, populism, asceticism, and self-reliance, associated with Mao Zedong and the utopian wing of the Chinese Communist movement, were superimposed on both Chinese tradition and Leninism-Stalinism. Each overlay interacted with the layers beneath it, reinforcing some of the characteristics of earlier periods, while uprooting, transforming, or modifying others.

THE ECONOMIC LEGACY

The economy of traditional China was grounded in agriculture and in the individual peasant families who were the heart of the rural economy.[4] The technology of the country's agriculture can be described as "advanced traditional." It relied on human effort, animal power, and natural fertilizers, rather than on mechanized energy or manufactured inputs. But by more intensive cultivation—expanding the area sown to crops, adding more water, improving the strains of seeds, and growing two or even three crops a year—China's rural sector supported an increase in population from about 60 million in 1400 to about 200 million in 1750. Though still prone to drought, flood, and plague, China's rural economy could, in most years, also produce the surplus to support one of the world's most advanced urban civilizations and most highly developed bureaucratic states. But the distribution of that output was increasingly unequal. Although some peasants owned their own land, others rented their fields, all or in part, from landlords.

Traditional China also possessed a growing national urban economy, although until the coming of foreigners entrepreneurship remained focused on commerce rather than on manufacturing. For the privileged, there was a national trade in highly valued commodities like silks, teas, ink, brushes, and porcelains. There was also a national commercial network in staples like salt and grain, based largely on the extensive natural waterways that facilitated the movement of goods from west to east, and on the Grand Canal and the Pacific Ocean, which permitted the shipment of supplies from south to north. A growing system of traditional banks and money shops supported this commerce. The state, while permitting the development of some commerce, also sought to regulate it through a system of monopoly licenses and to tax it through levies on merchants.

From the middle of the eighteenth century to the middle of the twentieth, both internal and external factors affected China's relatively advanced traditional economy. In one sense, China's rural economy was the victim of its own success. The country's population, which had already reached 200 million by 1750, doubled again to attain 400 million within the next hundred years. But agriculture had, by this time, encountered the problem of diminishing marginal returns to the rather stagnant level of technology. New arable land was becoming increasingly scarce, and further inputs of available seed, fertilizer, and labor could not keep up with the growing population pressures. As per capita incomes fell, poverty and despair in the countryside increased, fueling first the great peasant uprisings of the nineteenth century, and then, in the mid-twentieth, the Chinese Communist movement.

The coming of Westerners in force toward the end of the eighteenth century was China's first contact with a technologically superior group of foreigners. China's stunning military defeats in the two Opium Wars of 1840–42 and 1856–60 convinced some Chinese of the need to combine the efforts of both officials and merchants to absorb foreign technology and launch a program of industrialization to meet the military challenge of the West. After 1895 foreigners also gained the right to invest in industrial and commercial enterprises and to build a network of telegraph lines and railroads. By 1949, as a result of the efforts of both foreigners and Chinese, China had a small industrial base, concentrated in Manchuria and along the eastern coast. Fully one-third of its output was from foreign-owned plants, and the bulk was in light manufactures such as textiles, cigarettes, matches, and other consumer goods. Moreover, the economy had been disrupted by years of confiscatory taxation, foreign invasion, civil war, and inflation. Still, this industrial base—when coupled with China's rich supply of raw materials and energy supplies—provided the foundation for further economic development under Communist leadership.

After the establishment of the People's Republic in 1949, the Chinese Communist Party chose to rely heavily on Soviet models of economic structure and development strategy. This decision was ironic, for the Party had succeeded in its struggle for power only when it rejected the Soviet model of urban uprisings in favor of a strategy of protracted peasant warfare. This declaration of ideological independence, which also served to consolidate Mao Zedong's personal authority in the Party, had required the purge of many Soviet-trained leaders from key posts within the CCP, and the attenuation of the Party's relations with both Stalin and the Comintern. But in the mid-1950s, the Chinese Communist Party relied heavily on Soviet models in the spheres of economic structure, development strategy, and political organization. This decision was partly based on the fact that the Korean War had foreclosed the possibility of gaining technology, capital, markets, and advice from the West; whereas the Soviet Union, especially under Nikita Khrushchev, seemed willing to give China technical assistance and economic aid. Even more, adopting the Soviet model reflected Peking's lack of self-confidence in its ability to achieve economic modernization and industrial transformation on its own and its conviction that the Soviet Union, as the world's first socialist state, offered valuable experience that China could emulate.

The adoption of the Soviet model meant a fundamental transformation of the pattern of ownership in the Chinese economy, with the means of production transferred from private hands to public or collective ownership through a continuous series of mass movements in the mid-1950s.[5] Agricultural land and capital, which had been redistributed to the tillers during the land reform earlier in the decade, was amalgamated first into "mutual aid teams," then into cooperatives, and then into collective farms. In the cities, compulsory state contracts and other forms of state regulation restricted the operation of private industry and commerce. Ownership was finally transferred to the state or worker collectives in 1956. The environment for foreign-owned firms was made more and more burdensome, until most foreign ventures disbanded, assigning their assets to the government. In all these ways, the Soviet model served largely to suppress the entrepreneurial qualities that had once characterized both urban and rural China.

After the collectivization of agriculture and the nationalization of industry, the Chinese economy was governed, as in the Soviet Union, by a system of mandatory central planning, thus intensifying the tendencies toward control over the economy that had been a principal feature of traditional China. Though the process of central planning was always incomplete and imperfect, it regulated the distribution of capital goods, the allocation of investment, and the utilization of labor more tightly than was true in most other Soviet bloc countries.[6] As two Chinese economists have put it, enterprises "had to seek approval for doing everything, big and small, from the higher departments which were divorced from the frontline of production, had no responsibility for the results of the operations of the enterprises and often gave impractical and disconnected mandatory directives." In many factories, managers had to obtain authorization from their superiors before they could make expenditures greater than 50 *yuan* .[7]

Moreover, as in other Soviet-style economies, the state exercised its planning function primarily through mandatory procurement and allocation of key agricultural and industrial products and through rigid control of the prices of major goods. Together, this led to the identification of quantity of output, rather than quality of product or efficiency of production, as the target that the state emphasized and the enterprises sought hardest to reach. Some goods in high demand were hoarded, as enterprises and consumers sought to lay in large amounts to guard against future shortages and bottlenecks; other goods in low demand were stockpiled, since, although no consumers could be found, factories could not get permission to stop production.[8]

A further characteristic of the Soviet model was a high rate of investment, allocated to ministries and enterprises through a system of state grants. State control over wages and prices ensured that industrial enterprises enjoyed high profits, which were then transferred directly to the central state treasury to fund new investment. Similarly, the state's ability to procure necessary agricultural products at administered prices enabled it to extract large amounts of resources from rural areas at low cost. The effect was to enforce high levels of mandatory savings, amounting to an average of 24.2 percent of national output during the First Five-Year Plan (1953–57).[9] But these vast sums of investment capital were then distributed to enterprises as a government grant, without expectation that either interest or principal would ever be repaid. The lack of economic discipline in the allocation of investment permitted long periods of construction, low efficiency in the use of equipment, and investment decisions on the basis of political rather than economic criteria.

China's investment patterns in the 1950s closely followed Stalinist priorities, with heavy industry favored at the expense of all other sectors of the economy. Thus agriculture, which in 1952 provided more than 55 percent of the country's national output and accounted for more than 85 percent of employment, received only about 7 percent of investment capital during the First Five-Year Plan.[10] Similarly, prices were set to favor industry over agriculture so that peasants were forced to sell their output to the state at low prices, but were required to pay high prices for many necessary capital inputs and consumer goods. The intention was to accelerate the growth of heavy industry, which had previously been a lagging sector, but the effect was to retard the development of light industry, commerce, and social services such as housing, education, and transportation.

Within only a few years' time, many Chinese leaders had become uneasy with what they regarded as serious shortcomings in the Soviet model.[11] Leninism-Stalinism, they believed, enlarged the gap between city and countryside, brought economic activity under excessively tight central control, created an unresponsive bureaucracy interested only in perpetuating its own power and privilege, and produced serious tensions and contradictions between the Party and the ordinary citizen. Chinese leaders also came to fear that the comprehensive adoption of the Soviet model gave Moscow too much influence over Chinese affairs. The Soviet Union, they concluded, sought to create a situation in which the Chinese economy would be closely integrated with the rest of the socialist bloc, the main lines of Chinese foreign policy would follow decisions made in Moscow, and the Chinese military would become linked with the Red Army.

But in which direction should the Soviet model be reformed? Some leaders wanted to adopt a somewhat more liberal course, loosening state controls over the economy, slowing the pace of economic growth, establishing greater commercial ties with the West, and allowing greater freedom of expression in both politics and the arts. Such a program was adopted, briefly, during the Hundred Flowers period of 1956–57. But it immediately encountered grave difficulties. Despite Chinese overtures, the United States proved unwilling to relax its embargo on trade with Peking. The relaxation of the political and intellectual environment produced an outpouring of bitter criticism of the Communist Party from many non-Party intellectuals. And experiments with a more gradual pace of economic growth, and with disbanding some of the agricultural collectives formed in haste in 1955–56, were dismissed by Mao Zedong as unnecessarily conservative and unacceptably retrogressive.

By the middle of 1957, therefore, Mao had concluded that it would be necessary to move in the opposite direction, tightening political controls over both the economy and society and resurrecting the utopian elements in the Marxist-Leninist heritage that he believed Stalin and Khrushchev had successively abandoned. Ultimately, after Mao's death, the liberal remedy would prevail under the leadership of Deng Xiaoping, but from 1957 until 1976, the Maoist critique of the Soviet model dominated the Chinese political agenda.

During such mass movements as the Great Leap Forward and the Cultural Revolution, Mao attempted to introduce more egalitarian and populist elements into the Soviet economic model. But although his criticism of the Soviet model was intense, Mao never succeeded in thoroughly uprooting all the characteristics of the Soviet system in China. Instead, Maoist components were grafted onto Leninism-Stalinism, much as the Soviet model had been superimposed on the traditional Chinese economy. The resulting amalgam modified some features of the Soviet model, but unintentionally served to reinforce and intensify others.

In economics, Mao stressed egalitarianism—a principle that he believed had been honored in theory but ignored in practice in the course of economic development in the Soviet Union. Mao and his followers disdained the use of material incentives to stimulate more productive or efficient labor. Maoist policy in agriculture attenuated the connection between work and reward, favoring systems of remuneration based either on perceived need (during the Great Leap Forward) or on political commitment and compliance (during the Cultural Revolution). In industry, although the system of graduated salary scales connected with the Soviet model was never completely eliminated, Mao showed his disregard for material incentives by freezing wage rates, slowing promotions to a glacial pace, and finally, in the 1970s, eliminating the bonuses that had once been awarded for superior performance.

Mao's egalitarianism extended to the allocation of tasks, as well as to the distribution of rewards. Mao was contemptuous of the concepts of specialization and comparative advantage, whether applied to people or to geographic regions. Instead, he favored the notion that every sector of society should be engaged in the same set of economic activities as all the others. This principle was reflected in the insistence that all of China's agricultural communes, which numbered about 50,000 in the mid-1970s, should devote paramount attention to the production of grain, despite differences in terrain and climate. It was also seen in the attempt to turn all provinces into "small but complete" industrial systems, relatively self-sufficient in the production of raw materials, machinery, and consumer goods.[12] Maoism encouraged each factory and enterprise to become a "miniature society," engaged in running stores, hospitals, schools, day care centers, and apartment complexes, as well as in producing goods or providing services.[13] And, in similar fashion, Mao's ideal citizen was the *duomianshou,* the jack-of-all-trades, whose life would combine in equal measure the responsibilities of the worker, the peasant, the soldier, and the student.[14]

The concept of a cellular economy was related to another aspect of Maoist economics that departed sharply from the Soviet model: the mistrust of systematic central planning. Mao concluded that central planning agencies would become conservative, allowing much slack in the economy and permitting bottlenecks and lagging sectors to set the pace for development as a whole. And he also may have shared the view of many Chinese economists that it was impossible for a central planning bureaucracy, operating without computers, systematically and comprehensively to set quotas, determine prices, and allocate goods for a country of China's scale.

But unlike the economists, Mao was unwilling to substitute markets for planning. He preferred a highly decentralized system in which Peking would set bold targets, the lower levels of government would establish even more ambitious goals, China's vast supply of human resources would be mobilized in their pursuit, and the transfer of financial resources and material output among provinces would be minimized.[15]

The darkest side of Maoist egalitarianism was the contempt for intellectuals and the neglect of science and technology. Although he was a poet, calligrapher, and philosopher of no small accomplishment, Mao was also in large measure an anti-intellectual, who believed that scholars and scientists represented an elite, divorced from the ordinary concerns of the masses of citizens. He also believed that artistic and intellectual activity undermined ideological commitment by spreading contaminating ideas from the past and from abroad. This skepticism toward intellectuals had profound economic implications. The open contempt for the work of scientists and technicians that characterized the Great Leap Forward wasted untold human and material resources in ill-conceived projects that proved technically infeasible. A decade later, China's educational system was debilitated in the latter part of the Cultural Revolution, when university enrollment was based on class background rather than academic ability, and curricula emphasized physical labor and ideological training rather than technical substance.

Although Mao's egalitarianism modified some of the Leninist-Stalinist features of the Chinese economy, in several other respects Maoist economic policies reinforced some of the principal characteristics of the Soviet model. To begin with, Mao's opposition to private economic activity yielded a level of collectivization that went even beyond that attained in the mid-1950s. During the Great Leap Forward, Mao sponsored the further amalgamation of collective farms into even larger communes, with abortive experiments with communal housing, cooking, and eating arrangements. From the late 1950s onward, Mao favored periodic attempts to restrict or eliminate the private plots on which peasants raised vegetables, chickens, and pigs, and to limit the operation of the rural and suburban markets, where the output of the private plots could be sold to others. In the cities, too, the individual tradesmen who had survived the wave of nationalization and cooperativization in the mid-1950s were forced to abandon their private entrepreneurial activities and to join others in collective enterprise.

Second, in the quest for even faster rates of economic growth, Maoist economic policy maintained, and even exaggerated, the high rates of accumulation and investment characteristic of the Soviet model. Investment rose from about one-quarter of national output during the First Five-Year Plan to about one-third in the early 1970s, on the eve of Mao's death. It is true that the allocation of investment was altered somewhat as part of China's reaction to the Soviet model. The gap between agricultural and industrial prices— the so-called price scissors—was gradually narrowed, agriculture obtained a somewhat higher share of state investment, and greater priority was given to the production of such agricultural inputs as machinery and chemical fertilizer.[16] But agriculture still received, on the average, only about 10 percent of state investment between 1971 and 1975, and agricultural products were still purchased by the state at prices far below market value. Furthermore, the slight increase in the share of investment of agriculture came at the expense of light industry and services, rather than heavy industry. The average rate of investment in heavy industry increased from 36.1 percent during the First Five-Year Plan (1953–57) to about 50.0 percent in the Fourth Five-Year Plan (1971–75), while the share of investment devoted to light industry fell from 6.4 percent to 5.8 percent, and the ratio allocated to nonproductive investment dropped from 33.0 percent to 17.5 percent, during the comparable period.[17] Consequently, Maoism did little to alleviate the "heavy, unpredictable, and counter-productive" burdens on the peasantry or to relieve the chronic shortages and bottlenecks of grain, consumer goods, and housing that the Soviet model had created.[18]

THE TRADITION OF FOREIGN ECONOMIC RELATIONS

Just as China has a long history of domestic trade and commerce, so too does it have a rich tradition of economic relations with foreign nations. During such cosmopolitan dynasties as the Han (206 B.C.–A.D. 220) and the Tang (618–907), China had extensive dealings not only with other Asian societies but also with the Romans, the Byzantines, the Arabs, and the Persians at the other end of the fabled Silk Road. Ideas, as well as commodities, came to China from abroad in those times. In the late Han period, Buddhism entered China from India, to become the country's principal organized religion. By the Tang, Buddhism had been joined by Islam, which took root in the western reaches of China. In the Ming and early Qing dynasties, Jesuit missionaries arrived in Peking and forged close relationships with the imperial court.[19]

Alongside these periods of cosmopolitanism, there was also a strong and enduring suspicion of foreign contacts in China. Particularly in the late imperial period, the prevailing view was not only that Chinese culture was immeasurably superior to that of any other society, but also that contact with foreign barbarians, except in limited ways, could lead to intellectual confusion, cultural contamination, and social disorder. Over the years, therefore, foreign merchants who came to China by sea were restricted to a handful of ports at which they could conduct their business: the Arabs at Canton, Quanzhou, and Ningbo; the Portuguese at Macao and Canton; and other Europeans at Canton, Amoy, Fuzhou, and Ningbo.[20] Similarly, traders from China's vassal states usually had to accompany the regular tribute missions from their countries, entering China through specified border crossings where they would be permitted to set up temporary fairs or bazaars.

By 1760, in a further restriction on foreign trade, the Qing dynasty specified that Europeans could conduct trade only through the port of Canton, with the right of permanent residence restricted to the Portuguese enclave at Macao. The essence of the Canton system, as it came to be known, was to make trade inconvenient to the foreigners. Foreign traders were allowed to deal only with a few Chinese merchants licensed by the state, were given no right to see or deal with Chinese officials, and were subjected to arbitrary and irregular tariffs and capricious punishment for those who violated Chinese law.

As Western gunboats and troops opened China to foreign merchants, investors, and missionaries, it was no longer possible for China to limit the geographical scope of foreign contacts. More and more ports were open to trade with the West, and foreigners established extraterritorial enclaves within many of these cities. By the beginning of the twentieth century, seven ports had been either ceded or leased to foreign nations, and vast spheres of influence had been granted to the imperial powers all along the Chinese coast.

The advance of the West into China only intensified the intellectual ambivalence about dealings with foreigners.[21] On the one hand, there were those who, humiliated by China's technological backwardness, were persuaded that their country needed to undergo complete Westernization if it were to survive. At the other extreme were those who wanted to exclude all foreign influence and to seek national salvation through a process of self-reliance. To some in this latter category, such as the conservatives in the late Qing court, the solution was the revitalization of traditional Chinese culture and institutions. Increasingly, others came to rely on mass antiforeign movements, such as the Boxer Rebellion at the turn of the century, the boycotts of the 1910s and 1920s, and finally the Communist movement.[22] But the most prevalent view throughout the modern period was a compromise between these two positions: a willingness to accept advanced science and technology from abroad, but a determination to preserve some elements of Chinese culture from contamination by foreign influences. The formula of the nineteenth-century scholar-official Zhang Zhidong, "Chinese learning as the foundation, Western learning for its practical applications," has continued greatly to appeal to Chinese intellectuals ever since.

This traditional Chinese ambivalence about foreign economic relations echoed throughout the Maoist period. The Sino-Soviet alliance involved intensive interaction between China and the socialist bloc, with Moscow giving Peking sizable quantities of financial credit, advanced equipment, and technical advice. The Soviet experience was conveyed to China by about 10,000 advisers, who helped restructure the economy, draft the First Five-Year Plan, design new political and social institutions, and construct 156 key projects that, even today, underpin much of China's industrial economy. An equal number of Chinese students and scholars received education or conducted research in Soviet and Eastern European universities and research centers during the same period, and nearly 30,000 Chinese technicians and workers obtained on-the-job training in Soviet factories.[23]

And yet, Chinese leaders were never comfortable with this relationship. As just noted, they feared that the Soviet Union sought to exercise unwarranted influence over Chinese domestic and foreign policy and concluded that the Soviet model was not fully appropriate to Chinese social and economic conditions. Thus one result of the Great Leap Forward was the rapid attenuation of China's economic ties with the Soviet Union. Partly in response to Mao's criticism of the shortcomings of the Soviet model, Moscow withdrew its advisers and technicians from China in the summer of 1960, and trade between the two countries fell from a high point of $2.1 billion in 1959 to a low of $47.0 million in 1970.[24]

China's foreign economic relations after the Sino-Soviet split were not as autarkic as has often been believed. Mao continued to welcome economic relations with Western Europe and Japan through most of the 1960s, and with the United States following the Sino-American *rapprochement* of the early 1970s. China's foreign trade increased rather steadily from 1957 onward, dropping only temporarily in response to the economic and political disruptions caused by the

Great Leap Forward and the Cultural Revolution. Indeed, as a share of national output, two-way trade rose from about 8 percent in the late 1950s to 11 percent in the mid-1970s.[25]

Nonetheless, during the Maoist period, China's foreign economic interactions took on even more restricted forms than in the period of strict adherence to the Soviet model. Economic relations with foreign countries were, after the late 1950s, limited essentially to trade for cash. Peking did not accept foreign investment and, after the repayment of the last Soviet credits in the mid-1960s, refused any further foreign loans except for short-term letters of credit. China also forged "arms-length" relationships that minimized the points of contact between China and foreign societies. It had only a few scientific exchanges with foreign countries and sent few students abroad. It imported technology, but in ways that required little permanent foreign presence in China. Trade was conducted through a few centralized foreign trade corporations, which limited direct contact between Chinese exporters and their foreign customers, and between Chinese importers and their suppliers overseas.

Moreover, in a curious echo of the past, Chinese officials resurrected the policy of the mid-Qing dynasty that restricted the points of access through which foreigners could conduct business with China. Peking was the principal location for contacts between foreign business executives and China's trade bureaucracy, and the site of several trade exhibitions organized by Western Europeans in the early 1960s.[26] Like their Manchu predecessors, Communist leaders also identified Canton as the principal point of contact between Chinese businesses and foreign traders. The city became the site of a semiannual trade fair at which foreign merchants could meet with potential customers and suppliers, always through the intermediacy of the state trading companies.

Chinese leaders today blame the Western embargo of their country for the autarkic policies that Peking adopted during the Maoist period. They are partly correct. The restrictions that Washington imposed on American trade with China, and that it urged its allies to place on their commercial relations with Peking, did make it difficult for the People's Republic to look to the West for technology, capital, or markets while Mao was alive. But the Western embargo was not the entire problem. Like Chinese officials a century before, Chinese Communist leaders in the 1960s and 1970s feared that contact with Western culture would erode their country's established values and institutions. The only difference was that, whereas the scholar-officials of the Qing dynasty had sought to defend the tenets of neo-Confucianism, the cadres of the Chinese Communist

Party were attempting to maintain popular commitment to revolutionary Maoism. Moreover, most Chinese leaders in the late Maoist period were convinced that economic relations with the international capitalist economy would inevitably be exploitative and would cripple the independent development of China's indigenous industry. Both these forms of protectionism—cultural and economic—led China to forgo the benefits of a closer integration with the world economy.

THE POLITICAL HERITAGE

If the traditional Chinese economy was rooted in small-scale peasant agriculture, the foundation of the traditional Chinese political order was the national bureaucracy, with its origins in the Han dynasty, and with a history of nearly 2,000 years. As E. A. Kracke has pointed out, Chinese bureaucracy and Greek democracy, one authoritarian and the other polyarchic, one vast in size and the other intimate in scale, represent the two most important and most enduring traditions in the political history of mankind.[27]

As noted, the combination of relatively primitive technology and relatively high output suggests the "advanced traditional" character of Chinese agriculture in premodern times. The same term applies to the Chinese bureaucracy in the late imperial period.[28] The Chinese state was advanced in its evolution of an unusually elaborate set of rules and regulations governing the recruitment, ranking, promotion, responsibilities, and discipline of officials. It also enjoyed a clear hierarchy of offices and considerable specialization among those institutions charged with administering the affairs of state. But China remained traditional in several important ways: it undertook a rather limited range of activities; considerations based on family, friendship, and place of origin strongly influenced the performance of officials; and chronic tendencies toward corruption and graft plagued the civil service.

One feature of the premodern Chinese political order that set it apart from many other traditional bureaucracies was the importance assigned to creating and maintaining an official political philosophy as a principal instrument of governance. Chinese officials were selected largely because of their mastery of an official political doctrine, which eventually evolved into the neo-Confucianism of late imperial times. Those who wished to compete for positions in the civil service were thus forced to spend a lifetime in the study of the prescribed political texts, and periodic efforts were made to spread the basic principles of Confucianism to the ordinary peasantry as well. From early times, Chinese rulers believed that social order could be ensured as much by the indoctrination of moral values as by the enactment of formal rules and regulations. Politics was traditionally regarded in China as a pedagogic process. National unity was maintained through the promulgation of a single national philosophy, and proper conduct was fostered through moral education by the state.

The combination of a national bureaucracy and an official ideology produced, as Etienne Balazs first noted, strong totalitarian proclivities in traditional Chinese politics.[29] As in almost all traditional bureaucratic systems, the Chinese state was supervised only by the emperor and his advisers, not by powerful, independent institutions reflecting the popular will. Members of the ruling class of scholar-officials, whether inside or outside government, might be brave enough to challenge imperial decisions that they considered unwise or unjust, but they did so at grave risk to their lives and careers. And the state regularly sought to suppress or restrict any other institution—be it guild, clan, or secret society—whose power grew to the point that it could challenge the state's monopoly on political power.

That these totalitarian tendencies were never realized was primarily because of the limited resources available to the state, rather than any accepted limitations on the proper extent of state power. Because the state bureaucracy was fairly small in size, and because it extended only down to the county level, it did not have the resources to penetrate deep into the countryside. Control over rural areas was, therefore, usually a process of negotiation between county magistrates and local leaders, rather than one of unilateral state *diktat* and local compliance. As the power of the national government decayed during the late imperial period, the power of the localities grew correspondingly, setting the stage for the disunity and warlordism of the first half of the twentieth century.

In the early 1950s, the newly victorious Communist government imported much of the political structure, as well as the economic system, of the Soviet Union. Paradoxically, this new political order could draw on many of the traditions of the *ancien regime* that it had overthrown. Like its predecessor, the new Communist system was bureaucratic and authoritarian, even though it adopted some of the formal practices of modern democracies.[30] A government structure was created that featured indirect, noncompetitive elections to essentially powerless bodies, with real power vested in the executive agencies. And the Communist system, like the traditional

Chinese political system, sought legitimacy in an official ideology, in this case Marxism-Leninism, which claimed to provide both a set of policy guidelines for China's economic and social development and a set of moral standards for the behavior of both officials and ordinary citizens.

What distinguished the new Communist political system from its predecessors was that modern transportation and communications now made possible the creation of a genuinely totalitarian state. All sectors of society were penetrated by a network of mass organizations, so that nearly every Chinese man, woman, and child was a member of a trade union, a student organization, a professional association, the militia, the women's association, or a combination of several. These mass organizations, and the government bureaucracy, were controlled by a network of Party cells and committees, which made or approved all their important decisions on policy or personnel, monitored their loyalty and performance, and dispatched its own members to occupy their key leadership positions. The extensive propaganda network created in the early 1950s—which included both the impersonal mass media and small discussion groups—provided a way of conveying official policy and doctrine to the mass of Chinese far more effectively than any traditional Confucianist dared to dream.

Over time, however, Mao Zedong altered the structure and operation of this Leninist system, just as he significantly transformed the workings of the Soviet economic model.[31] Most of these changes were based on Mao's conviction about the need to continue the revolution well after the establishment of Communist rule and the revolutionary transformation of the economy and the political system. Mao conducted this struggle not just against the imperialists outside China and their agents inside the country, nor even the members of the former "exploiting classes" who had been dispossessed of property and power during the revolution, but also against ordinary workers and peasants, and even the leaders of the Communist Party. To Mao, the principal threat to communism was the selfishness within each individual from almost any social class. Mao became convinced that many Party leaders, intellectuals, and even workers and peasants, would come to tolerate or even welcome an unacceptable degree of economic inequality and political elitism. As Mao saw it, the task of politics throughout the socialist period was not routinized administration of socioeconomic modernization, but, rather, protracted and continuous struggle against these tendencies that, if unchecked, would prevent the attainment of communism and might even threaten the restoration of capitalism.

Mao's desire to wage continuing struggle against revisionism had several concrete manifestations. First, especially compared with Stalinism, Maoism retained a strong bias for "redness" over "expertise"—for political commitment over technical competence—in the structure and staffing of the political system. The transfer of power from veteran revolutionaries to younger technocrats, a process that was undertaken so violently through Stalin's great purges, never occurred in Mao's China. Instead, Mao emphasized class origin and political commitment in recruitment to the Party and state bureaucracies. It is true that, during the Cultural Revolution, Mao criticized senior officials and sought to bring younger men and women to power, much as Stalin did during the 1930s. But the beneficiaries of the Cultural Revolution were political activists, rather than technical specialists, drawn from the urban proletariat and rural peasantry, not from the ranks of the intellectuals or technicians. Moreover, in practice, the Cultural Revolution did not produce a significant reduction in the average age of the upper ranks of Chinese officials.

For much the same reasons, the Party under Mao acquired even greater powers over enterprise management and the state bureaucracy than it had gained under the Leninist model. The Party increasingly arrogated to itself the administrative responsibilities that had, in the early 1950s, originally been the preserve of the state. The Party Secretariat and its functional departments replaced the State Council as the main arena in which policy options were clarified and policy decisions translated into administrative guidelines. Party secretaries at all levels supplanted government officials and enterprise managers as the cadres responsible for day-to-day decisionmaking. During the Cultural Revolution, of course, the Party apparatus was seriously weakened by factional conflict and social turmoil. But the Cultural Revolution nonetheless reinforced the power of the debilitated Party organization by relegating government agencies to serve as administrative arms of the Party committees.

Furthermore, Mao believed that maintaining—even intensifying—the role of ideological and charismatic authority in Chinese politics was essential to mobilize and maintain support in his continuing campaign against revisionism and capitalism. From the anti-Rightist movement of the mid-1950s until his death in 1976, Mao sought to sustain the centrality of ideology in the Chinese political system. He and his advisers advanced the theory of "continuing the revolution under the dictatorship of the proletariat" to justify the intensified struggle against "class enemies" in the Party, which they described as the greatest theoretical advance in Marxism since the days of Lenin. Equally important, the style of political discourse and behavior became increasingly dogmatic during Mao's later years. Decisions on almost any subject, no matter how technical or trivial, were supposed to be made by explicit reference to Mao's writings and instructions. A long list of programs, labeled the "new born things" of the Cultural Revolution, were declared above criticism; and an equal number of policy options were removed from consideration on ideological grounds. Political and intellectual discourse was limited to exegeses of, and panegyrics to, the chairman's works.[32]

Mao and his lieutenants sought additional legitimacy through the deliberate promotion of a cult of personality surrounding the chairman. Mao had always enjoyed considerable charisma, as a result of his leadership of the Party during the revolution and his authorship of the works that were the foundation of the Party's ideological indoctrination programs. Beginning in the mid-1960s, however, the cult of Mao assumed even greater proportions. Mao was described in the official media as the greatest Marxist-Leninist of the contemporary period, and by his heir-apparent, Defense Minister Lin Biao, as the greatest genius in the history of mankind. "Every sentence of Chairman Mao's works is a truth," Lin declared on the eve of the Cultural Revolution; "one single sentence of his surpasses ten thousand of ours."[33] Chinese and foreigners alike were depicted as extending boundless love and limitless devotion to Mao.

Mao therefore retarded what, given the history of other communist states, would have been the normal evolution of the Chinese political system. He delayed the progress toward pragmatism, the routinization of charisma, the relaxation of totalitarian controls, and the emergence of a better-educated, technocratic elite that occurred in most other socialist countries in the post-Stalin era. Except for a brief period in 1956–57, Mao never accepted Khrushchev's notion that class struggle would come to an end in a mature socialist state, or that the dictatorship of the proletariat could be replaced by a "state of the whole people." Instead, Mao insisted on the artificial perpetuation of revolutionary struggle against ill-defined "capitalist roaders" and "class enemies."

What was distinctively Maoist was his strategy for carrying out this struggle. Rather than relying on internal Party investigations and purges, as Stalin had done, Mao encouraged many ordinary Chinese to criticize the Party establishment through meetings, wall posters, and demonstrations. He believed this mobilization would be the most appropriate and effective way of combating revisionism in the Party. It was not that Mao placed great trust in the political orientation of the groups that he encouraged, such as the poorer peasants during the Socialist Education Movement of the early 1960s or the high school and university students during the early stages of the Cultural Revolution. On the contrary, Mao worried that both the peasantry and the urban youth were in danger of falling victim to the same forces of selfishness and materialism that had corrupted China's Party and state officials. But Mao was confident that relying on these apparently unreliable elements to rectify the Party would, in the end, have a dual value. In the first instance, it would give the younger peasants and students of China a revolutionary experience comparable to that enjoyed by older generations in the 1930s and 1940s, which would inoculate them against ideological laxity. Simultaneously, it would also encourage the Party to abandon revisionist programs and recommit itself to a more revolutionary and utopian vision.

For all its utopian rhetoric, the Cultural Revolution served to reinforce some of the more sordid aspects of traditional Chinese political culture. Mao recreated, in revolutionary dress, a modern variant of some of the worst imperial tyrannies of the past. The leader exercised immense arbitrary power, unchecked by effective institutions of collective decisionmaking. Independent intellectual and cultural activity was ruthlessly suppressed in the name of ensuring ideological unity. National politics degenerated into a ruthless struggle for power among rival factions of courtiers. The legal system atrophied, the bureaucracy decayed, and representative bodies became little more than servile instruments of national and local leaders. The principal cities of the country were terrorized by a mass movement that its own creator found difficult to control. As one Chinese intellectual said, "Under the most revolutionary slogans . . . , the most backward, conservative, and decadent elements in Chinese tradition were revived" during the Cultural Revolution.[34]

A BALANCE SHEET

What sort of balance sheet can be drawn for the Maoist period of Communist rule in China? A few years after Mao's death, Chen Yun, one of China's leading economic planners, allegedly told a national Party work conference: "Had Chairman Mao died in 1956, there would have been no doubt that he was a great leader of the Chinese people. . . . Had he died in 1966, his meritorious achievements would have been somewhat tarnished. However, his achievements were still very good. Since he actually died in 1976, there is nothing we can do about it."[35] Chen's statement summarizes the prevailing view held by most thoughtful Chinese. Mao's record was a mixed one, combining great achievements with great short-comings. But it was also a record that deteriorated over time. The accomplishments were scored, for the most part, in the earlier years, and the failures occurred in the latter part of Mao's life. At the time of Mao's death, therefore, China was facing chronic economic problems that were serious, if not yet intense, and an acute political crisis that threatened the stability of the regime itself.

To be sure, China in 1976 had some notable economic accomplishments to its credit. Despite the depression and famine occasioned by the Great Leap Forward and the political instability created by the Cultural Revolution, China had, in the aggregate, achieved respectable rates of growth between 1952 and 1975, exceeding those of such other large Asian countries as India and Indonesia. These growth rates, which averaged 11.5 percent in industry, 3.1 percent in agriculture, and 8.2 percent overall, had increased the country's gross national product from about $67 billion in 1952 to more than $210 billion in the mid-1970s, or from about $117 to about $230 in per capita terms.[36] By the mid-1970s, whether measured in terms of the production of electric power, steel, or cement, China had created an industrial base comparable in scale to those in the Soviet Union or Japan in the early 1960s.[37] China had exploded its own nuclear bomb, launched earth satellites, built primitive computers, and synthesized insulin. A country with only a small heavy industrial establishment in 1949 had already achieved impressive economic successes.

China's distribution of income and quality of life were even more remarkable by third world standards. The gap between city and countryside, when measured in average income, was about the same as in most other developing Asian countries. But income differentials within rural areas, and those within cities, were significantly lower than elsewhere in Asia.[38] In both primary and secondary school enrollment, China ranked well ahead not only of other developing countries but also of most middle-income nations. The rate of adult literacy, at about 65 percent, was just below the average of middle-income countries, and above that of low-income nations. Basic means of subsistence, including both food and medical care, were widely available throughout the country, and average life expectancy—sixty-four years at birth in the late 1970s—was again higher than in middle-income, as well as low-income, nations. In short, as the World Bank has concluded, the Chinese people, although poor in monetary income, enjoyed a standard of living far above what might have been expected for a country at China's level of development.[39]

These achievements should not, of course, be exaggerated. In the remoter parts of rural China, life was still desperately poor, and the floor supporting human subsistence could be broken during periods of depression such as the one that followed the Great Leap Forward.[40] Although income was distributed relatively equally, access to scarce consumer goods often depended more on formal rank and position than on monetary wealth. Much of the population was undernourished, even though its life expectancy was high. And China was, as we shall see shortly, lagging behind much of the rest of East Asia. But its aggregate performance was little short of extraordinary when compared with broader third world standards.

The chronic economic difficulties that China faced in 1976 must also be set against these achievements. China's problems were largely the result of the inefficiencies inherent in a Soviet-style centrally planned economy, including irrational prices, isolation from foreign competition, lack of contact between supplier and consumer, and a pervasive emphasis on quantity rather than quality of output. Many problems were further exacerbated by the Maoist biases against material incentives, markets, and the division of labor.

The most important dilemma was the contradiction between rising investment and sluggish growth. The rate of investment, already high during the First Five-Year Plan, had been rising rather steadily ever since, from about one-quarter of national output in the mid-1950s to one-third in the early 1970s. But rates of growth were declining, from 11 percent to about 8 percent over the same period.[41] In short, the Chinese economy was requiring more and more investment to obtain smaller and smaller increases in output.

The same phenomenon can be measured in productivity. The increase in national output resulting from each additional one hundred yuan in investment had fallen from fifty-two yuan in the First Five-Year Plan to thirty-four yuan in the early 1970s.[42] Labor productivity in industry, which had risen rapidly during the mid-1950s, had increased only very slowly thereafter. Labor productivity in agriculture, which had risen somewhat sluggishly during the First Five-Year Plan, had declined in the 1960s and 1970s so that by 1977 it had dropped below the level of 1952.[43]

Levels of consumption were also rising slowly because of the decelerating rates of economic growth, rising rates of investment, and poor quality of much of the nation's annual output.[44] This was particularly evident in the countryside, where per capita incomes increased by an average rate of only 1.6 percent between 1957 and 1979, and where per capita consumption of grain was no higher in the late 1970s than in the mid-1950s. The situation in the cities was somewhat better, if only because the state heavily subsidized staple commodities, and because a growing number of families had more than one wage earner. But even urban dwellers faced serious shortages of housing, services, and consumer goods. In the mid-1970s, the living space available for each urban resident amounted to only a few square feet—the size of a dining room table or a double bed. Other urban services—from public transportation to parks, and from stores to restaurants—were in short supply, because of the continuation of Leninist neglect of state investment in "nonproductive" projects and Maoist mistrust of private urban enterprise. The availability of foodstuffs and clothing depended, in the final analysis, on increasing imports of grain, cotton, sugar, and vegetable oils from abroad. And a growing list of agricultural and manufactured goods was subject to rationing and queuing and delivery delays.

Of particular concern for the longer term were two other problems. The first concerned employment. For much of his life, Mao was an anti-Malthusianist, who regarded each newborn Chinese as a set of productive hands waiting to work, rather than as a hungry mouth waiting to be fed. Mao was persuaded that labor was the most important factor of production and that national output would not be limited by shortages of land, capital, or raw materials. Under this set of assumptions, family planning was seriously neglected in China between the onset of the Great Leap Forward and the end of the Cultural Revolution, even as an improvement in public health was producing a fall in the death rate. The rate of population growth soared from 1.6 percent in 1949 to 2.8 percent in 1965. Only in the early 1970s did Mao change his mind, authorizing one of the third world's most effective, if draconian, birth control campaigns, which brought China's rate of population growth down to 1.2 percent by 1976.[45]

The revival of family planning occurred too late to prevent the Chinese population from nearly doubling from 540 million in 1949 to more than 930 million in 1976. And as the young people born during the Maoist "baby boom" of the 1960s and early 1970s began to reach working age in the mid-1970s, unemployment and underemployment became serious problems, particularly in the countryside. Unemployment at that time was estimated to be about 9 percent of the urban labor force, and underemployment had probably reached between 10 percent and 30 percent of the total national population of working age. Furthermore, the problem was certain to intensify in the years ahead, as those born later in the 1960s sought employment. One estimate is that China would have to create 80 million jobs between 1980 and 1990 to absorb the new workers entering the labor force. An even larger number of jobs must be created to resolve satisfactorily the problem of underemployment in the countryside.[46]

The second longer-term problem that China confronted in the mid-1970s concerned technology. China's relative technological autarky after its break from the Soviet Union in the late 1950s—particularly its minimal program of sending students and scholars abroad for training and its refusal to welcome foreign investment—meant that there were few opportunities, other than the purchase of complete plants and occasional equipment, to import technology from abroad. At the same time, even though the Maoist emphasis on popularizing education had produced impressive rates of attendance in primary and junior middle schools, these gains had come at the expense of advanced science and technology and even secondary vocational education. Less than 2 percent of the labor force had completed university training or secondary schooling, and the ratio of scientific and technical manpower to the labor force was far below the average of other large developing countries. Moreover, the work of China's few scientists and technicians—except for those working in national defense industry—had been seriously disrupted by the political disorder and the anti-intellectual climate of the Cultural Revolution.[47]

Consequently, despite impressive achievements in certain high-priority areas, Chinese technology in the late 1970s lagged ten years to twenty years behind world levels overall, with a gap of thirty years to forty years in some fields. The technological base provided by the Soviet Union and Eastern Europe in the mid-1950s was slowly decaying and was not being renovated by either imports or indigenous invention. The Chinese have estimated that fully 60 percent of the technology employed in their industry in 1980 was completely obsolete and that much of the rest was in dire need of upgrading.[48]

It is not altogether clear how aware Chinese leaders—or even Chinese economists—were of these problems in the mid-1970s. Economic research had, like that in the natural sciences, been seriously disrupted by the decade of the Cultural Revolution; and the statistical system was in a similar state of disarray. Nonetheless, although their understanding of their economic difficulties may not have been exact, it is likely that at least some economists, officials, and political leaders knew that their economy was facing serious, if chronic, problems, and believed that drastic measures would be necessary to remedy them.

In the realm of political organization, a similar pattern occurred— initial achievement followed by steady decline. The administrative system created by the Chinese Communist Party had been reasonably effective in reunifying the country after a century and a half of rebellion, revolution, and civil war, and in designing and implementing a sweeping program of social transformation and economic development. Like the Soviet-style economic system they administered, the Party and state bureaucracies were cumbersome and inefficient; and like the traditional officials they supplanted, Chinese Communist cadres were often tempted to abuse their powers, seek special privilege, and engage in corruption. On balance, however, the inefficiency, malfeasance, and corruption in China was no worse, and probably much less severe, than in other Asian countries at China's level of development.[49]

But just as the efficiency of the Chinese economy was declining over time, so too was the effectiveness of the Chinese administrative apparatus. By the time of Mao's death, China's bureaucratic establishment was ill qualified—by age or level of education—to administer a program of sustained economic modernization.

When the new regime was organized, it was ruled by a remarkably young leadership—men and women born in the early twentieth century, who had joined the Communist movement in their twenties and thirties and who in the early 1950s were between forty and fifty years of age. But, without any regular system of personnel rotation, this generation of leaders remained in office throughout the 1960s and 1970s. Even the vast personnel turnovers during the Cultural Revolution produced little rejuvenation of the bureaucracy, and whatever progress may have been made was undone by the political rehabilitation of great numbers of senior officials once the movement came to an end. By the late 1970s, most top national and provincial leaders were in their sixties and few municipal or prefectural officials were under forty-five. Especially at the county, prefectural, and provincial levels—the crucial middle layer of the Chinese bureaucracy—the ranks of cadres were characterized by poor health, low vigor, and even senility.

The Chinese bureaucracy was as undereducated as it was overaged. The Communist Party, except for a few intellectuals at its head, had been the product of a revolutionary movement, whose members were recruited on the basis of political enthusiasm rather than formal education. Mao's disdain of technical expertise and his distrust of intellectuals, reflected in the recruitment patterns of both the Party and state bureaucracies, only served to exacerbate this problem. In the early 1980s, only 20 percent of provincial leaders, and about one-third of ranking central officials, had a college education. And the qualifications of officials at lower echelons were even less impressive. The detailed sample census conducted in 1982 implied that, of the nation's state and Party employees, only 6 percent had received higher education, and only 22 percent had received senior middle school training. The remaining three-quarters had received education at or below the level of junior middle school.[50]

Bureaucratic inefficiency, like the irrationalities in the economy, represented serious chronic problems that could have been expected to become more serious and debilitating over time. What distinguished the political situation from the economic arena, however, was the immediate, acute crisis in politics resulting directly from the trauma of the Cultural Revolution. This crisis involved both intense factional conflict within the highest level of leaders and the growing alienation of the Chinese populace from the regime as a whole.

Given his enormous personal prestige, the grievances held by many sectors of urban youth, and the backing of the Chinese military, Mao was able to launch an unprecedented mass assault against the Party and state bureaucracies in late 1966 and early 1967. But he was not able to bring his Cultural Revolution to a successful conclusion. He encouraged high school and university students, and then elements of the urban proletariat, to criticize "revisionists" in the Party, but he was unable to create new political institutions that could absorb the waves of political participation that he had unleashed. He called in the army to restore order and allowed military officers to assume key positions in the Party and state bureaucracies, but then he concluded that military involvement in civilian affairs had exceeded proper limits. Mao rehabilitated many of the veteran civilian officials who had been purged during the Red Guard movement as a way of bringing the army to heel, but he continued to view many of them as "unrepentant capitalist roaders." He criticized his most radical lieutenants, including his wife, Jiang Qing, for fostering division and instability, but he refused to repudiate the Cultural Revolution itself or to dismiss the radicals from office.

As a result of these half measures, China's central leadership in 1976 was deeply divided between those who had been the victims of the Cultural Revolution, those who had been its principal beneficiaries, and those who had made enough compromises with the movement to survive. Moreover, there were no longer any mechanisms for resolving the conflicts within the elite. Mao's decision to launch the Cultural Revolution against his own colleagues discarded with one stroke most of the basic norms of high-level politics in the Communist movement, and those traditional rules of political competition were weakened further during the intense factional struggles between military and civilian leaders in the early 1970s, and between radicals and moderates later in the decade.[51] The years 1966–76 were therefore characterized by unrelenting intrigue, betrayal, and violence at the highest levels of leadership. The millions of officials who had been branded counterrevolutionaries or capitalist roaders during the Cultural Revolution, and who had been placed under house arrest, imprisoned, or sent into internal exile, formed a powerful constituency for political change.

The Cultural Revolution also produced a severe crisis of confidence among large sectors of Chinese society, especially in the cities. Intellectuals had, as a group, been one of the principal targets of the Cultural Revolution. Accused by Mao of "bourgeois tendencies" and described by the radicals surrounding Jiang Qing as the "stinking ninth category" of counterrevolutionaries, intellectuals experienced a virtual reign of terror throughout the decade of the Cultural Revolution. The indictment presented against the Gang of Four during their trial in 1980 charged, probably conservatively, that more than 200,000 intellectuals had been "framed and persecuted" during the Cultural Revolution.[52] Of those, an unspecified number were physically tortured, as well as psychologically intimidated. Some were killed, and others committed suicide. Indeed, intellectuals were treated far more severely than most Party or state officials, and the impact on them has been likened to that of the Holocaust in Nazi Germany.[53]

For urban youth, the process of disillusionment was different, although the final results were in many ways similar. Many young high school and college students were originally the shock troops of the Cultural Revolution, rather than its victims, joining the movement out of a sense of a combination of idealism, adventure, and rebellion. But in mid-1967, after the Red Guard movement had produced division and chaos, rather than renewed revolutionary commitment, Mao ordered the People's Liberation Army to intervene to restore order; and little more than a year later, after the violence and turmoil had failed to abate, Mao further instructed the military to disband the Red Guard organizations and dispatch their members to the factories or the countryside for further "tempering." Mao's change of heart caused many of the former Red Guards to reassess their commitment to the principles of the Cultural Revolution. All were angered at the prospect of permanent exile in the countryside; many were astonished and disheartened by the poverty and backwardness they discovered there. Most must have been angered to watch a political movement intended to strengthen and purify their country degenerate into chaos and petty factionalism. Some had the opportunity to read and reflect on the developments that had transformed them from students to revolutionaries to outcasts, and of these some would become leaders in the reform movement of the early 1980s.

The urban proletariat represented a third group that harbored serious grievances against Maoist rule. China's workers had not been the targets of the Cultural Revolution, as the intellectuals had been; nor were they dispatched to the countryside during the course of the movement, as was the fate of many high school and college students. But they still suffered from the impact of Maoist economic policies: wages were frozen throughout the Cultural Revolution, and the bonus system effectively suspended. The average wage earned in the state sector in 1964 was not exceeded until 1979, after the inauguration of the post-Mao reforms.[54] Moreover, the urban workers were the principal victims of the cramped housing, inadequate city services, and shortages of consumer goods already described.

Thus, in the mid-1970s, dissatisfaction prevailed in urban China with the political and economic trends that had emerged in the latter years of Mao's life. The intellectuals were angered at the persecution they had suffered at the hands of the radicals; young people resented Mao's betrayal of the Red Guard movement; workers were tired of stagnant levels of consumption and crowded living conditions. All were weary of continuous mass movements and ideological indoctrination, and dismayed by the intense factionalism that still plagued the leadership of the Party after ten years of Cultural Revolution. For the superstitious, the devastating earthquakes that struck north China in the summer of 1976 were a sign that the regime was losing its mandate of heaven; for the more pragmatic, the fact that the radicals continued to describe criticism of "unrepentant capitalist roaders" as more important than earthquake relief work was equal evidence that the regime had forfeited its right to rule.[55]

In a totalitarian system such as China's during the late Maoist period, expressions of dissent are risky and rare. But China's crisis

of confidence was manifested in a series of dramatic protests against
the regime in the mid-1970s. A wall poster written in Canton in
November 1974 by three former Red Guards described China as a
"caricature of the old imperial system" and as a "feudalistic socialist-
fascist" state.[56] And a massive demonstration in the central square
of Peking in April 1976, nominally in memory of the late Zhou
Enlai, featured poems and posters that likened Mao to the most
tyrannical emperors of the past and compared Jiang Qing to the
Empress Dowager Tz'u-hsi of the late Manchu dynasty. In the eyes
of many of its citizens, the Chinese political system had become a
mixture of feudalism and fascism: feudal because it was tyrannical
rule masquerading as a reign of virtue, and fascist because it
employed the modern techniques of political manipulation, including the mass media and mass organizations, to ensure control.

THE PRESSURES FOR REFORM

In themselves, China's internal political and economic problems
were powerful forces for change as the country entered the post-
Mao era at the end of 1976. But they were intensified by certain
international factors, some of which increased the pressures for
reform, and others of which helped facilitate China's eventual
structural transformation. One was the unfavorable comparison
between China's economic performance and that of the rest of East
Asia. As China's rate of economic growth declined to an average of
7.4 percent between 1965 and 1973, growth rates accelerated in
Japan (9.8 percent), Taiwan (10.3 percent), South Korea (10.0 percent),
Hong Kong (7.9 percent), and Singapore (13.0 percent).[57] Moreover,
given the technological disparity between China and the rest of
East Asia, those gaps could only be expected to widen over time.
To China, which had traditionally regarded itself as the most
advanced country in East Asia, its poor performance relative to that
of the rest of the region was particularly galling. Many intellectuals
and leaders became determined to make up for what was increasingly
described as the "ten lost years" of the Cultural Revolution.

At the same time, Chinese economists were aware of the experiments in economic reform that had been undertaken in Eastern
Europe—particularly in Yugoslavia and Hungary—since the 1960s,
and of the debates over economic theory that had been conducted
in the Soviet Union during the same period. Chinese leaders were
familiar with the critique of the structural problems of the Soviet-
style economy, and, at the same time, had somewhat more freedom

of action than their counterparts in either Eastern Europe or the Soviet Union. Chinese scholars and intellectuals stress that the Soviet Union will find it difficult to renounce the economic model that its own Party had devised, while China can easily justify reform as a necessary adaptation to Chinese conditions. Moreover, unlike the Soviet Union and Eastern Europe, China need not worry about the reaction to its reform elsewhere in the socialist camp.

Finally, the international environment offered Chinese leaders a great opportunity, as well as a challenge. Ever since the Soviet invasion of Czechoslovakia in 1968, the Sino-Soviet border clashes of 1969, and the Sino-American *rapprochement* of the early 1970s, Peking's leaders had explicitly acknowledged that the Soviet Union, and not the United States, posed the greatest threat to their country's security. This idea meant that China and the West—first implicitly, and then explicitly—had a common interest in opposing the expansion of Soviet influence in Asia. These parallel perspectives, Chinese leaders correctly believed, meant that the United States and Japan, as well as Western Europe, would now be willing actively to cooperate in China's modernization if Peking encouraged them to do so. In addition, Peking's links with the many overseas Chinese both in America and in the rest of Asia offered a ready bridge for facilitating the transfer of capital and technology.

Under these circumstances, it would be tempting to conclude that the difficulties China faced at the time of Mao's death were so massive, the inefficiencies so glaring, and the advantages of political and economic liberalization so obvious, that the reforms later undertaken by Deng Xiaoping were inevitable. To some degree, this may be true. The situation in the political sphere was too explosive for the status quo to remain intact. The divisions within the leadership at the time of Mao's death were so deep that compromise and coexistence were impossible. In the same way, it was probably also necessary to design some change in economic policy that could halt the decline in growth rates, increase consumption levels, and thus help restore political confidence.

But the objective problems at the time of Mao's death still do not explain the extent of the reforms that have occurred under Deng Xiaoping. Indeed, Mao's immediate successor, Hua Guofeng, seemed convinced that fairly modest changes would be sufficient to restore political normalcy and economic vitality. The immediate cause of reform was the existence of a reform faction within the Chinese Communist Party, its successful struggle to gain supremacy over more conservative rivals, and its skillful strategy for launching and sustaining a bold program of political and economic renewal.

CHAPTER 3

The Rise of the Reformers

A T the time of Mao Zedong's death in 1976, the Chinese political spectrum consisted of three broad schools of thought. On the left of the spectrum was a group of revolutionary Maoists, headed by Mao's wife, Jiang Qing, who wished to preserve the values and policies of the Cultural Revolution. In the center was a second group of leaders, symbolized by Premier Hua Guofeng, who believed that the wounds of the Cultural Revolution could be healed by restoring, in modified form, many of the political and economic institutions that had existed in the mid-1950s and early 1960s, before the onset of the Cultural Revolution. At the other end of the spectrum, on what the Chinese call the "right," were leaders who sought to make significant changes in both the Maoist legacy and the Soviet model of politics and economics. This coalition of reformers was assembled and led by Deng Xiaoping, who has proved to be one of the most colorful and skillful leaders in contemporary China.

The political history of China since the mid-1970s has been characterized by a rapid and decisive movement rightward along this political spectrum. During the last years of Mao's life, Chinese politics seemed dominated by the revolutionary Maoists under Jiang Qing, with their incessant calls for class struggle against revisionists within the Party leadership. Within a month of Mao's death, however, these leftists were overthrown in a coup d'état and were replaced by a group of officials, led by Hua Guofeng, from the middle of the political spectrum. For two years, Hua attempted to find ways of reviving the sluggish Chinese economy and resolving the political crisis produced by the Cultural Revolution, while still remaining loyal to the memory of Mao Zedong. But by the end of 1978, this centrist program had encountered serious economic difficulties, without alleviating the crisis of confidence that plagued much of urban China. At that point, Chinese politics swerved even further to the right, with Hua Guofeng steadily losing power to the coalition of reformers headed by Deng Xiaoping. When Hua was finally removed from his leading posts in the Party in 1981–82, the political and economic reforms of the post-Mao era could finally get fully under way.

THE CHINESE POLITICAL SPECTRUM IN 1976

A brief description of these three schools of thought—the revolutionary Maoists, the restorationists, and the reformers—can facilitate an understanding of the dramatic changes that have occurred in China since the death of Mao.[1] Each of the schools espoused distinctive political values, advocated particular economic policies, and found inspiration in its own historical models and international reference groups. The programs associated with each school have set the terms for political discourse and competition throughout the post-Mao period.

Revolutionary Maoism

The program of the revolutionary Maoists in 1976 was to preserve the legacy of the Cultural Revolution: to uphold its ideological rationale, defend the methods by which it had been conducted, and carry on the socioeconomic programs introduced over the course of the movement. The watchword of the revolutionary Maoists was struggle: intense, protracted, even violent struggle against any sign of revisionism in policy or ideology.

The revolutionary Maoists placed their imprimatur on a long list of programs that had been developed in the early 1970s as part of an effort to apply the Maoist values of populism and egalitarianism to the formulation of social and economic policy. They included the politicization of educational curricula, the recruitment of university students on the basis of class origin and ideological orientation, the provision of rural public health through the "barefoot doctor" program, the restriction of theatrical performances to a few "revolutionary dramas," the maintenance of a high level of collectivization in agriculture, and relative autarky in foreign economic relations. The revolutionary Maoists sought to defend these "socialist newborn things" of the Cultural Revolution against any modification or abandonment, and opposed any attempt to assign greater priority to the restoration of political order or to economic development and modernization. "Rather socialist trains [running] late," the Maoists were said to have declared, "than revisionist punctuality."[2]

The revolutionary Maoists vehemently opposed the tendency, apparently supported by Mao, to rehabilitate many of the senior Party and government officials, including Deng Xiaoping, who had been purged during the Cultural Revolution. To the revolutionary Maoists, the reappearance of these leaders in the early 1970s symptomized a slackening of class struggle against "revisionists" and "capitalist roaders" in the Party. The resurrection of veteran officials from the past not only increased the possibility that the policies and values of the Cultural Revolution would be altered or overturned, but also suggested that the political position of the revolutionary Maoists could be effectively challenged once Mao Zedong had left the Chinese political stage. As early as 1973, using the highly allegoric style then characteristic of political commentary, the revolutionary Maoists complained of the policy of "reviving states that had been extinguished, restoring families whose line of succession had been broken, and calling to office those who had retired into obscurity." Instead, they proposed the rapid promotion of younger cadres who had supported the Cultural Revolution to leading positions in the Party, the government, and the army.[3]

Finally, the revolutionary Maoists attempted to mobilize mass protest against any indication that the "newborn things" of the Cultural Revolution were being modified or that the "revisionist" leaders and policies of the past were being rehabilitated. Throughout the early 1970s, they encouraged workers to write wall posters complaining of any signs of the neglect of ideological education, the restoration of material incentives, or the reimposition of administrative discipline in their factories. They also instigated their supporters to "rebel" against "unrepentant capitalist roaders," and to refuse to work for the "incorrect political line." They called for continuous "revolutionary great debates" among workers and peasants, which would presumably identify and criticize any tendency to abandon the programs and values of the Cultural Revolution. Any attempt by more moderate leaders to restore order, either in the workplace or the political arena, was condemned by the revolutionary Maoists as the "suppression of the masses."

The proponents of revolutionary Maoism were largely the activists and beneficiaries of the Cultural Revolution. The leaders of this school of thought were the critics, writers, and leftist scholars in Shanghai and Peking who had served as the propagandists and theoreticians of the movement. Two members of the Gang of Four, Zhang Chunqiao and Yao Wenyuan, for example, had been part of the municipal propaganda apparatus in Shanghai and had contributed important theoretical essays to the radical press throughout the Cultural Revolution. At lower levels, revolutionary Maoism was supported by many of the "mass representatives" appointed to Party committees and government bodies in the mid-1970s (including Wang Hongwen, another member of the Gang of Four), and by a network of radical workers in factories and government offices who favored the egalitarian and populist programs introduced during the same period. Some individuals supported this school of thought because of conviction, many others because the Cultural Revolution had provided opportunities for rapid promotion in a political system where upward mobility would otherwise have been slow or impossible.

To the extent that the revolutionary Maoists had a model that they sought to emulate, it was the Cultural Revolution. Nothing of use could be learned from the West, for all its institutions and programs were irremediably capitalist, and its values were irretrievably bourgeois. No other socialist country, least of all the Soviet Union, was combating revisionism as effectively as China. A few, like Albania, might be following the correct course of continuous revolution, but Albania would, in this process, be a student of China, and not the reverse. No other period in the history of the People's Republic offered any positive lessons for the revolutionary Maoists, for they regarded the seventeen years from 1949 to 1966 to have been dominated by a revisionist line in social, economic, and organizational policies. Their goal was to carry forward the quest for revolutionary purity that they believed was embodied in the Cultural Revolution.

Restorationism

The leaders of the restorationist tendency—the midpoint on the Chinese political spectrum in 1976—sought to restore the economic and political institutions that had existed before the Great Leap Forward and the Cultural Revolution. If the shibboleth of the revolutionary Maoists was continuous revolution, the watchword of the restorationists was stability and harmony. As Hua Guofeng would put it in 1976–77, their goal was to restore "great order across the land."[4]

In the political sphere, the restorationists offered a program of national unity under Party leadership. There would be no more uncontrolled mass mobilization, as the revolutionary Maoists had sponsored during the Red Guard movement of the late 1960s and the "revolutionary great debates" of the early 1970s. The Party would be rebuilt from the ravages of the Cultural Revolution, and its control over all aspects of life would be reinforced. There might be mass campaigns in politics, aimed at criticizing ideas that differed from those of the central leadership; and there might also be mass movements in economics, aimed at mobilizing greater effort and resources for national development. But all of these movements would be kept under careful organizational control and directed toward the purposes specified by the Party.

The restorationists took an ambivalent position toward Mao. They acknowledged the disastrous consequences of the Great Leap Forward and the Cultural Revolution, but, since they did not want to criticize Mao for these problems explicitly, they blamed the weather and the Russians for the failure of the Great Leap Forward and the revolutionary Maoists for the violence and disorder of the Cultural Revolution. The restorationists attemped to produce a sanitized version of Maoism, purged of the distortions allegedly introduced by the revolutionary Maoists, that they hoped would provide an adequate base of legitimacy for the regime and could retain a central position in intellectual matters. They endorsed Mao's original design for the Cultural Revolution, but they also claimed that interference from the ultra-left had sabotaged Mao's intentions.

In economics, the restorationists devoted much higher priority than did the revolutionary Maoists to resuming rapid economic growth and raising popular living standards, and proposed to abandon some of the more extreme economic policies connected with Mao Zedong. They sought to restore effective central control over the economy and end the Maoist experiment with radical decentralization; and they were willing to restore some material incentives in both agriculture and industry and end the Maoist flirtation with egalitarian systems of remuneration. But the central Stalinist priorities, as reiterated by Mao, were to remain intact: high levels of investment, rapid rates of economic growth, and the development of a large, heavy industrial base. Nor were the restorationists interested in any sizable increase in the place of market forces in the Chinese economy.

In foreign economic relations, the restorationists were willing to look abroad for foreign technology, whereas the revolutionary Maoists were not. Furthermore, given China's hostile relations with the Soviet Union and Eastern Europe, and the wide gap between Soviet technology and the technology of Japan and the West, the restorationists regarded the developed capitalist world as the most appropriate source of advanced equipment. But they were not eager to expand the range of China's international economic relationships. Essentially, the restorationists sought to import technology for cash. They were leery about accepting foreign credits, opposed to allowing foreigners to invest in China, and cautious about sending many Chinese students and scholars abroad for research and training.

Support for restorationism was rooted in the vast bureaucratic networks that had been the main beneficiaries of the Soviet model. These organizations included the ministries responsible for heavy industry, the state planning apparatus, the Ministry of Public Security, important segments of the military, and much of the rank and file of the Party. Their chief representatives in Peking in the mid-1970s were a group of five central leaders who had risen from second-echelon posts to national prominence during the Cultural Revolution. Hua Guofeng, the prime minister; Wang Dongxing, a public security official who commanded the elite force of Party bodyguards; Chen Xilian, the commander of the Peking military region; Ji Dengkui, a middle-level Party official from Henan, responsible for agricultural policy; and Wu De, mayor of Peking. For a time, the restorationists also enjoyed the support of some senior military and civilian leaders who had survived the Cultural Revolution, including Defense Minister Ye Jianying and vice-premier Li Xiannian.

The restorationists' program was based on the assumption that China did not require any serious structural reforms. They were confident that renewed economic growth and an end to political disorder would resolve the crisis of confidence that gripped urban China. They also were convinced that the vitality of the nation's economy could be revived through the restoration of political stability and effective central planning. To the restorationists, the previous periods that had embodied these values—notably the First Five-Year Plan of the mid-1950s, and the era of economic recovery following the Great Leap Forward in the early 1960s—were appropriate models for post-Mao China as well.

Reform

Compared with the restorationists, the third school of thought in Chinese politics in the mid-1970s, the reformers, wished a sharper and more decisive break from both Maoism and the Soviet model. The reformers proposed to restructure and revise the institutions and policies of the mid-1950s and early 1960s that the restorationists wanted to reactivate and revitalize. Whereas the restorationists sought simply to blame the revolutionary Maoists for the tragedy of the Cultural Revolution, the reformers were willing to assign much of the responsibility to Mao. The restorationists tried merely to redefine the content of Maoist doctrine to create the basis for greater unity and stability in politics, but the reformers were prepared to reduce the role of ideology in political and intellectual life.

At the time of Mao's death, the reformers were led by an extraordinary group of veteran Party leaders who had been the principal victims of the Cultural Revolution. Some, like Peng Zhen, the head of the Peking municipal Party apparatus before the Cultural Revolution, were especially interested in promoting political reforms that would repudiate the latter years of Mao's life and preclude the recurrence of a similar tragedy in the future. Others, like Chen Yun, one of China's leading economic planners, had long proposed economic reforms that would allow greater room for the market and for individual ownership. The most prominent reformer, Deng Xiaoping, placed special emphasis on the need to modernize and restructure the armed forces, link China more closely to the international economy, and reduce the role of the Party apparatus in making technical and administrative decisions. Reform was also supported by most of China's intellectuals, who, like veteran Party leaders, had been brutally persecuted during the Cultural Revolution. And the evolution of post-Mao China would show that reform could achieve broad-based support if it could produce a more relaxed political climate and raise urban and rural standards of living.

In economics, the reformers favored maintaining the dominance of the central state plan. Within this context, however, they were also willing to expand considerably the role of market forces in the economy, particularly in the distribution of agricultural products and smaller consumer goods; grant greater autonomy to factory managers, especially in the determination of levels of output and the methods of production; and give local governments greater authority to make decisions about investments in their jurisdictions. Similarly, the reformers were prepared to expand private ownership of small service enterprises in the cities, and household management of agriculture in the countryside, as long as the state and collective economy retained the preeminent position. Chen Yun, one of the leading spokesmen for moderate reform, has likened the economy to a bird and the plan to a cage: if the cage is too small, the bird will die; but if there is no cage at all, the bird will fly away, unrestrained.[5]

In political affairs, the reformers envisioned much greater freedom in matters of scientific inquiry and artistic expression than either the revolutionary Maoists or the restorationists. They favored greater pragmatism in policymaking, in the spirit of "seeking truth from facts," and greater professionalism in public administration, in the direction of rule by technocrats. The reformers also sought to reduce the Party's involvement in detailed administrative matters, assigning those responsibilities to government bureaus, economic enterprises, and other grassroots organizations.

But the moderate reform program of the late 1970s treated politics, as well as economics, like a bird in a cage. The reformers characteristically insisted that writers and artists should avoid vulgarity, obscurantism, or modernism and should create their works with an eye toward social responsibility. Although the reformers favored the professionalization of policymaking and administration, they also believed that the Communist Party should retain ultimate leadership. Above all, although the reformers were prepared to allow freer debate over the details of social and economic programs in those years, they considered the essential structure of the political system, and a basic commitment to socialism, above question.

Compared with those further to the left on the Chinese political spectrum, the reformers proposed a much wider range of economic and scientific relations with the West. They welcomed foreign investment in China, loans from abroad, and academic exchanges with foreign countries. Once again, however, there were limits on how far the reformers were prepared to go in the late 1970s. They remained concerned about the "contaminating" influence of cultural contacts with capitalist countries and about the loss of national sovereignty that might accompany extensive economic interaction with foreigners. Thus they were protectionist in both culture and economics, seeking to exclude many Western ideas, values, and institutions from China—and to limit the access of foreign enterprises to the domestic Chinese marketplace—even as they enthusiastically welcomed the import of foreign technology and capital.

The moderate reform measures of the late 1970s had their roots both inside and outside China. Domestically, their origins can be traced to the proposals for political and economic liberalization that surfaced in 1956–57 as part of the increasing dissatisfaction with the undesirable consequences of the Soviet model. At that time, as noted in chapter 2, some Chinese leaders had suggested greater freedom for intellectuals and greater pragmatism in policymaking in the hope of discovering appropriate revisions in the policies and institutions imported from the Soviet Union during the First Five-Year Plan. In this spirit, some professional economists, with the support of Chen Yun, had advocated more liberal economic policies, including more moderate rates of economic growth, greater attention to consumer needs, less reliance on mandatory planning, greater use of market mechanisms in the economy, greater autonomy for factory managers, and more emphasis on profitability, rather than physical quantity of output, as an indicator of economic performance. Similar ideas were expressed again in the early 1960s, in the aftermath of the Great Leap Forward. Although Mao Zedong rejected these proposals each time they were introduced, regarding them as evidence of emerging revisionism in the Party, the new ideas formed the intellectual basis for reform after the chairman's death in 1976.[6]

This reformist tendency in Chinese Communism has been consistently linked to similar developments elsewhere in the socialist world. The discussions of political liberalization in China during the Hundred Flowers period of 1956–57 were the direct result of the process of de-Stalinization in the Soviet Union and Eastern Europe following Nikita Khrushchev's speech to the Twentieth Party Congress in Moscow in February 1956. The Chinese economists calling for a less tightly controlled economy, and for the greater use of profit as a criterion of economic performance, were certainly aware of the work of Yevsey Liberman and like-minded economists in the Soviet Union in the late 1950s and early 1960s. And since 1976, the reformers have investigated with great interest the experiments with economic restructuring that have been conducted in Eastern Europe and, more recently, in the Soviet Union under Mikhail Gorbachev.[7]

In sum, the core of the reform program in post-Mao China has been neither struggle nor order, but limited liberalization. Whereas the revolutionary Maoists took inspiration from the Cultural Revolution, and the restorationists regarded the First Five-Year Plan as their point of reference, the reformers saw themselves as part of a tide of socialist reform that began with de-Stalinization in the mid-1950s, spread to Eastern Europe in the 1960s, and now is inundating the entire communist world.

THE EVOLUTION OF THE POLITICAL SPECTRUM
SINCE THE DEATH OF MAO

China's political history between 1976 and 1982 can be divided into three stages. The first was the decisive showdown following the death of Mao Zedong, in which the restorationists under Hua Guofeng decisively defeated the revolutionary Maoists, headed by Mao's widow, Jiang Qing. During the second period, from October

1976 to December 1978, China experienced a brief interregnum under Hua Guofeng, during which the restorationists attempted to devise a program of economic recovery and political rehabilitation that could heal some of the wounds of the Cultural Revolution. Then a third period, from 1978 through 1982, saw a struggle between the restorationists and the reformers, leading to the steady erosion of Hua's position and his replacement by Deng Xiaoping as China's paramount leader.

The Fall of the Revolutionary Maoists, 1975–76

By 1975 both Mao Zedong and Premier Zhou Enlai, China's principal leaders after the manic stage of the Cultural Revolution, were old and ailing men. Mao, who had turned eighty-one at the end of 1974, was a victim of Parkinson's disease. He was rapidly becoming more feeble physically and, by most accounts, less lucid mentally. Zhou Enlai, five years Mao's junior, was diagnosed with cancer in 1972 and hospitalized for long periods beginning in 1974. With the end near for both men, the struggle over political succession intensified. The chief participants were, on the one hand, the group of revolutionary Maoists later described as the Gang of Four, including Jiang Qing, Zhang Chunqiao, Wang Hongwen, and Yao Wenyuan, and, on the other, a group of senior leaders, headed by Deng Xiaoping, who had been purged during the Cultural Revolution but rehabilitated in the early 1970s.

Through the middle of 1975, the veteran cadres led by Deng Xiaoping seemed to be on the ascendancy. In January 1975, in rapid succession, Deng was named a vice-chairman of the Party, first vice-premier, and chief of staff of the People's Liberation Army. Together, these appointments returned Deng to the highest levels of party leadership, gave him operational authority over the armed forces, and perhaps most important, placed him first in line to succeed Zhou Enlai as prime minister. Through the rest of 1975, Deng supervised the drafting of three important Party documents that, if formally adopted, would have launched China on a far more moderate and pragmatic course than the one followed during the Cultural Revolution. These comprehensive programmatic statements called for the revitalization of higher education, the revival of scientific research, a return to material incentives in industry and agriculture, a purge and rectification of the Party to reduce the influence of the leftists, and, above all, the reassertion of political discipline and Party control over a deeply divided country.

To try to stem this moderate tide, the leftists launched, almost certainly with Mao's general support, what would be their last great political campaign: a movement against "capitulating to class enemies" and against "reversing the correct verdicts" of the Cultural Revolution. Using their control of the press, the educational system, and the Party's propaganda apparatus, the revolutionary Maoists mobilized their supporters in the universities and the mass media to write and publish vitriolic criticisms of Deng Xiaoping and his moderate policies. When Zhou Enlai died in January 1976, the radicals had gained enough political momentum to deny the premiership to Deng Xiaoping, the man who, only twelve months before, had been in line to succeed Zhou. They were also able to prevent much more than a brief formal obituary from appearing in the Chinese press to honor Zhou's passing.

But the leftists were not powerful enough to secure the appointment of their own candidate, Zhang Chunqiao, as prime minister. Instead, the post went on a temporary basis to a relatively obscure Party official from Hunan province named Hua Guofeng. Hua was not a revolutionary Maoist like the Gang of Four: he had not served on the Cultural Revolution Group during the late 1960s, nor had he been active in the mass movement in his province. Nor was Hua one of the leading Party officials who had been attacked and purged during the upheavals of the period. Instead, Hua was a typical representative of a different group of Chinese leaders: the second-echelon Party and state officials, primarily in the provinces, whose superiors were swept aside by the Cultural Revolution, but whose own commitment to Maoist principles seemed sufficiently deep that they were promoted to succeed them. Hua was a member of what would later be described as the "weathervane" faction: men and women who were already in positions of power on the eve of the Cultural Revolution, who made their own accommodation with the movement, and who secured significant promotions as a result.[8]

In 1966, when the Cultural Revolution swept across China, Hua was second vice-governor, and concurrently a junior Party secretary, in Hunan. The dismissal of provincial leaders of higher rank opened the way for Hua's ascendancy, and when a revolutionary committee was formed in 1968 to replace the discredited provincial Party committee and local government, Hua was named its first vice-chairman. This promotion led to Hua's election to the Central Committee at the Ninth Party Congress in 1969 and to his selection as first secretary of the Party apparatus in Hunan when it was reorganized the following year.

The fact that Hua was working in Mao's native province, and had been responsible earlier in his career for the administration of the chairman's home county, probably facilitated his rise from provincial to national leadership. Hua was called to Peking in 1971 to help investigate the death of Lin Biao, who had been slated to become Mao's successor. Lin had allegedly launched an abortive coup against Mao in September 1971 and then died while trying to flee to the Soviet Union. After the Central Committee had issued its report on the Lin Biao affair, Hua was named a vice-premier of the State Council, gradually assuming responsibility for public security, agriculture, and science and technology. In 1973 at the Tenth Party Congress, Hua was promoted from Central Committee membership to a position on the Politburo.

Hua was probably not fully welcomed by either of the two principal factions in Chinese politics in the mid-1970s. To the veteran leaders of the pre-Cultural Revolutionary Party establishment, Hua was an opportunist who not only had survived the Cultural Revolution but had benefited from it. Conversely, the revolutionary Maoists saw Hua as a professional Party bureaucrat and criticized him periodically throughout the early 1970s for insufficient commitment to Maoist principles. Nonetheless, when Zhou Enlai died in early 1976, Hua was a plausible compromise as acting premier, whose selection allowed Mao to avoid a choice between the representatives of the two contending factions.

The continued influence of the revolutionary Maoists and the struggle surrounding the succession deeply disturbed many thoughtful urban Chinese. Angered at the media's failure to memorialize the death of Zhou Enlai, thousands of residents of Peking used the annual Qingming festival on April 5, 1976—traditionally when Chinese pay homage to their dead ancestors—to place tributes to Zhou at the base of the Monument to the People's Heroes in the heart of Tiananmen Square. Although this spontaneous demonstration purported to honor Zhou Enlai, its undertone was a denunciation of the Gang of Four and a display of support for Deng Xiaoping.

The infuriated revolutionary Maoists were able to use the demonstrations—which devolved into outright riots after the wreaths to Zhou Enlai were removed overnight—as a pretext for securing the dismissal of Deng Xiaoping from his positions in the Party, state, and army. But they were still not able to obtain any promotions for themselves. Instead, the chief beneficiary of the Tiananmen incident was Hua Guofeng. At Mao's request, the same meeting of the Politburo that removed Deng Xiaoping also confirmed Hua as prime minister, removing the label of "acting premier," which he had carried since the death of Zhou Enlai. It also appointed him as first vice-chairman of the Party Central Committee, which made Hua Mao's heir apparent as well.

The decisions of the April Politburo meeting did not end the maneuvering by the revolutionary Maoists.[9] Still claiming that they were resisting a "right deviationist wind of reversing the verdicts" on the Cultural Revolution, the leftists intensified the mass campaign against the moderates that they had launched the year before. With Mao's health now in rapid decline, their goal was to displace many of the veteran Party officials at the central and provincial levels who had been rehabilitated since the early 1970s. To achieve this goal, the leftists were prepared to foment political instability and political disorder across the country. The mass media under their control described rehabilitated cadres as "bourgeois democrats" who were "holding back the wheel of revolution."[10] Representatives of the revolutionary Maoists were dispatched from Peking to organize demonstrations and sit-ins in provincial capitals. Strikes and slowdowns crippled China's ports, railways, and several major cities. By the end of the summer, the leftists had secured the dismissal of the minister of railways, the minister of education, and the director of the New China News Agency, as well as the suspension of several provincial-level officials.

The death of Mao on September 9 only spurred the revolutionary Maoists to further action. The Gang of Four apparently fabricated what they described as Mao's final behest—"act according to the principles laid down"—and presented it as his final endorsement of the principles, programs, and leaders of the Cultural Revolution. With this as justification, the leftists attempted to mobilize support for the notion that Jiang Qing, and not Hua Guofeng, should succeed Mao as Party chairman. To further this plan, they tried to gain control over the central Party offices in Peking, seized some of Mao's private papers from the central Party archives, and threatened mass struggle against any leader who attempted to "tamper" with the principles Mao had specified.[11]

Realizing that the Gang of Four was not about to accept Hua's leadership, and apprehensive that the group might be plotting some kind of *putsch* or rebellion, the moderates decided to strike first. With the support of Hua Guofeng, Ye Jianying and Wang Dongxing, the Politburo members who controlled the military and the public security forces, launched a preemptive coup against the leftists on October 6, arresting the Gang of Four and the central officials most closely associated with them. A rump meeting of the Politburo the following day confirmed Hua's appointment as chairman of the

Central Committee and of the Party's Military Affairs Commission, as well as his continuing position as premier of the State Council. Shortly thereafter, military units loyal to the moderates seized control over Shanghai, the radicals' chief base of power outside the capital.

The Restorationists' Interregnum, 1977–78

Hua Guofeng thus emerged from the showdown with the Gang of Four with impressive official posts, placing him atop each of the three chief institutions that govern contemporary China. No one in the history of the People's Republic, not even Mao, had ever monopolized the positions of formal leadership in the Party, state, and military bureaucracies.[12] But Hua lacked the informal bases of power that, in the end, count for more than official titles in the relatively personalized and uninstitutionalized Chinese political process.[13] Although he had a reputation for sincerity and modesty, he had not earned distinction for innovative or decisive leadership. Since he had spent most of his career in Hunan, he had not had much opportunity to forge a national network of political supporters. Even more important, at age fifty-five in 1976, Hua was a relatively junior official, with only seven years' membership on the Central Committee and only three years of service on the Politburo. He remained the protégé of more senior leaders—first Mao and Zhou, and then Marshal Ye Jianying and Li Xiannian—rather than a strong political force in his own right. Moreover, it soon became apparent that both Ye and Li were prepared to abandon Hua in favor of a more seasoned and more qualified leader.

After his appointment as Party chairman, Hua tried to enlarge his power base by defining national policies that could attract and maintain a broad coalition of national leaders and political institutions.[14] His overall strategy was to maintain some continuity with the recent past, but to redefine some of the Maoist legacy to promote faster economic modernization and greater political stability. In so doing, Hua was responding to the contradiction between his own path to power and the political and economic crises that China faced in 1976. Hua's rise to national prominence had been the direct result of the Cultural Revolution. His selection as Mao's heir apparent was the immediate consequence of Mao's intervention. In such a situation, for Hua to repudiate either the man or the movement risked fatally undermining his own position. Accordingly, Hua continued to deify the late chairman and to endorse Mao's decision to launch the Cultural Revolution. Yet Hua also seemed to recognize the country's need for a period of political normalcy and economic development to heal the wounds of the previous decade. This realization explains not only his involvement in the purge of the Gang of Four in October 1976, but also his selection of the phrase "great order across the land" as the principal political slogan of his administration, and his sponsorship of an ambitious ten-year development plan for the Chinese economy.

Hua's programs, as they unfolded in 1977 and 1978, reflected both aspects of this contradictory political imperative. Even though Hua brooked no criticism of Mao, describing him as the "greatest Marxist-Leninist of our time," he appeared to place Zhou Enlai, widely regarded as the leader who had tried hardest to moderate the ravages of the Cultural Revolution, on an equal footing with the chairman in the hagiography of the Chinese Communist movement.[15] Similarly, although nothing Mao said or wrote was ever repudiated under Hua's leadership, the official exegeses of the chairman's works produced under Hua's sponsorship stressed the mid-1950s, when Mao was emphasizing economic development and the conciliatory management of "non-antagonistic contradictions" among the people, rather than the early 1960s, when Mao was developing the rationale for the Cultural Revolution.

Hua's attitude toward the Cultural Revolution was equally ambivalent. He criticized the Gang of Four for their exaggerated assault on the Party apparatus during the movement. But he continued to describe the doctrines that had justified Mao's decision to launch the Cultural Revolution—the theories of permanent class struggle and continuous revolution under socialism—as the "fundamental concepts" in Mao's political thought. Hua announced the end of the Cultural Revolution and acknowledged the country's need for unity and stability. But he still depicted the Cultural Revolution as an event that will "shine with increasing splendor with the passage of time" and promised that more "political revolutions in the nature of the Cultural Revolution will take place many times in the future" as needed to prevent the reemergence of revisionism in the Party. Moreover, Hua pledged to prolong the "revolution in the fields of education, literature and art, public health, and science and technology," thus endorsing the "socialist newborn things" in at least these areas of national policy.[16]

Although Hua took credit for the arrest of the Gang of Four, he tried to restrict the subsequent purge of the Party to the fairly small number of central and provincial leaders who had participated directly in the "conspiratorial activities" of the revolutionary Maoists. In mid-1978, he announced the completion of the campaign against leftist influence in the Party, well before any large number of the Maoists had been dismissed from positions of leadership or from Party membership. Hua sponsored the rehabilitation of many of the intellectuals persecuted during the Cultural Revolution, but he resisted the reinstatement of the most prominent victims of the movement, including Deng Xiaoping, and the posthumous rehabilitation of others, including former head of state Liu Shaoqi.

In the economy, Hua announced a "new leap forward," intended to transform China into a "great, powerful, and modern socialist country before the end of this century." As set out in his ten-year development program introduced in 1978, Hua's strategy assumed that higher rates of growth could be stimulated by political stability, higher investment, and greater incentives, without any basic structural reforms.[17] Accelerating mechanization and reestablishing material incentives for peasant families would stimulate agricultural output. Higher levels of state investment, a crash program of importing technology, heavy reliance on foreign loans, and increases in urban wages would increase industrial productivity. Under Hua's leadership, the rate of investment rose to 36.5 percent of national output in 1978, higher than at any time in the history of the People's Republic except for the Great Leap Forward. A surge of foreign borrowing that same year suggested that a large share of the capital and technology for Hua's "new leap forward" would come from abroad.[18]

Hua and his advisers did suggest modest structural changes in both the urban and rural economies. In agriculture, while aiming for higher levels of collectivization, they allowed the limited revival of private plots and free markets. In industry, they proposed the reestablishment of multiprovincial economic regions and the transformation of some industrial ministries into state corporations. But the basic character of the Chinese economy would have remained unaltered. Hua still envisioned an economy whose units would interact with one another through the mechanism of central planning rather than through the marketplace, and he still pledged to "deal blows at capitalism in both town and countryside," rather than encouraging private entrepreneurship.[19]

Hua's strategy, which retained some aspects of the Maoist legacy while rejecting others, was meant to build and expand a political coalition that would be strong enough to keep him in power. By launching a "new leap forward," with continued emphasis on investment in heavy industry, Hua sought to maintain the support of those institutions, particularly the military, the planning apparatus, and the machine-building industry, which had been the bulwarks of such policies in the past. By limiting the rectification of the Party to those directly linked to the Gang of Four, Hua sought to protect other leaders who, like himself, had also seen their careers flourish as a result of the Cultural Revolution. By rehabilitating the intellectuals who had been persecuted during the Cultural Revolution, and by sponsoring hefty increases in urban wages, Hua was appealing for support to two of the most alienated sectors in Chinese society. By stressing the need for loyalty to Mao's memory and past decisions, Hua sought to link his own legitimacy to the charismatic authority of the late chairman. But by obstructing the reinstatement of the veteran officials purged in the late 1960s and early 1970s, Hua was also trying to prevent the reemergence of more senior leaders who might threaten his political dominance.

Unfortunately for Hua, this strategy met increasing difficulties throughout 1977 and 1978. His economic program did yield relatively high rates of growth, nearly 11 percent in 1977 and more than 12 percent in 1978. But, as with similar movements in the past, the cost of these achievements was high. The rapid growth of imports— 85 percent in the two years 1977 and 1978—was not fully matched by the concurrent increase in exports, and in 1978 China ran its largest trade deficit since the First Five-Year Plan.[20] The expansion of capital investment far exceeded that which the state's industrial resources could sustain and created acute bottlenecks of both construction materials and capital goods. These inflationary pressures were exacerbated by increasing wages faster than expanding the production of consumer goods. Accordingly, Hua's ten-year plan was shelved in early 1979, only a year after it had been announced.[21]

If Hua's economic "leap forward" could be criticized for going too fast, many judged his political and organizational program as proceeding too slowly. Hua's defense of the Cultural Revolution was unacceptable to the victims of the movement, who wanted a decisive repudiation of the events of the late 1960s and early 1970s. Hua's leniency toward those officials who had collaborated with the Cultural Revolution was resisted by those individuals, particularly in the military, who advocated a thoroughgoing purge of the Party. And Hua's attitude toward Mao Zedong—summarized in an ill-chosen formula, later known as the "two whatevers," that Chinese should "resolutely defend whatever policies Chairman Mao has formulated, and unswervingly adhere to whatever instructions Chairman Mao has issued"—was opposed by those who sought an objective evaluation of the decisions of the late chairman, especially during the latter years of his life. In short, Hua was unable or unwilling fully to confront and resolve the deeper political crisis that China faced at the time of Mao's death.[22]

Above all, Hua Guofeng faced, in Deng Xiaoping, a powerful political rival waiting in the wings of the Party, with enormous personal prestige and an attractive alternative program. In the end, Hua's political resources were not great enough, nor his policies appealing enough, to beat back Deng's challenge. From the middle of 1977 to the fall of 1982, when Hua was finally removed from his last leadership positions in the Party, Hua Guofeng's political coalition gradually withered and collapsed under Deng's determined assault.

The Struggle between Restorationists and Reformers, 1978–82

Outsiders may never know with certainty the motives behind Deng Xiaoping's decision to challenge Hua Guofeng's position as China's paramount leader in the early post-Mao years. But three factors were probably crucial. Deng almost certainly believed that, by dint of both seniority and skill, he was more qualified than Hua to lead the Chinese Communist Party and thus the nation's 900 million people.[23] At seventy-two years of age in 1976, Deng was seventeen years older than Hua and had outranked the younger man at every point in their careers. In the late 1940s, when Hua was the political commissar of county-level Red Army forces in northwest China, Deng was the political commissar of the field army to which Hua's superiors reported. In the mid-1950s, when Deng was appointed secretary-general of the Chinese Communist Party, Hua headed only a prefectural Party committee in Hunan. Deng joined the Politburo in 1955; Hua was elected to membership eighteen years later, in 1973. Moreover, Deng had a reputation for an encyclopedic memory and prodigious administrative skills, whereas Hua's reputation was more for loyalty, modesty, and deference to more senior officials.

Second, Deng doubtless resented the different fates that the two men experienced during the Cultural Revolution. Deng was, after all, one of the movement's chief victims. He had been identified in 1966 as the "number-two capitalist roader" in the Party, second only to Liu Shaoqi, jailed in 1967, and then sent to Jiangxi province in 1969, where he worked parttime as a fitter in a country tractor plant. His eldest son, a student at Peking University at the onset of the Cultural Revolution, had been crippled by Red Guards and confined to a wheelchair for the rest of his life. Hua Guofeng, in contrast, had seen his political career prosper during the movement, rising from a second-echelon position in 1966 to Politburo member, prime minister, and, finally, Party chairman. Whatever his role in arresting the Gang of Four in October 1976, Hua Guofeng may well have appeared to Deng Xiaoping as little more than a collaborator in one of the darkest periods in Chinese history.

Perhaps most important, by the late 1970s Deng Xiaoping had become convinced of the need for much more sweeping political and economic reforms than Hua Guofeng was willing to undertake. His daughter's account of his internal exile suggests that the reading, physical labor, and contemplation that Deng conducted during the early 1970s produced a "maturing of the mind" about what he hoped to accomplish should he ever gain political rehabilitation.[24] But Deng's reflections in Jiangxi seem to have reinforced earlier proclivities toward political liberalization and economic pragmatism. More than any other senior Party leader, Deng had supported Mao's encouragement for intellectuals to criticize the Party during the Hundred Flowers movement of early 1957; similarly, he was one of the few to endorse the chairman's call for an "open door" rectification of the Party's rural organization in the early 1960s. In the economic sphere, Deng had long enjoyed a reputation as a leader who supported the expansion of private plots and free markets to increase agricultural production. His oft-quoted statement, "No matter whether the cat is black or white, if it catches mice, it's a good cat," well summarized an underlying realism and flexibility in Deng's approach to economic policy.[25]

By the time of Mao's death in 1976, Deng had become a man with a mission: to launch a fundamental restructuring of the Chinese political and economic order. Though he did not necessarily have a detailed or systematic program in mind, his main priorities were clear. In the political realm, he sought to resolve China's political crisis by repudiating the Cultural Revolution, rehabilitating its victims, and conducting a thorough reassessment of Mao's career as China's paramount leader. He wanted to relax the Party's controls over social and political life, widen the range of issues that could be discussed without explicit reference to doctrine, and restaff the Party and state bureaucracies with younger, better-educated, and more liberal leaders. In economics, Deng was strongly committed to a more broad and sustained interaction with the rest of the world, particularly the West, as a way of overcoming China's backwardness. He also came to support the critique of the Soviet economic model that had been put forward in the mid-1950s and early 1960s by men like Chen Yun who believed in a greater use of market mechanisms in the economy, a larger role for individual entrepreneurship, and more stress on profitability, rather than physical output, as the main indicator of economic performance.

At the time of Mao's death, however, Deng was again in internal exile, this time in south China, as the result of Mao's decision to expel him from all his leadership positions after the Tiananmen incident in April 1976. To carry out his ambition to launch China on the road to reform, therefore, Deng first had to regain political power. His strategy had three components: securing his formal rehabilitation as a member of the Party's highest-level leadership; developing an alternative to Hua's economic and political program and securing its adoption; and gradually altering the balance of forces within the central organs of the Party to ease Hua Guofeng out of the prime ministry and the Party chairmanship.[26]

Deng's restoration to the central Party leadership was the element of the strategy accomplished most easily and rapidly, given the widespread belief that he had been unfairly dismissed from office in April 1976. Hua Guofeng, with many of his closest associates, probably resisted Deng's rehabilitation and advocated continued criticism of Deng's alleged "revisionism" to ensure that he would not return from political obscurity to challenge their position. But seven or eight provincial Party committees and several Politburo members petitioned the Central Committee for Deng's rehabilitation. These demands were supported by an ingenious form of popular protest in a few places: small bottles were placed along major streets and even at the base of the monument to revolutionary martyrs in Peking, for the Chinese phrase meaning "small bottle" (*xiao ping*) is a homophone for Deng's given name.[27]

Finally, in March 1977, Hua Guofeng agreed to Deng's return to active political life by acknowledging that Deng had had no responsibility for the Tiananmen protests of April 1976. But Hua extracted, in return, a letter in which Deng acknowledged his past errors, accepted the validity of Mao's criticism, and expressed his "sincere support" for Hua's appointment as Party chairman. Deng also promised to accept whatever work assignment the Central Committee might give him. This seeming compromise was formally endorsed by the Third Plenum in July 1977, the first meeting of the full Central Committee since 1975, which reconfirmed Hua's selection as Party chairman and reappointed Deng to the same positions—vice-chairman of the Party, vice-premier, and chief of staff of the People's Liberation Army—that he had held before his purge in 1976.[28]

Despite these protestations of loyalty, there were already signs that Deng planned to challenge Hua's leadership by offering an alternative to the policies that Hua was sponsoring and encouraging the Central Committee to adopt them. Deng presented the outlines of his program in a series of speeches to major Party and state meetings and in articles in leading newspapers and journals. Some of these statements were written by Deng, some by senior leaders who shared his views on the need for reform, and others by sympathetic intellectuals. Lobbying for the adoption of this program represented the second element of Deng's strategy for gaining power over Hua Guofeng.

Initially, the presentation of Deng's alternative emphasized its political and ideological elements. Whereas Hua hailed the "victorious conclusion of the first Cultural Revolution," Deng and his supporters began to criticize the shortcomings of the movement and to call for a "reversal of verdicts" on more of its victims. Hua continued to describe class struggle as the "key link" in the present political situation, but Deng's followers argued that it was no longer appropriate to consider it the principal feature of Chinese politics. And although Hua portrayed the Gang of Four as "ultra-rightists," a label that complicated a full criticism of the origins and evolution of the Cultural Revolution, Deng and his associates were prepared to depict the gang more accurately as having followed an "ultra-leftist" line, an assessment that would have opened the way to more thoroughgoing reform.[29]

The most important element in the ideological controversy between Hua and Deng was a debate over the criteria for evaluating policy alternatives. Hua Guofeng, as noted earlier, proposed the doctrine of the "two whatevers," implying that Mao's decisions and predispositions should still limit the alternatives considered by Chinese leaders in the formulation of the country's development strategy. In contrast, Deng's supporters began to argue for a more pragmatic approach to policymaking, suggesting that, within broad limits, it was perfectly proper, indeed necessary, to move in new directions if they proved more effective. At a Party meeting in September 1978, for example, Deng Xiaoping explicitly criticized Hua's theory of the "two whatevers." "According to this doctrine," he complained, "whatever documents Comrade Mao Zedong read and endorsed and whatever he did and said must always determine our actions, without the slightest deviation. . . . If this goes on, it will debase Mao Zedong Thought." The correct approach, Deng argued, was to "seek truth from facts" and to adapt Marxism pragmatically to meet China's present conditions.[30]

Somewhat later, Deng and his supporters also began to introduce the rudiments of a new economic reform program. In an important presentation to the State Council in July 1978, Hu Qiaomu, a leading Party intellectual then closely associated with Deng, presented some of the basic principles of moderate economic reform, including the idea that enterprises should be given greater initiative and authority over production planning. He believed that prices should be readjusted to reflect accurately the balance between supply and demand, regions should be encouraged to specialize in those products for which they enjoyed a comparative advantage, and economic levers should gradually replace administrative orders as the mechanisms for state regulation of the economy. Although Hu noted that Hua Guofeng also had called for attention to "objective economic laws," the general propositions outlined in his report implied a far more wide-ranging reform of the structure of the economy than Hua had advocated. That Hu Qiaomu's presentation aroused intense controversy at the highest levels of the Party was suggested by the fact that its publication was delayed for nearly three months after its delivery.[31]

Deng's strategy was to mobilize support not only from within the highest level of the Party but also from vocal sectors of the broader population. He encouraged popular pressure for a more explicit repudiation of the Cultural Revolution and a more rapid and thoroughgoing rehabilitation of its victims. This pressure was reflected most vividly in the "Democracy Wall" movement that swept Peking at the end of 1978, when the Party was convening an important work conference and Central Committee plenum to discuss Deng's proposals for reform. Some of the wall posters and underground journals written during this period called for a change in the structure of the political system to permit greater democracy and legality, presaging the similar calls for political reform at the end of 1986. But most of the appeals were a poignant call for a redress of grievances resulting from the Cultural Revolution, reflecting public dissatisfaction with the slow pace of rehabilitations under Hua Guofeng.[32]

Largely because of this public pressure, the Party work conference of November-December 1978, and the Third Plenum of the Eleventh Party Central Committee that followed it, produced a breakthrough for Deng Xiaoping. The plenum explicitly endorsed several key elements of Deng's program and implicitly supported many others. Henceforth, economic modernization would replace class struggle as the focus of the Party's work, the plenum announced, and, it said, the era of mass movements, whether in political or economic affairs, had come to an end. These decisions explicitly modified policies connected with Hua Guofeng, for Hua had insisted that class struggle remained the "key link" in governing the country and had suggested that mass movements like the Cultural Revolution would recur "many times in the future" as conditions warranted. In endorsing experiments with the household responsibility in agriculture for a few backward regions, the plenum also distanced itself from the highly collectivist "Dazhai model," which Hua had been advocating for the rural areas.[33]

The Central Committee also strongly encouraged, though it did not explicitly support, two other key elements of Deng Xiaoping's program. The committee "highly evaluated" the debate about whether practice was the sole criterion of truth and promised a full reassessment of Mao and the Cultural Revolution in the near future. Though falling short of explicitly endorsing Deng's position, these passages in the communiqué of the Third Plenum acknowledged the legitimacy of the issues he was raising. By doing so, the plenum seriously questioned the "two whatevers" associated with Hua Guofeng.

The Third Plenum set the stage for further victories for Deng Xiaoping the following year, when the Fourth Plenum of the Central Committee endorsed a brief but important speech by Ye Jianying in honor of the thirtieth anniversary of the founding of the People's Republic. In that statement, the Central Committee explicitly supported Deng's position on the two issues that the Third Plenum had treated more tentatively. It declared that the principle of "seeking truth from facts" was the essence of Maoism and, while still postponing a detailed accounting, acknowledged that the Cultural Revolution had been, not a glorious moment in contemporary Chinese history, but a "great calamity for the Chinese people." The fact that the statement was read by Ye Jianying, the veteran army marshal who had previously been one of Hua Guofeng's principal supporters on the Politburo, illustrated the rapid erosion of Hua's political base. To make matters worse, the Fourth Plenum also rejected another position associated with Hua Guofeng when it decided that the Gang of Four had been "ultra-leftists," rather than pursuing, as Hua had called it, an "ultra-rightist" line.[34]

Having achieved great victories on the ideological and programmatic fronts, Deng then proceeded with the third element of his strategy: to strengthen his own power base within the leading organs of the Party and to remove those leaders associated with Hua Guofeng. Once again, Deng's approach was gradual and incremental. At first, he secured the appointment of his own supporters to influential administrative positions in the Party, army, and government. In 1977–78, Wei Guoqing, one of the Politburo members who had pressed hardest for Deng's rehabilitation, became director of the General Political Department of the People's Liberation Army, finally filling the vacancy created by the purge of Zhang Chunqiao in 1976. Hu Yaobang, former head of the Communist Youth League who had worked closely with Deng in the mid-1970s, became director first of the Party's organization department, and then of its propaganda department. Yao Yilin, an economic planner long associated with Chen Yun, was placed in charge of the Central Committee's administrative office, responsible for the day-to-day work of the Party. And Deng seemed to benefit more than Hua from the recomposition of provincial Party committees following the purge of the Gang of Four.[35]

Deng scored similar gains on personnel matters at the successive plenary sessions of the Central Committee between December 1978 and February 1980, and at the meeting of the National People's Congress in June 1979. Chen Yun, the veteran proponent of economic liberalization, was raised to membership on the Standing Committee of the Politburo. Several leaders sympathetic to reform, including Zhao Ziyang, Hu Yaobang, Peng Zhen, and Wang Zhen, were added to the Politburo or its Standing Committee. Still others, such as Chen Yun, Yao Yilin, Bo Yibo, and Wan Li, were appointed vice-premiers of the State Council. Zhao Ziyang was also appointed vice-premier. Some of these men would later come to differ with Deng over the pace and scope of reform, but for now they acted as his allies in his struggle against Hua Guofeng.

If Deng could not immediately secure the removal of Hua's supporters from the Politburo or from government ministries, he could create new Party and state agencies that would make Hua's political strongholds less important. Thus a Party Secretariat, headed by Hu Yaobang, was created at the Fifth Plenum in February 1980, and gradually assumed the responsibility for national policymaking that had previously rested in the Politburo under Hua's chairmanship. A Central Discipline Inspection Commission, under Chen Yun, was established at the Third Plenum in December 1978 and was given authority for undertaking the reconstruction and rectification of the Party that Hua Guofeng had hindered. An independent Chinese Academy of Social Sciences, created the same year, became a major center for the academic study of economic reform measures. Three new supraministerial committees, established to promote reform within the economy, were headed by leaders associated with reform: a finance and economic commission under Chen Yun, a machine building commission under Bo Yibo, and an agricultural commission under Wang Renzhong.

Deng's relative power gradually increased to the point that he could begin to remove his rivals from leading positions. First, Deng moved against the four central leaders who had risen from second-echelon posts to national prominence during the Cultural Revolution and who were regarded as Hua's closest supporters in the Politburo. This "little Gang of Four," comprising Wang Dongxing, Chen Xilian, Ji Dengkui, and Wu De, were stripped of their administrative responsibilities in the late 1970s and then removed from the Politburo in February 1980 on the grounds that they had supported the theory of the "two whatevers."

Later that same year, an offshore oil rig being towed into position in the Bohai Gulf sank in rough seas with a great loss of life. This incident offered Deng an opportunity to weaken another set of leaders to whom Hua had turned for support: a group of officials from the energy sector, who had helped formulate Hua's ambitious ten-year economic development scheme in 1978. This so-called petroleum faction was subjected to intense criticism at a meeting of the National People's Congress in mid-1980, and several of its members were disciplined. The petroleum faction also lost control of both the State Planning Commission and the State Economic Commission, the two state agencies most directly responsible for the administration of China's planned economy.[36]

Finally, Deng moved against Hua Guofeng. In 1980, in the name of fostering a clearer division of labor between the Party and the state, Deng persuaded the Central Committee to limit the practice of holding concurrent positions in the two bureaucracies. This enabled Deng to exchange his own resignation from his vice-prime ministerial position for Hua's removal from the premiership and to secure the appointment of Zhao Ziyang, who would soon prove to be one of China's most devoted and effective reformers, as Hua's successor. By the middle of 1981, Hua was forced to step down as Party chairman in favor of Hu Yaobang and was then dismissed from the Politburo at the Twelfth Party Congress in 1982. Within six years, Hua Guofeng, who had entered the post-Mao era at the pinnacle of all three of China's major political institutions, was left with only a junior position on the Central Committee.

The capstone to Deng's successful struggle against Hua Guofeng was the adoption of an authoritative Party resolution on the history of the Chinese Communist movement since its founding in 1921. This document marked the Party's formal acceptance of Deng's political and economic program. It repudiated the Cultural Revolution and the ideological tenets connected with the later years of Mao Zedong. It called for a reform of the economy and for the development of "methods other than class struggle" to resolve the "diverse social contradictions in Chinese society." It described "seeking truth from facts" as one of the most important components of Maoism. And it offered a blunt, if concise, assessment of the shortcomings of Hua Guofeng when it declared that he had "promoted the erroneous 'two-whatevers' policy," opposed seeking truth from facts, "obstructed" the rehabilitation of the veteran cadres purged during the Cultural Revolution," sought "quick results" in economic work, and "fostered the personality cult around himself while continuing the personality cult of the past." In short, Hua had persistently committed a "'left' error in guiding ideology" during his service as chairman of the Party.[37]

Hua and his followers vigorously resisted Deng's assault only until the Third Plenum of December 1978. Indeed, for a brief period after that crucial meeting, Hua's supporters encouraged the display of wallposters accusing Deng and his followers of "revisionism." But the plenum convinced Hua that Deng had already gained the initiative in the struggle between them, and he therefore changed his strategy from vigorous resistance to a more passive holding action. Hua refrained from expressing his differences with Deng, gave grudging verbal support to the new policies being adopted under Deng's sponsorship, and sacrificed his associates to save his own position—perhaps calculating that, if he could only hold on, he might outlive his older rival and emerge the victor. Only at the very end, in late 1980 and early 1981, when Hua's continued membership on the Politburo was at stake, did he fight to maintain a position as the senior vice-chairman of the Party, if not the chairmanship itself. At that critical moment, Deng defeated even this rearguard maneuver by reiterating the issue on which Hua had always been most vulnerable in high Party councils: his obstruction of the rehabilitation of the veteran Party cadres who had been the victims of the Cultural Revolution.[38]

With the removal of Hua Guofeng from the Party chairmanship in 1981 and from the Politburo in 1982, the reformers made further progress in the reconstitution of national leadership. At the Twelfth Party Congress in 1982, and at the National Party Conference in September 1985, they almost completely reshuffled the highest organs of the Party and state, retiring senior officials to prestigious advisory positions and securing the appointment of younger, reform-minded cadres to succeed them. The extent of leadership rotation achieved by the reformers during this period can be gauged by comparing the composition of the State Council, the Secretariat, and the Politburo at the end of the Party conference in 1985 with that at the beginning of 1980, when the removal of Hua Guofeng's supporters first got under way. Of eighteen vice-premiers in early 1980, only eight remained on the State Council in 1985. Similarly, twenty-one of twenty-six Politburo members, and eight of eleven members of the Secretariat, were replaced during the same period. The survivors (older men like Deng Xiaoping, Chen Yun, Wan Li, Hu Yaobang, and Zhao Ziyang) and the replacements (particularly younger leaders like Hu Qili, Qiao Shi, Li Peng, and Tian Jiyun) gave the reformers dominance on all three of these central leadership bodies.

In summary, Hua Guofeng did not prove an effective or appropriate leader for China in the post-Mao era. His vision of China's future was limited. He was unwilling to break decisively with the follies of the past, and he was unable to resolve the political crisis or the economic ailments plaguing his country in the late 1970s. His political resources were outmatched by Deng's personal prestige and network of contacts, and his political strategy was soon reduced to one of passively waiting for Deng to die first. Still, it is possible to have some sympathy for this tragic figure. Hua was, literally, betrayed by Deng Xiaoping, who had pledged his loyalty to Hua as a condition for his own political rehabilitation. But despite this betrayal, Hua refused to use Cultural Revolutionary mechanisms, such as the mobilization of mass opposition to Deng, to defend himself against attack. Hua's contribution to contemporary Chinese history was the purge of the Gang of Four in the name of restoring political stability and normalcy. To Hua's great credit, he steadfastly refused to abandon this same principle to save his own political position. Instead, he agreed to pass quietly into obscurity.

CONCLUSION

In the nine years between the death of Mao Zedong in 1976 and the National Party Conference in 1985, the center of gravity of the Chinese political spectrum shifted rapidly to the right. The revolutionary Maoists were purged from the Politburo with the purge of the Gang of Four in October 1976. Their followers at the central and provincial levels were dismissed from their posts in the months that followed, and the revolutionary Maoists at lower levels of the Party and state bureaucracies were gradually removed during the waves of Party rectification and bureaucratic restaffing that occurred in the early 1980s. The influence of the restorationists was reduced in stages: first by the removal of the "little Gang of Four" in February 1980, then by the humiliation of the petroleum faction in the summer of 1980, and finally by the demotion of Hua Guofeng from his leading positions in the Party in 1981–82.

A powerful coalition of leaders emerged in place of the revolutionary Maoists and the restorationists. Committed to economic and political reform, the newly empowered leaders secured political rehabilitation in 1977–78, gained support for their general program at the Third Plenum in December 1978, obtained control of the Politburo at the Twelfth Party Congress in 1982, and consolidated their authority over the Politburo, the Secretariat, and the Central Committee at the National Party Congress in 1985. Moreover, recent years have seen proposals from radical elements of that coalition for even more wide-ranging and thoroughgoing reform of China's economic system and political structure. As a result, the reform programs that seemed visionary in the late 1970s seemed conservative, even orthodox, by the mid-1980s.

How can one explain this rapid change in political climate in less than a decade? To begin with, the revolutionary Maoists had a far weaker political base than the rhetoric of the early 1970s might have suggested. At the time of Mao's death, revolutionary Maoism was represented primarily by a small coterie of central leaders who had risen to prominence because of their involvement in the mass movements of the Cultural Revolution. They had fairly strong footholds in a few Party and government agencies, particularly those responsible for propaganda, culture, and education, which they had been able to staff with their own followers. They had also gained control of leadership positions in a few provinces and municipalities and had attempted to cultivate a handful of opportunistic military officers who sought influential positions in civilian affairs. And they had woven their supporters into a network of political action that could effectively disrupt and criticize the policies of more moderate leaders.

On balance, however, the political base of the revolutionary Maoists was fragmented and shallow. As suggested in chapter 2, the objective political and economic problems that had emerged under the leadership of Mao Zedong had drastically eroded the popular base for the policies and institutions of the Cultural Revolution. Consequently, the Gang of Four had some followers in many places, but they had gained majority support or administrative control in very few. Moreover, the death of Mao Zedong removed their most important source of political power, for although Mao was not always an uncritical supporter of the revolutionary Maoists, he protected them while he was alive from a concentrated attack by others.

Explaining the fall of the restorationists presents a somewhat more difficult problem. The key elements of the restorationist program—rapid growth, central planning, political order, Party leadership, ideological conservatism—were deeply rooted in some of the most powerful institutions in Chinese society. Hua Guofeng's ten-year development program must have strongly appealed to the heavy industrial ministries, the foreign trade apparatus, and the central planning establishment, all of whom would have benefited from its provisions. Similarly, Hua's calls for continued loyalty to Mao Zedong, but for the restoration of stability and the reconstruction of the Party, were designed to gain the support of the public security organs, the military, and the Party apparatus.

But, like the Gang of Four before him, Hua Guofeng suffered from some fatal flaws in his political base. In a society that places great weight on the personal qualities of its leaders, Hua never developed the individual authority that would have enabled him to consolidate his position. He was too junior, too inexperienced, too tainted by his association with the Cultural Revolution, and too reliant on the political patronage of others. His ten-year development program, like the Great Leap Forward on which it was loosely patterned, stretched the Chinese economy nearly to the breaking point, producing serious bottlenecks in supplies and generating the largest deficit in the country's current accounts for two decades. Furthermore, Hua failed to provide a fundamental solution to the acute political crisis that the nation faced in the late 1970s. He had refused to repudiate decisively the Cultural Revolution or to rehabilitate all the veteran Party officials who had been victims.

The shift in the Chinese political spectrum cannot be attributed simply to the weaknesses of the left. A further explanation must also be sought in the strengths of the right, especially in the skill and vision of Deng Xiaoping. The sluggish economic growth, the stagnant levels of consumption, the decaying administrative bureaucracy, and above all the political turmoil and persecution of the late Maoist period had created large potential constituencies for political and economic reform. But these supporters still had to be mobilized in ways that could offer a successful challenge to Hua Guofeng.

It was here that Deng Xiaoping's role was critical. His vast connections in both the army and the Party, dating in the first instance from his service as political commissar in one of the four

Communist field armies during the revolution, his position on the Party's Military Affairs Commission in the 1950s and 1960s, and his position as secretary-general of the Party from 1954 until the onset of the Cultural Revolution, gave him a personal network of colleagues and clients unmatched by any other leader. Deng's reputation as a talented administrator and a pragmatic policymaker had made him the leading candidate to succeed Zhou Enlai as premier, until the Gang of Four was able to use the Tiananmen incident to send Deng yet again into internal exile. Moreover, Deng personified the issue on which Hua Guofeng was most vulnerable: his travails in Peking and Jiangxi between 1967 and 1973 exemplified the persecution experienced by senior Party leaders during the Cultural Revolution, and his second purge in 1976 exemplified the continuing struggle of those veteran cadres to secure their political rehabilitation.

Deng supplemented this powerful political base and attractive policy program with a skillful strategy for regaining political power. Step by step, Deng whittled away at Hua Guofeng's position, first by creating new positions for his own lieutenants, then by dismissing Hua's more controversial associates, and finally, when the time was ripe, securing the removal of Hua. Even as he sought their political defeat, however, Deng dealt with his opponents in a relatively humane manner. Although they were sometimes the target of official criticism, and although they were dismissed from their positions in the central leadership, many remained on the Central Committee or were transferred to honorific positions on the newly created Central Advisory Commission. None was subjected to the political persecution that was the fate of Mao's defeated rivals during much of the chairman's rule.

In short, the shift in the Chinese political spectrum since 1976 has been only in part the inevitable result of the acute political crisis and the chronic economic difficulties that the country experienced at Mao's death. Equally, the change resulted from extraordinary political engineering, led by one of the most colorful leaders of contemporary China. It is never wise, of course, to place too much emphasis on the role of any individual leader in history. In this case, however, one might be forgiven for asking whether the changes in post-Mao China would have been as rapid or as dramatic if Deng, like so many of his colleagues, had died during the tragedy of the Cultural Revolution.

CHAPTER 4

The Course of Reform

THE historic shift from revolutionary Maoism to restorationism to reform was a surprisingly smooth and rapid affair, basically accomplished between 1976 and 1978. In contrast, the implementation of reform measures since the Third Plenum of the Central Committee in 1978 has seemed more halting and tentative. A wavelike pattern has characterized the process, as periods of consolidation or retreat have followed periods of advance, and periods of rapid momentum have given way to a more measured or tentative pace.

In part, the cycles have resulted from the complex economic, social, and political problems encountered during the course of reform. The loosening of administrative controls over the economy has frequently produced inflation, budget deficits, excessive investment, and surges of imports. Similarly, the relaxation of the political climate has allowed the emergence of crime, corruption, political dissent, and cultural experimentation, all of which many Chinese have regarded as unacceptable. These difficulties have required the reformers to slow down and take remedial measures to restore economic equilibrium and political stability before resuming the pace of reform.

The cyclical pattern of reform has also reflected a growing division of the reform coalition into moderate and radical wings since the early 1980s. Both groups of reformers have agreed on the need to depart decisively from both the policies and programs of the late Maoist period and the institutions of the Soviet model. But when compared with its moderate counterpart, the radical wing of the reform movement has been willing to move farther and faster toward political and economic liberalization. Conversely, the moderate reformers have been more concerned with maintaining economic balance and political stability and have been willing to take fewer risks along the road to reform than have their more radical colleagues.

These divisions between moderate and radical reformers have

exacerbated the cyclical character of reform in China since 1978. When reform has produced economic or political difficulties, the moderate reformers have been emboldened to call for protracted periods of retrenchment, or for a tightening of administrative controls. Conversely, when political and economic normalcy has been restored, the radical reformers have felt it possible to insist on accelerating the reform program. The cycles of reform have, in this way, reflected an interweaving of a struggle for power within the reform coalition with the attempts to remedy the problems that reform has produced.

A CHRONOLOGY OF REFORM

A brief review of the evolution of reform between 1978 and 1987 illustrates the cyclical character of the reform process and provides a chronological background for the more thematic analysis that is presented in later chapters. Although political reform and economic reform are closely intertwined, the chronology is clearer if these two elements are discussed separately.

Economics

China began experimenting with economic structural reform soon after the reformers achieved dominance over the restorationists during the Third Plenum at the end of 1978. In agriculture, first the production teams, roughly equivalent to a village, and then individual families, were assigned state production quotas and allowed control over the disposal of any above-quota output. Similarly, some state enterprises were allowed to retain a share of their profits and to sell independently the part of their output that exceeded mandatory state quotas. In both industry and agriculture, markets were opened to handle the distribution of above-quota production.

These early reforms threw the Chinese economy into serious imbalance. As enterprises and local government agencies retained a larger share of their profits, state revenues declined, and the national budget went into deficit. Investment, particularly at local levels, vastly exceeded government targets, as enterprises and local governments rushed to invest their retained profits into new projects. Imports, especially of capital goods, increased faster than exports, and China experienced a combined foreign trade deficit of $3.9 billion in 1979–80, the largest in its history.

At a central work conference at the end of 1980, Chinese leaders accepted a proposal from Chen Yun for a period of retrenchment and readjustment to remedy these imbalances.[1] Investment was slashed, the economy slowed, budget expenditures reduced, and the trade deficit trimmed. Further economic reform was also postponed in the apparent belief that the restructuring of the economy could be successfully undertaken only in a period of economic vitality, not economic weakness.

After two years of concerted retrenchment, economic reform entered a second period of advance between 1983 and 1985. A full set of moderate economic reforms was introduced, refined, expanded, and systematized during this period. In agriculture, critical decisions were promulgated by the Central Committee regularly, every January. In 1983 Peking announced the universal implementation of the household responsibility system; in 1984 it pledged to leave the resulting division of land unchanged for at least fifteen years; and in 1985 it replaced mandatory state purchases of grain with a more voluntary procurement contract system. In the urban economy, important components of structural reform were also introduced in 1983–84, including a reduction in the scope of mandatory planning, further increases in the autonomy of state enterprises, a decentralization of the foreign trade apparatus, the identification of fourteen open cities along the Chinese coast with greater flexibility to attract foreign trade and investment, reforms in the system of state finance, and changes in the wage system. These piecemeal measures were then codified in two major policy statements: a comprehensive outline of urban economic reform in October 1984 and a proposal for the Seventh Five-Year Plan (1986–90) in September 1985.[2]

Like their predecessors several years earlier, these reforms also caused the economy to overheat. The economic growth rate, measured in terms of national output, rose from 8 percent at the end of the retrenchment period in 1982 to 10 percent in 1983 and exceeded 12 percent in both 1984 and 1985. State investment increased by 25 percent in 1984 and by another 43 percent the following year. The wage bill, swollen by the bonuses distributed as part of wage reform, rose by more than 17 percent during the same two years. Despite these conditions, Peking then introduced another key rural reform: the relaxation of administrative controls over the prices of many agricultural products, including meat, eggs, and vegetables, which the state had previously subsidized. The result was predictable. The average retail price of agricultural produce rose 9 percent in 1985—a very high rate of inflation for a society accustomed to price stability—with the prices of those commodities that had been decontrolled rising by one-fifth to one-third.[3]

The overheating of the economy was evident in China's foreign exchange accounts as well. As in the late 1970s, the rise in domestic investment sparked a surge of imports of foreign equipment. This time, however, a simultaneous rise in the imports of consumer goods exacerbated the problem, as the central government sought to absorb the excess wages and bonuses that had been awarded at the end of 1984, and as local enterprises and governments tried to profit from the growth in consumer demand. As a result, China's merchandise trade balance, which had returned to equilibrium and then entered a surplus during the period of retrenchment, went into the deepest deficit yet: $1.3 billion in 1984, $15.1 billion in 1985, and another $6.4 billion in the first half of 1986.

Consequently, Chinese officials were forced to impose a second period of consolidation. Once again, import controls were tightened, the rate of investment slashed, the growth in the money supply slowed, and production quotas reduced—all in an effort to cool the economy down. The central government placed new restrictions on the ability of the open cities to conclude their own investment contracts with foreign firms, and limited their access to foreign exchange. And, as they had done at the end of 1980, Chinese officials announced at the beginning of 1986 that economic reform would be delayed during this period of readjustment. No new price or wage reforms would be undertaken for twelve months, they said, for 1986 would be a year of "consolidation, assimilation, supplementation, and improvement."[4]

This period of retrenchment was much shorter than the one that occurred between 1981 and 1983. By the end of 1986, in fact, several aspects of economic reform had regained momentum. The implementation of some elements of the urban reforms of 1983–85 resumed in the fall, with the adoption of a new labor system, the relaxation of price controls on some manufactured consumer goods, and the promulgation of a draft law on enterprise bankruptcy. Moreover, a set of more radical economic reforms was placed on the Chinese political agenda in the middle of the year. There was a lively discussion of the desirability of the creation of markets for the factors of production, and some experiments with capital markets were conducted in some of China's principal cities. The reform of the system of state ownership of industry was also the subject of intense scrutiny; some state and collective enterprises were leased to individual entrepreneurs or to groups of workers, while others issued shares of stock and formed boards of directors to supervise their management.

Still, by early 1987, the Chinese economy had still not completely recovered from the overheating of 1984–85. Although the trade deficit fell somewhat in 1986, it remained, at $12 billion, much higher than normal, and forced Peking to expand short-term borrowings on international capital markets. The government budget deficit, too, increased a bit, as the devaluation of the yuan and increases in the prices of raw materials lowered the profits earned by Chinese industry and reduced the taxes they paid to the state. Grain production, which had slumped in 1985 when mandatory production quotas were terminated, recovered somewhat in 1986, but still fell short of target. The rate of growth of investment fell from 38.7 percent in 1985 to 16.7 percent in 1986, a figure that Chinese leaders still thought excessive. Partly as a result, the general level of retail inflation remained high, at 6 percent, and the cost of living index for urban workers stayed at 7 percent—well below the levels of 1985 but substantially above those for the early 1980s.[5]

Thus, as 1987 began, Chinese leaders were still calling for economic retrenchment and consolidation. For the first time in many years, Peking launched a national economy campaign, saying its aim was to "reduce [consumer] spending, boost production, practice economy, increase revenue, and cut expenditure." Price reform was postponed again, with the State Council announcing at the beginning of 1987 that no increase would be made in the number of goods whose prices could fluctuate in response to market conditions. But other aspects of reform continued, including the drive to increase the autonomy of industrial enterprises, the creation of capital markets in major cities, and the experiments with leasing smaller state enterprises to those who had applied to manage them. These steps suggested that China was entering a complex period. Some aspects of reform maintained momentum, even as Peking delayed others in its fight to bring the economy into greater equilibrium.[6]

Politics

China's political reform shows a wavelike pattern similar to that of economic reform. In politics, however, two surges of reform occurred between 1978 and 1987, rather than three.

The main elements of moderate political reform were introduced between 1979 and 1983. By 1979 most of those who had been labeled "capitalists," "landlords," "counterrevolutionaries," or "rightists" during the Maoist period had secured their political rehabilitation. Steps were taken between 1979 and 1982 to construct a new legal order, with the adoption of new state and Party constitutions and the promulgation of codes of criminal law, criminal procedure, and civil procedure. Elections to local people's congresses, involving some competition among candidates nominated by the Party, were held in 1980. At about the same time, the National People's Congress began to take a more active and assertive role in discussion of national policy and to form specialized committees to examine proposed legislation. The restructuring and rejuvenation of the state bureaucracy started in 1982, and the rectification and restaffing of the Party finally got under way the following year.

Like economic reform, political relaxation in post-Mao China has had costs, particularly in the eyes of more conservative members of the Party leadership. The price has included the rise of crime and corruption, the expression of unorthodox opinions by intellectuals and students, experiments with new styles of expression by writers and artists, and the emergence of a materialistic, often vulgar, popular culture among ordinary Chinese. To address these problems, the authorities have periodically employed judicial measures, administrative sanctions, public criticism, and ideological education to reassert their control over Chinese society. Thus there was a suppression of political dissent following the Democracy Wall movement in 1979; a period of criticism of "bourgeois liberalism," particularly in the arts, in 1980–81; a campaign against "spiritual pollution" in the ideological and cultural sphere in 1983–84; and a crackdown against corruption in 1985–86. But in each case, once the social and political problems that were the target of the campaign had been identified, and some progress made in addressing them, the movement for political liberalization soon regained momentum. Indeed, some more conservative leaders began to conclude that the officials responsible for the day-to-day conduct of the Party's political education, including General Secretary Hu Yaobang, were insufficiently interested in thoroughly criticizing and eliminating these "unhealthy tendencies."

A second wave of political reform began to rise in 1986, when Deng Xiaoping again placed the issue on the Chinese political agenda. Deng never specified exactly what he meant by political reform. But with his general support as encouragement, some prominent intellectuals began to complain that some important elements of the political reforms of the early 1980s had not been adequately implemented. They mentioned the separation of the Party from the government, the rejuvenation and professionalization of the Party and state bureaucracies, and the expansion of political participation. Other leaders called for a streamlining of the state's economic agencies to reduce the government's ability to exercise direct administrative control over the economy. And some reform-minded officials, such as Hu Yaobang and Hu Qili, implied that discussions about the future course of political liberalization and reform should be unconstrained by ideological preconceptions.

Emboldened by these developments, some intellectuals began to introduce truly radical ideas into the debate. Some began to talk about the desirability of a multiparty system, with competitive elections. Others suggested abolishing basic-level Party committees in factories and universities to prevent the Party from interfering in the day-to-day operation of these grassroots units. Still others proposed the adoption of a law that would guarantee the freedom of the press and demanded the acknowledgment of the inalienable civil rights of Chinese citizens.

These ideas were embodied in a massive wave of student protests that spread through a score of Chinese cities in November and December 1986. Most of the demonstrators initially focused on local university issues, including poor food, crowded living conditions, and rising tuition. But others expressed dissatisfaction with the procedures for selecting delegates to local people's congresses, charging that university students were underrepresented and that genuinely independent candidates were disregarded. Over time, the protests began to coalesce around the issue of fundamental structural reform, with many participants calling for greater "freedom" and "democracy" for China.

Even as these events were occurring, dissatisfaction mounted at the highest levels of the Party with the leadership of Hu Yaobang. Hu's somewhat flamboyant, rash, and idiosyncratic style irritated many senior leaders who believed that the chief spokesman for the Party should possess a more grave, discreet, and collaborative demeanor. His call for accelerated economic growth, and for rapid economic reform, alarmed those more moderate reformers who were convinced of the need for steady and balanced economic development. Other officials were aghast at Hu's apparent sponsorship of radical political reform and his relative disinterest in maintaining an active program of political education. Perhaps the most serious problem was Hu's willingness to defy important elements of the political establishment: his demands that elderly leaders retire, his reluctance to give promotions to the children of senior officials, and his denigration of the role of the military in civilian affairs. By the summer of 1986, pressure was increasing in the Party for Hu's removal from the position of Party general secretary.

Perhaps the students felt their demonstrations would strengthen the hand of leaders who wanted more thoroughgoing political reform against those who were more cautious and orthodox. Conceivably, some intellectuals associated with Hu Yaobang encouraged the students to carry their demands into the streets. But the demonstrations had just the opposite effect than intended. At first, China's leaders adopted a conciliatory tone toward the students, expressing sympathy with their motives but questioning the methods they were using to express their views. As the ranks of the demonstrators swelled, however, the Party felt that it had no choice but to restore order by ending the protests. The authorities began to publish more critical accounts of the dissidents, promulgate more stringent regulations governing street demonstrations, arrest nonstudents involved in the protests, and threaten student participants with undesirable job assignments after their graduation.

By the middle of January 1987, the student demonstrations had occasioned a renewed campaign against "bourgeois liberalization." As in previous movements of this kind, intellectuals associated with proposals for radical political reform, and those who had expressed the sharpest criticism of the Party, were singled out for particular criticism. Some were dismissed from their administrative positions in universities, and some were expelled from the Party. Officials in the propaganda department of the Party were dismissed, and several newspapers and magazines were ordered to suspend publication on the grounds that they had not given students proper political education and guidance. But this time the backlash claimed even higher victims. Hu Yaobang was forced to resign as general secretary of the Party, to be replaced, at least temporarily, by Zhao Ziyang. Again, China seemed to be entering a period of political retrenchment and consolidation.

THE DIVISION BETWEEN MODERATE AND RADICAL REFORMERS

The purge of the revolutionary Maoists, and the submergence of the restorationists, greatly narrowed the differences among the leaders at the pinnacle of the Chinese political system. But the resolution of the debates of the 1970s gave rise to another cleavage as a gap emerged between the moderate and radical wings of the reform movement. The tensions between these two groups should not be characterized as a struggle between those who favor reform and those who oppose it. Both groups have agreed on the need for significant changes in the structure of the Chinese political and economic system. Instead, the difference between the moderate reformers and their more radical counterparts has concerned the questions of how fast to reform and how far to proceed, with the moderates at once more deliberate and more orthodox than their radical colleagues. Where one group is bold and enthusiastic about reform, the other tends to be cautious and skeptical.

The Radical Reformers

In economics, the radical reformers have favored a much greater role for the market than have the moderate reformers. Chen Yun, the chief spokesman for moderate reform, has proposed making the market an important supplementary mechanism for the allocation of goods and services and the determination of prices, with the state continuing to occupy the dominant position. The radical reformers would turn this formula on its head: the market, they believe, should be paramount, and the plan secondary. Moreover, the moderate reformers would restrict the operation of the market to agricultural goods and a few small manufactured commodities. The radical reformers, in contrast, favor the development of markets for almost all factors of production, including capital and labor, as well as for every type of raw material and industrial machinery.

The radical reformers have welcomed more extensive economic and cultural relations with foreign countries than have the proponents of moderate reform. They have been less worried by the danger of "spiritual contamination" from contact with capitalist countries and, indeed, have usually argued that the main cultural obstacles to socialist reform come not from foreign bourgeois influences, but from China's own "feudal" and "small peasant" traditions. Similarly, the radical reformers are also less protectionist on economic matters. Many favor opening the Chinese market to imports from foreign countries and the products of foreign ventures in China, asserting that only by doing so can Chinese enterprises increase their ability to compete in the international marketplace.

In politics, the radical reformers have favored greater pluralization than do the moderate reformers. They would allow writers, artists, and intellectuals greater freedom to explore hitherto forbidden subjects and to experiment with new styles of expression. They would open basic political questions, including the structure of the state and the role of the Party, to more candid and probing examination. Some would favor a restructuring of the Party to reduce its control over personnel appointments in non-Party organizations and minimize its interference in the day-to-day operations of factories, universities, and other enterprises. Others have proposed expanding the role of national and local legislatures, granting greater freedom to the press, and enlarging the authority of provincial and local governments to prevent the arbitrary exercise of political power by the central Party authorities. Some radical reformers have suggested direct elections to leading positions at all levels of government; others have recommended competitive elections to expand the opportunities for popular participation.

Many of those most active in radical reform have been a group of intellectuals in their thirties and forties. Some of them were sent to the countryside during the Cultural Revolution (1966–76), and others have been trained in the United States since 1978. They have formed study groups, salons, and, more recently, research institutes. They have suggested a wide range of sweeping reform measures and presented some of them to sympathetic higher-level leaders for consideration. The sponsors of radical reform in the central Party leadership have included Hu Yaobang, who served as general secretary of the Party from 1982 to 1987; Zhao Ziyang, prime minister since 1980, who was Hu's immediate successor as head of the Party apparatus; and Hu Qili, Tian Jiyun, and Wang Zhaoguo, younger leaders appointed to the Party Secretariat in the mid-1980s. To a degree, the radical reformers have been protected by Deng Xiaoping, who has shown great sympathy for much of their program.

At the extreme right of the Chinese political spectrum, a few radical reformers, mainly younger intellectuals, have posited some basic principles that are nothing less than revolutionary in character: the economy should be grounded in the sanctity of private property rights; political legitimacy should be derived from the consent of the governed; the government and Party should unconditionally respect certain basic human and civil rights; and China's culture can be modernized only if it rejects most of its past culture and absorbs Western values and institutions. As of this writing this group represents a small minority of those interested in radical reform. But the group may become more vocal, and possibly more influential, in the years ahead.

The reference points for the radical reformers are not in China's own history, or even in Eastern Europe and the Soviet Union, but in the experience of the North Atlantic and East Asia. Some radical reformers have been attracted to the pluralistic political institutions of the United States or to the social democracy of Western Europe. Even more find inspiration in the newly industrialized countries of East Asia: the ability of Japan, South Korea, and Taiwan to blend private entrepreneurship with public ownership, market forces with government regulation, and organizational pluralism with political order.

The Moderate Reformers

Compared with these radical reformers, more moderate elements in the reform coalition have wanted to proceed with reform more slowly, gradually, and deliberately. In keeping with the development strategy of Chen Yun, their principal spokesman on economic issues, the moderate reformers have emphasized preserving an equilibrium in the management of the Chinese economy: balance between government revenues and expenditures, balance between exports and imports, and balance between supply and demand for major commodities. The moderate reformers have feared, often correctly, that a rapid relaxation of administrative controls over the economy will create severe disequilibrium in all three areas, as local governments launch new investment projects, workers demand higher wages and better standards of living, and enterprises import capital equipment and consumer goods from abroad. The moderate reformers see economic liberalization as fostering a growing gap between supply and demand, a deficit in the state budget, and a shortage of foreign exchange.

This difference of opinion between moderate and radical reformers can also be seen as a debate over how much risk is acceptable in the course of economic reform. The moderate reformers are averse to risks. They wish to maintain fairly stringent administrative control over certain aspects of the economy, especially investment and foreign exchange, in order to preserve economic balance. The radical reformers, in contrast, are more willing to take risks for the sake of improved economic efficiency, even if the result is a temporary disequilibrium in the national economy. In this sense, the radical reformers are, paradoxically, similar to Mao Zedong, who also believed that imbalance and disequilibrium should be seen as a motivating force in the economy, rather than a destabilizing factor.

An example illustrating this difference concerns opening the domestic market to the output of foreign investment projects in China. The moderate reformers have been reluctant to permit the repatriation of profits earned in *renminbi* because of fear that the resulting outflow of hard currency would lead to an imbalance in China's foreign exchange accounts. The radical reformers, in contrast, believe that such a policy will produce countervailing inflows of foreign exchange. Not only will more foreigners be persuaded to invest or reinvest in China, but the competition from foreign ventures will improve the ability of Chinese enterprises to produce for world export markets.

In short, whereas the radical reformers have stressed the necessity for rapid structural reform, the moderate reformers have emphasized the desirability of continuous "readjustments" to maintain economic equilibrium. The moderate reformers would prefer a protracted process of structural reform, with lengthy periods of readjustment during which the imbalances generated by reform can be repaired. The radical reformers, in contrast, have favored far more rapid structural change to remove quickly the inefficiencies and rigidities of the previous economic system. According to some accounts, this debate was especially severe when the Party was drafting a comprehensive proposal for the reform of the urban economy in 1984. At that time, Chen Yun suggested structural reform over a period of thirty years, while Hu Yaobang insisted on completing the process in three to five years. In 1985, when reform had created serious imbalances, Chen reportedly recommended slowing the process of structural reform to the point that it would take a full century to complete.[7]

A second issue chronically dividing the moderate reformers from their more radical counterparts concerns culture and public morality. The moderate reformers particularly interested in this question have included Peng Zhen, the chairman of the National People's Congress Standing Committee; Hu Qiaomu, a leading ideologist who was elected to the Politburo in 1982; and Deng Liqun, the member of the Secretariat with overall responsibility for the Party's propaganda work. These three leaders have been concerned about how much political and economic reform has eroded the "socialist spiritual civilization," which they believe the Party should be committed to protect.

The moderate reformers have been sympathetic to a relaxation of the ideological constraints that once stifled Chinese art, distorted scientific inquiry, and hampered the objective consideration of policy questions. Chen Yun, after all, was one of the first of China's leaders to endorse Deng Xiaoping's attempt to substitute the principle of "seeking truth from facts" for Hua Guofeng's theory of the "two whatevers." But, over time, the moderate reformers have become disturbed by a decline in commitment to basic ideological principles and values, not only among Chinese society at large but also within the Party. The moderates decry insufficient attention to political education in schools, universities, and the workplace.

They believe too much stress is being placed on the shortcomings of the classic Marxist works and too little attention given to their enduring value.

The fascination with Western culture, particularly among youth, and a disinterest in values that are distinctively Chinese also troubles the moderate reformers. They fear that their country is falling victim once again to the belief, recurring periodically since the late nineteenth century, that anything foreign is superior to its Chinese counterpart. They complain that this tendency, which they variously describe as "total Westernization" or "national nihilism," will undermine the traditional virtues of Chinese culture, particularly diligence, frugality, and patriotism. They see the materialism and selfishness of the West giving rise to crime, corruption, and inflation. They believe that literature, art, music, and film are being excessively influenced by avant-garde ideas from the Western intellectual community and by vulgar and tasteless styles from capitalist popular culture. One prominent moderate reformer, Hu Qiaomu, has been linked with the complaint that the Shenzhen special economic zone has been modeled on Hong Kong, Guangdong province is being modeled on Shenzhen, and the entire country is being modeled on Guangdong. The result will be the "Hongkongization" of the rest of China.[8]

The appropriate limit on political and economic reform is the third point of contention between moderate and radical reformers. The radical reformers have tended to give a much less restrictive definition of socialism than have their more moderate counterparts. Moderate reformers, for example, have usually defined socialism as requiring a "planned economy," state or collective ownership of the means of production, and distribution according to labor. Radical reformers, in contrast, have offered a looser definition. As early as November 1979, Zhao Ziyang excluded the planned economy from the list of principles implied by a commitment to socialism; and by late 1985 Deng Xiaoping had done the same. The radical reformers also recast the principle of public ownership more flexibly, so as to allow for the "existence of a variety of economic forms" while ensuring the "dominant position of the economic sector under public ownership."[9]

The moderate reformers have resisted several reform proposals that have been proposed by their more radical colleagues. In the economy, these radical proposals include eliminating mandatory planning, developing markets for the allocation of land, labor, capital, and other factors of production, and restructuring the system of state ownership of industrial and commercial enterprises. In the political sphere, the radical reformers have considered structural reforms that would limit the role of the Party, provide greater opportunities for contested elections, and offer more freedom to Chinese journalists to report on political matters.

In contrast, the moderate reformers have insisted on maintaining the basic principles that they believe a commitment to socialism requires. Planning should lie at the heart of the Chinese economy, they say, and while the scope of mandatory planning should be reduced, administrative guidance from the planning agencies must always control certain critical sectors of the economy. The moderate reformers do not see land and labor as exchangeable commodities on the marketplace, but rather as a means of production whose distribution should be directly controlled by the state. Moderate reformers have been far more skeptical than their radical colleagues about the growth of individual ownership in the Chinese economy, and more doubtful about the experiments with the sale of stock in state enterprises to individual workers and investors. And, perhaps most important, the moderate reformers seem committed to an orthodox Leninist view of the political system. Although they agree that policymaking should become more consultative, Party leadership more collective, and direct Party intervention in economic management reduced, they are opposed to any sign of political pluralization that would challenge the dominance of the Party in Chinese political life.

THE POLITICS OF REFORM

The competition between the moderate and radical wings of the reform coalition has helped create the cyclical pattern that has characterized the course of reform in China throughout the post-Mao years. Each of the two groups has had its own strategy. The moderate reformers have attempted to capitalize on the political and economic problems produced by reform in order to limit the pace and extent of the reform program. Conversely, the radical reformers have tried to devise ways of maintaining the momentum of reform or reviving it after a time of retrenchment. The interaction of these two strategies has caused the alternation of periods of advance and periods of retreat since 1978. But the cyclical pattern has also been reinforced by Deng Xiaoping who, in an effort to maintain a consensus between the two groups, has characteristically supported both the periods of advance advocated by the reformers and the periods of retrenchment proposed by more conservative leaders.

The Strategies of the Moderate Reformers

Although the moderate reformers have professed enthusiasm for the general principle of reform, they have also been quick to point out the concrete shortcomings of the reform program. They have identified problems like the increase of crime and corruption, the expression of unorthodox political ideas, the emergence of avant-garde styles in literature and art, and the development of popular culture that draws inspiration from Hong Kong and the West. The moderates have criticized the inflation created by price reform, the decline of central control over investment and the expenditure of foreign exchange, the emergence of inequality in the countryside, the failure of grain production to meet state targets after mandatory planning in that sector had been eliminated, and the sudden outbreak of political dissent during the student movement at the end of 1986.

In each case, the moderate reformers have blamed the emergence of these problems on the failure of their more radical colleagues to proceed cautiously and prudently and to set clear limits on political discourse and intellectual activity. In such circumstances, the skeptics have usually called for a slowdown in the pace of reform, a tightening of administrative controls over the economy, a crack-down against crime and dissent, the reassertion of the fundamental principles of Marxist-Leninist ideology, and the inauguration of propaganda campaigns against unorthodox ideas in politics, litera-ture, and art. Many of the periods of political and economic retrenchment since 1978 have reflected the influence of the moderate reformers, as they insist on remedial measures to restore equilibrium to the economy and stability to the political system.

The radical reformers have been sensitive to this skepticism, often describing their position as precarious and the long-term survivability of their reform program as in doubt. As Hu Qili said in the spring of 1986: "Whenever [the overall concept of] reform is mentioned, everybody expresses support without reservation and nobody raises an objection. However, when concrete reform meas-ures are taken, some people become anxious and worried; and they may even get alarmed at, and make much fuss over, the problems appearing in the course of reform, and become doubtful about reform."[10]

Since the purge of Hua Guofeng in 1982, the Chinese policymaking process has become more regularized and consultative and has once again centered on the drafting and promulgation of lengthy statements of policy on various aspects of political and economic reform. The moderate reformers, strongly represented in the Party Politburo, have tried to slow the pace and limit the extent of reform by participating actively in the drafting of these documents. They have worked for the deletion of new, unacceptable reforms, advocated the insertion of passages that would limit political and economic liberalization, and proposed statements to reassert the importance of subjects, such as political education, that they consider important.

Several documents reflect the influence of the moderate reformers on policymaking. The Central Committee decision on urban economic reform in October 1984, for example, followed an extensive debate between the moderate reformers and their radical counterparts over whether the plan, or the market, should be seen as the foundation of the Chinese economy. The document reflected a compromise between the two groups. It pleased the radicals by calling for a reduction in the scope of mandatory planning, but it satisfied the moderate reformers because it identified planning as a basic characteristic of a socialist economy.[11] Similarly, the Party statement on "socialist spiritual civilization," adopted at the Sixth Plenum of the Twelfth Party Central Committee in September 1986, may well have been inspired by the moderate reformers' desire for an authoritative statement on questions of ideology and public morality. Here, too, a debate apparently took place between the two wings of the reform faction, with the moderate reformers successfully insisting on the inclusion of passages that denigrated "bourgeois democracy" and "bourgeois liberalization" and that upheld the leadership of the Party and the "people's democratic dictatorship."[12]

In other cases, too, the moderate reformers may have succeeded in removing objectionable passages from central Party documents. This action is suggested by the fact that Chinese and foreign observers have often been led to expect the Party resolutions to contain far more radical policies than proves true in the end. For example, some of the proposals for urban economic reform that Deng Xiaoping had discussed with foreign visitors in August 1984 did not appear in the resolution on the subject approved by the Third Plenum of the Twelfth Party Central Committee in October.[13] Many Chinese intellectuals apparently expected the resolution on spiritual civilization in September 1986 to contain a fairly detailed statement cn political reform, but in the end, the document said that a program for reform of the political structure could be drawn up only "after exhaustive investigation and study."[14] And representatives of the foreign business and diplomatic communities in

Peking expressed disappointment with the Twenty-two Articles on foreign investment adopted in October 1986, because they did not contain the guarantees for the repatriation of profits that they had been told to anticipate.

Finally, the moderate reformers have, naturally, tried to maximize their representation in the leading bodies of the Party and state. Although it is impossible to assess with any great accuracy the balance in the national Chinese leadership, it seems that the radical reformers made some gains at the National Party Conference in the fall of 1985, when several younger leaders, sympathetic to radical reform, were elected to the Secretariat and Politburo. Nevertheless, the radical reformers were unable to secure the retirement of several senior leaders, including Chen Yun, Peng Zhen, Hu Qiaomu, and Deng Liqun, widely regarded as more sympathetic to the moderate wing of the reform movement. The dismissal of Hu Yaobang in early 1987, in turn, enabled the moderate reformers to remove some of his protégés from key positions in the propaganda apparatus, the Party's organization department, and the Ministry of Public Security, and raised the possibility that younger representatives of the moderate political tendency might secure appointment to leading Party bodies at the Thirteenth Party Congress in the autumn of 1987.

The Counterstrategies of the Radical Reformers

Faced with the continuing skepticism of the moderate reformers, as well as the more fundamental opposition of the remaining restorationists deep in the Chinese bureaucracies, the radical reformers have been pressed to find techniques for maintaining the momentum of the reform program. They have not been at a loss to do so. The radical reformers have adopted a strategy that features an incremental method for undertaking reform, a preemptive orientation toward the problems that reform creates, a spirited defense of the reform against its critics, and a cooptative approach to the periods of economic and political retrenchment launched by the skeptics. The incremental and cooptative approach undertaken by the radical reformers has reinforced the cyclical character of the reform effort.

The radical reformers have implemented reforms in stages, beginning with the easier and less controversial problems, in the hope that the success of the initial reforms will create enough political momentum and support to permit the adoption of more complex and less popular measures later on. In the economic realm, this incremental approach to reform is reflected in the decision to begin serious structural reforms in the countryside, where the problems are better understood and less complicated, before undertaking comprehensive reforms in urban areas. It is also evident in the decision, taken against the advice of some of East Europe's leading economists, to conduct price reform in stages, rather than to readjust or decontrol all prices at once.[15]

The adoption of an incremental strategy did arouse controversy in the ranks of the radical reformers. The critics of incrementalism warned that, by extending the process of reform, the strategy almost guaranteed that problems would grow, inconsistencies multiply, and pressures for retreat and retrenchment mount. Some reformers have advocated, instead, that China take a more synoptic approach, quickly implementing the entire package of reforms before the potential opposition can mobilize. They think incrementalism will only inhibit the momentum of reform, which will then grind to a halt before the reform agenda is complete. According to some accounts, Hu Yaobang was a leading advocate of a "blitzkrieg" strategy of political and economic change.[16]

However, most radical reformers believed that no feasible alternative to an incremental strategy existed. Some have acknowledged the desirability of a more rapid approach, but they think China's size, backwardness, and lack of expertise make it impossible to design and implement a comprehensive reform program at one stroke.[17] One Chinese university specialist has said privately that it would be preferable to undertake price reform quickly, but this move would "require theory and technology that we just do not have." The proponents of incrementalism have also emphasized that a gradual strategy enables the reformers to avoid making any large mistakes, and that they do not yet have the political strength to secure consent for the entire range of reforms that they have in mind.

Closely related to incrementalism is the experimental approach that has been taken to reform in post-Mao China. Potential reform programs are adopted and implemented in selected sectors, regions, or enterprises in order to judge their effectiveness and feasibility. Those that succeed can then be adopted on a wider basis, while those that fail can be abandoned or modified, without inflicting much damage on the overall reform effort. In the words of Deng Xiaoping: "We are engaged in an experiment. For us, it [reform] is something new, and we have to grope around to find our way. . . . Our method is to sum up experience from time to time and correct mistakes whenever they are discovered, so that small errors will not grow into big ones."[18]

Examples of this experimental approach to reform can be drawn from a variety of fields. In agriculture, the household responsibility system was first authorized in poorer parts of the country and was not extended to other regions until its effectiveness had been demonstrated and its political base had been solidified. In industry, certain enterprises were selected as early as 1978 as experimental sites for profit retention and management autonomy.[19] In more recent years, several cities have been authorized to experiment with capital markets, bankruptcy, and bureaucratic reform. And one prominent justification for the establishment of special economic zones along the Chinese coast has been the possibility of using them to adopt, evaluate, and absorb new macroeconomic policies and management strategies from the West.

When the reforms have encountered problems, the radical reformers have adopted a preemptive approach, attempting to find effective remedies in keeping with the spirit of reform. When the first wave of agricultural reforms led to large state subsidies for agriculture, the reformers proposed eliminating mandatory procurement contracts as a way of reducing the financial burden on the government treasury. When shortfalls occurred in grain production in 1985 and 1986, the reformers sought to identify and employ economic levers— higher prices, lower interest rates, and subsidized agricultural inputs—that would encourage peasants to grow more grain. When foreign investment began to decline in early 1986, the reformers drafted a set of regulations intended to create a more hospitable climate for investment. And when socioeconomic inequalities began to increase in rural areas, the radicals began to consider the extension of a graduated income tax into the countryside. In each case, the radical reformers have tried to use the problems encountered along the road to reform as a stimulus for deepening and broadening the reform program.

In so doing, they have had to develop effective remedial measures for coping with the shortcomings of reform, as well as devise a persuasive rhetorical defense of the reform problem against skeptics and critics both in the Party leadership and in Chinese society. They have argued that the difficulties experienced during reform result from the irrationalities of the old economic system, and not from flaws in the reforms. Corruption, the radical reformers have insisted, results from lingering feudal ideas among officials; inflation is the consequence of having frozen prices for so long at irrational levels; imbalance in China's current accounts is due to the inability of a formerly closed economy to produce competitive goods for export; and so on. Furthermore, the radical reformers often accuse the skeptics of applying unreasonable standards in the evaluation of the consequences of reform. Inequalities should be welcomed, not resisted, because they show that those with greater ambition and diligence can achieve economic success. Similarly, new ideas in politics and culture should be tolerated, not suppressed, because they show that Chinese intellectuals are now able to advance innovative solutions to the nation's problems.

When more conservative leaders have called for a retrenchment in the economy or a movement against "unhealthy tendencies" in political or intellectual affairs, the radical reformers have adopted a cooptative approach. While accepting the need for such remedial measures, they have also tried to find ways of redirecting and limiting them to maintain the momentum behind their reform program.

Their strategy has contained several components. First, they have attempted to restrict the movements against deviance in the political and intellectual spheres. During the campaign against spiritual pollution in 1983–84, for example, the radical reformers attempted to narrow the range of criticism to a fairly small number of issues in the cultural and intellectual spheres and to exempt from attack most other subjects, including industrial bonuses, the agricultural reforms, economic and cultural exchanges with the West, and the tolerance of more colorful clothing. Two years later, the radical reformers also tried to set limits on the conduct of the drive against bourgeois liberalization. The radical reformers did not want the campaign to be carried out in the countryside, nor did they want individuals criticized by name or economic reform obstructed. They sought to conduct the drive primarily within the Communist Party and keep it from extending into the "people's daily lives."[20]

Furthermore, just as their more conservative colleagues have been quick to identify the shortcomings of reform, the radical reformers have spared no time in pointing out the difficulties caused by periods of political retrenchment. In 1983–84, for example, they warned that the campaign against spiritual pollution was alienating many Chinese intellectuals and causing apprehension among many over- seas investors by creating a "chill" in the political climate. Urban Chinese were beginning to worry, noted one article, that "a mo- notonous situation will once again emerge in which many restric- tions are imposed on reading books, singing songs, putting on performances, and even clothes," and admitted that "their worries are not without reason." Unless the purpose of the campaign were more narrowly defined, the article continued, "we will be divorced from the masses." In the same vein, radical reformers such as Hu

Yaobang also utilized the adverse foreign reaction against the campaign to urge limiting its scope.[21]

On this basis, the radical reformers have attempted to redirect the periods of retrenchment or to bring them to an end. In February 1984, while acknowledging that the main problem in the ideological realm might well be excessive laxity and tolerance, Hu Yaobang insisted that the principal shortcoming in concrete policy matters was the sort of leftist thinking that obstructed reform. Within a few days, the focus of much of the nation's propaganda had therefore been shifted to emphasize not the elimination of spiritual pollution, but rather the orthodox ideology, force of habit, and "negative wait-and-see attitude" that prevented the smooth implementation of reform policies. Similarly, a campaign against "unhealthy tendencies" launched at the conclusion of the National Party Conference in late 1985 was soon transformed by the radical reformers into an attempt to mobilize greater support for reform. And in May 1987, Zhao Ziyang insisted that the best way to combat "bourgeois liberalization" was to resume reform, for only reform could demonstrate the superiority of the socialist road. This speech, too, was an effort both to coopt one of the retrenchment drives launched by the critics of reform and to bring it to an end.[22]

Finally, like their more conservative counterparts, the radical reformers have wanted to strengthen their representation on central Party and state bodies and to limit that of other political tendencies. Radical reformers have tended to push for the retirement of elderly Party officials in the awareness that some of them take a skeptical and cautious approach to reform. Some, in fact, have even advocated the early retirement of Deng Xiaoping, believing that Deng's departure from the Politburo would facilitate the removal of more conservative leaders of Deng's age and rank. While seeking to add their own voices to the Politburo, the Secretariat, and the State Council, the radical reformers have also tried to prevent the emergence of younger, moderate leaders, who might be expected to serve as effective spokesmen for a more orthodox approach to reform in the years after Deng Xiaoping and his contemporaries leave the Chinese political stage.

The Role of Deng Xiaoping

No account of the course of reform in the post-Mao era would be complete without at least a brief reference to the part played by Deng Xiaoping. As already noted, in the late 1970s Deng developed a set of political and economic reforms to replace the restorationist programs of Hua Guofeng, offered himself as an alternative to Hua as the country's paramount leader, and mobilized a coalition of senior officials and elements of urban society powerful enough to remove Hua from office. Since 1982, Deng's role in Chinese politics has been equally central but substantially different: he has attempted to strike a balance between the two wings of the reform movement, but in ways that have usually supported the more ambitious objectives of the radical reformers.

One of Deng's objectives has been to maintain a consensus at the highest level of the Party, particularly among the most senior leaders who are, in age and seniority, his peers. To do so, Deng has not only supported the demands of the moderate reformers to tighten controls or postpone reform when serious difficulties have emerged but has even placed himself at the forefront of the retrenchment effort. In early 1979, when some local Party leaders began to grumble that the decisions of the Third Plenum were nothing less than revisionism, and when some participants in the Democracy Wall movement began to demand a more thoroughgoing liberalization of Chinese politics than most leaders were prepared to accept, Deng established the "four cardinal principles"—a commitment to Marxism-Leninism and Mao Zedong thought, Party leadership, socialism, and the existing state structure—as limits to permissible political discourse.[23] In late 1980, when the urban economy was overheating, Deng quickly endorsed proposals by Chen Yun and others for a period of economic retrenchment.[24] In 1981, 1983, 1985, and 1986, Deng responded to signs of crime, corruption, and dissent—and above all to growing criticism of those problems from his colleagues within the Party—by sponsoring campaigns against "right deviations," "laxity and weakness," "bourgeois liberalism," "spiritual pollution," or "erroneous tendencies."[25]

In the course of these retrenchments, Deng has sacrificed a few leaders and intellectuals to symbolize his commitment to setting limits to reform. His attack on the playwright Bai Hua in 1981, his sanctioning of the reassignments of Wang Ruoshui and Hu Jiwei in 1984, his expulsion of the dissident intellectuals Liu Binyan, Wang Ruowang, and Fang Lizhi from the Party in 1987, and, above all, his consent to the dismissal of Hu Yaobang from the general secretaryship that same year give evidence of Deng's ability to remove those radical reformers whose outspokenness has made them unacceptable to more conservative leaders. Deng's consistently tough line on young dissidents—from Wei Jingsheng of Democracy

Wall to the student protesters of late 1986—also exemplifies Deng's intolerance of anyone who criticizes the fundamentals of the Chinese political system.

However, Deng has also shown, at least in general terms, his support even for some of the most controversial elements of the radical reform program. Deng's *Selected Works* has given extensive and impassioned support for the principle of opening China to the outside world. In his discussions of domestic economic policy, Deng has refrained from mentioning state planning as one of the defining characteristics of a socialist economy. Deng first placed political reform on the Chinese political agenda in 1980 and reemphasized its importance in 1986. Deng has, in fact, been particularly insistent about the need to limit the control of the Party over both economic and administrative matters. And although Deng has always sponsored the inauguration of movements to criticize "unhealthy tendencies" that have arisen in the course of reform, he has also helped the radical reformers rein in those campaigns shortly after they were launched. Moreover, in supervising appointments to high-level Party and state bodies, Deng has consistently sought to ensure a balance in favor of radical reform.

At the same time, Deng has rarely committed his personal prestige to any particular reform programs. When the Central Committee adopted a comprehensive program of urban reform in 1984, for example, Deng indicated that he approved of the document, but he took pains to point out that he had neither added nor deleted a single word.[26] He has presented potentially controversial reforms, such as the special economic zones, as experiments that can always be modified, or canceled, should they encounter insurmountable difficulties. He has clearly committed himself to certain, basic principles of reform, including a significant redefinition of the role of the Party in domestic affairs, but he leaves to others the development of concrete proposals. This detached posture preserves Deng's ability to intervene to correct the errors of his subordinates and maintain consensus in the Party to preserve support for the overall reform program.

In short, Deng's goal has been to preempt and coopt potential criticism so that a consensus in favor of reform—and even many elements of radical reform—can be developed or preserved. To achieve this goal Deng has depicted himself as occupying the middle of the political spectrum, rather than either extreme. Deng has argued strongly in favor of fundamental reform and has characterized those who resist sweeping change as dogmatists wedded to outmoded ideological principles. At the same time, Deng has presented himself as a committed communist who seeks to defend the essentials of socialism against those who would move too far toward economic or political liberalization. Like many skillful politicians, Deng has sought the middle ground, portraying himself as an opponent of both stagnation and disorder, of both dogmatism and "bourgeois liberalization."[27]

CONCLUSION

Economic and political reform in China has followed a tortuous course. In certain years—for example, 1978 and 1984—the tide of reform has been at its height, with comprehensive programs adopted, bold new proposals placed on the agenda, and great progress made toward enlivening the economy and relaxing political life. Other years—for example, 1981 and 1982—have been times of retrenchment, in which the economic disequilibrium produced by reform has been redressed and the political ferment encouraged by reform has been restrained. In some years, such as 1986, the fluctuations have been intense, with China lurching from retrenchment to advancement to renewed retrenchment in a single, twelve-month period.

Official Chinese spokesmen prefer to describe these cycles as the product of the rational decisions of a unified national leadership, slowing the pace of reform when problems arise and restoring momentum when economic and political normalcy has been restored. This interpretation does contain an important element of truth that should not be overlooked. For the most part, Chinese leaders since 1982 have been unified in their desire for reform and united in their willingness to undertake serious changes in the institutions and policies that were the legacy of Mao Zedong. A consensus has also formed on the need to remedy the problems emerging as reform is carried out. The economy must be slowed when it becomes overheated, foreign exchange accounts must be balanced after imports surge, and limits must be set on political discourse when Party leadership is challenged.

But the cyclical pattern of reform must also be attributed to the differences within the reform coalition over how far and how fast reform should proceed. The moderate reformers have been eager to set limits on the extent of reform and to reduce the speed at which it is implemented. In contrast, the radical reformers have attempted to sustain the pace of reform and to win acceptance of hitherto unorthodox ideas. As is normal in any political system, each group has also tried to strengthen its position in Party councils at the expense of its rival; and each has been quick to identify and criticize the shortcomings of the other's programs.

Although the course of reform since 1978 has been uneven, the cycles of the mid-seventies to the mid-eighties have nonetheless traced an upward spiral. Temporary retrenchments, modifications, and retreats notwithstanding, the trend has been toward the diversification of the economy, greater autonomy for producers, a larger role for the market, more freedom both for intellectuals and for the average citizen, and a more professional and regularized policymaking process.

The progress that reform has made, despite ebbs and flows, is attributable to several factors. Under the leadership of Deng Xiaoping, the reform coalition scored a decisive victory over Hua Guofeng in 1981–82 and succeeded in excluding most representatives of the restorationist tendency, let alone the revolutionary Maoists, from leading positions in the Party and government. For many years after 1982, moreover, the reform coalition remained united on the necessity of the first package of political and economic reforms, even if the members of that coalition may have differed somewhat at the pace at which they should be adopted. The incremental nature of reform—starting with the easier problems first, where the gains were likely to be rapid, and where the benefits would far outweigh the costs—helped develop and maintain a popular base for the reform program. Great credit must also be given to Deng Xiaoping, who used his prodigious political skills and his unique standing within the Chinese Communist movement to manage the tensions within the reform coalition and to supervise the amelioration of the problems created by reform.

Such an analysis of the past, however, suggests some troubling questions for the future. Inherent in the incremental approach that has been applied to reform is the attempt to secure the easy gains early and to postpone the more difficult and controversial aspects. As the reformers are forced to address the more troublesome problems, the base for reform both inside and outside the Party may begin to erode. Furthermore, as the first package of reforms is completed, and as new reform measures are placed on the Chinese political agenda, the differences within the reform coalition between radicals and moderates are likely to increase, with the radicals proposing more individual entrepreneurship, less state control over the market, and greater liberalization of politics than their moderate colleagues will enthusiastically accept.

Finally, Deng Xiaoping is, like all men, mortal. Despite his efforts to institutionalize the Chinese political system, his death will leave a vacuum at the highest level of Chinese leadership. Without a Deng Xiaoping, it is less certain that the differences within the reform coalition can be managed effectively. And the departure of Deng may well lead to more intense competition between the moderate reformers and their radical counterparts, as each group seeks to install its representative as China's paramount leader. Consequently, despite the sometimes dramatic cycles in reform since 1978, the most difficult stage in the course of China's second revolution may still lie ahead.

The Content of Reform

CHAPTER 5

Restructuring the Economy

B Y 1976 China suffered from the chronic malaise characteristic of many relatively mature socialist economies. Despite a continuous increase in the share of national output devoted to investment, the country's economic growth rates were declining and patterns of consumption were stagnating. During the brief interregnum of Hua Guofeng in the late 1970s, economic policy was still based on the optimistic premise that the decline in growth rates had resulted from political circumstances, rather than any underlying structural problems. Hua and his advisers were persuaded that the restoration of political stability after a decade of turmoil would stimulate popular enthusiasm for production and increase the efficiency of state planning and administration. In this context, high levels of investment would once again produce high rates of growth, even without a basic change in the structure of the economy.[1]

Hua Guofeng's "new leap forward" fell victim, however, to the same difficulties encountered by similar movements in the past. The expansion of state investment strained supplies of construction materials and capital goods. The surge in imports of foreign technology produced serious balance of payments difficulties. The increases in wages granted to urban workers were not matched by comparable increases in the production of consumer goods. By the end of 1978, many Chinese leaders and economists felt that the Chinese economy had again entered a familiar "blind alley." In the words of Xue Muqiao, one of the country's senior economists who had served as director of the State Statistical Bureau in the 1950s, China's economic policy was still producing "high speed, high accumulation, [but] low results, and low consumption."[2]

Since then, Chinese leaders have reached a consensus on the need for systematic structural reform that would break decisively with the institutions and policies of Leninism and Maoism. The complex domestic economic reform program undertaken since 1978 can be summarized in three propositions: private ownership can occupy a useful place in a socialist economy, market forces should be allowed to influence the allocation of goods and the determination of prices, and material incentives should be the principal mechanism for stimulating greater productivity and efficiency. Based on these three principles, Chinese leaders have envisioned an economy in which individuals can start their own small businesses, managers enjoy greater autonomy in running their factories, state officials exercise less direct administrative control over economic activity, and productive workers are rewarded with higher levels of consumption.

Although China's post-Mao leaders are devoted to reform, they also remain committed to socialism. And each of the three principles of economic reform just outlined conflicts with a crucial element of the socialist ethic in contemporary China. The spirit of reform calls for an increase in private enterprise, but the socialist ethic demands the predominance of public ownership of the means of production. Reform allows a greater role for market forces in the economy, but the socialist ethic insists on the continued primacy of state planning. And reformism emphasizes the use of material incentives to stimulate production, but socialism warns against a polarization of rich and poor and extols the spirit of "plain living and hard struggle."

This tension between the reformist spirit and the socialist ethic has been the foundation of a debate over economic reform that has continued throughout the post-Mao era. The moderate reformers have placed high priority on maintaining an economic system that embodies traditional socialist values, whereas the radical reformers have been more willing to accept a higher degree of private ownership, market mechanisms, and even economic inequality.

The two groups of leaders were able initially to agree on a preliminary set of moderate economic reforms, implemented between 1978 and 1985. Taken together, these measures granted greater autonomy to factory managers, created a lively market in the distribution of both industrial and agricultural commodities, decollectivized agricultural production, and allowed greater room for individual entrepreneurship. Over time, however, some more skeptical leaders began to express their doubts about some of the unintended consequences of this early reform package: the shortfall in grain output created by the retreat from mandatory production quotas, the growing inequalities resulting from the rise of profitable private and collective enterprises, and the inflation caused by the relaxation of administrative controls over prices.

Moreover, the radical reformers placed another set of proposals on the Chinese political agenda in 1986. If adopted, these more radical measures would make the market, rather than the mandatory plan, the heart of the Chinese economy and would establish markets for land, labor, and financial capital, as well as for goods and services. Moreover, the measures would also make further changes in the system of state ownership of industrial enterprises, leasing out some factories to individual managers and making others responsible to boards of directors elected by shareholders. This second package of economic reforms has proved far more controversial than the first and has increasingly become the focus of the ongoing controversy between the radical reformers and their more moderate counterparts.

THE MODERATE ECONOMIC REFORMS

For the sake of convenience, the moderate set of reforms can be discussed under four broad headings, according to particular economic units affected by them. For the peasant, the reforms have transformed agricultural production from a collective undertaking into a family enterprise. For the state, the reforms have greatly reduced, although not eliminated, the government's role in the establishment of production targets and the determination of prices. For the enterprise, the moderate reforms have given managers more autonomy in making decisions, more control over the allocation of profits, and more responsibility for the outcomes of their decisions. For the industrial worker, the reforms are slowly changing the systems of education, employment, discipline, and remuneration.

Thus far, the moderate reforms have been more successful in the rural areas than in the cities. This is largely because the Chinese leaders have not yet fully implemented those politically difficult measures—such as price reform, enterprise autonomy, and enterprise bankruptcy—that will be necessary for the first wave of urban reforms to be completely effective. Over the longer term, however, the situation may reverse itself. The rural reforms seem to have produced a sharp reduction in agricultural investment and are contributing to shortfalls in grain production. Conversely, if the Chinese leaders can find the political resources with which to bite the bullets of price reform, enterprise autonomy, and bankruptcy, then the urban reforms may begin to have a greater impact on the productivity and efficiency of China's industrial enterprises.

Peasants

The virtual decollectivization of agricultural production, and the return to individual family farming under the "household responsibility system," has been the most notable reform in the rural sector.[3] But this policy has been only one of a series of measures, implemented sequentially since the late 1970s, that have been designed to improve rural productivity and increase agricultural output. Taken together, these reforms have transformed agricultural production from a collective to a private undertaking. At the same time, however, the state remains heavily involved in procuring agricultural output, and much subsidiary activity surrounding the planting, cultivation, and harvesting of crops is still likely to retain a collective character.

In one of the earliest and most effective agricultural reforms, the state increased procurement prices in 1979–80. In part, this was accomplished by increasing the prices that the state paid farmers for their agricultural products. In addition, the quotas for mandatory deliveries to the state were frozen, allowing farmers to sell an increasing share of their annual output at the higher price paid for above-quota production. Although these price increases affected some crops more than others, a 40 percent increase resulted in the overall prices paid for agricultural products in 1979–80 alone.[4]

The agricultural reforms also encouraged substantial diversification and specialization in rural areas. Chinese leaders have now abandoned the Maoist principle that, regardless of comparative advantage, every rural area should place the highest priority on the cultivation of grain. The more diverse cropping patterns prevalent before the Cultural Revolution have been restored. Under the rural reforms, peasant families are now permitted to abandon grain and vegetable cultivation to engage in more specialized occupations. Some families now produce industrial crops; others engage in individual or collective industry; and still others provide the rural services, such as transportation or the use of agricultural machinery, that are needed by their neighbors.[5]

In this way, the rural reforms are intended to absorb most of the surplus labor power that is being created in the countryside by population growth and greater productivity, while at the same time restraining migration to China's large, overcrowded cities. By the summer of 1985, specialized households in rural China employed about 10 million to 15 million people, while collective rural industry employed 60 million more people.[6] The expansion of these alternative employment opportunities is intended to permit the percentage of the rural labor force engaged in agricultural production to decline steadily from 85 percent in 1984 to about 30 percent by the year 2000.[7]

A third major rural reform linked income ever more directly to production output, replacing the more egalitarian criteria common during the Cultural Revolution. Beginning in 1978, several provinces conducted experiments with various kinds of "responsibility systems," in which peasants were offered material incentives for fulfilling the responsibilities assigned them by the state. These local experiments continued throughout the late 1970s and early 1980s until a uniform national policy was finally announced in early 1983.[8] Under the policy, known as the "household responsibility system," the collective assigned plots of land to individual peasant families—not to own, but to farm. The family then had to provide its share of the agricultural tax due to the government, the agricultural products purchased by the state under the system of mandatory production quotas, and fees owed to the collective. Whatever the households produced above these quotas could be disposed of as they wished: they could consume it, sell it to the state at a premium procurement price, or sell it to other peasants and urban dwellers at market prices.[9]

The household responsibility system has permitted the abolition of the communes, formerly the highest level of collective organization in the countryside. Their control over agricultural land has been transferred to the smaller production brigades. Their responsibility for agricultural services and local industry has frequently been shifted to government agencies, collective enterprises, or even individual peasant households. And administrative functions—public security, public health, education, civil affairs, and the like—have been assigned to newly established township and village governments.[10]

The achievements of these early rural reforms came at a very high price to the government. Peasants were selling more produce to the state; the state was paying higher prices for the agricultural output that it procured; but the rising cost of agricultural products was not being passed on to urban consumers. Consequently, a rapid increase occurred in state subsidies for agricultural products, which by 1981 had already reached about 25 billion yuan, nearly one-quarter of all state revenues for the year.[11]

To solve this problem, the state announced at the beginning of 1985 a big change in how it procured agricultural output from the countryside.[12] No longer would it issue mandatory purchase quotas to the agricultural community. Instead, the state would set a target for the procurement of a relatively small number of products, particularly grain, cotton, and certain other important industrial crops, and offer to sign purchase contracts for those amounts. In theory, at least, peasants are free either to accept or reject these government contracts. Even if the peasants decide to try to sell their output on their own, the state still guarantees to purchase, at a minimum floor price, agricultural products for which no other market can be found.

The system, as designed, is supposed to offer advantages to both the state and the peasant. The government hopes the procurement contract system will reduce the burden of agricultural subsidies on the state by reducing the amount of produce purchased by government agencies and by lowering the average price that those agencies pay. The peasants face a wider range of marketing options. If they sign a contract with the state, they can obtain a guaranteed market, at a known price, through familiar delivery channels, well before the harvest. They can also receive a fraction of the purchase price in advance. Alternatively, peasants can attempt to sell their product on the open market, at a higher price than that offered by the state, but must assume the risk and inconvenience of doing so.[13]

In many areas, the procurement contract system has retained a highly compulsory flavor, with peasants coerced by local officials into signing contracts.[14] Even so, the immediate effect of the adoption of the new procurement system in 1985 was a 6 percent drop in grain output, as millions of peasants, freed from the mandatory quotas of the past, shifted from the production of grain into the cultivation of more lucrative crops. Given the historical importance of grain production in China, and the importance of grain in the Chinese diet, it was not surprising that many Chinese leaders became alarmed. At the national Party conference in September 1985, Chen Yun warned that further "grain shortages will lead to social disorder," and there is some reason to believe that some leaders called for reviving the previous system of mandatory grain quotas.[15]

But the reformers were committed to coping with the problem by finding the economic levers that would encourage the production of grain, rather than by resorting to administrative measures to compel it. In some areas, controls were imposed on the use of land to prevent peasants from shifting out of grain production into other crops. But more commonly, the government increased the incentives to the peasants to grow grain under contract to the state. The state gave peasants who were willing to sign state procurement contracts scarce agricultural inputs, such as fertilizer and diesel fuel, at subsidized prices. The government also offered tax reductions and low-interest loans to peasants who agreed to grow and sell grain.[16]

By the end of 1986, these remedial measures had achieved only partial results. The 1986 grain harvest, at 391 million metric tons, was 3.2 percent higher than in 1985. But it had not matched the record harvest of 407 million metric tons reaped in 1984, nor did it reach the target of 400 million tons reportedly set by Peking for the year.[17] If grain production continues to lag in the years to come, Peking will face some difficult and unpalatable choices. It can raise the state purchase price of grain or provide more subsidized agricultural inputs to the rural sector. These measures may encourage peasants to produce more grain for the state under the purchase contract system, but these steps will also place a heavy burden on the state treasury. Alternatively, the state could reduce purchases of grain, allow peasants to sell more on the open market, and assume that grain shortages would force the market price up. But if the government did not provide wage supplements to offset the resulting increases in urban food prices, it would doubtless encounter urban unrest at the higher cost of living. Third, it could increase imports of foreign grain. But this move would impose a further demand on the nation's scarce foreign exchange reserves. Or, finally, the government could end the experiment in grain procurement contracts and return to compulsory grain production quotas, thereby acknowledging that a major agricultural policy initiative had failed. And it would suffer the inefficiencies that would result from mandatory planning.

The agricultural reforms have had a remarkable impact on rural output and productivity. With village industry included, agricultural output has grown at an average annual rate of 10.5 percent between 1978 and 1986 (table 5-1), compared with 4.0 percent in the late 1960s and early 1970s. The productivity of both land and labor since 1978 has risen at twice the average rate between 1953 and 1978.[18] Many factors—the rural reforms, political stability, and good weather— were responsible for this extraordinary performance. One careful econometric model of Chinese agriculture between 1978 and 1984 suggests that three-quarters of the gains in productivity can be attributed to the increased incentives offered to peasant families by the inauguration of the household responsibility system, and the credit for the rest can be given to the higher prices paid by the state for agricultural products.[19]

Over the longer run, however, sustaining this impressive progress will require maintaining investment in the agricultural sector. Thus far, one unfortunate consequence of the rural reforms is that neither the state, nor the collective, nor the individual peasant family seems to be investing capital in agriculture at the requisite level.

The allocation of agricultural land to peasant families transfers responsibility for investment in machinery, improved seed strains,

Table 5-1. *National Output and Real Growth Rates, 1979–86*
Billions of 1980 yuan and, in parentheses, percent growth rate over previous year

Output	1979	1980	1981	1982	1983	1984	1985	1986	Average annual growth rate, 1979–86
National output	347	369	387	419	460	522	586	630	
	...	(6.3)	(4.9)	(8.3)	(9.8)	(13.5)	(12.3)	(7.5)	(8.9)
Gross value of agricultural output[a]	214.0	222.3	236.9	263.2	288.4	339.1	387.3	429.3	
	...	(3.9)	(6.6)	(11.1)	(9.6)	(17.6)	(14.2)	(10.8)	(10.5)
Nonindustrial rural production[b]	192.7	196.4	209.1	232.8	250.8	281.6	291.2	301.4	
	...	(1.9)	(6.5)	(11.3)	(7.7)	(12.3)	(3.4)	(3.5)	(6.6)
Village industrial output	21.3	25.9	27.8	30.4	37.6	57.5	96.1	127.9	
	...	(21.6)	(7.3)	(9.4)	(23.7)	(52.9)	(67.1)	(33.1)	(29.2)
Gross value of industrial output[c]	457.2	497.2	517.8	557.7	616.4	703.0	829.5	902.8	
	...	(8.7)	(4.1)	(7.7)	(10.5)	(14.0)	(18.0)	(8.8)	(10.2)

Sources: These data are drawn from Rock Creek Research, 1985 *China Statistical Handbook*, and 1987 *China Statistical Handbook* (Washington, D.C.: Rock Creek Research, 1985 and 1987); and Guojia Tongjiu [State Statistical Bureau], *Zhongguo tongji zhaiyao, 1987* [Peking: Chinese Statistical Publishing House, 1987]. Data that were expressed in 1970 yuan have been converted to 1980 yuan. I am grateful for Robert M. Field's assistance in compiling these figures.

a. Including village industry.
b. Farming, forestry, animal husbandry, fisheries, and sideline production.
c. Including township industry.

fertilizer, and pesticides to the individual households who farm the land. But even though the rural reforms have greatly increased incomes and rural savings, the peasants seem to be spending little of the increase on productive investment. Uncertain of the long-term fate of the household responsibility system, peasants have been reluctant to make permanent, nonmobile investments in their land, because of fear that improvements would be confiscated if their plots were later reabsorbed into a collective farm. Instead, farmers have devoted their savings to building new private housing. To alleviate peasants' doubts, the Central Committee announced in early 1984 that the division of land would remain in effect for at least fifteen years, enough time to allow for the amortization of any peasant investment.[20] It remains to be seen whether such reassurances, when combined with the gradual satisfaction of pent-up demand for a higher standard of living, will lead to increases in private investment in the agricultural sector.

At stake in the countryside, however, is not simply the stimulation of new investment in agriculture but also the maintenance of the infrastructure supporting agricultural production and social services. As the communes have been disbanded, the large transportation and irrigation facilities for which they were responsible have often fallen into disrepair. As collective control over land has weakened, some agricultural land has been transferred to nonagricultural use.[21] The inauguration of the household responsibility system has also reduced the resources available to the collectives to support rural welfare, public health, and educational facilities.[22]

Recognizing this problem, the state has attempted to strengthen the control of local government agencies over land usage, agricultural infrastructure, and social services. In many places, however, this aim has led to the imposition of rather arbitrary fees on peasant households to maintain these collective investments. Over the longer term, the Chinese are encouraging the creation of various forms of rural cooperatives to provide many of the rural services that were previously the responsibility of the communes. Cooperatives have been formed, on an experimental basis, to provide agricultural inputs, process and market agricultural products, offer mechanical services to peasants, and provide financial capital. If such a policy is more widely implemented—and Chinese officials have suggested that it may even become compulsory in the future— it would mean that many of the subsidiary activities surrounding agricultural production would be organized on a cooperative basis, even as production itself remains the province of the individual peasant family.[23]

Attention must also be paid to the decline in state investment in agriculture. Although the Third Plenum of the Eleventh Party Central Committee announced that state investment devoted to agriculture would be increased, agriculture's share of state capital construction has fallen, in both absolute and relative terms. In 1986, agriculture received only 3.3 percent of state investment, compared with 10.6 percent in 1978. And during the Sixth Five-Year Plan (1981–85), the total amount invested in agriculture was 30 percent less than it had been during the Fifth Five-Year Plan (1976–80).[24] Other state outlays relevant to agriculture, including those for rural transportation and rural electrification, have also fallen or stagnated. What is more, the Seventh Five-Year Plan, covering the years from 1986 through 1990, calls for a further 15 percent reduction in state investment in agriculture, which would reduce agriculture's share of total investment to slightly more than 2.9 percent.[25]

The State

During the Maoist period, the government, at either the state or the provincial level, directly controlled the production, procurement, and allocation of all the chief industrial and agricultural products and set the prices for the exchange of these goods. Changes in economic policy sometimes reallocated the division of responsibility between Peking and the provinces. These cyclical changes in the structure of the economy, however, never challenged the essential premise of direct state control over all significant economic activity.

The goal of the post-Mao reforms has been to reduce the control of the state over both production and pricing. Now a wider range of output can be distributed through the marketplace, a greater number of prices can rise and fall in direct response to market conditions, and the state increasingly employs indirect economic levers, rather than direct administrative controls, to influence the decisions of individual enterprises.[26]

These reforms have been evident, in the first instance, in a restructuring of the planning system. Like the Hungarians, the Chinese have established three channels for the circulation of commodities: mandatory planning (the state directs production by administrative orders), guidance planning (the state encourages production through various economic levers), and the marketplace (the state intervenes through the control of prices, if at all).

Most descriptions of the reform of the planning system have suggested that the plurality of commodities—perhaps 40 percent to

60 percent of total output value—will eventually be governed by guidance planning, defined by the Chinese as using "indirect methods of readjusting the economic benefits" to enterprises to encourage or discourage the production of certain commodities.[27] One set of economic levers is familiar in Western societies: the reduction of tax rates and the provision of credit to industries selected for preferential treatment. But in China, the state can also use the selective rationing of key inputs, at subsidized prices, as an economic lever. Enterprises that accept guidance planning receive the inputs, and those that balk at the planning are denied them. In this sense, the new procurement contract system in agriculture, which provides subsidized diesel fuel and fertilizer to peasant households that sign purchase contracts with the state, may be the prototypical form of guidance planning in post-Mao China.

Some cynics have suggested that the power of the state over Chinese enterprises is so great that guidance planning may be indistinguishable from mandatory planning, especially after the target figures leave Peking and are in the hands of local authorities. One American scholar has described guidance planning as mandatory planning by local governments, while another has depicted it as "mandatory plans with a 'please' in front of them."[28] But in both industry and agriculture evidence is growing that the relaxation of mandatory planning is indeed affecting the operation of enterprises. As noted earlier, the elimination of mandatory planning in agriculture caused an immediate drop in grain production. Similarly, in industry, the reduction of mandatory plans for export goods has led to a decline in production for the export market as enterprises have shifted production in more profitable directions.

Clearly, the number of commodities subject to mandatory planning has already been greatly reduced and may fall further in the years to come. The number of industrial products allocated under mandatory planning, which had been more than 500 at the height of central planning in the 1950s, was reduced first to 120, and then to 60. The comparable number of agricultural commodities was reduced from 29 to 10 in 1984 and then to zero in 1985 with the adoption of the procurement contract system.[29] The decision on urban economic reform adopted by the Central Committee in 1984 stipulated that mandatory planning would, in the future, "be applied [only] to major products which have a direct bearing on the national economy and the people's livelihood . . . , as well as major economic activities that affect the overall situation."[30] Most Chinese economists have interpreted this passage to mean that a small minority of products, perhaps 20 percent to 30 percent of total output value, will continue to be allocated under mandatory planning. But some more radical reformers favor eliminating mandatory planning altogether.

With the relaxation of mandatory planning, factories have been authorized to sell first their above-quota output, and later their nonplanned output, on what have gradually become regular wholesale markets, where they can also purchase some of the inputs they require. Over time, the scope of these wholesale markets has expanded beyond the administrative boundaries of a single city or province to encompass a larger natural economic region.

Indeed, the movement away from mandatory planning has encouraged the Chinese to reconsider the geographic organization of their economy. During the Maoist period, the Chinese economy was organized in cellular fashion. Economic regions corresponded to administrative boundaries, sought great self-sufficiency, and closely duplicated one another's production. Under the post-Mao reforms, the economy has been seen as a set of more open and interactive economic regions, each centered on a major commercial city rather than on a provincial capital, and following natural economic boundaries rather than administrative jurisdictions. In this reconceptualization, economic regions should "overlap and permeate" one another, and each major city should develop a distinctive mixture of industrial, cultural, commercial, and financial undertakings.[31] Enterprises in each region should be able to expand their sales into other areas and, in turn, should face increasing competition from factories in other parts of the country.

But the concept of cellular economy still enjoys strong support in China, especially in less advanced regions. Less efficient factories are not eager to encounter competition from their more efficient counterparts and seek to maintain the protected local markets provided by the cellular economy. Similarly, provincial governments, which draw most of their revenues from the profits of the enterprises under their jurisdiction, are unwilling to see local markets captured by industry in other parts of the country. By working together, local industry and local governments have been able to maintain "blockades" preventing outside industry from gaining access to local markets.

The heart of the Soviet economic model, which China imitated in the mid-1950s, was the system of mandatory procurement and allocation of major agricultural and industrial commodities. An important subsidiary feature was state control of the prices charged for the exchange of those goods. Because those prices were changed infrequently during the late Maoist period, relative prices had become distorted by the end of the 1970s. The prices of most primary products, including grain, energy, and raw materials, were too low. The fees charged for many services, including transportation, rent, and public utilities, were often below cost. The prices of manufactured goods, including processed materials such as steel, were set too high. And prices were not allowed to vary because of transportation costs, seasonality, or differences in quality.

By the late 1970s, most officials and economists acknowledged that these distorted prices needed to be readjusted to better reflect relative costs and relative scarcity. But a debate arose over how to accomplish this task. Some believed that prices could be changed through administrative adjustment, and work was begun on a large input-output table of the Chinese economy that could serve as the basis for the calculation of new prices. In keeping with this approach, several sets of prices have been changed administratively since 1978. As noted earlier, state agricultural procurement prices were raised in 1979–80. The prices of petroleum, coal, textiles, and rail transportation have also been changed to make them somewhat more rational.

But gradually an alternative approach gained ascendancy. Zhao Ziyang, after his accession to the premiership in 1980, supported a strategy to modify the price system to give market forces a greater role in the determination of prices. In keeping with this philosophy, and again following closely the Hungarian example, the Chinese have now established three categories of prices: fixed prices, floating prices, and market prices.

Generally speaking, the goods governed by mandatory planning are still sold at prices fixed by the state. As mandatory planning is reduced, however, the number of fixed prices also declines. The number of industrial products sold at fixed prices has already fallen from 256 to 29, the number of categories of consumer goods sold at state-set prices has been reduced from 85 to 37, and the comparable number of agricultural commodities has dropped from 113 to 25. As a result, goods sold at fixed prices now account for only 30 percent to 40 percent of total sales volume.[32] Many fixed prices are, in fact, no longer mandatory, but represent the terms under which the state offers to purchase products from potential suppliers. The prices offered to peasant families for agricultural output under the procurement contract system exemplify this variant of fixed prices.[33]

Second, many industrial products are now subject to floating prices. Under this system, the state establishes a range within which prices can vary. The exact price is then determined either by market conditions or through negotiations between producer and consumer. The concept of floating prices was first implemented in 1978, when some factories were authorized to market their above-quota production directly to potential buyers, at prices that could range within 20 percent of the fixed price. Many goods produced under guidance planning are also sold at floating prices.

Finally, prices of many small consumer goods and agricultural products are now allowed to fluctuate according to market conditions. In September 1982, for example, enterprises were permitted to set their own prices for 160 commodities, and in 1983, they were given similar authority for another 350 categories of goods. In 1985, with the end of mandatory purchasing of agricultural products, the prices of meat, fish, poultry, and vegetables were also released from state control and were allowed to move freely on the marketplace.[34]

As in most socialist countries, the most serious problem connected with price reform in China has been inflation. The establishment of floating prices for many raw materials in the late 1970s and early 1980s caused the retail price index, which had been stable during the late Maoist period, to rise at an annual rate falling between 1.5 percent and 2.5 percent. The relaxation of controls over agricultural prices in 1985 caused retail prices to soar even further, with inflation running at almost 9 percent in 1985 and 6.6 percent in 1986. The price of foodstuffs has risen at a double-digit level: the price of meat and eggs rose 22 percent in 1985 and 10 percent in 1986, the price of fish rose 34 percent in 1985 and 12 percent in 1986, and the price of vegetables rose by a third in 1985 alone.[35] The prices of manufactured consumer goods might well drop if price controls were relaxed and if there were meaningful competition among light industrial enterprises, but raising the price of urban services (particularly the cost of housing) to more rational levels would almost certainly be an explosive political problem.[36]

As the state relaxes controls over the allocation of commodities and the setting of prices, the reformers intend that it develop other mechanisms for regulating the economy. One of the most important will be monetary and fiscal policy. The People's Bank of China is being recast as the nation's central reserve bank, with the ability to determine the money supply, adjust the volume of credit, and set interest rates. The allocation of investment capital is being assigned to the Industrial and Commercial Bank of China and to other specialized banks. National bond issues are being used to finance government deficits and to absorb excessive liquidity in the economy.[37]

Thus far, however, the central government has not been able to get a firm grip on these new economic levers. The explosive growth of the money supply in late 1984 and 1985, largely at the behest of the local authorities, demonstrated the limited power of the People's Bank over even this crucial aspect of national economic policy. The state budget is still hostage to unpredictable fluctuations in the amount of taxes received from, and subsidies granted to, the nation's state-owned enterprises. And the specialized investment banks have not been able to evade political interference in their allocation of investment. Although the state has relaxed administrative controls over the economy, therefore, it has not yet adequately developed effective regulatory devices to replace them.

Enterprises

Under the economic system at the end of the Maoist era, industrial and commercial enterprises were little more than appendages of the state bureaucracies that administered them. Enterprise managers had little ability to make decisions about sources, product line, marketing, or pricing. They had little power over investment and minimal access to capital for new equipment. The post-Mao economic reforms have given managers greater independence in running their enterprises, the ability to retain more financial resources and decide on their use, and more responsibility for their enterprises' profitability. But of all the urban reforms, the attempts to promote greater autonomy in enterprise management have been among the most difficult to implement effectively.[38]

The reduction in the scope of state planning and in the number of prices determined by the state requires an increase in the operational autonomy of state enterprises. If the government bureaucracy is not going to determine the level of output, or the prices at which to sell goods, then that responsibility necessarily devolves to the enterprises. Since 1984, therefore, enterprises have been granted greater power over the production, pricing, and distribution of above-quota or nonplanned output; and over the hiring, promotion, remuneration, and dismissal of their workers. Moreover, within each factory, these expanded powers were granted to the enterprise managers, who were to be subject to less interference from their superiors in the state bureaucracy, their enterprise Party committee, or the workers' committees in their plants.[39]

Even in theory, however, this reform has been subject to rather stringent limits. The Party, the state, and the workers' congress all retain significant residual powers that limit the autonomy of factory managers. As of the end of 1986, the state preserved control over an enterprise's product line, decisions to start up new factories or close old ones, and the appointment and promotion of the managers. The state still had the right to review the salaries, promotions, and disciplinary actions given to key personnel in a factory and to establish the size of the labor force. And the state could still set an enterprise's annual production quota for that share of output that is subject to mandatory planning, allocate or withhold key inputs that fall under state allocation, and, at least for a transitional period, adjust the tax rates for individual product lines.

Nor, under the new regulations, is the factory manager completely free of supervision by the Party committee and workers' organizations in his factory. The enterprise Party committee retains broad powers to monitor the implementation of Party policies, ensure that enterprises meet their obligations under state plans, and review serious personnel matters. The workers' congresses have some authority over decisions about workers' welfare, patterns of remuneration, and the annual production plan. And a manager must consult with the trade union if he wishes to dismiss any factory employee.

Moreover, both the Party and the government bureaucracies have tenaciously maintained their control over state enterprises. In many cases, government agencies at the provincial and municipal levels have simply transformed themselves into "state corporations," in order to retain authority over their factories.[40] Some state industrial bureaus have used their control over raw materials allocated by the state to pressure enterprises into following their instructions. Party committees have employed their power to correct "unhealthy tendencies" to ensure that factory managers comply with their wishes. Factory managers describe the Party and state as having "handed down the bowl, but not the chopsticks" and are said to be "burning with anger and anxiety" that they have not received the powers to which government regulations have entitled them.[41]

Autonomy for enterprises would mean little if the enterprises did not have greater financial resources at their disposal. In the Maoist era, factories had almost no discretionary funds: net revenues, except for a small depreciation fund, were remitted to the cognizant state agencies, which provided investment capital, at no cost, for projects they had approved. Thus reform has focused on giving enterprises greater access to financial resources while making them more responsible for the profitability of their investment.[42]

When the urban reforms were first introduced on an experimental basis in the late 1970s, enterprises were granted the right to retain some of their profits, which they could then employ, under state restrictions, for investment, worker welfare, bonuses, or research and development.[43] Beginning in 1983, however, the enterprise's responsibility was gradually redefined. The enterprise had to move from submitting profits to paying taxes to the state, on the grounds that a tax system could more accurately measure, and stimulate, the economic performance of the enterprise. Under this policy, enterprises will not only pay a tax on their income but also a tax on total sales. They must also pay fees for various resources that, despite the preliminary price reforms, remain underpriced, including taxes on the use of land, capital, and equipment. In addition, pending the full implementation of price reform, enterprises must also pay a "regulatory" tax on the part of their profit that can be attributed to irrationally favorable prices—a Chinese version of a windfall profits tax. All earnings that remain after the payment of these taxes are largely at the disposal of the enterprise.[44]

These reforms, designed to reward enterprises for earning profits, are supposed to be supplemented by measures to make businesses more responsible for their losses. One mechanism is a shift from grants to loans in financing investment. Under this reform, enterprises obtain an increasing share of their investment capital from banks, rather than from government agencies, and are supposed to repay their loans according to a fixed schedule. But the financial discipline on enterprises remains weak. The interest rates charged for investment loans remain too low. Enterprises encountering financial difficulties can receive tax remissions to enable them to repay their loans, or they can have their loans guaranteed by their superior administrative departments. Banks are still subject to political interference from local governments, which can press them to renegotiate the terms of loans to local enterprises. At the same time, the banks operate in a relaxed regulatory environment, in which the issuance of bad loans is of little consequence. As a result, the system of loans to enterprises has not been significantly more stringent than the previous use of state grants.[45]

Indeed, taken together, several of the urban industrial reforms have greatly increased the amount of investment capital at the disposal of state enterprises. Over time, the profit retention mechanisms have been successively redesigned to allow enterprises to keep more than 40 percent of the profits they earned in 1986, compared with less than 4 percent in 1978.[46] The growing role of banks has meant the emergence of a new channel for funneling local funds into enterprise investment, independent of central control.

These changes in China's financial and tax systems have produced a revolution in the funding of new investment. The share of national investment in capital construction occurring outside the state budget, which had been only 16.7 percent in 1978, rose to 61.5 percent in 1986. Local governments and enterprises initiated a flood of projects in areas such as cigarette manufacture and wine distilleries that seemed to promise quick profit, but that expanded the nation's productive capacities far beyond what the market could support. In turn, the increase in new projects has placed great pressure on supplies of materials, and the relaxation in the planning system has enabled some suppliers to divert construction materials and equipment away from state projects to local projects that are willing to pay a higher price. Given these considerations, the central government has adopted measures to bring extrabudgetary investment under control, including levying taxes on it. However, the government action has not been successful. From 1981 to 1986, extrabudgetary investment in capital construction by state-owned units increased at an average rate of 30 percent a year, whereas investment in capital construction included in the state budget grew at an average annual rate of only 12 percent.[47]

The ultimate form of financial discipline on state enterprises would, of course, be bankruptcy for those that ran chronic losses. The appropriateness of bankruptcy for a socialist economy was debated intensely in academic circles and in the press throughout 1985 and 1986. Draft bankruptcy regulations were implemented on a trial basis in a few cities, and a few enterprises, mostly collective undertakings, were declared bankrupt.[48] But when a national bankruptcy law was presented to the National People's Congress in 1986, it encountered stiff opposition.[49] Some delegates argued that the institution of bankruptcy proceedings against unprofitable enterprises would be unfair in the absence of a more reasonable price structure and true enterprise autonomy. Without such preconditions, they pointed out, managers might be held responsible for the consequences of decisions over which they had no control or for losses produced by prices that they had no power to adjust. Further, the opponents of a national bankruptcy law also insisted that more preparation was needed to provide unemployment compensation, retraining, and relocation of those put out of work when an enterprise failed.

After tabling the issue for several months, the Standing Committee of the National People's Congress finally adopted a provisional bankruptcy law in early December 1986, but it remained uncertain how rapidly, or how stringently, it would be enforced. Until the danger of bankruptcy becomes significant in the calculations of

Chinese managers, the budgetary constraints on Chinese enterprises will, in the familiar phrase of the Hungarian economist Janos Kornai, be "soft" rather than "hard." Enterprises, in other words, will enjoy the benefits of any profits they earn, but they will not be responsible for the losses they suffer.

The problem of bankruptcy illustrates perfectly the interconnectedness of economic reform in China. Giving enterprises greater access to financial resources, whether from retained profits or from bank loans, produces little benefit and can even be counterproductive in the absence of the tight financial discipline symbolized by bankruptcy. But bankruptcy is difficult, and can even be unfair, in the absence of rational prices, unemployment compensation, and greater labor mobility. Moreover, both bankruptcy and price reform are among the most sensitive issues on the Chinese political agenda. They represent a conundrum for Chinese reformers: failure to adopt them may condemn other, more popular, reforms to failure; but attempts to implement them may seriously reduce the political support for the reform program.

Workers

Urban workers, too, face a much different economic environment under the post-Mao reforms than they did during the late Maoist period. Then the urban labor force was trained in a system of comprehensive secondary schools that might have provided some opportunities for part-time labor but offered little rigorous technical or vocational training. Following graduation, state labor bureaus assigned workers to industrial enterprises and commercial establishments for what amounted to unconditional lifetime employment. As state employees, urban workers were paid according to national wage scales, with fairly little variation according to performance and with few opportunities for promotion or bonuses.

Under the post-Mao reforms, changes have occurred in all three elements of this picture: education, employment, and remuneration. Under the reform of the educational system announced in the spring of 1985, the content of the middle school curriculum in the cities will be altered to stress vocational training to provide a better match between the skills of the labor force and the demands of the industrial sector. Extending the length of vocational training can also help regulate the flow of a vast number of Chinese urban youth into the labor market during the next five years.[50]

The system of employment has been modified to give urban workers greater opportunities to find work outside the state sector and limited opportunities to change jobs within the network of state enterprises.[51] The more dramatic reform has been the encouragement of individual and collective labor, especially in the underdeveloped service sector, as a way of absorbing new entrants into the labor force. The number of privately employed urban workers remains a small fraction of the total labor force, constituting 3.6 percent in 1986. But the nonstate sector employed more than its share of young workers entering the labor force in the early 1980s: more than 13 percent of the new urban workers employed for the first time in 1983, for example, found work in privately owned and operated establishments, and another 27 percent were employed by collective enterprises—enterprises owned collectively by their workers that belong to neither the state nor the private sector. Only 60 percent of the new entrants into the labor force were hired by state enterprises.[52]

In the state sector, workers are encountering a more flexible labor market, although its operations remain extremely restricted. Under some reform experiments, workers seeking employment are allowed to apply for the jobs that they find attractive and to refuse assignments offered them by state labor bureaus. Those with technical training who believe that their skills are not being adequately utilized can apply for transfer to other positions, or they can leave the state sector to seek employment in collective enterprises or to engage in private entrepreneurial activities. Enterprises are permitted to use their own recruitment procedures, including advertisements and examinations, to select the most suitable employees from a pool of applicants.

The limits on the operation of China's fledgling labor market are apparent in two somewhat different areas. Although technicians are being given greater freedom to change jobs, college students are still required for the most part to accept the initial assignments given them by the state immediately upon graduation. In the mid-1980s the government experimented with allowing college graduates to take more initiative in selecting their own employers, which apparently led to shortages of young intellectuals in certain regions and sectors regarded by the state as having high priority. Accordingly, in a reversal of this aspect of economic liberalization, the percentage of university graduates receiving assignments from the state returned from 24 percent in 1985 to 69 percent in 1986.[53]

Furthermore, China still does not allow much rural-to-urban migration, except to some of the new smaller cities being established in the countryside to absorb surplus agricultural labor. Although some young peasant women can find jobs in Shanghai and Peking as domestic servants, and many more peasants enter the cities illegally, residents of the Chinese countryside still have little hope of finding legal employment in any of the country's larger urban areas. Workers, too, are restricted by labor regulations from transferring to cities larger than the one in which they are already employed. Thus, despite some exceptions, labor mobility in China exists primarily for those who are willing to stay in the same city or to move to a smaller one.

In 1985, following more than five years of experimentation, China changed the terms under which young workers became employees of state enterprises. Rather than hiring for life, the state now gives employees contracts with a specified term and a detailed set of responsibilities. After consultation with the trade union, supervisors can dismiss workers who do not perform their duties satisfactorily or who violate the disciplinary regulations of the enterprise. Workers relieved of their jobs, whether for poor performance, disciplinary transgressions, or because of the bankruptcy of the enterprise, will become eligible for unemployment compensation for a period of up to two years.[54]

Finally, the government is also changing the salary system. As early as 1977, most state employees finally received the promotions and salary increases that had been denied them for so long during the late Maoist period. Shortly thereafter, enterprises were authorized to grant bonuses to deserving workers from the profits they were now permitted to retain. In late 1984, in its decision on urban economic reform, the Party announced that it was planning to develop measures that would "better link wages and bonuses with the improved enterprise performance." Economists explained that the government would actually abolish the system of national wage scales that had been in effect for more than thirty years and would replace them with a set of formulas under which an enterprises's total wage bill would be related to its economic performance.[55] For an industrial enterprise, for example, the state might specify the ratio according to which the total amount of wages and bonuses paid in a year would be related to the level of taxes remitted or sales generated. For a transportation company, wages might be linked to tonnage carried; and for a construction company, salary might be determined by the value of projects completed. After the total wage bill was set by the state formula, the management of each enterprise would have almost complete freedom to establish a system of wages and bonuses.

As might be imagined, these adjustments of the wage and employment systems have been difficult to implement successfully, since they run counter to the principles of egalitarianism and job security that occupy a central place in the socialist ethic. By the early 1980s, it was already clear that bonuses were not being awarded on the basis of a worker's effort and productivity, but were being distributed to all an enterprise's employees on a relatively egalitarian basis. The reform of the wage system, announced in 1985, has apparently not been widely implemented, since it is virtually impossible to link wages to a factory's profits before price control has been completed. And the system of state employment contracts was variously denounced as being a "capitalist system," benefiting the enterprise but not the workers, and denying workers the position of being "masters of their own house."[56]

The opposition to labor reform was so intense that it could only be implemented in the most gradual fashion. The employment contract system has, in effect, a grandfather clause so that workers already employed in October 1985 preserve their guarantee of lifetime employment. Only new workers entering the labor force after that date are subject to employment contracts, thus ensuring that it will take more than thirty years for the new system to be universally adopted. Moreover, to compensate for the greater uncertainty inherent in employment contracts, new workers will be paid at a higher wage than those with total job security. Even so, only 31 percent of a sample of new workers surveyed in Canton said they supported the new system.[57]

THE RADICAL ECONOMIC REFORMS

Generally speaking, the urban economic reforms undertaken in post-Mao China have been less successful than those in agriculture. It is true that the average rate of growth of urban industrial output was 9.3 percent between 1979 and 1986, slightly higher than the rate China had experienced in the early 1970s before the urban reforms had been put into effect (table 5-1). But China's industrial problem has been a shortage of efficiency and quality, not any lack of speed or quantity. And on these other dimensions the urban economic reforms have, as yet, had little beneficial effect. Although labor productivity in state-owned industrial enterprises has increased, capital productivity apparently fell between 1978 and 1983.[58] After an initial drop in the early 1980s, the financial losses incurred by state enterprises have risen again, mostly because of the periodic surges of unprofitable new investments and the rising costs of raw materials. And the quality of industrial output has not been improved.

As they examined the incomplete accomplishments of urban economic reform in late 1985 and early 1986, Chinese economists and political leaders identified three possible courses of action, each of which had strong advocates and equally committed opponents. One group would reverse course, restoring tighter administrative controls over the economy to remedy the problems of excessive investment, chronic losses, corruption, and inflation. Another group would continue the changes already agreed to, but make them more effective by proceeding in a more determined manner with such politically sensitive programs as price reform, labor reform, and enterprise bankruptcy.

But a third option—even more sweeping reform—dominated the Chinese political agenda in 1986. A group of radical reformers, including both economists and politicians, decided that the limits placed on the initial reform program were partly responsible for the country's economic difficulties. According to this group, moderate economic reform had tried to secure the benefits of the marketplace while preserving the dominance of the state plan. Initial reforms had been aimed at exploiting the gains of increasing the autonomy of enterprises while making few alterations in the system of state ownership of industry. But the radical reformers believed that economic reform could be successful only if the marketplace were expanded to include critical industrial inputs, including capital and labor, and if there was a significant change in the structure of public ownership in the urban economy. If adopted, these proposals would constitute a second package of reform measures that would build on, but go far beyond, the first set of moderate reforms launched in the late 1970s and early 1980s.

Enlarging the Marketplace

The radical reformers proposed a new way of looking at the market. In the most basic and controversial element of their plan, they favored making the market the foundation of the Chinese economy.[59] In the past, the prevailing view had been that only a limited number of commodities—notably agricultural products and consumer goods— should properly be exchanged in the market. As one representative article published in 1982 put it, only "small consumer goods" and "small natural [meaning agricultural] products," which were "produced in greater varieties but have a low output value," could reasonably be exempted from mandatory state planning.[60] Other commodities, including basic raw materials and capital goods, would have to remain the province of the state system of procurement and allocation. In a concise formula presented by Chen Yun, "the plan should be the foundation, and the market should serve as a supplement."[61]

In contrast, China's radical reformers have proposed that the market, rather than the plan, become the principal allocative mechanism in the Chinese economy, and that regulation, rather than planning, become the most important device for state intervention in the nation's economic life. For some, this concept would mean eliminating mandatory planning and creating a "market system under guidance planning."[62] Others would go even further and restrict the use of both mandatory and guidance plans. In their view, the function of the state should be limited to regulating, through the legal system and through macroeconomic policy, what would become a market economy. As one young reformer, drawing an analogy with soccer, said privately, the government should have three roles in the economy: "setting out the playing field, determining the rules, and being the judge."[63]

By the end of 1985, this idea was the subject of intense debate in the Chinese press. Some warned that economic activity would become "blind" or "chaotic" in the absence of effective national plans. Others cautioned that it would be impossible, under present conditions of scarcity, to eliminate planning without engendering an unacceptable level of inflation. While acknowledging that China's planning system has its faults, the defenders of planning have argued that the appropriate response should be to "consolidate and perfect socialist methods of production," rather than to eliminate them.[64] Perhaps the most succinct and authoritative expression of this point of view was Chen Yun's brief address to the National Party Conference in September 1985. The veteran economic planner insisted once again that socialism required the "primacy" of the planned economy, and that planning, and not merely regulation, should remain the "essence" of the state's macroeconomic policy.[65]

The radical reformers' interest in marketization of the economy led them to propose that China develop markets for the factors of production—including technology, capital, land, and labor—as well as for final products and services. Some of these more specific proposals are less controversial than others and have already been implemented on an experimental basis. Others appear to produce many more practical and ideological objections.

The principle that technology is a commodity that can legitimately be traded in the marketplace is at the foundation of the redesign of

China's scientific and technological institutions that was announced in 1985. Fewer research centers are to receive unconditional financial support from the state—the pattern of funding that was the norm in the past. Instead, they are to obtain funding from a competitive system of government grants and by accepting research contracts from industrial enterprises that want to employ the technology invented or improved as the result of a research project. The institutions and individuals who make technological discoveries are, under the new system, to receive financial benefit from their accomplishments, and their rights are protected under a new national patent law. Although the Chinese have found it difficult to agree on a formula for determining the price or value of new technology, the basic concept of a market for technology now seems to be broadly accepted.[66]

The creation of capital markets has proceeded more rapidly than many observers anticipated, even though it remains a controversial subject. Several state and collective enterprises in a few cities have sold shares of stock to both employees and nonemployees as a method of raising investment capital.[67] These shares, currently without any form of voting rights, are guaranteed to pay a certain minimal rate of interest and promise a share of the enterprise's profits over and above that basic amount. The shares can be traded on nascent stock exchanges in a few cities, but it is not yet clear that the price of stock will be permitted to vary to reflect the total rate of return on the investment.

Though these experiments in shareholding have received the greatest amount of attention abroad, they are in fact only one aspect of China's emergent capital market.[68] Several cities have begun to issue municipal construction bonds to domestic investors.[69] Besides the investment capital given to them by the state, banks are now able to issue, as loans, funds that they have raised from their depositors.[70] At least nine cities have begun interbank lending on a modest scale, and Shanghai has permitted the establishment of a new local bank to compete with the People's Bank of China and the specialized central investment banks.[71]

The more conservative economists have been skeptical about giving the marketplace so much responsibility for the mobilization and allocation of capital. In their view, the creation of capital markets would make it much more difficult for the state to retain control over credit, currency, and the scale of investment. They worry that private investors might lose their savings by purchasing stocks in companies that later suffered losses or even went bankrupt. Moreover, the conservatives have also cautioned that trading of shares by private citizens would lead to "blind development" rather than promote a "reasonable investment structure" and would generate differences in wealth and income on a scale unacceptable in a socialist society.[72]

In 1986 the radical reformers also made controversial proposals for the creation of markets in labor and land. If adopted, these proposals would give workers greater freedom to change their place of work and even their residence if they could find more attractive opportunities for employment elsewhere. An increase in labor mobility would, according to the radical reformers, also force state enterprises to use this crucial factor of production more efficiently. A land market would enable enterprises, collective farms, and even private individuals to buy and sell the rights to use land, even though these entities could not own the land. Indeed, by the end of 1986, Shanghai had launched, on a small scale, the first urban housing market, and prospective homeowners were lining up to purchase apartments from the municipal government's housing authority.

To orthodox Marxists, of course, neither land nor labor has traditionally been regarded as a marketable commodity in a socialist society. If limited experiments with capital markets raised the specter of opportunistic investors living off unearned income from stocks and bonds, then proposals for land and labor markets suggested even uglier images: a new class of landlords earning exorbitant rents from their large landholdings, and selfish industrial and commercial employers manipulating a revived labor market to drive wages down to subsistence levels. To defend their unorthodox proposals, the radical reformers were forced to develop rather arcane arguments to the effect that the creation of land and labor markets would not necessarily violate the Marxist premise that neither of these two factors of production could ever become commodities under socialism.

Reforming the Pattern of Ownership

In 1986 the radical reformers revealed the second principal component in their program. They wanted to change the system of ownership in the urban economy. Shortly after the purge of the Gang of Four, a rapid expansion had occurred in the number of privately owned and operated enterprises in China's major cities. The expansion had led to increased job opportunities for unemployed urban residents and an improvement in the provision of scarce urban services. But important as it was, the new enterprises remained, at least on paper, limited in scope. They were allowed to employ only five employees or apprentices from outside the employer's family and were restricted to such sectors of the economy as catering, services, and handicrafts.

By 1986 the government was contemplating whether to relax these limits to encourage the further expansion of private enterprise in urban China. Some of the radical reformers suggested lifting or removing the restrictions on the number of employees that private entrepreneurs could hire. Others proposed legislation to guarantee the right of private property against unwarranted expropriation or harassment by the state.

The debate hinged largely on the experiments with private ownership in the city of Wenzhou, to the south of Shanghai. There, families and private entrepreneurs had been encouraged to launch small industrial enterprises, specializing in the production of such items as buttons, zippers, badges, and yarn, which were then traded on free markets outside the scope of the state plan. The size of these private enterprises, and their importance in the local economy, had become far greater than in the rest of the country, with family industries reportedly accounting for 60 percent of the city's total industrial output. To radical reformers, the "Wenzhou miracle" had succeeded in increasing output and living standards in an area previously plagued by surplus rural labor and high levels of urban unemployment.[73] But others regarded the problems encountered in Wenzhou—tax evasion, fraud, moonlighting, and growing inequality—as symptomatic of private industry. One article noted that the Wenzhou experiment could be described as the "'assault' of the individual economy" against the state and argued that, as an experiment, it should not be "widely emulated."[74]

Proposals for changes in the ownership of state enterprises, including even the largest ones, were also part of the radical economic reforms put forward in 1986. The radical reformers argued that the benefits of greater autonomy for enterprise could not be fully realized so long as factory managers were administratively responsible to their superiors in the cognizant ministry of the state bureaucracy. The reformers want to find ways of redefining the concept of state ownership so as to give enterprise managers greater freedom from interference by the government and greater freedom to respond creatively and flexibly to signals from the marketplace. Li Yining of Peking University has therefore insisted that a transformation in the system of state ownership was just as important to the success of overall reform as was the tendency toward more rational prices. In his words, "the failure of price reform could be the reason the [broader] reforms will fail, but the success of reform will require a change in the ownership pattern" in state industry.[75]

The radical reformers have shown interest in two proposals for reforming the system of industrial ownership. The first leases state enterprises to individuals or, more commonly, groups of workers for terms of three to six years. Potential lessees must secure backing from financial guarantors and must pass an examination of their managerial skills. Those whose applications are approved by the state become the managers of the factories for the term of their lease. During that period, in return for their regular lease payments to the state, they acquire full power over the enterprise's operations and personnel. At least in theory, they have full rights to determine the disposition of the enterprise's annual profit. With their guarantors, they are responsible for any losses their enterprise might incur. Some radical reformers have apparently proposed that all small state enterprises, with fixed assets of less than 1.5 million yuan (about $400,000), be leased in this manner. By mid-1987, about three thousand state enterprises had been transferred to new management through some form of leasing.[76]

For larger state enterprises, reformers have proposed a second ownership reform scheme known as *gufenhua,* which can be translated into English accurately, if rather awkwardly, as "stockification." Under this proposal, ownership in these enterprises would be vested in shares of stock, which would then be assigned or sold to various government agencies, public organizations, the enterprise's workers, and individual citizens, who would then elect a board of directors to appoint and supervise the enterprise manager.[77]

The radical reformers argue that this type of reform would create a better balance between autonomy and responsibility within each enterprise. The autonomy of factory directors would be enhanced by attenuating the connection between the enterprise and its cognizant government ministry. At the same time, however, the factory would become responsible to a broadly based board of directors, who could better represent the general social interest than could any single government ministry. Indeed, one reformer has described stockification as "precisely a form of the 'common ownership' that Marxism once put forth."[78]

The radical reformers have argued among themselves about the details of stockification. Some, like Liu Guoguang of the Academy of Social Sciences, have suggested that government agencies maintain control of 51 percent of the shares of each state enterprise to guarantee continued state control. Others, like Li Yining, have been more flexible, declaring that the state could still preserve its ability to guide the economy even if it had only a minority interest in some enterprises.[79]

Thus the radical reformers have envisioned an economy in which direct state ownership of industry and commerce plays a minimal role. In one version, proposed by Li Yining, state ownership would be restricted to major public utilities, such as banks, railroads, and communications facilities that already exist. Stockification would be the predominant system of ownership for all medium and large state enterprises and for all newly established state utilities. Small commercial and industrial enterprises would be leased out or transformed into collectives controlled by their workers. In particular, Li has implied that no new state enterprises should ever again be created.[80]

Not surprisingly, stockification has proved every bit as controversial as the proposals for marketization have been. Conservative economists have maintained that continued state ownership is necessary in order to realize collective and national interests and have warned that transferring ownership outside the state bureaucracy would produce a form of "state capitalism" rather than socialism.[81] They have also pointed out, quite correctly, that China already has a shortage of skilled managers and have asked how it will be possible to find a qualified board of directors for each state enterprise that has undergone stockification. As one critic has warned, "If promoted blindly, it [issuance of stock] may cause the dislocation of the already accumulated power of ownership by the whole people of the means of production, disrupting the fiscal revenues of the state and [the] capital accumulations of enterprises. Hence it is not acceptable."[82]

Advocates of radical economic reform fell silent in early 1987, in the aftermath of the resignation of Hu Yaobang. The campaign against bourgeois liberalization offered the opponents of radical reform the opportunity to defend the continuation of mandatory planning, criticize proposals for enterprise bankruptcy and stockification, and warn of the economic polarization that might result from expanding private enterprise. Moreover, some elements of moderate economic reform also came under fire. Conservative officials in both Peking and the provinces alleged that the household responsibility system in agriculture was "undermining" the basis of the collective economy, that the growing role of market forces was tantamount to the restoration of capitalist practices, and that expanding the autonomy of factory managers was "abolishing the Party's leadership" in state enterprises. Some skeptics also charged that the basic cause for the emergence of political dissent and cultural experimentation was the encouragement of individual entrepreneurship in the economic sphere.[83]

By the middle of the year, however, the radical reformers seemed to have regained the initiative and had resumed the defense both of the moderate economic reforms of the early 1980s and the advocacy of the more radical measures first introduced in 1986. It seems, therefore, that the radical reformers' proposals to expand the role of the market in the Chinese economy and to revise the system of state ownership of industry will continue to occupy a critical and controversial place on the Chinese political agenda for many years to come.

CONCLUSION

Dramatic, palpable changes have occurred in the Chinese economy since the death of Mao Zedong. A stroll down a street in urban China is a vastly different experience today than in 1976. Cars, trucks, and buses now crowd thoroughfares once devoid of motor vehicles. Small shops that were shuttered during the Cultural Revolution have now reopened, some as restaurants, some as stores, some as barber shops, and some as billiard halls. Private vendors throng on the street corners, and some now sing or shout the characteristic calls that were so familiar in years past. Free markets are full of fresh meat, fish, and produce, and they are crowded with shoppers. Young people are more fashionably dressed, and avidly search the department stores for cassette recorders, television sets, refrigerators, and other prized consumer goods. In the suburban areas, construction materials for private housing line the major roads, and many peasant homes now display television antennas.

Confronted with changes such as these, some observers have concluded that China has abandoned socialism to follow a capitalist course. Writing in the *New York Times* at the end of 1984, for example, William Safire declared that the "biggest event" of the past year had been the "embrace of capitalism" by the Chinese Communist Party. In a similar vein, *Business Week* published a cover story on the Chinese economic reforms entitled "Capitalism in China."[84] Others, unwilling to jump to extreme conclusions, have suggested that China is engaged in an experiment with market socialism.

Private proprietorship is important at the margins of the Chinese economy. In 1985, for example, nearly half of the increase in national retail sales was accounted for by the private sector of the economy.

Table 5-2. *Urban Employment, Industrial Output, and Retail Sales by Sector, Selected Years and Period, 1978–86*

Aspects	Private	Collective	State	Other
Urban employment				
Percent of total, 1978	0.2	21.5	78.3	0.0
Percent of total, 1986	3.6	25.7	70.2	0.4[a]
Average rate of increase, 1980–86	34.7	5.9	2.6	n.a.
Industrial output				
Percent of total, 1978	0.0	19.2	80.8	0.0
Percent of total, 1986	0.3	29.2	68.7	1.8[a]
Average rate of increase, 1980–86	80.3	16.9	7.9	33.2
Retail sales				
Percent of total, 1978	2.1[b]	7.4	90.5	0.0
Percent of total, 1986	23.9[b]	36.4	39.4	0.3[c]
Average rate of increase, 1980–86	55.3	38.3	1.4	83.4

Source: *Zhongguo tongji zhaiyao, 1987*, pp. 17, 22, 40, 82.
n.a. Not available.
a. Includes foreign ventures.
b. Includes sales by peasants to non-peasants.
c. Indicates joint state-private ownership.

Similarly, of the urban workers newly employed in that year, almost 14 percent found jobs as individual laborers or in privately owned enterprises. Private enterprises have been the most rapidly growing sector of Chinese industry, averaging growth rates of 80 percent per year between 1980 and 1986 (table 5-2). Individuals made nearly 10 percent of the investment in productive fixed assets. And if housing were added to that total, then the private sector was responsible for more than one-fifth of the nation's total investment in 1985.[85]

Still, despite the rapid growth in private and collective enterprises, the core of the economy remains state owned and state operated (table 5-2). The state sector of the economy accounts for about 70 percent of urban employment and industrial production; the collective sector, for about 25 percent to 30 percent; and the private sector, for less than 5 percent. Even in retail sales, where the state's presence has declined precipitously since the late 1970s, the government still has the largest single share, 39 percent, compared with 36 percent for the collective sector and 24 percent for the private sector. Despite the rapid growth in private employment, the number of workers in the private sector in 1985 (4.8 million) was only slightly more than those who were unemployed (about 2.6 million).[86]

With the growing role of market forces, the state is playing a smaller part in the allocation of goods and services in the Chinese economy. In 1986, about 18 percent of all marketed agricultural output was sold directly by peasants on free markets.[87] A sizable share of industrial commodities, ranging from a third to a half in some cases, was being traded outside the system of state allocation, for prices that could fluctuate with the forces of supply and demand. And many younger and more radical Chinese reformers would like to see a further reduction in the scope of mandatory planning and the development of factor markets for technology, capital, land, and labor.

Still, the Chinese economy remains highly regulated. The state still issues detailed annual plans and five-year plans. About 30 percent to 40 percent of industrial output remains subject to mandatory planning, and another 40 percent to 50 percent is governed by guidance plans. The state continues to set many key prices: interest rates, the prices offered for agricultural output under the purchase contract system, the retail price of state-distributed agricultural commodities, the prices for industrial commodities produced according to mandatory planning, and the range within which the prices of other industrial products can fluctuate. Even if, in the future, China should abolish all mandatory planning, the bulk of production and allocation decisions will still be made under heavy state influence, although not direct state control.

Thus China is moving neither toward capitalism nor orthodox socialism, but rather toward a mixed economy that combines state planning, government regulation, and market forces, and that melds private, collective, and state ownership. The debate in China, as in much of the Asian-Pacific region, is over the optimal balance among these different aspects of the economy. Radical reformers are eager to expand the role of the market, increase opportunities for private enterprise, and revise the system of state ownership. Their more conservative colleagues want to maintain a higher level of central planning, place restrictions on the size of the private sector of the economy, and retain more traditional forms of state ownership in industry. The issue is not whether to adopt any pure economic model, but how to select the blend that will be most appropriate to China's circumstances.

CHAPTER 6

Opening China to the World Economy

As noted in chapter 1, Peking's foreign economic policy during the late Maoist period was neither as self-reliant as its leaders claimed, nor as autarkic as foreign observers commonly perceived. China's foreign trade did fall seriously during the early years of the Cultural Revolution, declining by 13 percent in absolute terms between 1966 and 1969. This drop occurred partly because the radical doctrines of the day denigrated international economic relations and partly because the turmoil of the period disrupted both China's export economy and its diplomatic ties with trading partners. In 1970, just after this low point in China's foreign economic relations, two-way trade amounted to about $4.6 billion, and exports constituted less than 3 percent of national output.[1]

But once the Cultural Revolution had passed its peak, China's trade quickly recovered from its temporary slump. In the early 1970s, even before the death of Mao Zedong, Peking dramatically increased imports of industrial supplies and foreign technology, particularly whole plants, and expanded the export of agricultural goods, raw materials, and manufactured goods in order to pay for them. By 1975 the country's total foreign trade had reached nearly $15 billion, an increase of more than 250 percent in only six years; and exports rose to 5 percent of national output, the highest level in the history of the People's Republic. The "great leap outward" associated with Hua Guofeng saw another surge in trade, which passed $20 billion in 1978, more than 40 percent higher than it had been only three years earlier.

Thus the 1970s witnessed a big increase in the volume of China's imports and exports and in the importance of trade to the domestic economy. But even though the level of trade increased markedly during the last years of Mao Zedong and the short interregnum of Hua Guofeng, until late in the decade stringent limits remained on the types of international relationships that China was prepared to enter. Under the prodding of the Gang of Four, for example, Chinese leaders in the mid-1970s refused to accept foreign investment, foreign aid, or foreign loans, except for short-term suppliers' credits, to finance their imports.[2] Similar restrictions were restated in early 1977 when, five months after Mao's death, an authoritative discussion of China's foreign economic relations emphasized that Peking would never allow foreigners to dump consumer goods in its domestic markets, "mortgage" its natural resources to import advanced technology, or accept loans or investments from abroad.[3] For most of the 1970s, in other words, China may have been interested in purchasing foreign equipment, but it was not willing to engage in the full range of practices that characterize international economic relations in the contemporary world.

The reforms undertaken since 1978 in the sphere of foreign economic policy have greatly increased China's interaction with the international economy.[4] Decentralizing and liberalizing the mechanisms by which trade is conducted have led to further increases in the volume of trade, important changes in its composition, and, to a somewhat lesser degree, a redirection of imports and exports to new sources and markets. Furthermore, the post-Mao reforms have broadened the range of international economic relationships that China considers acceptable. In contrast to the early and mid-1970s, let alone the 1960s, Peking now welcomes direct foreign investment; accepts aid, loans, and credits from foreign governments, international organizations, and commercial banks; and has multiplied the channels through which it hopes to acquire advanced technological know-how and managerial experience. Finally, Peking has designated certain parts of the country—first four special economic zones in the Southeast, then fourteen "open cities" and Hainan Island, and most recently, three larger "development zones" along the southern coast—to be front-runners in absorbing foreign technology, introducing foreign capital, and expanding Chinese exports to foreign markets. In all these ways, the post-Mao reforms have produced not just a quantitative increase in China's economic exchanges with the rest of the world but also a qualitative change in the nature of its international economic relationships.[5]

These wide-ranging reforms are based on a single critical assumption: that China will not be able to modernize rapidly or effectively unless it expands economic relations with the outside world. Most Chinese leaders and intellectuals now understand that an autarkic strategy of development will prevent China from absorbing the advanced experience and modern technology of other countries, and that an isolated China will remain relatively poor and weak. Chinese economists have acknowledged that China's relative autarky in the 1960s, when most of the rest of East Asia was enjoying rapid economic growth, caused Peking to lag farther and farther behind its neighbors. Conversely, Chinese analysts have also stressed the benefits—especially the lower costs of production, greater economic efficiency, and technological advance—that can be gained from more active participation in the international economy.[6]

This premise is one of the themes that has permeated the published writings and speeches of Deng Xiaoping during the past decade. As early as 1975, in a major Party document outlining a strategy for industrial development, Deng warned that China should not "adopt a closed-door attitude and refuse to learn from the good things of foreign countries." More recently, Deng has cautioned that "any country that closes its door to the outside world cannot achieve progress" and has attributed the slow pace of China's modernization to its international isolation from the middle of the Ming dynasty through the Opium War, and from the Sino-Soviet split of the late 1950s through the Cultural Revolution.[7]

As reform-minded Chinese officials and economists have examined the patterns of international economic interaction in the 1980s, they have discovered a single world economy, within which developing countries such as China can work effectively. In the words of one academic analysis, "The present world is an open world, in which economies of all countries are more and more closely interrelated and interdependent."[8] In addition, Chinese reformers have also accepted the proposition that a universal set of international economic mechanisms and instruments exists, which China should learn to employ. In opening its doors to the rest of the world, therefore, China should not restrict economic and technological ties solely to other socialist countries, nor limit international economic relations to the methods and strategies customarily employed by other socialist states.

This assessment differs sharply from the one common in the 1950s, when China, like the Soviet Union, believed that the world was divided into two competing economic blocs, one socialist and one capitalist, between which there could be little mutually beneficial interaction. It also stands in considerable contrast to the prevailing interpretation of the 1970s, when Chinese leaders insisted that large, industrialized, capitalist countries dominated the international economic order, which was structured in ways detrimental to the interests of the developing nations. Today, Chinese reformers assert that tensions remain between North and South, but increasingly insist that compromise and cooperation, rather than confrontation, is the most effective way to find solutions to these problems.

The internationalist tendencies increasingly evident in post-Mao China must still compete, however, with a strong and resilient strain of Chinese protectionism—a way of thinking that draws not only on Marxism, Leninism, and Maoism but also on China's experience with Western and Japanese penetration and aggression in the late nineteenth and early twentieth centuries. Just as the tension between the reformist spirit and the socialist ethic has been the principal characteristic of the continuing discussions of domestic economic reform, so has the interplay between the elements of internationalism and protectionism been the critical dynamic in the evolution of China's foreign economic policy in the post-Mao era.

As in many developing countries, protectionism in China possesses both economic and cultural dimensions. In the cultural sphere, many Chinese officials and intellectuals continue to believe, as they have for more than a century, that extensive contact with foreigners will produce an infusion of unorthodox ideas—including individualism and consumerism, political pluralism and human rights—that will endanger their country's political stability, social order, and cultural integrity. Repeatedly, both leaders and scholars in China have stressed the need to protect their society from "spiritual pollution" and "unhealthy tendencies" from abroad to preserve a "spiritual civilization" that is identifiably socialist and distinctively Chinese.

Similarly, many planners and managers fear that, if the Chinese economy were fully opened to the outside world, domestic firms would be unable to compete effectively with foreign imports, Chinese consumers would demand expensive foreign products, and local manufacturers would become dependent on external sources of supply. Using the rhetoric of self-reliance, both officials and economists have called for continued restrictions on the import of foreign products, even advanced technology. As Vice-Premier Li Peng said in mid-1986, "China should rely mainly on its own products to push ahead with the modernization drive instead of importing large amounts of foreign equipment."[9]

Disputes over these issues have been apparent ever since the reform of China's foreign economic policy began in 1978. In 1980–81 vigorous debate occurred over the costs and benefits of the "self-strengthening" movement of the latter half of the nineteenth century, and the lessons drawn from this reassessment were believed to be directly relevant to the contemporary period.[10] At about the same time, critics of the new foreign economic policies introduced arguments that would be repeated frequently in later years: the balance of payments deficit of 1978 had been a direct and inevitable consequence of the opening to the West; importing goods from abroad harmed domestic industry; and the export of China's coal and petroleum meant the mortgaging of the nation's resources to foreigners.[11] One theme of the campaign against spiritual pollution in 1983–84 was that the creation of the special economic zones and the opening of China to the outside world had been responsible for the flow of contaminating ideas from abroad.

In 1985 debate over foreign economic policy culminated in an unusual mass protest. In September, on the anniversary of the all-out Japanese attack against China in 1937, university students in Peking staged a protest against, among other things, what they described as the "second Japanese invasion" of their country. By this term they referred not only to some incidents earlier that year in which imported Japanese products, including several thousand Mitsubishi trucks, had been shown to be defective, but also to the influx of Japanese cars and consumer goods and to the prevalence of Japanese advertising on billboards and television. When the protests spread to several other big cities, Chinese leaders felt obliged to launch a nationwide campaign to persuade the country's youth of the merits of expanding China's economic links to the rest of the world.[12]

Chinese leaders have attempted to resolve this tension between internationalism and protectionism by promising to use the power of the state to regulate their country's cultural and economic relations with the rest of the world. They have insisted that, as a large country with a strong national government, China now has the ability to secure the gains of international involvement but to avoid the costs. For one thing, since a relatively centralized Chinese system now confronts many foreign countries and firms, the Chinese government possesses considerable leverage over trading partners and foreign investors. China can avoid dependence on any single supplier, press to gain access to new markets, close its national market to goods that would compete with domestic industries, control the level of national indebtedness, and insist that all foreign investment projects carry advanced technology or some other obvious benefit for China. Similarly, Peking can protect China from cultural contamination by maintaining substantial control over who goes abroad, who comes to China, and what forms cultural and educational exchange can take.[13] Borrowing a familiar analogy from earlier times, Chinese leaders speak of having created an "open door" between China and the rest of the world, but also emphasize the need to place a screen across this passageway, allowing China to admit the technology it wants and the capital that it needs while excluding the ideas, products, and influences it fears.[14]

This formulation still begs a critical and controversial issue: how many doors should be opened to the outside world and how fine a mesh should be placed across them? The radical reformers have been more willing than their more cautious counterparts to establish special economic zones along the Chinese coast, adopt flexible policies to attract foreign investment to China, expand academic exchanges in the social sciences, and even open the Chinese marketplace to competition with foreign firms. Conversely, more conservative elements in Chinese society have been more critical of the special economic zones, more concerned about the contaminating influence of foreigners, and more resistant to imports, even of advanced technology.

THE DECENTRALIZATION AND EXPANSION OF TRADE

Throughout the Maoist period, a highly centralized system of foreign trade agencies, modeled after those in the Soviet Union, governed China's international economic relationships. The disadvantage of such a system, especially for trade outside the socialist bloc, was that it interposed a large and cumbersome bureaucratic organization between Chinese exporters and their foreign customers, and between Chinese importers and their suppliers overseas. Indeed, direct contact between buyers and sellers was strongly discouraged, if not completely prohibited. Consequently, imports were not well suited to Chinese needs, and Chinese exporters could not easily learn how to adapt their products for foreign markets. Moreover, given the complicated and lengthy procedures for making trading decisions, neither exporters nor importers could react quickly and efficiently to changes in the international marketplace. Neither local governments nor enterprises had any incentive to promote exports, other than passively to fulfill the export plans passed down to them by higher authorities, since the foreign trade agencies retained all foreign exchange earnings for remission to the central government.[15]

In restructuring China's foreign trade apparatus, the reformers have applied to the foreign economic sphere many of the same concepts that have guided reform in the domestic economy, including the principles of diversification, responsibility, and incentive.[16] To begin with, they have expanded the number of channels by which products are exchanged with the outside world and through which producers and consumers can meet. As yet, only a few enterprises have been granted permission to export or import directly. Most must still conduct business through the intermediacy of the government trading companies.[17] But the number of state trading agencies has been greatly increased. There are now a large number of provincial and municipal trading companies responsible for serving the enterprises in their localities, and ministerial trading firms are authorized to buy and sell on behalf of their subordinate state corporations. Increasingly, too, the government encourages foreign trade companies to form joint operations with productive enterprises so that, for the first time, a single organization will be responsible for production and marketing. All told, though only a handful of state trading corporations monopolized China's foreign trade in the mid-1970s, now about two thousand channels link Chinese buyers and suppliers to the rest of the world. Conversely, the central Ministry of Foreign Economic Relations and Trade now enjoys a monopoly over only seven categories of import goods and over sixteen categories of exports.[18]

To increase the initiative and responsibility of these foreign trade companies, they were transformed under regulations announced in September 1984 from government agencies with an official monopoly over certain product lines into competitive economic enterprises responsible for their own profits and losses. Each trading company may expand beyond the limited geographic scope and product lines that it had originally been chartered to serve and compete with others for the import and export business of Chinese enterprises and wholesalers. Under the same reforms, the Ministry of Foreign Economic Relations and Trade lost the direct managerial authority over the state trading companies that it once enjoyed. The ministry's principal responsibilities are now to issue plans for China's foreign economic relations, conduct international market research, administer China's shrinking foreign aid program, and conduct formal trade negotiations with foreign countries. The ministry has also slowly accumulated regulatory powers over foreign trade, including the authority to license foreign trade companies, issue import permits, and determine quotas for export.[19]

Finally, to give localities and enterprises greater incentive to produce for the international market, they have been allowed to retain a portion of the foreign exchange they earn through foreign trade. From early 1981, when the internal rate was established, until 1984, when it was eliminated, the local enterprises were permitted to convert their foreign exchange earnings into Chinese currency at a highly favorable internal exchange rate that, in effect, subsidized exports. Though the retention rates seem to have varied from province to province, commodity to commodity, and year to year, at the end of 1985 it was reported that the central government received only 75 percent of the country's foreign exchange receipts. The rest was retained at the local level, where it was divided (usually equally) between local governments and the exporting enterprises.[20]

The Chinese, however, have not yet struck the ideal balance between initiative and autonomy in the conduct of foreign trade. Just as in the domestic sphere, exporting enterprises and foreign trade corporations have indeed gained substantial control over their foreign exchange receipts, but they are not completely responsible for their profits and losses. This situation has contributed to distortions in the patterns of exports. Some factories that can directly market their output abroad do so at prices well below cost, knowing they can retain a portion of their foreign exchange receipts but will not be held responsible for the losses they have suffered in domestic currency. Similarly, some foreign trade corporations have been willing to pay high prices in Chinese currency for export products, which they then sell on international markets for a relatively low price. The corporation retains some of the foreign exchange revenues, while the state bears the loss. The commodities sold in this way are described by the Chinese as "parallel goods": goods exported at a loss for the foreign exchange that they will generate.[21]

The results of these reforms have been, in the first instance, a continued increase in the level of China's foreign trade. The combined total of Chinese imports and exports, which had been a bit more than $20 billion in 1978, rose above $70 billion in 1986 (table 6-1). The ratio of exports to national output—a good measure of the importance of trade to the national economy—increased from less than 6 percent in 1978 to nearly 14 percent in 1986.

Predictably, as its level of foreign economic relations rose to a more normal level, China was not able to sustain the rate of growth in foreign trade that it had enjoyed in the 1970s. The nominal increase in two-way trade slowed from more than 200 percent in 1971–75, to about 180 percent in 1976–80, to 60 percent in 1981–85. For the period of the Seventh Five-Year Plan (1986–90), Peking has officially projected a further increase of 40 percent in foreign trade. Since this figure is slightly less than the planned rate of

Table 6-1. *China's Commodity Trade, 1978–86*

Year	Billions of current U.S. dollars				Billions of current yuan		Ratio of exports to national output (percent)
	Total	Exports (FOB)[a]	Imports (CIF)[b]	Balance	Exports (FOB)	National output	
1978	20.6	9.7	10.9	−1.2	16.8	301	5.6
1979	29.3	13.7	15.7	−2.0	21.2	337	6.3
1980	38.1	18.1	20.0	−1.9	27.1	369	7.3
1981	44.0	22.0	22.0	0.0	36.8	394	9.3
1982	41.6	22.4	19.3	3.1	41.4	426	9.7
1983	43.6	22.2	21.4	0.8	43.8	473	9.3
1984	53.6	26.1	27.4	−1.3	58.1	563	10.3
1985	69.6	27.4	42.2	−15.1	80.9	682	11.9
1986	73.8	30.9	42.9	−12.0	108.2	779	13.9

Sources: For imports and exports, Guojia Tongjiju (State Statistical Bureau), *Zhongguo tongji zhaiyao, 1987* (Chinese statistical abstract, 1987) (Peking: Chinese Statistical Publishing House, 1987), p. 89; for the 1978–79 figures for national output, World Bank, *China: Socialist Economic Development*, vol. 1: *The Economy, Statistical System, and Basic Data* (Washington, D.C.: World Bank, 1983), p. 281; for the 1980 figures, Rock Creek Research, *1985 China Statistical Handbook* (Washington, D.C.: Rock Creek Research, 1985), p. 1; and for the 1981–86 figures, Rock Creek Research, *1987 China Statistical Handbook* (Washington, D.C.: Rock Creek Research, 1987), p. 1.
a. Free on board.
b. Including cost, insurance, freight.

growth in national output, the importance of exports to the domestic economy may now begin to decline somewhat.

Together with the changes in domestic economic policy discussed in chapter 4, the reforms of China's foreign trade structure have also produced big shifts in the composition of the nation's exports and imports. In many cases, however, these changes have simply accelerated or reinforced trends that were already evident during the Maoist era.

The most dramatic changes have occurred on the import side of the ledger (table 6-2). To begin with, the share of consumer goods in China's imports has dropped dramatically in the past twenty years, from more than 18 percent in 1970 to less than 10 percent in the mid-1980s. From the late 1950s through the late 1970s, China purchased large quantities of grain from abroad, not only to supplement inadequate domestic harvests, as was the case immediately after the Great Leap Forward, but also to ease the strain on the nation's overburdened transportation system. The success of the rural reforms in the early 1980s, however, has enabled Peking drastically to reduce imports of foreign foodstuffs, which have fallen from a bit more than 13 percent of total imports in 1978 to about 4 percent in 1986.

Table 6-2. *Commodity Composition of Chinese Imports, including Consumer Goods and Industrial Goods, 1970, 1978–86*[a]

Percentage of total imports

Share of imports[b]	1970	1978	1979	1980	1981	1982	1983	1984	1985	1986
Total consumer goods	18.3	14.3	15.4	19.0	22.8	25.3	18.5	13.7	9.8	7.5
Foodstuffs	17.6	13.2	13.2	15.8	18.0	21.4	14.1	8.1	4.3	4.0
Consumer durables	0.7	1.1	2.2	3.2	4.7	3.9	4.4	5.6	5.5	3.5
Total industrial goods	81.7	85.7	84.6	81.0	77.2	74.7	80.6	85.4	90.3	84.1
Industrial supplies	65.0	66.3	58.8	51.5	49.6	53.1	56.2	53.6	45.5	42.4
Capital goods	16.6	19.4	25.9	29.4	27.6	21.5	24.4	31.8	44.8	41.7
Selected commodities										
Fibers and fabrics	6.8	10.5	10.2	11.9	13.7	9.6	11.4	10.8	9.3	6.2
Iron and steel	18.1	27.8	23.2	11.5	7.4	11.3	17.9	16.5	14.9	15.7

Sources: Percentages for 1970, and 1978–82 were calculated from John L. Davie, "China's International Trade and Finance," in *China's Economy Looks toward the Year 2000*, vol. 2: *Economic Openness in Modernizing China*, Committee Print, Joint Economic Committee, 99 Cong, 2 sess. (Government Printing Office, 1986), pp. 311–34, p. 332, table 4. Percentages for 1983–85 were calculated from two-digit SITC data in Central Intelligence Agency, *China: International Trade, Fourth Quarter, 1985* (Washington, D.C.: CIA, 1986), pp. 10–11, table 6, according to the concordance contained in National Foreign Assessment Center, *China: Real Trends in Trade with Non-Communist Countries since 1970* (Washington, D.C.: CIA, 1977), p. 26, table A-1. Since three-digit SITC data were not available, all tobacco products (SITC 12) were assigned to consumer goods, and all essential oils and soaps (SITC 55) and textile yarn and fabrics (SITC 65) to industrial supplies. Of the total for metal manufactures (SITC 69), 25 percent were assigned to industrial supplies, 55 percent to capital goods, and 20 percent to consumer goods. Similarly, of the total for precision instruments (SITC 86), 55 percent were assigned to capital goods and 45 percent to consumer goods. Percentages for 1986 were calculated from two-digit SITC data in PRC General Administration of Customs, *China's Customs Statistics*, various issues, compiled and converted to U.S. dollars by Rock Creek Research, Washington, D.C. The SITC data were then recompiled according to the procedures given above with one exception: since Chinese customs data do not report precision instruments (SITC 86), the data for scientific and professional equipment (SITC 87) and cameras and optical goods (SITC 88) were combined to provide an estimate for this category.

SITC = Standard International Trade Classification. Figures are rounded.

a. Imports for 1970 and 1978–85 are FOB; imports for 1986 are CIF.

b. Miscellaneous commodities are not assigned to any category.

During the same period, China's imports of durable consumer goods have increased noticeably, rising from about 1 percent of total imports in 1978 to more than 5 percent in 1984 and 1985, before dropping off a bit in 1986. The rising purchasing power of China's urban workers encouraged the Chinese government to approve the import of large quantities of radios, televisions, watches, and refrigerators from Japan in the mid-1980s. These official imports were supplemented by additional purchases, made through semilegal or illegal channels, by local governments and enterprises eager to profit from the rapid increase in Chinese consumer spending. Even so, the increase in the importation of durable consumer goods did not completely offset the decline in the purchase of foreign food-stuffs. The result, as just noted, is that consumer products are a smaller share of Chinese imports today than they were in the 1970s or early 1980s.

The relative decline of consumer goods has further increased the share of producer goods in the country's import mix. Equipment and supplies for Chinese industry constitute the overwhelming majority of Chinese imports—about 80 percent of the total import bill—as they have for most years since 1949. But within this broad category a great change has taken place. In periods of relative self-reliance, such as the 1960s and early 1970s, China imported industrial supplies (chemicals, raw materials, and metals) rather than capital equipment. Now that it has broken decisively with the autarkic policies of the past, however, China has begun to import more machinery and fewer materials. Industrial supplies, which constituted nearly two-thirds of imports in both 1970 and 1978, have fallen back to well below one-half of the country's total import bill. Iron and steel are still China's single largest import in this category (at nearly 30 percent of total imports in 1978 and about 15 percent in the mid-1980s), with fibers and fabrics accounting for the next largest share (about 10 percent in 1978, and slightly less in more recent years). Conversely, capital goods, which accounted for less than 20 percent of total imports in the late Maoist period, have come to account for a 40 percent share, as Chinese planners concentrate greater amounts of foreign exchange on the purchase of foreign technology and equipment.

On the other side of the ledger, the changing composition of Chinese exports in the post-Mao era has reinforced three developments that were already apparent in earlier years: the growing importance of manufactured goods in China's exports, the steady decline in the importance of agricultural output, and the rise (and more recent decline) of the products of extractive industry, particularly petroleum and coal (table 6-3).

Table 6-3. *Commodity Composition of Chinese Exports, FOB, 1970, 1978–86*
Percentage of total exports

Share of exports[a]	1970	1978	1979	1980	1981	1982	1983	1984	1985	1986
Agriculture	46.6	31.8	28.2	24.7	23.8	21.6	18.2	17.4	16.7	18.7
Extractive	5.3	13.1	15.0	19.0	18.4	17.3	22.1	22.5	25.0	14.0
Manufacturing	48.0	55.1	56.8	56.3	57.7	61.1	59.3	59.6	56.6	62.5
Selected commodities										
Total energy	n.a.	13.4	17.2	23.1	22.2	22.4	20.2	20.7	23.0	12.2
Coal	n.a.	1.0	1.3	1.3	1.2	1.4	1.3	1.1	1.8	1.5
Petroleum products	n.a.	2.3	4.4	6.7	6.4	6.9 ⎫	18.9	19.6	21.2	10.7
Crude oil	n.a.	10.1	11.5	15.1	14.6	14.1 ⎭				
Total textiles	28.5	27.9	28.1	26.2	26.4	25.4	27.9	30.5	29.7	26.7
Fibers[b]	4.9	4.0	3.7	2.9	2.4	2.4	3.0	3.5	3.7	3.7
Yarns and fabrics	16.2	16.7	16.2	14.6	14.3	12.5	13.3	14.7	14.0	13.6
Clothing	7.4	7.2	8.1	8.8	9.7	10.4	11.5	12.2	12.0	9.4
Firearms	n.a.	n.a.	n.a.	0.0	0.0	5.5	6.5	4.5	2.5	5.3[c]

Sources: Percentages for 1970, and 1978–82 were calculated from Davie, "China's International Trade and Finance," p. 331, table 3. Percentages for 1983–85 were calculated from two-digit SITC data in CIA, *China: International Trade, Fourth Quarter, 1985, China: Real Trends in Trade with Non-Communist Countries,* p. 26, table A-1. Since three-digit data were not available, all tobacco products (SITC 12) were assigned to the agricultural sector; all crude rubber (SITC 23), all petroleum products and crude oil (SITC 33) to the extractive sector; and all textile fibers (SITC 26) to manufacturing. Percentages for 1986 were calculated from two-digit SITC data in PRC General Administration of Customs, *China's Customs Statistics,* recompiled according to the procedures given above. I am grateful to Albert Keidel for making these data available to me. Figures are rounded.

n.a. Not available.

a. Miscellaneous commodities are not assigned to any of these categories.

b. Percentages for 1970, and 1978–82 are for natural fibers only; percentages for 1983–86 include natural and synthetic fibers.

c. Chinese customs statistics do not contain data for the export of firearms. The figure for 1986 is derived by subtracting the exports for 1983–85 from the total for 1983–86 in Richard F. Grimmett, *Trends in Conventional Arms Transfers to the Third World By Major Supplier, 1979–1986,* report 87-418 F (Washington, D.C.: Congressional Research Service, 1987), p. 46, table 2F.

In the early 1950s, China mainly exported agricultural products, which accounted for about 80 percent of foreign sales, and a small quantity of light industrial products. As a result of the emphasis on industrialization since the mid-1950s, however, the relative importance of these two groups of commodities has undergone a striking change. By 1970 the agricultural and industrial sectors had come to occupy roughly equal shares in China's export mix. By 1978 the share of the agricultural sector had fallen further to about 32 percent, and the share of industrial exports had risen to about 55 percent. In the mid-1980s, the gap had become wider: industrial products accounted for about three-fifths of China's export earnings, while agricultural produce was responsible for less than one-fifth.

The decision to sell China's energy resources on international markets, first taken by Mao in the early 1970s over the objections of leftist leaders, has also transformed the composition of Chinese exports. In 1970 the products of extractive industry accounted for only about 5 percent of China's foreign trade receipts. By 1978 the share of the energy sector in China's export earnings had risen to 13 percent, and then peaked at between 20 percent and 25 percent in the early 1980s. Of that, crude oil and petroleum products provided the overwhelming majority of energy exports, supplemented by much smaller sales of coal (and, later, natural gas). Unfortunately for China, the collapse of the international oil market in 1985–86 caused a marked reduction in the earnings from the export of oil and petroleum. Not only did the volume of oil exports decline from 36 million tons in 1985 to 34 million tons in 1986, but the falling price of oil led to an even sharper decrease in revenues, from $6.7 billion in 1985 to $3.1 billion the following year.[22]

As was already true in 1970, textiles are China's most important export commodity, accounting for 25 percent to 30 percent of foreign sales. But within this broad category, China has been able to shift somewhat from the export of basic products like fibers and fabrics into more profitable product lines such as clothing. This development has directly resulted from the change in the structure of China's foreign trade apparatus. As Chinese textile mills have forged closer contacts with wholesalers and retailers abroad, they have increased their ability to produce finished garments, according to foreign designs, and often under foreign labels. Consequently, the share of clothing in China's textile exports has risen noticeably, from 25 percent in 1978 to 40 percent in 1985. (It remains to be seen whether an apparent drop back to 35 percent in 1986 is a temporary phenomenon or a more permanent reversal of the trend.)

Most of the rest of China's manufactured exports constitutes a mix of chemicals, machinery, metals and minerals, and handicrafts, each accounting for about 5 percent of China's total export receipts in the post-Mao era. In addition, China has also dramatically increased its sale of weapons, from less than 1 percent of the nation's exports in 1978 to an average of nearly 5 percent between 1982 and 1986. In the process, China has become, by some estimates, the world's fourth largest merchant of arms to the third world since 1983.[23]

China has also looked to its services account to find new sources of foreign exchange.[24] Revenues from tourism rose from $263 million in 1978 to $1.5 billion in 1986, thus increasing from the equivalent of 2.7 percent of exports to 4.9 percent.[25] The value of the labor services that China has contracted to provide in foreign countries— largely for construction projects in developing nations in Africa and the Middle East—reached $950 million in 1986, another 3 percent of China's export earnings. In both 1985 and 1986, China's foreign trade deficits were partly offset by $3.5 billion to $3.8 billion surpluses in its services account. Indeed, Peking has enjoyed a surplus in services each year from 1981 through 1986.[26]

The foreign economic reforms have also contributed to a shift in the direction of China's international trade (table 6-4). Although the noticeable increase in Sino-Soviet trade in recent years has doubtless been of geopolitical significance, China's foreign economic relations remain heavily oriented toward noncommunist countries. Indeed, the share of Chinese trade directed toward other communist countries has fallen steadily in the last decade, dropping from 15 percent in 1978 to 7 percent in 1985. At the same time, China's trade has also been shifting from the Atlantic to the Pacific, with Western Europe's share falling from 18 percent to 13 percent between 1978 and 1985, and the share of trade conducted with East Asian, Southeast Asian, and North American countries rising from 54 percent to 70 percent during the same period.

In the Asian-Pacific region, Japan remains China's largest trading partner, accounting for about 25 percent of Peking's two-way trade. Japan's exports to China have mostly consisted of machinery and steel, but automobiles and durable consumer goods accounted for much of the increase in Japanese sales to China in 1984 and 1985. However, China's purchases from Japan have not been fully offset by its exports, mainly petroleum and coal. Consequently, China ran trade deficits with Japan for all but one year between 1978 and 1985 and amassed a cumulative deficit of more than $9.4 billion over that period. The fact that Chinese imports from Japan tripled between 1978 and 1985, while Chinese exports only doubled, has been a source of both irritation and concern to leaders in Peking.

Although Japan still accounts for the largest single share of China's two-way trade, the United States and Hong Kong have been able to increase their shares since China began expanding its foreign trade in the late 1970s. The United States has benefited from the normalization of diplomatic relations with China in early 1979 and from China's growing interest in importing Western technology. The U.S. share of China's trade has increased from 6 percent in 1978 to 10 percent to 12 percent in the mid-1980s. Moreover, the composition of American exports to China has also undergone rapid change. In the early 1980s, wheat was the single biggest American export commodity to China, accounting for nearly 50 percent of American sales in 1982. By 1986 transportation equipment and machinery held the largest share of American sales to China, with timber replacing wheat as the principal agricultural export commodity. The composition of Chinese exports to the United States, in contrast, has not changed considerably. Textiles have consistently accounted for the largest share (between 30 percent and 40 percent), with petroleum products supplying another 20 percent to 25 percent of Chinese sales to America.[27]

Hong Kong has become a major *entrepôt* through which China, and particularly its southeastern provinces, can sell exports and procure imports. Hong Kong's share of China's trade has risen from about 11 percent in 1978 to 22 percent to 23 percent in the mid-1980s. Of the Chinese exports to Hong Kong, only about 40 percent are consumed in the territory, while the remaining 60 percent are reexported to third countries. Similarly, about 75 percent of China's imports from Hong Kong come from outside the territory, including from trading partners, such as Taiwan and South Korea, with whom Peking has no diplomatic or direct economic relations.[28]

Farther to the south, the Association of Southeast Asian Nation's (ASEAN's) trade with China has also held fairly steady, at about 6 percent of Peking's total volume. Growing sales of Chinese petroleum to Singapore have more than matched Peking's purchases of primary and manufactured materials from other Southeast Asian countries, and China has therefore enjoyed a surplus with the region.

In sum, China today conducts about 55 percent of its trade with the developed countries of the West, 20 percent with Hong Kong, 20 percent with the developing nations of Asia, Africa, and Latin America, and 5 percent with the Communist bloc. In essence, this trading pattern is a triangular one, in which China generates deficits

Table 6-4. *China's Trade with Selected Countries and Regions, 1970, 1978–85.*
Millions of current U.S. dollars and, in parentheses, percentage of total trade

Trading partners	1970	1978	1979	1980	1981	1982	1983	1984	1985
Total trade[a]	**4,200** (100)	**20,230.8**	**28,224.3**	**38,719.1**	**41,003.4**	**39,586.0**	**42,198.7**	**53,132.5**	**70,804.1**
Developed countries	2,030 (48.3)	11,045.1 (54.6)	15,811.3 (56.0)	21,772.5 (56.2)	22,869.4 (55.8)	21,028.5 (53.1)	21,767.5 (51.6)	27,328.6 (51.4)	38,203.3 (54.0)
East Asia and Pacific	984 (23.4)	5,730.2 (28.3)	7,532.3 (26.7)	10,488.1 (27.1)	11,244.0 (27.4)	9,888.7 (25.0)	10,528.6 (25.0)	14,069.3 (26.7)	20,153.6 (28.5)
Australia	164 (3.9)	623.6 (3.1)	942.4 (3.3)	1,040.2 (2.7)	978.7 (2.3)	1,157.1 (2.9)	622.9 (1.5)	1,048.9 (2.0)	1,157.0 (1.6)
Japan	811 (19.3)	5,021.4 (24.8)	6,466.8 (22.9)	9,247.3 (23.9)	10,107.8 (24.7)	8,583.4 (21.7)	9,763.9 (23.2)	12,858.8 (24.4)	18,812.4 (26.7)
North America	153 (3.6)	1,713.2 (8.5)	2,968.2 (10.5)	5,684.7 (14.7)	6,437.2 (15.7)	6,357.4 (16.1)	5,918.9 (14.0)	7,303.8 (13.8)	8,921.2 (12.6)
Canada	153 (3.6)	524.9 (2.6)	649.5 (2.3)	874.2 (2.3)	959.6 (2.3)	1,170.5 (2.3)	1,494.2 (3.5)	1,225.5 (2.3)	1,225.3 (1.7)
United States	0 (0.0)	1,188.2 (5.9)	2,318.7 (8.2)	4,810.5 (12.4)	5,477.6 (13.4)	5,186.9 (13.1)	4,424.7 (10.5)	6,078.3 (11.5)	7,695.9 (10.9)
Western Europe	892 (21.2)	3,601.8 (17.8)	5,310.8 (18.8)	5,599.7 (14.5)	5,188.3 (12.7)	4,782.4 (12.1)	5,320.0 (12.6)	5,955.4 (11.2)	9,128.5 (12.9)

Less developed countries	1,301 (31.0)	6,099.7 (30.2)	8,715.2 (30.9)	13,229.1 (34.3)	17,465.5 (42.6)	15,862.8 (40.1)	17,018.3 (40.5)	21,365.2 (40.5)	27,733.0 (39.2)
Southeast Asia	770 (18.3)	3,567.7 (17.6)	5,153.9 (18.3)	8,245.8 (21.3)	12,315.1 (30.0)	10,537.0 (26.6)	11,195.0 (26.5)	16,097.9 (30.2)	20,449.5 (28.9)
Hong Kong	477 (11.4)	2,312.3 (11.4)	3,403.0 (12.1)	5,650.1 (14.6)	7,235.9 (17.6)	7,384.9 (18.7)	8,341.3 (19.8)	12,161.2 (23.1)	15,425.6 (21.8)
ASEAN[b]	267 (6.4)	1,112.5 (5.5)	1,560.3 (5.5)	2,326.8 (6.0)	2,303.1 (5.6)	2,533.4 (6.4)	2,093.1 (5.0)	2,987.0 (5.6)	4,008.0 (5.7)
South Asia and Middle East	258 (6.1)	996.4 (4.9)	1,348.9 (4.8)	2,142.8 (5.5)	2,231.2 (5.4)	3,394.0 (8.6)	3,388.1 (8.0)	3,389.0 (6.4)	3,318.9 (4.7)
Latin America	11 (0.3)	559.8 (2.8)	1,088.1 (3.9)	1,234.2 (3.2)	1,162.5 (2.8)	1,096.8 (2.8)	1,705.9 (4.0)	1,475.3 (2.8)	2,243.9 (3.2)
Africa	260 (6.2)	975.7 (4.8)	1,124.4 (4.0)	1,606.5 (4.1)	1,756.7 (4.3)	943.9 (2.4)	1,158.9 (2.7)	1,418.5 (2.7)	1,720.7 (2.4)
Communist bloc	869 (20.7)	3,085.9 (15.3)	3,697.8 (13.1)	3,717.1 (9.6)	3,152.0 (7.7)	2,991.4 (7.6)	2,983.1 (7.1)	3,694.0 (7.0)	4,867.8 (6.9)
USSR	47 (1.1)	499.5 (2.5)	508.8 (1.8)	523.4 (1.4)	247.6 (0.6)	307.8 (0.8)	647.6 (1.5)	1,199.8 (2.3)	1,931.4 (2.7)
Eastern Europe	480 (11.4)	1,936.0 (9.6)	2,335.4 (8.3)	2,413.7 (6.2)	2,073.1 (5.1)	1,701.1 (4.3)	1,484.4 (3.5)	1,700.9 (3.2)	2,213.9 (3.1)
Other communist[c]	342 (8.1)	650.4 (3.2)	853.5 (3.0)	790.1 (2.0)	831.2 (2.0)	982.5 (2.5)	851.1 (2.0)	793.3 (1.5)	722.5 (1.0)

Sources: CIA, *China: International Trade* (Washington, D.C.: CIA, various years); and Davie, "China's International Trade and Finance," pp. 329–31, tables 1, 2.

a. Total trade in this table differs from the trade figures given in table 5-1. Table 5-1 draws on Chinese government data, which give exports on an FOB basis but list imports as CIF. This table is based on U.S. governmental reconstructions, which give both imports and exports on an FOB basis and are based on data from China's trading partners. Figures are rounded.

b. Figures do not include exports from China to Brunei and, for 1970, to Thailand and the Philippines.

c. Kampuchea, Cuba, Laos, Mongolia, North Korea, and Vietnam.

Table 6-5. *China's Trade Balance with Selected Countries and Regions, 1970, 1978–85*
Millions of current U.S. dollars

Trading partners	1970	1978	1979	1980	1981	1982	1983	1984	1985
Total net exports[a]	**112**	**−297.0**	**−752.5**	**−35.3**	**−3,751.2**	**6,214.0**	**5,224.9**	**2,156.1**	**−8,154.9**
Developed countries	−714	−3,491.1	−4,524.7	−5,245.3	−2,817.0	−579.3	−1,885.1	−3,572.8	−11,104.5
East Asia and Pacific	−420	−1,513.6	−1,545.9	−1,643.1	−431.6	−996.7	−312.4	−2,045.7	−7,027.4
Australia	−94	−342.2	−609.8	−552.0	−299.3	−518.7	−162.7	−422.7	−572.6
Japan	−327	−1,126.4	−880.2	−969.9	−44.2	1,583.4	−71.5	−1,538.6	−6,367.6
North America	−117	−900.2	−1,492.8	−3,309.3	−2,320.8	−1,477.0	−1,016.7	−639.8	−649.0
Canada	−117	−359.3	−363.9	−609.8	−593.0	−839.9	−1,095.2	−709.5	−633.5
United States	0	−541.0	−1,128.9	−2,699.5	−1,727.8	−637.1	78.5	69.7	−15.5
Western Europe	−176	−1,077.2	−1,486.0	−292.9	−64.7	−99.0	−566.0	−887.3	−3,428.1
Less developed countries	735	3,156.2	3,959.7	5,322.1	6,400.2	7,234.7	7,360.8	6,491.4	3,469.4
Southeast Asia	660	2,853.5	3,388.5	4,295.8	4,864.6	4,543.8	4,703.6	3,991.9	2,249.7
Hong Kong	457	2,186.5	2,638.6	3,151.5	3,307.1	3,476.1	3,351.7	2,099.8	−289.6
ASEAN[b]	177	568.7	600.5	940.2	1,307.3	980.2	1,040.9	1,588.8	2,233.6
South Asia and Middle East	42	397.0	648.5	631.8	701.0	2,632.2	2,415.5	2,150.4	1,472.9
Latin America	3	−406.4	−575.3	−285.2	−9.5	−40.0	−354.1	−363.3	−888.9
Africa	30	312.1	498.0	679.7	843.9	504.3	595.7	683.5	635.7
Communist bloc	91	37.9	−187.6	−111.9	168.0	−441.4	−250.7	−462.4	−519.8
USSR	−3	15.1	−27.4	−63.6	15.8	−22.6	−31.8	50.6	57.0
Eastern Europe	30	26.0	−143.4	−61.9	57.9	−249.5	−134.6	−400.5	−605.9
Other communist[c]	64	−3.2	−16.7	3.5	94.4	−169.3	−84.3	−112.5	29.1

Sources: CIA, *China: International Trade*, various years; and Davie, "China's International Trade and Finance," pp. 329–31, tables 1, 2.
a. Net exports in this table differ from the trade balances in table 6-1. Table 6-1 draws on Chinese government data, which give exports on an FOB basis but list imports as CIF. This table is based on U.S. government reconstructions, which give both imports and exports on an FOB basis and are based on data from China's trading partners. Figures are rounded.
b. Figures do not include exports from China to Brunei and, for 1970, to Thailand and the Philippines.
c. Kampuchea, Cuba, Mongolia, Laos, North Korea, and Vietnam.

in trade with the developed world and usually earns surpluses in trade with the less-developed regions (table 6-5). In 1984, for example, China ran a deficit of some $3.6 billion in direct trade with the developed countries, but enjoyed surpluses of $1.6 billion in trade with ASEAN and $2.2 billion in trade with South Asia and the Middle East. However, China has encountered a problem in the balance of imports and exports. In 1985, for example, China's import of capital equipment and consumer goods from the developed countries surged, but exports to either the less-developed nations or to the developed world did not show a corresponding increase.

TRADE IMBALANCES AND CHINA'S USE OF FOREIGN CREDIT

As China tries to reform its system of foreign trade, it encounters difficulties similar to those encountered in its reform of the domestic economy. Domestically, the tendency toward excessive investment in unprofitable projects chronically recurs; internationally, periodic surges in imports that have not been counterbalanced by comparable increases in exports dismay the Chinese government. Both problems have resulted, at least partly, from the decentralization of the economic system that reform has brought about.

The first of these import surges occurred during the "great leap outward" in the late 1970s. The Ten-Year Plan adopted at the National People's Congress in early 1978 envisioned total capital investment of $300 billion between 1976 and 1985, of which $70 billion to $80 billion would be spent on the import of foreign equipment. Under the impetus of this ambitious plan, $40 billion in foreign contracts for complete industrial plants were discussed, and $7 billion in contracts were actually signed in 1978 alone, with contracts totaling $3 billion signed in ten frantic days at the end of December. A similar phenomenon occurred during an investment drive in 1980.[29] In each case, negotiations were halted or contracts suspended, pending reexamination by the central authorities of the desirability of the project in question or the prospects for external financing. Even so, Peking did not intervene quickly enough to prevent balance of payments deficits of $5.1 billion between 1978 and 1980.[30]

An even more alarming surge of imports took place in 1985, with China's imports increasing by 54 percent in comparison with the previous year.[31] This increase resulted partly from a deliberate central decision to increase the purchase of foreign consumer goods, and the production lines for manufacturing them, as a way of absorbing the excessive wage increases awarded to urban workers at the end of 1984. But, in equal measure, the problem occurred because of the loss of central control over imports, as localities acquired, through both legal and illicit channels, the foreign exchange with which to buy highly valued consumer goods, and as many small trading companies sprang up in the hope of earning large profits on the importation of popular foreign products.[32]

The most notorious example occurred on Hainan Island, off the southern coast of China. There, local authorities mobilized $570 million in foreign exchange, in part by drawing on their official annual allotments from the central treasury, in part by using the retained earnings from the island's own exports, and in part by purchasing foreign exchange from other localities on the black market. The half billion dollars that Hainan accumulated was then used to import nearly 90,000 motor vehicles, 3 million television sets, 250,000 video recorders, and 120,000 motorcycles, most of which were resold as "used" commodities on China's domestic market at double or triple the price. Local banks cooperated by lending the money with which to purchase foreign exchange from outside the island, and virtually every unit in Hainan, including kindergartens and medical clinics, allegedly participated in ordering and reselling foreign goods.[33]

The surge of imports in 1985 was exacerbated by a slowdown in the growth of exports that same year. The growth of imports, at 54 percent in 1985, was substantially faster than the average between 1980 and 1984, which had been about 8 percent. In contrast, although exports had also risen on an average of 10 percent between 1980 and 1984, they grew by only 5 percent in 1985. Although foreign protectionism undoubtedly contributed to the problem, it was rooted in the fact that many Chinese manufacturers preferred to produce for the domestic market rather than for export. In the past, mandatory export quotas, imposed by Peking, had been able to override this bias. But with the relaxation of central planning over foreign trade at the end of 1984, Chinese enterprises were free to refuse to sell their products overseas if they could find more attractive markets at home.

The Chinese economy's bias against exports can be attributed to several factors. The most basic one was that the renminbi, although it had been devalued by more than 50 percent since 1979, remained about 40 percent too high, thus encouraging imports but discouraging exports. Furthermore, in the absence of price reform, Chinese manufacturers could often obtain higher prices on protected do-

Table 6-6. *China's Balance of Payments, 1981–86*
Billions of current U.S. dollars

Item	1981	1982	1983	1984	1985	1986
Current account						
balance	3.0	5.7	4.2	2.0	−8.6	−4.9
Trade balance	2.6	4.2	2.0	0.0	−12.1	−8.7
Net noncommodity						
receipts ·	0.4	1.4	2.2	2.0	3.5	3.8
Net capital inflow	−0.7	0.3	−0.2	−1.0	3.8	3.2
Errors and omissions	0.2	0.3	−0.7	1.2	0.0	0.0
Increase in reserves	2.5	6.3	3.3	2.2	−4.8	−1.7
Year-end reserves	4.8	11.1	14.4	16.7	11.9	10.2

Source: Based on Rock Creek Research, *1987 China Statistical Handbook*, p. 24. The trade balance here differs from that in table 6-1 because both exports and imports are calculated on an FOB basis. Figures are rounded.

mestic markets than on competitive international ones. And finally, export markets required an attention to quality control and a willingness to meet foreign specifications that many Chinese enterprises regarded as too onerous.

In theory, reform measures, which allowed export enterprises to retain part of their foreign exchange earnings, were supposed to overcome these difficulties. In practice, however, the incentive was not great enough to overcome the bias against exporting. The part of export earnings retained by export enterprises was small: around 12.5 percent nationwide, and even less in some provinces. What is more, factories were required to deposit their foreign exchange in accounts in the Bank of China, from which it could be withdrawn only after a formal application was officially approved. To many enterprise managers, these incentives did not overcome the inconvenience of producing and marketing export products.

The combined effect of the surge of imports and the shortfall in exports was a serious deficit in China's trade account, amounting to $12.1 billion in 1985 and to $8.7 billion in 1986. Although the deficit was somewhat offset by a surplus in its service account, China was forced to draw heavily on the foreign exchange reserves that it had amassed in the 1970s and early 1980s. Peking's reserves fell precipitously, from $16.7 billion at the end of 1984 to $10.2 billion at the end of 1986, as the country attempted to pay off its burgeoning trade deficit (table 6-6). The speed with which this occurred offered Chinese leaders dramatic and sobering evidence of the extent to which they had lost control over imports, and the difficulties they were encountering in increasing exports to desired levels.

Faced with this crisis, China also had to increase its borrowing from the international financial market (table 6-7). Ever since December 1978, when China's minister of foreign trade announced that Peking would accept direct loans and developmental assistance from abroad, Peking has explored every conceivable route for acquiring foreign credit.[34] It has joined the International Monetary Fund, the World Bank, and the Asian Development Bank. It has welcomed credits from foreign governments, in the form of both official development assistance and government-backed export credits. It has negotiated extensive lines of credit with commercial banks, principally Japanese. And Chinese institutions at both the central and provincial levels have issued bonds to investors in Hong Kong, Japan, and Western Europe.

Despite this activity, China's policy toward the absorption of foreign credit was, at least until the mid-1980s, extremely cautious and conservative. Peking sought to obtain foreign capital on the most favorable terms possible, without accepting a high level of indebtedness. These considerations led Peking to limit its borrowings from commercial banks, seek medium- and long-term credits instead of short-term obligations, and limit debt service ratio to 15 percent of export earnings. According to official Chinese statistics, by the end of 1983 Peking had absorbed only $11.9 billion in foreign loans. Of this, about 60 percent had come from foreign banks, primarily during the import binge of 1979, and the remainder was almost entirely from foreign governments and international institutions (table 6-8). A Western estimate of Chinese debt at the end of 1983 shows a slightly higher total, but a similar composition: 60 percent from private sources and more than three-quarters in medium- and long-term loans (table 6-7).

The foreign exchange crisis of 1984–86 caused a rapid increase in China's indebtedness. Official Chinese data show that Peking accepted nearly $9 billion in new loans in those three years alone (table 6-8). Again, Western analyses are somewhat higher, suggesting an increase in gross indebtedness from $13 billion at the end of 1984 to $28 billion by the end of 1986 (table 6-7). Of particular concern to the international financial community, as well as to Chinese leaders, were three aspects of its debt: the speed with which it grew, the share that was borrowed for short terms at relatively high interest rates, and the fact that much of it was denominated in Japanese yen. At a time when the Japanese yen was being revalued against the American dollar, and when many Chinese exports were denominated in dollars, it was feared that Peking might begin to experience a high debt service ratio unless its trade deficits could quickly be reduced.

Table 6-7. *China's Debt at Year End, 1982–86*
Millions of current U.S. dollars, and, in parentheses, percentage of total debt

Debt	1982	1983	1984	1985	1986
Short term	1,200	3,260	6,410	10,866	7,500
	(11.0)	(22.6)	(49.5)	(56.3)	(26.7)
Medium and long term	9,720	11,177	6,546	8,446	20,578
	(89.0)	(77.4)	(50.5)	(43.7)	(73.3)
Foreign governments	1,377	1,883	2,170	2,500	3,000
International organizations	838	401	578	1,000	1,500
Private sources	7,504	8,893	3,798	4,946	16,078
Gross debt	10,920	14,437	12,956	19,312	28,078
Reserves	7,912	16,018	16,998	11,938	10,938
Net debt	3,008	−1,581	−4,042	7,374	17,140

Source: Wharton Econometric Forecasting Associates, "China's Overseas Debt and Debt Management," *Centrally Planned Economies Service: Analysis of Current Issues*, vol. 6 (March 20, 1987), p. 8, table 2.

After some debate, Chinese leaders adopted a package that included economic, administrative, and diplomatic measures to remedy its balance of payments crisis. To encourage exports and discourage imports, the renminbi was devalued by another 42 percent against the dollar between October 1985 and July 1986. Administratively, the central government reestablished mandatory quotas for exports, delayed important capital construction projects that required foreign goods, put tighter controls on the creation and operation of local foreign trade companies, and imposed various taxes, tariffs, and licenses against imports.[35] And on the diplomatic front, Peking increased the pressure on principal trading partners, including both Japan and the United States, to purchase more Chinese exports, particularly textiles. China also encouraged the creation of "export production networks" to coordinate the design, production, transportation, and marketing of export goods and provided those associations with investment capital, guaranteed supplies of raw materials and power, favorable rates of taxation, and increased access to foreign exchange.

China plans to increase exports more rapidly than imports and, in so doing, slowly reduce its current account deficit to $3.2 billion in 1990, lower its debt service ratio to 9 percent, and rebuild reserves to $15.5 billion. This plan will not permit Peking to stop accumulating foreign debt, but it will allow it to stop assuming new bank loans by 1988 and to rely entirely on the lower interest loans offered by foreign governments and international institutions. Whether China can meet these ambitious targets, however, will depend critically on Peking's ability to control imports and expand exports.

Table 6-8. *China's Absorption of Foreign Capital, 1979–86*
Millions of current U.S. dollars

Sources of capital	1979–81	1982	1983	1984	1985	1986	Total 1979–86
Loans	9,090	1,783	1,065	1,286	2,506	5,015	20,745
Foreign governments	925	553	716	723	486	841	4,244
International institutions	932	3	73	183	604	1,342	3,137
Buyer's credits	206	189	106	133	126	178	938
Foreign banks	6,700	860	0	122	526	1,495	9,703
Other	327	178	170	124	762	1,159	2,720
Direct foreign investment	1,121	649	916	1,418	1,956	2,155	8,215
Joint ventures	65	34	74	255	580	n.a.	n.a.
Joint production	353	178	227	465	585	n.a.	n.a.
Cooperation in offshore oil development	317	179	292	523	481	n.a.	n.a.
Wholly foreign-owned enterprises	1	39	43	15	13	n.a.	n.a.
Compensation trade	283	122	197	98	169	n.a.	n.a.
Other	101	97	83	63	129	n.a.	n.a.
Total	10,211	2,432	1,981	2,704	4,462	6,985	28,960

Sources: These figures may well underestimate the new loans China incurred in 1984 and 1985. Compare the data from Western sources in table 6-7. For 1979–83 figures, see *Zhongguo duiwai jingji maoyi nianjian, 1984* [Yearbook of China's foreign economic relations and trade, 1984] [Peking: Chinese Foreign Economic Relations and Trade Publishers, 1984], pp. IV-183 and IV-185; for 1984–85 figures, *1986 Almanac of China's Foreign Economic Relations and Trade* [Hong Kong: China Resources Trade Consultancy Co., Ltd., 1986], p. 1212; for 1986 figures, Xinhua News Agency, March 6, 1987, in Foreign Broadcast Information Service, *Daily Report: China*, pp. K17–19; and Daiwa Securities Co., Ltd., "Outlook for China in the International Capital Market," data presented to the conference, "China's External Financing Strategy: Changes Ahead?" sponsored by the Asia Society, New York, May 1987.

n.a. Not available.

By the middle of 1987, fortunately, China seemed to be on the way to doing so.

TECHNOLOGICAL EXCHANGE

By interacting with the international economy, China hopes to gain access to advanced technology, both from the West and from the socialist economies. It is true that many Chinese remain skeptical about the desirability of studying Western social science or adopting Western values, and that others wish to protect China's domestic industry from foreign competition. But today a consensus believes that China must master advanced foreign technology if it is to develop its economy, modernize military forces, and raise standards of living. In recent years, therefore, Peking has begun engaging in technological and scientific exchange with foreign countries and institutions.

China's dispatch of unprecedented numbers of Chinese students and scholars for training and research abroad has created an important channel for acquiring advanced technology. Between 1978 and 1985, the number of Chinese students and scholars sent overseas totaled about 38,000. Of these, about 90 percent studied some aspect of science or engineering, and about half were acquiring their education in the United States. Although most (about 30,000) were sponsored by the Chinese government, a large minority (about 8,000) took up their studies with private support from relatives overseas or from foreign universities.[36] Moreover, many students originally funded by the Chinese government have subsequently obtained fellowships or scholarships from foreign sources after their first year abroad. In the United States, for example, it has been estimated that American institutions have borne about 40 percent of the costs of the students and scholars sponsored by the Chinese government since 1978, with that ratio rising from 30 percent during the early years of the exchange program to about 50 percent in the mid-1980s. Moreover, Americans have assumed virtually all of the expenses of those studying here under private auspices.[37] As a result, China's scholarly exchange program has enabled foreign countries not only to transfer technology to China, on a scale triple that of the comparable program undertaken in the mid-1950s, but also to give financial assistance to China's modernization effort.

Nevertheless, the academic exchange programs have created some problems for China and, to a smaller degree, for Peking's relations with the countries to which Chinese students and scholars have been sent. In the early years, foreigners, particularly Americans, complained of a lack of reciprocity in the exchanges. China was sending far more students and scholars abroad than it received and offering far fewer opportunities for foreign researchers than its own scholars enjoyed overseas. More recently, however, the growth of China's research institutions, the livelier climate for academic inquiry, and the development of personal and institutional contacts between foreign scholars and their Chinese counterparts have made great strides toward resolving the problem. Today, financial issues are more dominant. Many American institutions resent Peking's efforts to reduce the economic burden of the program by requiring Chinese students and scholars to seek financial aid from American institutions immediately on arrival in the United States. The resentment occurs even though the share of the costs borne by the American side seems to be no larger than is true for students and scholars from most other developing countries.

China's concerns include what kind of students and scholars to send abroad, how to absorb those who return, and how to react to those who decide to remain overseas. In the late 1970s, when the exchange programs were just getting under way, the participants were primarily senior Chinese intellectuals, with fairly small numbers of students at either the undergraduate or the graduate level sent to study abroad. The Chinese government wanted to reactivate the personal ties that many older intellectuals had established with foreign colleagues before the Cultural Revolution. Officials also hoped to provide a quick "refresher course" for senior scholars so that they could offer more adequate training to a younger generation of Chinese students, and the use of study programs abroad served as a method of atoning for the persecution and neglect of China's elder academics during the Cultural Revolution.

By 1983, however, the Chinese participants in academic exchange programs in the United States were divided fairly evenly between students and scholars. At that point, the issue became what kind of students to send abroad and what disciplines they should study. In general, Peking has been reluctant to dispatch students for undergraduate education overseas, and, by 1986, was skeptical about the desirability of sending students abroad for master's degree programs as well. At the same time, most of the students and scholars sent to the United States have studied the sciences and engineering, with only about 3 percent studying humanities and 11 percent studying any form of social science.[38]

In making these decisions, two considerations have guided the Chinese: the reluctance to spend scarce foreign exchange on degree programs that Chinese institutions can provide at home and the desire to minimize contact with unorthodox political and social values and concepts overseas. The architects of China's academic exchange program seem convinced that older students, studying science and engineering, are less likely to bring "spiritual pollution" back to China than are younger students studying the humanities or social sciences.[39] Indeed, a senior Chinese official responsible for educational affairs once told a group of visitors from the United States that, in his opinion, some Americans hoped to use exchange programs in the social sciences and humanities to convert China into a capitalist country. More reform-minded leaders and intellectuals, however, believe that China can benefit from an expansion of exchanges in economics, political science, sociology, and international affairs.

Given the fairly short history of the exchange program, it is still not clear how many of the Chinese scholars dispatched abroad will return to their homeland, and how many will try to avail themselves of more attractive opportunities overseas. Not even the most pessimistic estimates anticipate that China will encounter the same difficulties as other developing countries, such as Taiwan, which routinely lose the services of most of their overseas students. But it is plausible that a sizable minority of government-sponsored students and scholars, and an even larger number of those who have traveled overseas under private auspices, will attempt to remain abroad. Even more important, it is almost certain that such a development will arouse resentment and controversy within the Chinese leadership. Already, some Chinese spokesmen have begun pointing to a "brain drain" from China to America, with some even suggesting that the United States has been discouraging Chinese students and scholars from returning to their homeland.

For those Chinese students and scholars that do return home, the issue is whether they will be employed in positions that will fully employ the skills and knowledge acquired overseas. Unfortunately, preliminary evidence suggests the contrary. Many returned students and scholars are assigned to administrative work; others are frustrated by the lack of laboratory equipment, libraries, or computer facilities comparable to those to which they had access overseas; and others find their career prospects blocked by older scholars, trained in the 1950s, who are jealously defending their positions and privileges. One specialist on China's academic exchange programs has estimated that only 25 percent of those returning to China have been effectively reabsorbed into the Chinese educational and scientific establishment. Of the others, perhaps 50 percent could be described as "mildly unhappy" with their new assignments, and the remaining 25 percent have skills that are not being used at all.[40]

Academic exchange is not the only way in which China has attempted to acquire advanced technology from abroad. Peking has also signed many government-to-government protocols with advanced industrial nations. As of mid-1985, these included no fewer than twenty-five exchange agreements with the United States, and a total of eighty-six arrangements with West Germany, Britain, France, and Italy. Management training programs, organized by the United States, Germany, and Japan, have been established in China for Chinese enterprise executives. One of the most successful, the National Center for Industrial Science and Technology Management Development, in Dalian, is run for the Chinese by the U.S. Department of Commerce.[41]

In addition, Chinese investments overseas also serve as training grounds for Chinese managers, as channels of access to foreign technology, and as sources of raw materials abroad. By the middle of 1986, China had invested $239 million in 144 projects in thirty-four countries.[42] Many of the projects were in banking, land development, manufacturing, and transportation projects in Hong Kong, making China one of the largest, if not the largest, investors in the territory.[43] But Chinese organizations, particularly the China International Trust and Investment Corporation, have also invested their capital in forest land and computer firms in the United States and in an aluminum smelter in Australia.

Foreigners who have served as advisers on Chinese development strategy and industrial management have provided another channel for technology transfer to China. The World Bank has prepared, at the request of the Chinese government, two comprehensive reports on the Chinese economy, which have contained detailed proposals about the structure of the economic system and the alternative paths for economic modernization. Various agencies of the United Nations have assisted China on projects ranging from birth control to trade development.[44] The Japanese government has served as a consultant on the modernization of the Chinese railway system, a former deputy prime minister of Singapore has been retained as a consultant on the development of China's special economic zones and "open cities," and American consulting firms have drawn up development plans for Chinese cities and provinces. Many foreign scholars and entrepreneurs, especially overseas Chinese, have offered to counsel China on various aspects of its modernization program, and the Chinese government has employed at least one foreigner, a West German, as the manager of a large state enterprise.[45]

FOREIGN INVESTMENT IN CHINA

In contrast to the late Maoist period, Chinese officials have also begun to welcome direct foreign investment in their country.[46] The idea that foreign entrepreneurs might play a constructive role in China's economic development emerged as early as 1975, when some senior leaders, particularly Deng Xiaoping, began to acknowledge that foreign investment projects might help absorb foreign capital, attract advanced technology, and market export products. To justify their proposal to welcome foreign investment to China, these leaders described it as a form of "state capitalism." The foreign investor's freedom of action would be constrained by the decisions of the Chinese state enterprise involved in the project and by the regulations and policies formulated by the Chinese government.[47] Because of the leftist political climate of the time, however, this visionary proposal was not approved. It was only in 1979 that Peking adopted a foreign investment law that established the legal basis for direct foreign investment in China.

At first, cautious Chinese leaders intended to limit the scope of foreign investment in their country to particular organizational forms and particular geographic regions. They identified, for example, the equity joint venture as the organizational format that most foreign investment projects should adopt. They implied that most foreign investment would be restricted to the four special economic zones that were established along the coast of southeast China in 1980. And there was even some suggestion that foreign ventures would be welcome in only a few sectors of the economy, such as hotel construction and energy extraction.

Over time, however, each of these restrictions has fallen. Virtually every part of China is now eligible for foreign investment, and almost every province has launched promotional schemes to attract it. Investment has been welcomed in every sector of the economy, from the new Sheraton Hotel in Shanghai to chicken ranches in Guangdong, from offshore oil fields in the South China Sea to wineries in Tianjin, and from Pepsi-Cola bottling plants in Shenzhen to French restaurants in Peking. Moreover, the range of organizational formats under which foreign capital can be invested in China has widened. Peking now permits the use of legal devices other than equity joint ventures, ranging from wholly foreign-owned enterprise to contractual joint ventures of various sorts.[48]

At first, the level of direct foreign investment in China was rather low. From the adoption of the joint venture law in 1979 until 1983, only about $1.8 billion in foreign capital was actually invested in China, even though foreign investors had signed agreements for projects totaling about $5.5 billion. Between 1983 and 1985, however, the rate of foreign investment in China rose more rapidly, as the legal framework for foreign ventures became more complete, and as the organizational forms that foreign investment could take became more flexible and diverse. In 1983 China absorbed $916 million in direct foreign investment, a 41 percent increase over the previous year. In 1984, the amount of foreign investment rose to $1.42 billion and increased again to $1.96 billion in 1985 (see table 6-8).

Even so, the progress in attracting foreign investment to China was not fully satisfactory to either Peking or the foreign business community. Although the Chinese have never announced any precise targets for the absorption of foreign investment, there is every reason to believe that the $6.06 billion invested in their country between 1979 and 1985 fell short of their expectations. Moreover, the nature of the foreign ventures in China has been disappointing to Peking. Most of the projects have been small enterprises, launched by overseas Chinese from Hong Kong, with low levels of capitalization and fairly unsophisticated technology.[49]

The relatively low levels of foreign investment in China, in turn, can be explained by some chronic problems leading many foreign business executives to believe that, for all its rhetoric, China did not truly welcome foreign investment except on exploitative terms. These have included the high cost of many important inputs, especially land, housing, labor, and office space; the poor training and discipline of Chinese workers; the low quality of Chinese components; the uncertain availability of some raw materials; the difficulties in obtaining loans in Chinese currency to cover local operating costs; the incomplete legal system; an overburdened communications and transportation infrastructure; and convoluted lines of authority in the Chinese bureaucracy. In a parody of official Chinese invocations of the "four modernizations," some cynical foreign business executives in Peking invented "four Ms" of their own: *mafan* ("it's too much trouble"), *meiyou* ("we don't have it"), *meibanfa* ("we can't do anything about it"), and *meiguanxi* ("it doesn't matter").[50]

Above all, because the Chinese have required each foreign venture to maintain its own foreign exchange balance, it has been difficult for foreign businesses to repatriate any profits not earned in hard currency. With only a few exceptions, repatriation has been permitted only if it is counterbalanced by an inflow of foreign exchange through exports or new investment. This has discouraged investment projects designed to produce for the domestic Chinese market, thus removing one of the principal incentives that the Chinese can offer to potential foreign investors.

These long-standing problems were exacerbated by China's balance of payments difficulties in 1985 and early 1986. As Peking tightened control over the expenditure of foreign exchange, it became more difficult for foreign ventures to import necessary equipment or components from abroad. At the same time, the devaluation of the renminbi also increased the cost of imported components and thus raised the price of the finished product on the Chinese market. For many prominent foreign ventures, especially those that assembled automobiles from components imported from abroad, these developments made the profitable conduct of business almost impossible.

The difficulties encountered by foreign ventures in 1986 compounded the dissatisfaction of overseas investors with the business climate in China. In April, the International Businessmen's Association of Peking wrote to Vice-President George Bush warning that, if the Chinese investment environment did not improve, some American firms might begin to withdraw from their projects in China. In a major speech delivered in Washington in May, U.S. Ambassador Winston Lord described the foreign business community as "frustrated by high costs, price gouging, tight foreign exchange controls, limited access to the Chinese market, bureaucratic foot-dragging, lack of qualified local personnel, and unpredictability." In July, a front-page article in the *Wall Street Journal* described the growing frustrations with the "costs and hassles" of doing business in China. And by early August, it was apparent that new foreign investment in China had fallen 20 percent in the first six months of the year.[51]

Faced with these pressures from the foreign business community, Chinese leaders began to consider new policies that would restore investor confidence by improving the business climate in China.[52] In the summer, both Zhao Ziyang and Deng Xiaoping held meetings with foreign business executives to discuss their complaints, and State Councilor Gu Mu, the senior Chinese official responsible for foreign economic relations, convened a meeting with the country's principal governors and mayors to discuss concrete measures for improving the foreign investment climate. A full set of draft regulations on the subject was issued by the State Council in October. Shortly thereafter, several provincial and municipal governments announced additional regulations that offered further concessions and incentives to foreign investors.[53]

In essence, the 1986 investment regulations offered four sets of incentives to the foreign business community. First, they were intended to lower the cost of conducting business in China, by reducing land use fees, taxes, the cost of some inputs, and the wage rates paid by foreign ventures. Second, the regulations promised improved access to crucial inputs controlled by the state, including water, electricity, communication, transportation, and renminbi loans. Third, the regulations were intended to increase the efficiency with which the bureaucracy approves foreign investment projects, by establishing deadlines for government decisions and by creating local service agencies that can expedite the review process. And finally, the regulations guaranteed foreign ventures greater authority over production plans, imports and exports, wages and bonuses, and the employment and dismissal of labor. In all these ways, these central and local provisions represented a sincere attempt to improve the climate for foreign investment in China. Still, a great deal will depend on the spirit and efficiency with which they are implemented.

Furthermore, the 1986 investment regulations did little to resolve what is perhaps the most fundamental issue dividing the Chinese government and the foreign investment community: access to the domestic Chinese market, and the repatriation of the resulting profits earned in renminbi. The regulations were written to ensure favorable treatment of foreign ventures that, because they earn a surplus of foreign exchange, can receive official classification as "export enterprises." They did not offer, as many foreigners had hoped, the unrestricted right to convert profits earned from domestic sales into hard currency for repatriation. This omission reflected the widely shared Chinese concern that permitting the repatriation of profits earned in Chinese currency would place an unacceptable additional burden on the country's limited foreign exchange earnings and reserves.

The Chinese have offered only a few mechanisms by which foreign ventures can circumvent the requirement to balance their foreign currency accounts. Foreign ventures that are classified by the Chinese government as "technologically advanced enterprises," or whose products are regarded as import substitutes, may require their Chinese customers to pay at least part of the purchase price in foreign exchange. Peking has also been willing to provide foreign exchange subsidies for technologically advanced enterprises that need to purchase critical components abroad. A limited foreign exchange market has been created in a few Chinese cities, in which foreign ventures with a surplus of hard currency are authorized to sell it, for a premium, to foreign ventures that are experiencing a shortage. And foreign ventures producing for the domestic market are encouraged to use their renminbi profits to buy Chinese goods for export abroad.[54]

It remains highly improbable, however, that these devices will solve the foreign exchange problems of foreign ventures in China. Chinese purchasers with access to foreign exchange may prefer to import directly, rather than pay hard currency for the products of China's own foreign ventures. The amount of surplus foreign currency that can be made available on the limited foreign exchange markets now being established is unlikely to satisfy the demands of the foreign business community. The use of countertrade to resolve the repatriation issue is also of doubtful effectiveness. Not only are foreign ventures finding such a mechanism cumbersome and inconvenient, but Chinese firms that produce export-quality goods are not eager to sell them to a foreign venture for renminbi when they could sell them directly on the international marketplace for hard currency.

Thus the climate for foreign investment in China remains cool, especially for those projects that envision the use of fairly simple technology to manufacture products for the domestic Chinese market. In 1985 and 1986 some radical reformers proposed that the interior of the country be opened to foreign investors, that foreign exchange markets be established to facilitate the repatriation of profits, that development zones in major cities be leased or sold to foreign investors, and that the Communist Party and Youth League organizations be banned from foreign ventures.[55] But it it unlikely the proposals will be rapidly adopted. Consequently, foreign investment will probably increase more slowly than Chinese leaders would prefer, and the shortcomings in China's investment climate will remain a contentious issue in China's relations with foreign countries.

SPECIAL ECONOMIC ZONES AND OPEN CITIES

As noted in chapter 1, China has long had experience with the selection of certain cities as points of contact with foreigners, including the trading ports of the Ming, the treaty ports of the Qing, and the extraterritorial concessions of the late Qing and early Republican periods. In a decision that carries intriguing echoes from the past, China's post-Mao leadership has also selected several parts of the country to serve as linkages between China and the rest of the world. But the differences between the contemporary period and its historical precedents are as important as the similarities. In the past, the Chinese government chose cities as trading ports more to restrict and channel trade than to expand or encourage it. Conversely, the emergence of cities as a means of access to the Chinese interior occurred at the initiative of foreign businessmen and local merchants, not at the behest of the central Chinese government. Today, for the first time, a strong Chinese state, wishing to promote, rather than discourage, foreign investment and trade, has selected certain parts of the country to spearhead economic relations with foreigners.

In its first and, in the end, most controversial measure, China designated four areas along the southeast coast—Shenzhen, Zhuhai, Xiamen, and Shantou—as "special economic zones" (SEZs) in 1979.[56] In some ways, the SEZs are similar to the export-processing zones established in Taiwan, South Korea, and other developing countries in the 1960s and 1970s. Like these counterparts abroad, China's SEZs were designed to encourage foreign investment in export projects. In these areas, the government would build a modern physical infrastructure, provide a well-trained labor force, and offer preferential tax rates, exemptions, and holidays. All four SEZs are coastal cities, with relatively convenient access to ocean transport routes. Two, Xiamen and Shantou, were selected partly because of their links to large overseas Chinese communities that could become sources of investment capital.

But China's SEZs are unique because they also have additional responsibilities. They are bridges linking China to Hong Kong and Macao, and through them to the rest of the world; laboratories in which new management techniques and economic policies can be tested before being adopted in the rest of China; filters that can screen out those aspects of foreign technology and culture that are not considered appropriate for Chinese needs; and lubricants that can facilitate the reunification of Hong Kong, Macao, and, Peking hopes, Taiwan, with the rest of the Chinese mainland.

One of the most important functions of the SEZs is to serve as mechanisms for the introduction, study, and absorption of technology in a wider range of industries than in most export-processing zones. The zones are to be centers of services, agricultural processing, and tourism as well as manufacturing; and these areas are designed to absorb advanced technology for capital- and technology-intensive industries. The SEZs are not meant just to attract the technology suited to the production of labor-intensive exports.

The SEZs were also meant to be arenas for testing economic and social reforms considered too radical or too experimental for the rest of China. Shenzhen, in particular, has progressed further toward a market economy than any other part of China. It has been the site for the testing of new wage systems and labor regulations and has modeled a new university along Western lines. Some Chinese intellectuals even proposed that Shenzhen be considered a "special cultural zone," with greater adoption of foreign culture, values, and institutions than the rest of China.[57] For this reason, in fact, several of the areas chosen to become SEZs were not the more advanced parts of Guangdong province, but rather relatively poor and under-developed regions in which a completely new economic system and physical infrastructure could be—indeed, would have to be—constructed from scratch.

The locations of the special economic zones provide further clues to their purposes: Zhuhai adjacent to Macao, Shenzhen next to Hong Kong, and Shantou and Xiamen opposite Taiwan. Both Zhuhai and Shenzhen have ready access to information in Hong Kong about international markets, advanced technology, and foreign design. Besides being used by the SEZs, the information can also be transmitted into the interior of China through the branch enterprises and representative offices established in Shenzhen by various ministries and provinces. Furthermore, with their large foreign presence, special culture, and market orientation, the SEZs are intended to facilitate the eventual reunification of China by blurring the differences between the mainland, on the one hand, and Taiwan, Hong Kong, and Macao on the other.

Examining the record of Shenzhen, the largest of the four zones and the one that has received the greatest attention from Chinese leaders, reveals the performance of the SEZs to date. To Shenzhen's credit, it has enjoyed rapid growth in both total output and foreign investment. Almost overnight, a sleepy county seat has become a bustling modern city, with high-rise office buildings, fashionable hotels, and broad streets that often rival those of neighboring Hong Kong. By October 1985, Shenzhen had attracted $840 million in direct foreign investment—one-seventh of the national total and more than half the original target established for foreign investment in the zone for the entire period from 1980 to the year 2000.[58]

But these impressive accomplishments were achieved at considerable cost. Shenzhen has imposed a greater burden on the central treasury—in investments made and taxes forgiven—than originally anticipated. A development plan, drawn up in 1982 to cover the years 1980–2000, called for an expenditure of 3.7 billion yuan in capital construction over that twenty-year period. Within two years, however, nearly the entire amount had been spent, and the projected investment for the next five years (1985–1990) had been increased to 7.5 billion yuan.[59] In only seven years, in other words, Shenzhen needed more than twice the investment initially forecast for twenty.

Nor has Shenzhen's economic performance met all of the leaders' expectations. As in the rest of China, foreign investment in Shenzhen has involved less advanced technology than originally anticipated, with only about one-third classified by Chinese analysts as "advanced or relatively advanced."[60] Perhaps most disturbing, Shenzhen has generated less foreign exchange from exports than it has spent on imports, with imports exceeding exports by a ratio of five to one.[61] More than two-thirds of Shenzhen's output, much of which required expensive imported components, was consumed inside China rather than exported. Indeed, Shenzhen served as a sales and purchasing agent for the rest of China, marketing (often through illicit channels) the export goods of other provinces and obtaining (again, often through illegal means) vast amounts of foreign capital goods and consumer products for resale to the interior. Thus far, Shenzhen has served more as an import-procurement region than as an export-processing zone.

Serious social and political problems have accompanied these economic shortcomings. In Shenzhen, both the local currency and the indigenous culture are being driven out by their counterparts from Hong Kong. The Hong Kong dollar, more than either the renminbi or Peking's "foreign exchange certificates," has become the prevalent currency, so that foreign entrepreneurs and local workers alike can be assured of total convertibility. Tipping, prostitution, smuggling, and corruption have become flagrant, and officials in Shenzhen have felt it necessary to deny widespread reports that they planned to establish brothels and casinos to attract more visitors from Hong Kong.[62]

The problems connected with the SEZs have caused great political controversy in China. But they have also encouraged Chinese leaders to reconsider their strategy for attracting and absorbing foreign investment. Peking is still using many of the policies first formulated for the special economic zones, but is now applying them to a much wider segment of the Chinese economy. This decision was encouraged by the resentment of leaders from other parts of the country, who felt that the emphasis initially placed on the SEZs would prevent their regions from gaining equal access to foreign investment.[63]

Beginning in late 1979, for example, Chinese leaders gave five provincial-level units—Fujian, Guangdong, Peking, Shanghai, and Tianjin—expanded authority over trade and investment decisions, comparable to that enjoyed by the special economic zones.[64] The size of projects that could be initiated without central approval was expanded, and the amount of foreign exchange placed at the disposal of local governments was increased. Other provinces and cities received comparable powers in later years. Under these regulations, the upper limit on projects that can be launched on local initiative was, at the end of 1984, $2 million or $3 million for most smaller cities, $5 million for larger cities and most provinces, $10 million for Liaoning, Dalian, Canton, and Peking, and $30 million for Guangdong, Fujian, Tianjin, and Shanghai (U.S. dollars). Even so, even the cities and provinces in the latter, most favored category fell short of the $50 million limit that had been established for the special economic zones.[65]

In a further step, taken after what the Chinese media have acknowledged to have been "heated discussions," fourteen coastal cities, along with Hainan Island, were permitted in 1984 to offer tax incentives for foreign investment similar to, although less generous than, those inducements offered in the special economic zones.[66] These cities were also encouraged to establish economic and technical development zones, usually in their suburbs, which were allowed to offer tax incentives to investors that were practically identical to those provided in the SEZs.[67] By the middle of 1986, many provinces were also allowed to offer tax exemptions, reductions, or holidays to targeted foreign ventures.[68]

Finally, three "development triangles" in southeastern and central China— the Pearl River, Min River, and Yangtze River deltas—have been identified as trade and investment promotion zones. Like the SEZs, these regions are a base for exports and a "filter to digest [the] world['s] modern science and technology and advanced managerial methods . . . so as to discard the dross and select the essential."[69] But the main emphasis of these zones is not on technology-intensive manufacturing, as in the SEZs or the economic and technical development zones in the open cities, but rather on growing and processing the agricultural products that can be sold on international markets.[70]

These decisions have transformed all of coastal China, with a population of about 200 million people, into a single "development belt," offering greater incentives to foreign investors, more freedom to approve contracts with foreign entrepreneurs, and increased control over foreign exchange. China's goal is to extend this belt to the north and west, into the country's interior. Conceivably, open cities or even special economic zones may be established along the Sino-Soviet frontier to stimulate trade with the Soviet Union and Eastern Europe. But since these initiatives were designed to deal with decentralized market economies and private investors, they may not prove appropriate for promoting economic relations with more centrally planned economies.[71]

In short, Chinese leaders have made a subtle but significant change in policy since the early 1980s. Originally, they seemed intent on creating a few special economic zones in parts of the country with good access to foreign markets and technology. Gradually, they have learned that the zones' lack of physical facilities, shortages of skilled labor, and relative isolation from the rest of the country have produced high economic and social costs for China. By creating a larger number of open cities, China's reformers now seem interested in attracting foreign investment into parts of the country that are already more highly developed and can absorb foreign technology more readily, and whose resistance to "spiritual pollution" will be somewhat greater. Such an approach is also more palatable to the powerful officials of China's other coastal and interior provinces, who want to see the benefits of foreign investment distributed more widely than in a few special economic zones.

The extension to other parts of China of some of the powers and privileges enjoyed by the SEZs did not, however, end the controversies over this aspect of China's foreign economic policies. The debate over the special economic zones became even more heated in 1984–86, as the economic and social costs of Shenzhen became increasingly apparent.[72] At first, the controversy focused on political and symbolic issues. One senior leader who had visited Shenzhen was quoted in the Chinese press as saying, "Apart from the five-starred red flag, everything in Shenzhen has turned capitalist." Another is alleged to have burst into tears during his inspection tour, declaring that he would never have joined the Communist revolution had he known that Shenzhen would be the result.[73] Hu Qiaomu, then a member of the Party Secretariat, publicly objected to the limited and docile role played by Communist Party branches and trade union organizations in joint ventures in Shenzhen.[74] And the Chinese press repeatedly acknowledged that high Party leaders were comparing the special economic zones and the open cities to the treaty ports and foreign concessions of the nineteenth and early twentieth centuries.[75]

The discussions took a somewhat more concrete and analytical tone in mid-1985 when Yao Yilin, a vice-premier responsible for economic matters and a long-time associate of Chen Yun, charged that Shenzhen survived only because of repeated "transfusions" from the state treasury. In his opinion, he announced, it was time to "pull out the 'syringe.'"[76] In a debate that lasted for another year, the critics of the special economic zones produced data to show that Shenzhen was experiencing chronic deficits in its balance of payments, exporting only a small fraction of total output, and failing to import advanced technology from abroad. In a commentary with implications far beyond foreign economic policy, one critic charged that Shenzhen's shortcomings were the direct result of the absence of central planning in the SEZs.[77]

In an unusually direct, spirited, and detailed response, the defenders of the SEZs replied that Shenzhen's development should be seen as a staged process in which results could only be achieved gradually.[78] Some even attempted to make a virtue out of necessity. An official of the provincial economic system reform commission in Guangdong tacitly rejected the basic assumption on which the SEZs had been created when he denied that Shenzhen should be primarily "outward oriented." Instead, he argued, the SEZs should adopt a "pivot role," in which they are "open to both the outside world and the areas at home," drawing capital from both and selling to both. Otherwise, they would develop a "self-enclosed market pattern," which would be of little benefit to either themselves or the state.[79] The supporters of Shenzhen could also take pleasure in a well-publicized statement made by Deng Xiaoping in mid-1985, to the effect that, although Shenzhen was still in an experimental stage, it represented the correct approach to China's foreign economic relations.[80]

The debate was resolved temporarily in late 1985 and early 1986, when Chinese leaders agreed to cut back sharply on central investment in the special economic zones and other open cities and give the SEZs a grace period in which to significantly improve their foreign exchange and capital accounts. Some reports suggest that Shenzhen was told to increase the share of total output that it exported from 40 percent in 1986 to 60 percent by 1990, reduce transshipment of foreign goods to other provinces, and cut back on imports of foreign components.[81] The SEZs will probably survive their present difficulties, if only because to disband them would do great damage to China's longer-term policy toward Hong Kong, Macao, and Taiwan. But probably no new special economic zones will be created, as Chinese leaders continue their policy of drawing foreign capital and technology into the areas considered to be the core of the Chinese economy, rather than to peripheral regions.

CONCLUSION

Because of its new foreign economic policies, China's relationship to the international economy has changed greatly. Between 1978 and 1986, China's trade with foreign countries increased two and a half times. The People's Republic has imported foreign technology valued at nearly $10 billion, attracted more than $8 billion in foreign investment, and borrowed more than $20 billion from international financial markets and institutions (table 6-7).

The foreign presence in China is found in many quarters: the new international hotels, the advertisements on Chinese television, the offices and shop floors of the new joint ventures and wholly foreign-owned enterprises, and the halls and libraries of Chinese universities. Many Chinese have gone abroad to work. They are officers in the World Bank and International Monetary Fund, and students and scholars in foreign universities. They negotiate deals in the boardrooms of major banks and corporations, float bond issues on world capital markets, and finance and manage their own investment projects overseas.

Given all the activity, it is tempting to describe China's new trade and investment strategy either as an "open door policy" or as "export-led growth," comparable to the strategies of development adopted by some of the smaller countries and regions in East Asia during the last several decades. But although both terms contain elements of truth, they also exaggerate and distort a complicated picture.

To begin with, China is not engaged in export-led growth, by any reasonable definition of the term. In 1986 exports amounted to 108 billion yuan, or about 14 percent of a national output of 779 billion yuan (see table 6-1). Although the ratio of exports to national output has risen greatly since the early 1970s, and although it is comparable to those in other large continental economies such as Nigeria or Brazil, it remains far below the ratios for such truly export-led economies as Taiwan and South Korea (55 percent and 37 percent, respectively), or even for Indonesia and Thailand (25 percent and 22 percent).[82] According to Chinese estimates, each 100 million yuan in industrial exports supports 12,000 jobs. If this ratio is correct, then China's export industries, which sold 39 billion yuan worth of goods overseas in 1985, employed approximately 4.7 million workers, or only about 6 percent of the industrial labor force. The expansion of the Chinese economy depends principally on the growth of the internal Chinese market, rather than on access to alternative sales opportunities overseas.[83]

Nor has China adopted the philosophy, or even the rhetoric, of free trade. Chinese economists remain outspoken in their defense of protectionist policies for developing countries, even as they harshly denounce any sign that protectionism is increasing in the developed world. In the words of one economist, "The state must take measures to protect national economic development" and must not permit a "free inflow of foreign capital and products." Although they have adopted an aggressive policy of importing technology, the Chinese seem committed to a long-term strategy of import-substitution, with the foreign capital and technology imported today meant to promote the development of indigenous industries in the years ahead.[84] According to one common saying, "The first product can be imported, but the second should be made in China and the third should be exported."[85] Or, to quote another common aphorism, the goal should be to "import fewer eggs and more chickens."

Thus China's foreign trade remains highly regulated. Some exports are still subjected to mandatory quotas to ensure an adequate flow of foreign exchange, while other goods are liable to heavy export tariffs to discourage their sale abroad. Imports are restricted by a complex system of licenses and duties designed both to ensure the avoidance of competition with domestic products and the expenditure of foreign exchange on items considered by the state to be "wasteful" or "unnecessary." China's foreign economic strategy can be described as one of "import-led growth," in which the principal aim has been to expand the country's purchases of advanced technology, with the final goal of producing as much at home as possible. In this sense, China, like much of the rest of East Asia, has adopted a neomercantilist strategy aimed at promoting foreign economic relationships that will, in the end, help produce a relatively self-reliant nation.

CHAPTER 7

Liberalizing Political Life

BY September 1976, China faced an acute crisis in domestic politics. Large segments of society were alienated from the Communist Party and from the government because of the violence, persecution, and disorder of the Cultural Revolution. The leadership was engaged in a savage internecine struggle unconstrained by the norms of civility and consensus that had once governed political debate. Official ideology had lost much of its ability to mobilize and sustain poular support. And the death of Mao had now removed the one remaining pillar on which the legitimacy of the regime rested.

Hua Guofeng responded cautiously and conservatively to China's post-Mao political crisis. It is true that he supported the arrest of the Gang of Four in October 1976 and charged them with plotting a coup against their colleagues on the Politburo. He inaugurated a conciliatory policy toward the urban intellectuals who had been persecuted during the Cultural Revolution and announced wage increases for the workers whose salaries had been frozen during the late Maoist period. He also sought to revive the traditional norms of open discussion, collective leadership, and strict discipline within the Party.

But this was virtually all that Hua was prepared to do. He proposed neither a thorough purge of the followers of the Gang of Four, nor sweeping changes in the structure of the Chinese political system, nor a broad reassessment of Maoist doctrine, nor a reappraisal of Mao's role in post-revolutionary China. Like other conservatives at previous times of crisis in modern China, Hua constructed a strategy aimed at restoring the vitality of traditional institutions and procedures rather than replacing them with anything new. His program called for stability, not for reform.

Other leaders, however, reached more radical conclusions about the nature of their country's political crisis and were willing to entertain wide-ranging proposals for political reform. By 1980 the reformers associated with Deng Xiaoping were prepared to admit that, despite the purge of the Gang of Four and the restoration of political stability, there was still a serious "crisis of confidence" among sizable segments of the Chinese population. Many young people, they acknowledged, still adhered to Mao's view that a separate class of Party bureaucrats ruled China solely in its own interest. If no measures were undertaken to create a reconciliation between the Party and the people, these reformers warned, then China would risk popular unrest comparable to what was then sweeping Poland. As the reformers saw it, they had to reshape the structure of political life in ways that would create a greater degree of democracy and legality. Only in doing so could popular support for the regime be rebuilt.[1]

The reformers also saw an economic rationale for a transformation of the political structure. Retaining the totalitarian system of the past would be incompatible with the economic reforms that they envisioned. Tight organizational and ideological controls would make it virtually impossible for scientists to innovate, technicians to invent, economists to develop new strategies for development, or entrepreneurs to launch new economic activities. Nor would foreigners, particularly those from the West, find it convenient to interact with a China that remained under rigid administrative controls.

For all these reasons, China's reformers have agreed on the necessity for a relaxation of political life. But most of them, including Deng Xiaoping, remain committed to certain fundamental Leninist principles that limit the political liberalization that has occurred. These principles, in turn, echo deeply rooted Chinese values that give the state the right—even the obligation—to promote moral conduct by educating citizens in an official doctrine believed to be morally valid. The state must also preserve social harmony by prohibiting the emergence of political organizations that would challenge the control of the central government. These Chinese values and Leninist principles permit the state to suppress dissent or heterodoxy in society, preclude the emergence of genuine political pluralism, justify the maintenance of broad Party leadership over all other political and social institutions, and preserve a significant, although attenuated, role for Marxist ideology in political affairs.

These limits, in turn, have been tested by growing popular pressures for further political liberaliztion. Ever since the end of 1978, small but influential sectors of urban society—particularly young intellectuals—have urged greater freedom in the arts, more opportunities for political participation, and a further relaxation of ideological constraints on the discussion of economic and political reform. Some of these demands were expressed in the wall posters and underground literature published during the "Democracy Wall" movement of 1978–79. Others were stated implicitly in the continuing experimentation with new styles and new subjects in literature and the visual arts. The most dramatic example of the pressure for further political reform occurred at the end of 1986, when tens of thousands of Chinese students launched demonstrations in a score of major cities across the country to demand more freedom and democracy.

Faced with these demands for political relaxation, Party leaders have responded by suppressing what they have successively labeled "spiritual pollution," "unhealthy tendencies," and "bourgeois liberalization." During these periods, the Party has tightened controls over publication, subjected unorthodox ideas to intense attack in the mass media, and disciplined those who have expressed unacceptable demands for reform. With the support of Deng Xiaoping, however, the radical reformers have insisted that these campaigns be limited in scope, short in duration, and mild in severity. Once the point has been made, therefore, the criticism of dissent and experimentation has tapered off, and the political environment once again becomes more relaxed.

THE MODERATE POLITICAL REFORMS

The political reforms launched in the late 1970s and early 1980s fall into three broad categories. These include promoting a reconciliation between state and society by reducing the scope and arbitrariness of political intervention in daily life; expanding the opportunities for popular participation in political affairs, although with limits on both the form and content of political expression; and redefining the content and role of China's official ideology to create a new basis for authority in contemporary Chinese politics.[2] Together, the reforms have greatly relaxed the degree of political control over Chinese society, without fundamentally altering the Leninist character of the Chinese political system.

Reducing and Regularizing the Role of the State

In post-Mao China the state has reduced both the scope and arbitrariness of political intervention in social life. The range of activities that the state attempts to regulate has been substantially restricted, and those controls remaining on certain activities have, with some exceptions, become more predictable and less arbitrary.

As a result, ordinary citizens now enjoy much greater freedom of belief, expression, and consumption than was true in the past. The Chinese Communist Party today places less emphasis on securing from non-Party members an active commitment to Marxist ideological principles, and pursues the less ambitious goal of obtaining popular compliance with national policy. Citizens therefore spend less time in political study than they did during the Maoist period, and those study sessions that do take place are more likely to deal with practical policy questions than with general ideological principles. Religion is no longer condemned as superstition: churches and temples in urban areas have been allowed to reopen, there has been a revival of folk customs and local religious practices in the countryside, and the recruitment and training of monks and priests have been resumed.[3]

The scope for expression is greater. In both the arts and intellectual matters, artists and writers are encouraged to revive traditional styles and to experiment with modern techniques. Popular tabloids, widely available in major cities, carry articles and pictures on subjects ranging from crime to romance. Foreign music and drama, from Shakespeare to *Death of a Salesman* to the British rock group Wham!, have returned to the Chinese stage. Foreign literature is popular among urban intellectuals, and foreign films, not always of the highest quality, appear on both theater and television screens. A wider range of intellectual issues is now debated relatively freely in academic circles, and the number of scholarly journals on specialized subjects has increased substantially.[4]

The change most readily apparent to foreigners visiting China has been the growing range of choices available to Chinese consumers, especially in urban areas. Hobbies banned during the Cultural Revolution—such as growing flowers, raising fish and birds, and collecting stamps—have again become acceptable and popular pastimes. Activities that were unthinkable in the past, including disco dancing and body building, have gained avid adherents among China's restless young people. Urban Chinese more commonly wear T-shirts, blue jeans, trench coats, Western suits, neckties, and down jackets. Fashionable women now sport cosmetics, permanent waves, and jewelry; and some even undergo cosmetic surgery to alter the appearance of their eyes and noses. Billboards that once carried political slogans now display advertisements for consumer goods from both home and abroad. Opportunities are increasing for leisure travel inside China and, on a much more limited basis, for tourism abroad. The emergence of a lively service sector in the country's cities and towns provides more options to those seeking either employment or entertainment.

One important aspect of political liberalization since 1976 has been the removal of the pejorative political and class labels that had been assigned to hundreds of millions of Chinese during the Maoist period. Beginning in 1978, political labels, such as "rightist," "capitalist roader," or "counterrevolutionary" were lifted from approximately three million people who had received them during the antirightist campaign of 1957 and the Cultural Revolution of 1966–76. In 1977 discriminatory class labels were lifted from almost all former landlords, rich peasants, and capitalists. At the same time, the significance of class background has been noticeably reduced. The pre-revolutionary occupation or social standing of one's family now has much less impact on one's chances for employment, for admission to a university, or even for membership in the Party. In a terminological change with considerable symbolic significance, the form of China's political system is now described as a "people's democratic dictatorship" rather than a "dictatorship of the proletariat." The change implies that the rights of citizenship are being granted to virtually every member of society, rather than only to workers and peasants.[5]

The creation of a legal framework that more fully specifies the substantive and procedural rights of Chinese citizens has been another feature of political reform. The state constitution of 1982 specifies, for the first time, that all Chinese citizens are "equal before the law" and includes new provisions granting citizens the rights of religious belief, the inviolability of the home, privacy of correspondence, and freedom from unlawful arrest. The constitution also stipulates that all government organs and political parties must "abide by the Constitution and the law" in conducting their work. The criminal law and the code of criminal procedure, adopted in 1979, guarantee against torture and arbitrary detention and specify the right to a trial with a courtroom defense. The new legal code also offers a more restrictive definition of "counterrevolutionary" offenses.[6]

Although these changes have been impressive, important limits remain on the extent to which the scope of state control over society has been reduced. Both the state and the Party continue to promote certain kinds of beliefs and to discourage others. The state constitution notes the responsibility of the government to "educate the people" in "dialectical and historical materialism" and, at the same time, to "combat capitalist, feudalist, and other decadent ideas."

The Party constitution stipulates that the development of a "socialist spiritual civilization," the struggle against "nonproletarian ideas," and the inculcation of "communist ideology" are all part of the Party's basic program. The state periodically reminds intellectuals and artists of their obligations to maintain a "socialist orientation" and to fulfill their "social responsibilities." The assumption that the state has the obligation to create and maintain public morality in China has justified the periodic movements against various forms of social and political deviance since 1978.[7]

The area in which the hand of the state remains particularly strong is family planning. The practice of birth control is, under the state constitution, the legal obligation of all Chinese families. To limit population growth, the central authorities have set annual targets for births. At the local level, these targets have often been translated into firm quotas and ceilings, and couples who want to have children must seek authorization from local officials before doing so. Couples who have only one child, and who do so only after receiving official approval, are granted economic rewards and moral commendation. But women who have more than one child, according to one careful study, have frequently been "lectured, harassed, publicly humiliated," fined, and on occasion subjected to even more severe abuse. In 1983 internal Chinese regulations apparently stated that women should be fitted with intrauterine devices after having their first child, persuaded to undergo an abortion if they became pregnant without authorization, and sterilized if they became pregnant a second time. However, no formal piece of legislation adopted by the national legislature establishes such a draconian birth control program, and no public set of regulations guides its implementation by Party and state officials.[8]

In the same way, limits remain on the extent to which state control has been made more predictable and universal. The revised legal system still lacks provisions seen as essential in much of Western law, including the presumption of innocence, protection against self-incrimination, and the practice of an aggressive courtroom defense.[9] Along with the formal system of criminal justice, there still exist more flexible administrative regulations and procedures that can be employed to deal harshly and arbitrarily with those whom the state does not choose to bring to trial. Dissidents have been subject to arbitrary arrest, lengthy detention without trial, torture and solitary confinement, and severe prison terms for loosely defined political offenses. In contrast, Party members are often subject to the more lenient internal disciplinary procedures, rather than to the jurisdiction of criminal courts.[10]

Perhaps most important, there is still no tradition of judicial independence in China. Although the Party seems to intervene less frequently in the treatment of ordinary cases, the handling of more important crimes is subject to review, and often to ultimate decision, by the cognizant Party committee. In addition, no provision is made for independent judicial oversight of the conduct of Party and state officials, except when the Party itself has chosen to bring errant cadres to trial. The process of codification remains incomplete, providing Party officials great leeway in interpreting the law and in acting outside the legal framework. Consequently, the importance of formal legal provisions in shaping the relationship between the citizen and the state should not be exaggerated.

Increasing Opportunities for Popular Participation

The increase of opportunities for political participation at both the grassroots and national levels constitutes a second aspect of political liberalization. The introduction of competitive elections to local legislatures, the expansion of the role of the people's congresses, and growing consultation with various social groups through several institutional mechanisms characterize the post-Mao reforms. Even so, the political participation that is allowed and the views that can be safely expressed are subject to important restrictions.[11]

During the Maoist period, elections in China were highly ritualized affairs. Only delegates to people's congresses at the lowest levels of Chinese society were directly elected by their constituents. The Communist Party controlled the process of nomination and put forward only as many candidates as there were vacancies to be filled. But under the election law of 1979, the use of direct elections was extended to the level of rural counties and urban districts. Even more significant, the number of candidates must now, by law, exceed the number of vacancies, and ordinary citizens may nominate candidates to stand for election.[12]

These elections would have little meaning, of course, if the legislative bodies to which delegates were chosen had only minor functions in the policymaking process. In the past, people's congresses served only to legitimize Communist Party decisions, holding short and infrequent meetings in which laws, policy documents, and personnel appointments were approved by acclamation. Since 1979, however, the role of the people's congresses has been expanded, especially at the national level. The National People's Congress (NPC) holds an annual plenary session, and its Standing Committee meets on five or six occasions over the course of the year. The NPC has established functional committees that specialize in particular aspects of foreign and domestic policy and that have played a more active role in drafting legislation. The meetings of the NPC—and, on rarer occasions, meetings of provincial and county congresses as well—have increasingly served as a forum in which delegates can fairly frankly discuss national and local policy, question government officials, and advance the interests of their regional or sectoral constituencies. By the spring of 1986, some members of the NPC were actually voting against nominations and reports presented to them.[13]

On several occasions, in fact, the NPC has been able to modify the text of proposed legislation or the details of the state budget. In 1986 the adoption of a national bankruptcy law was repeatedly delayed by opposition and reservations among members of the NPC, and it was approved only after significant changes were made in the text of the draft law. And on one occasion—its apparent refusal to adopt a resolution supporting the movement against "spiritual pollution" at the end of 1983—the Standing Committee of the NPC may have expressed the equivalence of a vote of no confidence on a significant Party policy.[14]

In factories, workers' congresses have been established in most large and medium-sized state enterprises, through which worker representatives can exercise some influence over welfare and safety, enterprise plans and budgets, and personnel appointments. Local branches of the trade union have been given a larger say in wages, labor insurance, safety, and discipline.[15] In some smaller enterprises, the workers' congresses directly elect factory managers.

At the national and provincial levels, the small "democratic parties," primarily associations of intellectuals, scientists, and former capitalists, have resumed the recruitment of new members, and some have exercised considerable influence on certain technical decisions.[16] The Chinese People's Political Consultative Conference, an umbrella organization representing various mass organizations, political parties, and social sectors, has been revived and reconstituted. The central office of the trade union has issued proposals on major policies and has participated in the drafting of laws and regulations concerning labor matters. The national government, and some provincial and municipal governments, have begun to use public opinion surveys to probe the popular mood on important issues.[17] Above all, the proliferation of research institutes and academic organizations has established a channel through which the opinions and suggestions of scholars and intellectuals can be considered in the determination of policy.

Further, while not encouraged by Party policy, direct political participation through popular protest and demonstration is more widespread today than in any other period in the history of the People's Republic, save for the chaotic years of the Cultural Revolution. Both workers and students have periodically held strikes and demonstrations in major Chinese cities on a number of political, social, economic, and foreign policy issues. There have been protests against nuclear testing in Xinjiang, against economic relations with Japan, against changes in university tuition policies, against price increases, and in favor of greater political liberalization. Wall posters are still displayed and underground political journals circulated, despite efforts to suppress them. There have been occasional reports of peasants protesting as well. All this activity reflects the greater opportunities for political participation that have emerged from the relaxation of Party and state control over the rest of society.[18]

But all these opportunities for political participation remain limited. The implementation of the new election law has encountered serious difficulties at local levels. Some cadres have refused to nominate more candidates than vacancies, harassed truly independent candidates who had not been nominated by the Party, and overturned election results whose outcomes they disapproved. The election regulations prohibit candidates from appealing to class or regional interests and discourage them from running on concrete political platforms. The minister of civil affairs has criticized candidates who ran active election campaigns in which they aggressively sought to mobilize popular support.[19] Nor has the scope of elections been extended to include delegates to provincial or national people's congresses, let alone to include executives, such as county magistrates or township mayors, who are still effectively appointed by Party organization departments at higher levels.[20]

Similar limits affect the functioning of the people's congresses. Despite the recent increase in the frequency of their meetings, the range of their activities, and the outspokenness of their delegates, the people's congresses in China remain, on balance, consultative and advisory bodies. They have not yet become independent legislatures that can routinely initiate legislation, veto state proposals, or impose accountability on government or Party officials. Delegates to assemblies can introduce motions, but these are treated as recommendations to be submitted to the relevant state agency, rather than as bills to be voted on and adopted as law.[21] Delegates who criticize local leaders who have violated the law or who have departed from national policy run the risk of being regarded as "anti-Party" elements.[22] Proposals made during the early stages of political reform to grant people's congresses the power of investigation and impeachment have not been implemented widely, if at all.[23]

Nor has there been much progress toward democratization within the Chinese Communist Party. The Party constitution does provide for competitive elections for delegates to Party congresses and for members of Party committees at every level. But these provisions have not been widely implemented. Only in a few places has the press reported the selection of Party leaders by competitive elections, without direct intervention by higher levels.[24]

One of the most intriguing proposals for democratizing the Party was made by Liao Gailong in October 1980. Liao suggested establishing three coequal central decisionmaking bodies, each of which could examine and veto one another's decisions. The establishment of the three bodies—the Central Committee, a Central Advisory Committee, and a Central Disciplinary Inspection Committee— was confirmed by the Party constitution of 1982, but with the provision that the latter two would be subordinate to the leadership of the Central Committee. Thus the Party proved unwilling to establish a system of institutionalized checks and balances to monitor its own organizational hierarchy.[25]

The other mechanisms for political participation also suffer from serious limitations. Early experiments in which workers' congresses became the principal source of authority in state enterprises have not been extensively popularized. Instead, power is concentrated in the hands of the factory manager, under the supervision of the Party committee, with the workers' congresses in an advisory or consultative position.[26] In the same way, the participation of the "democratic parties" in the political process is clearly limited. They are not considered opposition parties, but are advisory organizations that can offer suggestions to the Communist Party but are obliged to accept its leadership. They are not permitted to compete with the Party's nominees for electoral office. Indeed these smaller parties cannot even nominate their own representatives to serve on people's congresses and on the consultative conferences. That task is the responsibility of the United Front Work Department of the Communist Party, the agency responsible for the Party's relations with non-Party groups.[27]

Despite the constitutional provisions guaranteeing freedom of assembly, association, and press, there are restrictions on the rights of independent organization and publication. All organizations, especially those that may become national in scope, must receive the sanction of the state, and those that fail to do so are forced to disband. This residual power of the state has been used to prevent the emergence of independent trade unions, rural secret societies, religious organizations deemed to have political ambitions, and even academic organizations.[28]

Journals and newspapers, too, must register with the government. Those not approved are prevented from publishing, and those that later express unacceptable opinions are subject to suspension.[29] The official press remains under the close supervision of the Party and has been charged with the responsibility, as Hu Yaobang put it in 1985, to "unremittingly publicize, with vast quantities of facts and opinions, the views of the central authorities." Although the press is permitted to express a gamut of views on important issues before decisions are taken, such discussions "should not be turned into an open debate on the correctness of the Party's basic principles and policies" and should end once a final decision has been reached. Thus Chinese intellectuals look not to the domestic press but to foreign publications, which are rather widely available in translation in China, for more candid discussions of the successes and short-comings of the reform program.[30]

Particular forms of political participation have also been banned or restricted, although not always effectively. The right to strike, added to the 1975 state constitution at Mao's insistence, was removed when the document was revised in 1982, probably because of contemporaneous developments in Poland. The right to write and display wall posters, another legacy of the Cultural Revolution, was deleted from the constitution in 1980, on the grounds that such activities might libel innocent officials and were harmful to national unity. Though demonstrations have not been declared unconstitutional, and often do occur, those who organize them or participate in them are still subject to harassment, arrest, and punishment. The outbreak of student protests at the end of 1986 led to a series of municipal regulations seeking to discourage street demonstrations from occurring again.[31]

Most important of all, restrictions remain on the content of what can be said, through whatever organizational channel. The Party still holds that the freedom of speech is not absolute, but is constrained by principles of national unity, socialist morality, and, for Party members, Party discipline. The most important guidelines are the "four cardinal principles" identified by Deng Xiaoping in the spring of 1979, which establish the outer limits of political expression. The four principles call for upholding the leadership of the Communist Party, preserving the general structure of the Chinese state, following a socialist course in economic development, and maintaining Marxism as the official ideology of the nation.

Chinese are much freer now than in the past to reinterpret each of these four principles. There has been a lively debate over the essential characteristics of socialism and Marxism and growing discussion of how to reform the government and improve the leadership of the Party. But none of the four cardinal principles can be openly rejected or challenged without fear of punishment.

Changing the Basis of Political Authority

A crisis of political confidence, such as China experienced upon the death of Mao Zedong in 1976, is in essence a collapse of the legitimacy that a government enjoys in the eyes of its people. China's leaders agreed, after the purge of the Gang of Four, that the Party's authority had to be revived if the crisis of confidence was to be resolved. But some sought simply to revitalize the same elements of legitimacy that had so badly decayed, while others wanted to redefine the basis on which the Chinese Communist regime justified its rule.

Under the leadership of Hua Guofeng, the Chinese Communist Party sought to recapture the blend of ideological and charismatic authority that had been the hallmark of the Maoist era. The cult of personality surrounding Mao Zedong was retained intact: the chairman's remains were enshrined in a huge mausoleum in the heart of Peking, his portrait continued to grace public buildings, and his instructions still appeared on billboards across the land. All this was related to a deliberate effort to convey some of Mao's charisma to his successor. Hua Guofeng's portrait was hung next to Mao's in government offices and many homes, and he was officially described as the nation's "wise leader." A widely distributed painting of Mao and Hua sitting together in Mao's study, the older man's hand on the younger man's knee, encaptioned "With you in charge, I'm at ease," depicted symbolically the transfer of charismatic authority to Mao's personally chosen successor.

Similarly, even though Hua began the redefinition of the contents of Maoism, a process that would be carried to even greater lengths under the aegis of Deng Xiaoping, he attempted to preserve a distinctively ideological tone to Chinese politics. Hua supervised the compilation of a fifth volume of Mao's *Selected Works,* covering the period from 1949 to 1957, and he wrote what was intended to be the authoritative interpretation of this new volume.[32] Quotations from Mao continued to provide the justification for all important policy decisions, and, as a sign of respect, were printed in bold-faced type when they appeared in newspapers and periodicals. As indicated earlier, Hua was associated with the policy of "upholding whatever policy decisions Chairman Mao made and unswervingly carrying out whatever Chairman Mao instructed."

In contrast, the reformers have reduced the importance of both ideological and charismatic authority in China and have based the legitimacy of their regime on a different set of principles. Legitimacy in most political systems rests on both procedural and substantive considerations. Procedural legitimacy derives from the procedures through which political institutions assess public opinion, balance competing political interests, and reach policy decisions. Substantive legitimacy is grounded in the goals that the government pursues, the values that it espouses, and the results that its policies achieve. From this perspective, China's political reforms since 1978 can be described as the transformation of the regime's procedural legitimacy from charismatic to what Max Weber described as rational-legal authority. The regime's substantive legitimacy is, in turn, increasingly being based on the concepts of modernization and nationalism rather than on Maoist ideology.

The decline in charismatic authority began with the Third Plenum of December 1978, which criticized the personality cult that had surrounded Mao Zedong, implicitly condemned the recent attempts to inflate the personal prestige of Hua Guofeng, and announced a renewed emphasis on collective leadership. At that meeting, Hua announced that he should no longer be identified as a "wise leader," but simply as "Comrade Hua," and the propaganda establishment began to reiterate that political authority should rest with the entire Party organization and not with any one individual. Gradually, the display of Mao's portraits and the references to his writings became less frequent, and his memorial hall in the middle of Tiananmen Square was transformed into a monument honoring the entire generation of Long March veterans, rather than just Mao himself.[33]

In place of charismatic authority, the reformers have stressed the rational and legal procedures by which the political system now reaches decisions. Each time an important reform is announced, the official press has published a lengthy description of the processes of deliberation and decision. Press accounts emphasize the importance of intellectuals and experts in the policymaking process, the extent to which decisions are reached after broad consultations, and the degree to which policies are now grounded in constitutional provisions, legal codes, and statutory procedures. In so doing, these accounts are arguing, in effect, that the exercise of rational-legal authority now characterizes the Chinese political system. In the same way, the expansion of opportunities for political participation by ordinary citizens, although limited, is also designed to increase the regime's ability to claim that it is responsive to public concerns.

The Chinese are also reevaluating ideology as a source of authority for their political system. To begin with, they have extensively reexamined the content of doctrine. The Party has repudiated many of the ideological concepts associated with Mao's later years: that class struggle is the principal contradiction in socialist society, that "continuous revolution under the dictatorship of the proletariat" should be the basic line of the Party, and that cultural revolutions should be conducted every few years against "party people in authority taking the capitalist road." Other concepts, such as Mao's theory of the three worlds and Lin Biao's "people's war," have been quietly abandoned. Even Leninism has undergone a subtle reevaluation, with some theorists privately denying that Lenin's concepts of imperialism and the vanguard party have much relevance to contemporary Chinese experience, and others publicly extolling the contributions of other communist leaders, such as Rosa Luxemburg, who criticized the dictatorial tendencies inherent in the Leninist model of political organization.[34]

As a result of this sort of reassessment, the content of official doctrine has been transformed along several dimensions.[35] The main task of politics is now seen as promoting modernization and reform, rather than undertaking continuous struggle and revolution. The Maoist vision of a socialist society as one rent with conflict among antagonistic social classes has been replaced by a more consensual vision, in which class struggle plays a relatively minor role. The responsibility of the contemporary Chinese state is increasingly defined as expanding democracy, rather than exercising dictatorship. Accordingly, elements of the Marxist legacy that acknowledge the possibility of the alienation of people from their government even under socialism, and that acknowledge common bonds of humanity that cut across social classes, have been cautiously and gradually resurrected.[36]

Equally important, the Party today admits that many intellectual, scientific, and technical questions can and should be addressed on their merits, without regard to ideological considerations. This attitude presents a stark contrast to the Cultural Revolution period, when all decisions were supposedly taken only after a consideration of the relevant doctrinal principles. The list of socioeconomic policies and political institutions said to be required by a commitment to Marxism has been pared, and some of the most radical reformers believe that being a Marxist should not preclude adoption of any particular policy, so long as it can be shown effective.

Increasingly, doctrine is regarded as a set of broad goals for the future and a methodology for analyzing social and economic problems, rather than a list of detailed and infallible solutions to immediate policy problems. Ideology, in other words, no longer requires very many policies, but simply sets limits on those that can receive serious consideration.[37]

As the role of doctrine in Chinese political life recedes, the Party has come to base its substantive legitimacy on the concepts of modernization and nationalism. In early 1984, for example, Hu Yaobang announced that the principal goal of the Party was to "make people rich."[38] Eight months later, on National Day, one of China's two official news services declared that the Communist Party, unlike previous modern Chinese governments, had been able to unify and strengthen the country to the point that no foreigner could call the Chinese people a "sheet of loose sand" or the "sick men of Asia." "The Chinese," the editorial continued, "are no longer targets of attack and insult wherever they go."[39] And a few weeks later, Deng Xiaoping announced that one aim of reform was to turn China into a world power by the turn of the century.[40] In short, the Party is promising to create a powerful nation that will assume leadership in international affairs, raise the living standards of the Chinese people, and create a modern social, economic, and political system that embodies the best of the Chinese tradition.

Like the other aspects of political reform discussed in this chapter, there have been limits to the transformation of authority in post-Mao China. It would be incorrect to claim, as some Western observers did in late 1984, that China was "repudiating" or "renouncing" Marx.[41] The Chinese describe their task as the "enrichment and development" of doctrine, not as its abandonment. It is true that the Party now cares less about securing an active commitment to Marxism from every sector of society, and that it is willing to tolerate substantial apathy and indifference from large parts of the population. It is also true that the Party is willing to allow, and even encourage, some creativity in the interpretation of Marxism. But it still does not tolerate the active presentation of any ideological alternative.

The appeal of Marxism to the Party, and to many intellectuals, stems from several considerations. The Party's claim to leadership still rests on its assertion that it embodies a scientifically correct body of doctrine. If the Party were actually to repudiate Marxism, it would remove an important source of legitimacy. Moreover, many Chinese intellectuals continue to believe that maintaining the unity and coherence of so large and populous a country as China requires the adoption and promulgation of an official ideology. As one provincial official said in late 1983, "A ruling party and a state cannot do without its own guiding ideology, and the condition of its guiding ideology is related to the prosperity or decline of the state."[42]

In the same way, although rational-legal authority has become a more important aspect of the Party's procedural legitimacy, it has not totally supplanted charisma in post-Mao China. Although the Chinese political system is no longer organized exclusively around the rule of a single charismatic leader, as it was during the Cultural Revolution, it is still focused on the personal prestige of a single individual, Deng Xiaoping, who is widely regarded as having extraordinary qualities of leadership. Conversely, the development of either rational or legal authority in contemporary China remains limited. Intellectuals are still prohibited from freely investigating and debating certain basic economic and political issues, such as the leadership of the Party or the desirability of socialism. And, despite the development of legal codes, electoral mechanisms, and more powerful legislatures, powerful Party cadres, relatively unconstrained by formal legal procedures, still exercise political authority.

THE LIMITS TO THE MODERATE
POLITICAL REFORMS

In keeping with the Party's determination to promote "socialist spiritual civilization"—a term perhaps better translated as "socialist public morality"— it conducted campaigns against political dissent, intellectual heterodoxy, and social deviance periodically after the process of political liberalization began in 1978. Some of these efforts have had a fairly positive character, such as the rather vapid campaign to develop the "five stresses and the four beauties"— an all-purpose attempt to improve the nation's "decorum, manners, hygiene, discipline, morality, mind, language, behavior, and environment."[43] Others, more negative in tone, have been directed against dissidence, corruption, crime, and pornography.

Four campaigns swept the country between late 1978 and early 1986, each with a slightly different focus.[44] The first, in 1979–80, was a crackdown against the dissidents who had called for further liberalization of Chinese politics during the "Democracy Wall" movement. Leading dissidents, such as Wei Jingsheng and Fu Yuehua, were arrested and jailed, and underground newspapers and periodicals advocating democratization were banned.[45] In 1980–81 the Party conducted a campaign against "bourgeois liberalism" in literature and art. This movement was directed primarily against the most extreme examples of the "scar literature" of the early post-Mao period, which had depicted the tragedies of the Cultural Revolution and revealed the "darker side" of socialism. But it also saw some criticism of the "modernist" and "obscurantist" trends that were then becoming increasingly popular among writers and poets.[46] The third campaign—and the one best known in the West— was the movement against "spiritual pollution" in 1983–84. This campaign began as a criticism of the intellectuals who had redis- covered the early Marxist theories of humanism and alienation, and who had sought to apply them to socialist society. Over time, however, the movement also extended to ordinary citizens, with local leaders attempting to restrict the freedom of younger Chinese people to attend disco dances, grow long hair, or wear fashionable clothes.[47] Finally, a fourth campaign in 1985–86 addressed such "unhealthy tendencies" as vulgarity in the arts, corruption in the economy, and extravagance and waste in public life.

Despite their slightly different emphases, however, all four cam- paigns stressed several common themes. Each attacked the experi- ments in new forms and subjects in the arts and demanded greater fealty to the principles of "socialist realism." Each criticized ex- travagance and consumerism and called for a revival of the values of self-sacrifice and frugality. Each movement rejected the notion of unrestricted freedom and insisted on national unity and Party discipline. Each identified and denounced unorthodox new ideas then at the cutting edge of reform and advocated more traditional values, policies, and methods of analysis. Each campaign, while insisting that political liberalization would continue, warned against undue weakness or laxity on the ideological front. And the first movement announced, and each subsequent campaign reiterated, the primacy of the "four cardinal principles" formulated by Deng Xiaoping in 1979: preservation of the leadership of the Party, maintenance of the basic structure of the political system, adherence to Marxism-Leninism- Mao Zedong Thought, and pursuit of socialist development.[48]

The four campaigns were launched at the request of more con- servative Party leaders, such as Deng Liqun, Hu Qiaomu, Wang Zhen, and Chen Yun, who have been sensitive to what they regard as the undesirable consequences of political relaxation. In September 1983, for example, it was Deng Liqun who first developed the formula that educators, political instructors, and writers should "strive to eliminate spiritual pollution in all ideological spheres."

Deng Liqun's views were echoed the following month by Wang Zhen, who decried the lack of publicity given to communist ideology, and who declared that the "first question now on the ideological front" was the need to overcome "weakness and laxity."[49] Similarly, in September 1985, Chen Yun claimed that there had been a "decline in the function and authority of departments in charge of ideological and political work" and therefore "neglect" for the "building of spiritual civilization."[50]

These proposals for a tightening of political controls and a reassertion of intellectual orthodoxy have generally been supported by Deng Xiaoping. Deng, in 1979, set forward the four cardinal principles, which have been the theoretical underpinning of every political crackdown since then. In an important speech in the spring of 1981, Deng complained of "laxity and weakness" in ideological patterns and warned that some people "want to abandon the road of socialism, break away from Party leadership, and promote bourgeois liberalization." In 1983, in his speech to the Second Plenum of the Central Committee, Deng endorsed a campaign against "spiritual pollution" and set forward what later became the official definition of the term.[51] In part, this action has reflected Deng's strategy of maintaining support for his economic reforms by reassuring his more conservative colleagues that he would not allow political dissent or ideological laxity to get out of hand. But it may also reveal that Deng is not as flexible in political matters as he is in the economic sphere. Like the more cautious members of the Politburo, Deng too is concerned about the emergence of ideological trends that, if unchecked, might ultimately challenge political stability or the leadership of the Party.

Once these campaigns were launched, the radical reformers responded by trying to limit their scope and extent. The radical reformers have attempted to prevent both domestic economic policy and foreign economic relations from becoming targets of the campaigns. They have tried to exempt the rural areas from the implementation of the movement, to assure peasants that the agricultural reforms, especially the household responsibility system, would not be affected. They have emphasized that eliminating spiritual pollution and unhealthy tendencies can only be a gradual and protracted undertaking and should not involve the methods of mass mobilization and intense struggle characteristic of the Cultural Revolution. On occasion, too, the radical reformers have attempted to redefine the content of the campaigns, so that what began as a criticism of ideological laxity might later become a program of positive education in the goals and programs of reform.

In so doing, the radical reformers have been alert to signs that the campaigns were arousing opposition among intellectuals, uncertainty among foreign investors, or anxiety among peasants and workers that China might be swinging far back to the left. During the campaign against spiritual pollution, for example, the radical reformers assembled evidence that foreign business executives were concerned about the resurgence of radical economic policies in China and were considering withdrawing from their investments in the country. One news agency dispatch warned during the same period that the campaign was leading some workers to refuse bonuses and some peasants to question the sustainability of rural policies. Another newspaper article pointed out that some urban youth had concluded, "A monotonous situation will again emerge in which many restrictions are imposed on reading books, singing songs, putting on performances, and even clothes," and cautioned that the Party ran the risk of being "divorced from the masses" if it carried the campaign against spiritual pollution too far.[52]

The interaction between the attempts by conservative leaders to launch campaigns against intellectual deviance and the corresponding efforts by more reform-minded officials to limit the effects of those movements has created an ongoing cycle, in which political and social controls are successively tightened, relaxed, and reimposed again. In discussing this phenomenon, the Chinese often use a meteorological analogy, describing the political climate as alternating between "cold winds" and "warmer breezes." In the more frigid political climate, some political dissidents are often tried and imprisoned; controversial intellectuals and writers are dismissed from their posts, expelled from the Party, or criticized in the press; unorthodox ideas are expressed less frequently; and political conformity becomes the order of the day. In more relaxed periods, intellectuals are encouraged to speak freely, some of those punished or ostracized in earlier periods may be rehabilitated, and new ideas are put forward.

Although the alternation of the loosening and tightening of political controls has its precedents in the Maoist era, the scope of the periodic crackdowns has never resembled that of any of the political campaigns launched in the late Maoist period. The realm of politically acceptable discussion has been widened, the number of prohibited subjects and conclusions has been reduced, criticism is focused on a smaller number of people, the characterization of their political offenses is milder, and the punishments they receive are lighter. If restrictions are placed on what is politically permissible, in other words, limits are also set on the degree to which political controls are reasserted. On balance, the freedom of inquiry, expression, and life-style that today's Chinese citizens enjoy far exceeds that at any time since 1949.

PROPOSALS FOR RADICAL REFORM

After the high tide of political liberalization in 1978–82, political reform experienced a fairly long hiatus until the middle of 1986. This is not to say that there was no progress during this period. The power of the National People's Congress continued to expand, so that by the spring of 1986 some delgates were voting against some of the nominations, reports, and legislative proposals presented to them. The construction of a new Chinese legal system proceeded, with the adoption of a series of laws on economic matters and the passage of a civil code in April 1986. Successive regulations on factory management reinforced the authority of managers relative to Party secretaries. Nonetheless, these measures were efforts to elaborate or implement reforms that had been agreed on earlier. No new proposals for political reforms were put forward, and no new concepts were articulated.

In mid-1986, however, after these four years of relative neglect, the country's radical leaders reinserted the question of political reform on the Chinese political agenda. They did so for three reasons.

For one thing, they wanted to sustain the momentum of their broader reform program at a time when economic reform seemed to be faltering. The year 1986 was regarded as one of economic retrenchment, following the excessive growth of wages, investment, and imports that had occurred in late 1984 and through much of 1985. Few new policy initiatives were expected in the economic sphere over the course of 1986. If the radical reformers were to maintain the impression of continued progress, they would have to shift their focus from economic policy to political matters.

Second, the radical reformers had concluded that increasing economic efficiency and productivity would require a new wave of even more far-reaching economic reforms, including the extension of the marketplace to govern an increasing number of economic activities, the growth of private entrepreneurship, and changes in the structure of state ownership of industry. If these economic reforms were to be seriously considered, let alone adopted, there would need to be widespread agreement to reduce further the ideological constraints on the formulation of economic policy.

Finally, many of the radical reformers believed that a new round of political reforms was necessary as an end in itself. Further political liberalization would be needed to prevent abuses of power by Party and state officials, create greater stability, and make government more responsive to the will of the people. Many radical reformers were aware that the crisis of confidence of the late 1970s had not been completely resolved, and they concluded that a new round of political reforms would be required to restore the confidence of the Chinese people in their government.

On May Day, 1986, Hu Qili, a younger radical reformer who served on both the Secretariat and the Politburo, introduced the call for a new set of political reforms. Hu proposed a more creative and less dogmatic approach to ideological matters and, in somewhat more cautious terms, advocated further progress toward democratization and legalization of the Chinese political system. Hu Qili's views soon obtained the personal endorsement of Deng Xiaoping, who acknowledged that many "unhealthy tendencies" were the result of the "unconditioned power" held by many Party and state officials. Deng called for the mobilization of public opinion in support of a new round of political reform. By the fall, the Party Secretariat had established a small working group on political reform, headed by Zhao Ziyang, which was charged with drafting a program that would be comparable to the Party's earlier documents on reform of the urban economy, science and technology, and education.[53]

Deng's endorsement of a second round of political reform, and the formation of the Party's small working group on the subject, soon led to an outpouring of discussion of political restructuring in academic conferences and in the pages of the official press. The central leadership did not present detailed views on this aspect of political reform. But hints were given in a series of articles and interviews in mid-1986 by two individuals intimately involved in the political reform process: Wang Zhaoguo, a member of the Party Secretariat apparently responsible for the drafting of the Party's proposals for political reform, and Yan Jiaqi, a younger scholar who served as director of the Institute of Political Science of the Chinese Academy of Social Sciences.[54] Their comments helped launch a debate over political reform through the summer and early fall of 1986 that ran along two parallel tracks: calls for greater freedom of inquiry and discussion, and proposals for the further development of "socialist democracy." Together, the new ideas introduced during this period constituted a design for an ideological and structural pluralism unknown in the history of the People's Republic.

As the debate over political reform between the radical reformers and their more conservative colleagues intensified, tens of thousands of Chinese students launched protests in the streets of the nation's principal cities in November and December 1986, supporting the calls for greater freedom and democracy and producing the most serious crisis faced by the reform program since it was launched in 1978. The government immediately tightened political controls, this time targeting what was described as "bourgeois liberalization." Furthermore, the arrangements for political succession, which Deng Xiaoping had carefully crafted in preparation for his eventual death or retirement, collapsed. But the longer-term impact of the demonstrations may be an enduring pressure for political liberalization from Chinese students and intellectuals, crystallizing occasionally into outbursts of political dissent that will shape the Chinese political agenda for decades to come.

Expanding the Freedom of Inquiry and Discussion

The discussion of more radical political reform measures coincided with the thirtieth anniversary of the Hundred Flowers movement of 1956–57, the one previous period in contemporary Chinese history when the Party had invited intellectuals to think and speak freely. Encouraged by such radical reformers as Hu Qili, China's intellectuals used the events commemorating the Hundred Flowers movement to insist on greater freedom of inquiry about both the subjects that could be explored and the conclusions that could be reached. There are "too many fetters and forbidden zones," one complained. Intellectuals should be able to "discuss and analyze the concepts of freedom, equality, universal love, human rights, and humanitarianism [all subjects that had previously been proscribed] without hesitation."[55]

The demands for greater freedom of inquiry and discussion had several more specific implications. First, many intellectuals—including some Party leaders—now admitted publicly and explicitly that some Marxist tenets were obsolete, inapplicable, or incomplete. It would be necessary, the radical reformers declared, to make new theoretical innovations, rejecting old concepts that were no longer valid and creating new ones in those areas in which the classics were inadequate. As Hu Qili said in his May Day speech, Chinese intellectuals should have "the courage to break through the few conclusions that experience has already proven to be outmoded or not entirely correct." Other journalists and intellectuals similarly called for the repudiation of "outdated Marxist conclusions." As one put it, "it is impossible for us to devise a perfect once and for all theoretical system. It is impossible for an article or a book to be all-embracing, and it is impossible that every sentence is correct and that every article is the pinnacle of perfection." Indeed, the call for "breakthroughs in the theoretical work" now became one of the most important slogans of the radical political reform.[56]

Second, the radical reformers also proposed employing analytical concepts, research methods, and scientific conclusions that came from outside the world of Marxist analysis. In a highly controversial article published in late 1985, a young economist, writing under the pen name of Ma Ding, had criticized most Chinese research in economics as "abstract, empty commentary" that had fallen into the "quagmire of metaphysics," and he proposed greater use of Western economic methods and concepts. Although Ma Ding's article was sharply criticized at first, his viewpoint gained greater support as proposals for radical political reform multiplied in 1986. Su Shaozhi, a liberal intellectual who directed the Institute of Marxism, Leninism, and Mao Zedong Thought at the Chinese Academy of Social Sciences, noted that Marx had made use of the works of many bourgeois economists when writing *Das Kapital* and "would not turn a blind eye to all sorts of new ideas and concepts" were he alive today. Hu Sheng, the president of the academy, agreed that scholars should have the right to publish works that did not employ Marxist methods of analysis and even acknowledged that the achievements of some non-Marxist scholars were superior to the accomplishments of Marxist intellectuals.[57]

Some radical reformers went even further, suggesting that Chinese culture itself—and not simply the world of scholarship—should draw more heavily on Western ideas and values. Publicly, some intellectuals began to attack the traditional distinction between "culture" and "technology" and the related concept that China should import Western technology but not Western culture. China, they implied, should study and adopt some foreign cultural values and social institutions, as well as Western science and technology. Privately, some radical reformers were said to have called for the complete "Westernization" of China, on the grounds that there was little in traditional Chinese culture that was worth preserving.

If the Chinese intellectual community was to be able to make new ideological breakthroughs, adopt foreign scholarly methods, and even explore the suitability of Western values for the renovation of Chinese culture, then it would be necessary, many radical reformers insisted, to create an academic environment unconstrained by doctrinal preconceptions, censorship, or fear of political reprisals. A senior economist, for example, declared that the characterization of intellectual debates as a conflict between "correct" and "incorrect" political lines, and the labeling of scientists as "proletarian" or "bourgeois," was one of the flaws of the Soviet model that China should now move to remedy. Some intellectuals began calling for the end to political censorship, and others wanted to reduce the priority assigned to political education in schools and universities.[58]

The tide of political reform in mid-1986 led several officials responsible for propaganda and cultural matters to support the radical reformers' point of view. Zhu Houze, the newly appointed director of the Party's propaganda department, criticized the Party and the government for their "interference" in intellectual life in the past; and Wang Meng, the new minister of culture, suggested that the government should henceforth pay more attention to the financing and maintenance of the country's cultural institutions than to particular intellectual controversies.[59]

Toward Socialist Democracy

The second aspect of political reform discussed extensively in the latter half of 1986 was the restructuring of the political system to make it less arbitrary and more democratic. The Party never systematically spelled out what it meant by the development of "socialist democracy," but the term was apparently meant to include measures to increase the degree of legislative oversight over administrative officials and the establishment of mechanisms to increase the accountability of both legislators and administrators to their constituents. Experiments with political reform were launched in three cities that had, over time, developed close ties with the radical reformers. In the Shekou Industrial Area, part of the Shenzhen Special Economic Zone, a management committee was chosen through direct elections and was subjected to annual votes of confidence by staff and workers. In the Tianjin Economic and Technological Development Zone officials were subject to recall by the voters. In Wenzhou, the Communist Youth League conducted experiments in which its officers were elected through more democratic procedures.[60]

The calls for greater academic freedom were soon transformed into demands for the freedom to discuss the details of political reform. Intellectuals rejected the notion that the spirit of the "hundred flowers" should apply only to literary, artistic, and academic issues and not to matters of national policy or political structure. As one put it in late May 1986, "If our citizens do not have the right to express their opinions on political issues, if political issues still remain a forbidden area ... , [then] how can we call them masters of the country?"[61]

In this climate, some intellectuals began to introduce proposals for political refrom that were not necessarily sanctioned by the Party. Fei Xiaotong, China's leading sociologist, reintroduced an idea that had first been put forward in the mid-1950s: transform the Chinese People's Political Consultative Conference into an upper house of the National People's Congress, comparable to Britain's House of Lords. Others argued for the creation of an independent press that could serve as a mechanism for popular supervision of the Party and the government. Still others revived discussion of a national law that would guarantee the rights granted to the press, with one writer proposing that non-Party newspapers be exempt from the requirement to "obey the Party constitution, Party resolutions, and instructions from leading Party organs." Some younger intellectuals began considering the feasibility of a multi-party system with competitive elections to local and national legislatures.[62]

Perhaps the most radical concept advanced during this period was that Chinese citizens, like all other people, enjoyed inalienable human rights, and that the Chinese Communist Party should govern with the consent of the governed. The leading spokesman for this point of view was Fang Lizhi, an astrophysicist serving as vice-president of the Chinese University of Science and Technology in Anhui province, who soon became widely known as "China's Sakharov." In a speech delivered at Jiaotong University in Shanghai in November, Fang noted, "Men are born with rights," including the rights "to live, to marry, to think, to receive an education," and, as he said later in the same address, to enjoy "democracy." These rights implied, in Fang's analysis, that the citizens of a country bestowed upon the government the right to govern; it was not the government that bestowed any rights upon its citizens. In Fang's view, "it is the citizens who maintain the government ... [and] the government [that] must serve the citizens."[63]

THE CONTROVERSY OVER RADICAL
POLITICAL REFORMS

These calls for radical political reform soon aroused the opposition of some of China's more conservative leaders. They thought the political situation in 1986 had become both permissive and one-sided. There seemed to be no limits to the expression of unorthodox political ideas. No criticism was being raised against those who criticized the socialist political and economic system. Little positive propaganda was being conducted on the superiority of the socialist system. Indeed, as the conservatives perceived it, it was becoming increasingly difficult to publish articles that called for upholding traditional Marxist concepts and policies. As they would later complain, the Party appeared to be implementing a policy of "relaxation, leniency, and generosity" toward those who propagated bourgeois ideas, but was simultaneously trying to "tie up and gag" those who were "brave in upholding Marxism."[64]

Although relatively unimportant in itself, a small but bitter debate over music offers a revealing illustration of the mood of the conservatives in 1986. As it happens, many older Chinese still enjoy the popular music of the late Maoist era, including songs from the "revolutionary operas" composed in the 1960s and early 1970s under the patronage of Mao's wife, Jiang Qing. But it has become increasingly difficult for them to find theaters or radio stations that offer the music they want to hear. Younger people, of course, prefer rock and disco music from Hong Kong and the West, and they consider traditional music old-fashioned. Many intellectuals wished to ban the music from the revolutionary operas because of its association with the Cultural Revolution. As one put it, "Whenever I hear [the music from the] model dramas, . . . I immediately recall the ten years of bloody terror, with an involuntary shudder." To many conservatives, the bias against traditional revolutionary music well illustrated the growing tendency in the cultural and ideological spheres to slight the orthodox while favoring the vulgar. One article in a southern Chinese newspaper complained that the liberals "do not mind young people singing pop songs and dancing at discos, but they kick up a racket when we sing the songs of the model dramas. They turn a blind eye to the return of capitalist culture, but they cannot tolerate our great and perfect revolutionary heroes. What feelings do they really have?"[65]

In the midst of this growing debate between liberals and conservatives over the proper extent of cultural and political liberalization, Chinese leaders began consideration of a draft resolution on creating "socialist spiritual civilization" in China. The writing of the resolution had begun in January 1986, and it was scheduled to be adopted at a plenary session of the Central Committee in the fall. In the course of the drafting and redrafting, both groups tried to shape the document in ways that would support their position. Conservatives proposed inserting criticisms of "bourgeois liberalization" and adding limits to the process of political reform. Liberals wanted the resolution to have passages defending the absorption of some non-Marxist values and institutions from the West, and they hoped that the document might offer a strong endorsement of, and blueprint for, political reform.

The result of the heated negotiations was, as has so often been the case, a compromise between the two groups that was apparently forged by Deng Xiaoping. On doctrinal issues, the resolution reiterated both the liberal view that outmoded judgments and conclusions should be jettisoned and the more conservative position that it would be wrong to "negate its [Marxism's] basic tenets, view it as an outmoded theory, and blindly worship bourgeois philosophies and social doctrines." The resolution praised the concepts of democracy, liberty, and equality, which, it acknowledged, had originated in bourgeois philosophy, but it also insisted that the Marxist versions of these values are "different from them in principle." On political reform, the document said that the Central Committee intended to restructure China's political system in ways that would promote democracy, but that, in doing so, it would uphold "the leadership of the Party and the people's democratic dictatorship." Deng Xiaoping endorsed the proposals by more conservative leaders that the document contain a refutation of "bourgeois liberalization," thus revealing that he also believed the relaxation of controls over political and intellectual matters may have gone too far.[66]

The failure of the Party's resolution to set any timetable for political reform, and the extent to which the radical reformers had been forced to compromise with their more conservative colleagues, were disappointments to many of China's younger intellectuals. The students may well also have hoped that the elections then getting under way for delegates to local-level people's congresses would be conducted according to more liberal guidelines than had been the case in 1980. If so, they would soon be disillusioned. The National People's Congress made no major changes in the national election law when it considered the matter in mid-November, and students believed that their nominees for the people's congresses were being ignored by the Party-dominated election committees, which still controlled the nomination process.[67] The lack of progress toward political liberalization in China presented a sharp contrast to contemporary developments elsewhere in East Asia earlier in 1986: the overthrow of Ferdinand Marcos in the Philippines, the consideration of constitutional revision in South Korea, and the emergence of an opposition party on Taiwan. Some younger Chinese intellectuals began to argue that a tide of political liberalization was beginning to rise throughout the Asian-Pacific region and that China should be no exception to this trend.[68]

These developments helped spark a wave of spontaneous demonstrations that swept through a score of China's larger cities in December 1986 and included several tens of thousands of college and university students.[69] At first, the demonstrators were preoccupied with local campus issues: the rising cost of tuition, the poor quality of food, the manipulation of basic-level elections, and the like. Gradually, however, the theme of the protests began to center on the need for political reform. The program of the protestors in this regard was, to be sure, extremely inchoate, with their banners and wall posters calling vaguely for more "freedom" and "democracy" in China. But interviews with the students revealed that a sizable fraction had been strongly influenced by Western concepts of political democracy. The students were demanding a multiparty system, a free press, competitive elections, and the abolition of an official ideology.[70]

The Party moved quickly to suppress the student protests, busing participants back to their campuses, imposing new restrictions on street demonstrations, appealing for unity and stability, and arresting the small number of workers who had joined the students in their demands for political reform. The Party also expelled from its ranks three intellectuals, including Fang Lizhi, who had been particularly outspoken in their criticism of the Party or their demands for political liberalization. An intense propaganda campaign was launched against those who had allegedly advocated "bourgeois liberalization," "complete Westernization," or "national nihilism" in 1986.[71] Moreover, the crisis led to the forced resignation of Party General Secretary Hu Yaobang in January 1987 and the collapse of the arrangements that had been made for the succession to Deng Xiaoping.

CONCLUSION

Many aspects of Chinese political life have changed since the death of Mao Zedong in 1976. The reach of the state is less intrusive and less arbitrary than it was during Mao's lifetime. The Party no longer interferes in the details of the daily lives of most citizens. A system of law, which guarantees the Chinese people certain substantive and procedural rights, increasingly constrains the exercise of political power. Greater opportunities have been opened for Chinese outside government, particularly intellectuals, to express their views on national policy. Discussion of political issues, both in private occasions and in public forums, is more lively, frank, and detailed. And the tone of political discourse is less charismatic, more secular, less ideological, and more rational. On balance, the political system is more open and relaxed than at any time since 1949.

At the same time, the political reforms of the post-Mao era have not fundamentally transformed some of the basic Leninist features of the Chinese political system. Chinese politics is not characterized by pluralism in either the organizational or the ideological sphere. The Party may now consult with a larger number of individuals and institutions in its determination of national policy, but it still allows no independent political parties, no autonomous mass media, no independent social or professional associations, and no true contest for political power. The Party has relaxed control over large segments of Chinese society, but it has not yet acknowledged in any binding manner that there are spheres of life in which it has no right to interfere. The government employs administrative regulations and criminal codes to enforce policies in a predictable way, but it has not yet accepted enduring legal procedures that unconditionally protect citizens against the arbitrary exercise of power. The Party may now admit that Marxism is a living doctrine that must evolve in keeping with changing circumstances and may even tolerate the absence of a firm commitment to Marxist ideology among many Chinese. But it still does not tolerate the open competition of alternative social and political philosophies for the allegiance of China's intellectuals.

Thus China in the post-Mao period has become what might best be described as a "consultative authoritarian" regime, a significant departure from the totalitarianism of the recent past, but not a truly pluralistic, or even quasi-democratic, political system.[72] It increasingly recognizes the need to obtain information, advice, and support from key sectors of the population, but insists on suppressing dissent, cultivating its vision of public morality, and maintaining ultimate political power in the hands of the Party. In the spring of 1987, for example, shortly after the student protests, Zhao Ziyang reiterated the need to open "various channels through which to maintain a dialogue with the broad masses," but contrasted this form of "socialist democracy" with both the anarchy of "mass democracy" and the pluralism of "bourgeois democracy."[73] The successive relaxations and reimpositions of political controls reflect the uncertainty within the Party over the proper blend between consultation and authoritarianism, and over the proper boundaries between the permissible and the proscribed.

What explains the continued commitment of the Chinese Communist Party to an authoritarian system? One reason is that political liberalization, much more than economic liberalization or the policy of expanding economic relations with foreign countries, would challenge the dominant political position of the Chinese Communist Party and thus is completely unacceptable to an overwhelming majority of senior Party leaders. The creation of a genuine multiparty system, the development of independent mass organizations, the emergence of a truly independent press or judiciary, or the implementation of genuinely contested elections would create powerful political institutions outside the Party's control. Similarly, the tolerance of competing ideologies—let alone the repudiation of Marxism by the Party itself—would greatly weaken the Party's claim to exclusive political leadership.

Though many of the limits on political liberalization that have been evident in post-Mao China stem from the self-interest of the Party and its leaders, it is also true that the restraints conform to long-standing tenets of Chinese political culture. Many intellectuals apparently still believe that pluralism may promote chaos and that a more unitary form of politics is necessary to ensure unity and harmony.[74] Accordingly, consultative authoritarianism may well enjoy more support among Chinese intellectuals than does pluralistic democracy. Yang Xianzhen, who fell victim to the Cultural Revolution for his opposition to the dogmatization of ideology in the early 1960s, has still insisted that China needs a common doctrine to posit ultimate goals for society and to provide the basis for national unity.[75] Another senior intellectual, closely associated with the moderate political reforms in the early 1980s, has also asked privately, "What good would there be in having opposition parties here? What the Chinese people want is common goals." Their desire is not that the Party compete for power with other political organizations, but rather that its rule become more regularized, less arbitrary, more enlightened, and more consultative.

But the student demonstrations of 1986 suggest that a new strain has entered the discussion of political reform. Demands for fundamental political change may now have become a permanent and significant feature of the Chinese political agenda. These demands are likely to grow in influence as economic development and social modernization proceed. The interaction of popular pressures for liberalization with the Party's desire to maintain monopoly of political power will become an important, dynamic feature of Chinese politics, as has been true in many of the other rapidly developing political systems of East Asia.

CHAPTER 8

Institutionalizing the post-Mao Reforms

WHEN Deng Xiaoping achieved his final political victory over Hua Guofeng at the Twelfth Party Congress in 1982, he was seventy-eight years old. Obviously, he not only needed an effective strategy for securing the adoption and implementation of his reform program, but he also had to institutionalize the reforms to ensure their survival after his death. In the broadest terms, the challenge was to devise a way to sustain a controversial and problematic new course of policy after the demise of its champion.

Deng had, close at hand, an example of how quickly a leader's legacy could be undone after his death. In the late 1950s Mao Zedong had become obsessed with his own mortality and had begun devoting much attention to ensuring that his vision of revolutionary socialism would survive him. The Cultural Revolution was in large part a device enabling Mao to remove leaders who he felt would, in the end, betray his programs, select successors who would be more faithful to the Maoist vision, and embed his values and policies deep in the Chinese political system. Yet within a month of Mao's death, his succession arrangements collapsed, and within six years his economic and social programs had been explicitly repudiated.

Deng Xiaoping insists that his reforms have achieved much more success, and therefore enjoy much more popular support, than did Mao's programs. These factors, he believes, greatly increase the prospects that the reforms will survive him. But Deng has not been content to leave matters to chance. Like Mao, he has also undertaken an active program of political and organizational restructuring designed to institutionalize the reforms he has sponsored.

From Deng's perspective, the Chinese political system in the late 1970s and 1980s was characterized by three problems that threatened the long-term survival of his political and economic reforms. First, China was governed by overaged, undereducated, overstaffed, and poorly organized party and state bureaucracies. The policymaking process was in disarray, after the dogmatism and factionalism of the Cultural Revolution. And the rehabilitation of veteran officials who had been purged during the Cultural Revolution had increased both the size of the bureaucracy and the average age of China's leadership. All told, the Party and state organizations were ill prepared to design and implement a program of sustained economic modernization.

Second, the relationships among China's chief political institutions were seriously imbalanced. Thanks to Mao's preference for "redness" over "expertise," the Party had come to exercise tight control over both the government bureaucracy and the nation's state-owned enterprises, with state officials and factory managers alike shunted aside in favor of Party secretaries. As a result of the turmoil of the Cultural Revolution, the military had been able to expand its power over China's civilian affairs, and enjoyed a degree of representation and influence in the Party that threatened civilian control over the armed forces. Moreover, the political orientations of both the Party and the army ensured that these organizations were sources of powerful opposition to the reforms that Deng and his colleagues envisioned.

Finally, there were no clear mechanisms governing the political succession to Deng Xiaoping. Although Mao had been preoccupied with the question of succession for many years, he had failed to create an institutionalized process for handling it. Mao defined the succession in highly personalized terms as the transfer of unlimited power to another individual for life, but he consistently lost confidence in the men whom he selected as his heirs apparent. Moreover, by regarding Chinese politics as a Manichaean struggle between the "capitalist road" and the "proletarian line," Mao ensured that the political process would not simply be a debate over policy alternatives or a competition for marginal advantage, but a struggle for political—and even physical—survival. In the early 1980s, therefore, Deng Xiaoping could not be confident that his own death would not be followed by a protracted struggle for power, or a quick coup d'état, that would, in the end, overturn his reform program.

Accordingly, Deng has attempted to restaff and restructure the Chinese political system to maintain, perpetuate, and institutionalize the reforms. This aspect of Deng's broader reform program has had three principal components, each one designed to address one of the organizational problems just outlined. They include reforming the Party and state bureaucracies and the policymaking process to provide a solid base of political and technical support for Deng's reforms; redefining the roles and interrelationships of the Party, the army, and the government; and designing and implementing arrangements for the political succession to Deng Xiaoping.

Great progress has been made in the first two of these three areas and, until 1986, similar progress seemed to be under way in the third. But the removal of Hu Yaobang as Party general secretary in January 1987, until then the man whom Deng had identified as his successor within the Party apparatus, showed that the design and implementation of the succession arrangements were flawed and incomplete.

REFORMING THE POLITICAL PROCESS

China's post-Mao reformers inherited a bureaucratic establishment that was ill qualified—by age, level of education, or effectiveness of organization—to undertake successfully the ambitious program of reform and modernization that they wanted to launch. The bureaucracy was bloated; many cadres were too old to undertake a full day's work; few officials had higher education or technical training; lines of authority were muddied; and the responsibilities of office were poorly defined.

The reformers were intensely aware of the inadequacies of the Chinese bureaucracy and assigned a high priority to efforts to remedy them. In 1981 Zhou Enlai's widow Deng Yingchao complained that many of the country's officials "just sit there and do nothing." The following year, Deng Xiaoping criticized the "incompetent, irresponsible, lethargic, under-educated, and inefficient staff members" who filled the nation's bureaucracies. In 1983 an article in the *People's Daily* lamented, "After arrangements have been made for a job, nobody bothers about its actual implementation and also no one cares about the result." To cope with these problems, Deng Xiaoping called for an organizational "revolution" that would include a massive restaffing of the Party and state bureaucracies, an attempt to streamline and rationalize the country's administrative organizations, and the development of more rational and consultative mechanisms for decisionmaking.[1]

Restaffing the Party and State Bureaucracies

Remolding the bureaucracy to provide a firmer technical and political base for reform has been a principal aim of Deng and his associates, and they have faced difficult complications in the pursuit of their goal. On the one hand, they recognized that the institutionalization of reform would require a major restructuring and restaffing of the nation's major bureaucracies. But at the same time, the reformers also had to reassure the cadres who would be the targets of organizational reform that they would not be purged in a violent or humiliating manner, but would be eased out of office with their dignity and their perquisites intact. Indeed, one of the most remarkable accomplishments registered by the reformers has been to find ways of making wholesale organizational change acceptable to those very officials at whom it is directed.[2]

Transforming the Party and state bureaucracies into highly professional organizations has required, first of all, a massive program of organizational restaffing. The reformers are using a combination of retirement, purge, and recruitment to replace the old with the young, the poorly trained with the better educated, and the more conservative with the more reform minded. Since the late 1970s, the reformers have tried to remove from office those cadres who are deemed to lack the proper political and technical qualifications, and to replace them with officials who are more skilled, more capable, and more committed to reform.

In the past, the pruning of the bureaucracy was undertaken through the political purge, with officials summarily dismissed because of their supposed commitment to disavowed programs or their alleged loyalty to discredited leaders. And such a technique has also been employed in post-Mao China. Nevertheless, the use of retirement, rather than the purge, distinguishes the current restaffing drive from previous efforts. Mandatory retirement ages—65 for cabinet ministers and provincial governors, and 60 for all other leading officials—have been announced and, with some prominent exceptions, implemented. To make mandatory retirement more palatable, officials have been permitted to retire at full salary, and some have even received more compensation after retirement than when they were still serving as cadres. Senior officials have also been allowed to keep many of the perquisites of their former rank: cars and drivers, superior housing, and access to the best stores and hospitals. Many have been named to prestigious positions on Party advisory commissions and disciplinary commissions established at the central and provincial levels. Many more have received less formal appointments as advisers, consultants, or honorary directors in the Party or government agencies in which they formerly worked. Of the 2 million cadres still in office in the mid-1980s who had become officials in the Chinese Communist movement before 1949, almost half had retired by the end of 1985, and another 700,000 had retired by the middle of 1986.[3]

The cost of the arrangements has been high. Maintaining so many former officials at full salary has greatly increased the cost of government administration, and, in many places, the number of "investigators" and "inspectors" exceeds the number of regular staff members.[4] New appointees have been frustrated by the continued power exercised by their predecessors even after their retirement. And the provisions for mandatory retirement created much resentment among senior officials, a fact that may have helped speed the dismissal of Hu Yaobang in 1987.

Yet the accomplishments of the mandatory retirement program, when combined with the achievements of a concurrent Party rectification campaign, have also been substantial. Indeed, the turnover in Chinese bureaucratic leadership since 1977–78 rivals that of the Cultural Revolution, even though the methods employed have been very different. The rotation of leaders has occurred in two stages: an initial wave from 1977 to 1983, and a second thrust in 1984 and 1985 (table 8-1). The first wave of turnovers removed 84 percent of the nation's cabinet ministers, and the second wave retired another 47 percent. Fifty-nine percent of the Central Committee members elected in 1977 were removed from office by 1982, and another 20 percent of the Central Committee elected in 1982 were retired by the National Party Conference of 1985. The first round of rotations removed 60 percent of China's provincial first Party secretaries and governors, and the second round retired another 86 percent. Only four cabinet ministers who were in office in 1978 remained there in 1985, and only two first Party secretaries or governors survived the two rounds of turnovers at that level of the bureaucracy.

As older cadres retire or are dismissed, new officials are recruited to take their place. The reformers emphasize selecting cadres who are "younger, better educated, more professional, and more revolutionary," with commitment to revolution increasingly defined as support for economic and political reform. At each step in the restaffing process, Peking has established age limits for leaders at each organizational level and has set timetables for the reduction of the average age of cadres at each echelon of the bureaucracy.[5]

Newly appointed cadres tend to be about ten years younger than their predecessors and are much more likely to have had the benefit of higher education. At the central level, 75 percent of those newly

Table 8-1. *Turnover Rates of Party and State Officials, 1978–85*

Ministers of the State Council	Central Committee members	Provincial first secretaries and governors
Round one, 1978–83	*Round one, 1977–82*	*Round one, 1979–82*
Original pool: n = 37	Original pool: n = 333	Original pool: n = 29
Removed: 84%	Removed: 59%	Removed: 60%
New Pool: n = 45	New pool: n = 348	New pool: n = 58
New appointments: 87%	New appointments: 61%	New appointments: 81%
Retained: 13%	Retained: 39%	Retained: 19%
Round two, 1983–85	*Round two, 1982–85*	*Round two, 1982–85*
Original pool: n = 45	Original pool: n = 348	Original pool: n = 58
Removed: 47%	Removed: 20%	Removed: 86%
New pool: n = 44	New pool: n = 343	New pool: n = 58
New appointments: 46%	New appointments: 19%	New appointments: 86%
Retained: 54%	Retained: 81%	Retained: 14%
Retained in the pool, 1977–85	*Retained in the pool, 1977–85*	*Retained in the pool, 1977–85*
n = 4	n = 50	n = 2
Percent of original pool: 11%	Percent of original pool: 15%	Percent of original pool: 7%
Percent of final pool: 9%	Percent of final pool: 15%	Percent of final pool: 3%

Note: Removed = removed from the pool by promotion, demotion, resignation, or death.
    Retained = retained in the pool.
    New appointment = added to the pool.

appointed to the Central Committee in 1985, and all eight cabinet members added to the State Council that same year, had attended university. The average age of the new appointees to the Central Committee was 50; that of the new cabinet ministers was 56. At the provincial level, 71 percent of the party and government leaders had a college education. The average age of the new provincial officials, like that of their central counterparts, appeared to be the mid-50s.[6] Most of the new provincial and central officials were promoted from the ranks of the bureaucracy, rather than from the military or mass organizations, as had so often been the case during the Cultural Revolution.

At the bottom of the Chinese civil service, the criteria for recruitment have been changed in ways that, over time, should create more professional Party and state bureaucracies. New recruits for the Chinese civil service now come mostly from the nation's colleges and universities, rather than from the factory, the commune, or the barracks, as was true in the past. Meanwhile, for those cadres already in office and too young to retire, the Party has announced an ambitious retraining program. Nearly 40 percent of the present cadre force is slated for supplementary education by the end of the century: 3 million to 4 million are to receive the equivalent of a college degree, and another 5 million are to obtain secondary school education, through in-service training programs.

Through these programs of recruitment and retraining, Chinese leaders anticipate that, by the end of the century, half of the country's government and Party employees—who numbered about 22 million in 1985—will have a college education, and that the rest will have the equivalent of a senior middle school diploma. In 1985, in contrast, only 22 percent of the nation's cadres had graduated from universities, and only 29 percent had completed secondary education.[7]

The net effect of the replacement of older and less-educated officials by younger and better-trained successors has been a great change in the average age and level of education of Chinese officials. By the end of the second round of rotations in 1985, the average age of cadres at nearly every level had been reduced by about five years: the Politburo from 74 to 69, the Secretariat from 66 to 61; the provinces from 64 to 53; the central ministries from 64 to 58; the central Party departments from 64 to 60; and cities and prefectures from 58 to 50. Simultaneously, the percentage of leaders with a college education rose substantially: in the central state bureaucracy from 38 percent to 50 percent; in the provinces from 20 percent to 43 percent; in the prefectures and cities from 14 percent to 44 percent; and in the counties from 11 percent to 45 percent.[8]

It would be an exaggeration to conclude that the Chinese bureaucracy has, because of this personnel turnover, become highly professionalized. The level of education is still much lower than in many other countries and regions in East Asia. Most of the new appointments are political generalists, although with a higher level of education than their predecessors. There has been enormous resistance to the promotion of younger and better-educated cadres, and to the retirement of senior ones. And anecdotal evidence from several Chinese institutions suggests that younger and better-educated leaders are not necessarily more effective, efficient, or competent than their predecessors. Nonetheless, the speed of organizational turnover, and the relative ease with which it has occurred, has been impressive, and signs are increasing that the Chinese bureaucracy now has a greater ability and willingness to bring technical competence to bear on the assessment of policy alternatives.

Rationalizing China's Civil Service

To take greatest advantage of the turnover of administrative personnel, the reformers will have to find more efficient ways of managing China's civil service and of remedying the corpulence and disorganization of the Party and state bureaucracies. Chinese leaders have assigned high priority to developing a rational program of personnel management and reducing the size of the country's administrative apparatus. But progress has been slow, and they have achieved only partial results.

The search for a new cadre policy has been under way since 1979, when Hua Guofeng, in an address to the National People's Congress, called for more systematic procedures for the "examination, assessment, supervision, reward and punishment, removal, rotation, and retirement" of Party and government officials.[9] Since then, the goals of the reform of personnel management programs have been to end the system of lifetime tenure for officials, break up concentrations of administrative power by establishing fixed terms of office and provisions for rotation of cadres, provide clearer definitions of the responsibilities of each administrative assignment, and mandate procedures for evaluating, rewarding, and punishing the performance of state and Party cadres.

Since these goals were announced in 1979, pieces of a new personnel management program have been put in place, but only on a piecemeal and often experimental basis. Retirement ages have been established for state and Party officials. The state constitution has set a limit of two five-year terms for the president, vice-president, premier, vice-premiers, and state councilors; and comparable (though less formal) restrictions have also been established for the leading administrative positions in the Party. A network of Party disciplinary commissions was reestablished at the end of 1978, and a parallel system of state control commissions, headed by a Ministry of Supervision, was reestablished in 1986. There have been experiments with various mechanisms for the assessment of officials, including written examinations, surveys of their subordinates, and evaluations by their superiors; and there have been trials of new systems for the rotation and demotion of Party and state officials.[10]

On balance, however, the reform of the personnel management system has occurred at a glacial pace. It was only toward the end of 1986 that the state Ministry of Labor and Personnel and the Party's organization department jointly issued draft regulations on the recruitment and dismissal, promotion and demotion, and assessment and retirement of state officials.[11] No comprehensive civil service law has yet been adopted, and there is still no universal examination to assess the quality of new applicants for service in either the Party or state bureaucracy.[12] This absence of systematic personnel procedures may well reflect the resistance of China's administrative officials to any change in what is familiarly known as their "iron rice bowl": the previous system of complete job security, lifetime tenure in office, and blurred lines of responsibility.

The reformers have encountered similar difficulties in their attempts to streamline the bureaucracy. When the effort began in 1981–82, Deng Xiaoping announced that his goal was to cut the size of the bureaucracy by "several million people": by one-third at the central levels and by "more than one-third" at lower levels. Deng acknowledged the political obstacles to such an undertaking. Indeed, he even foresaw open defiance by some lower-level officials, warning of the possibility of "marches and demonstrations and . . . the appearance of big-character posters in the process of our organizational streamlining."[13]

At first, much progress seemed to have occurred. For example, it was announced in 1982 that the number of vice-ministers had been reduced by 80 percent, the number of directors and deputy directors of central government bureaus had been cut by more than 50 percent, and the size of the central Party staff had been trimmed by 17 percent. By the following year, the number of provincial-level Party and state officials had reportedly been slashed by 33 percent. Comparable cuts were also made in the number of bureaucratic agencies. The number of central ministries was reduced from 52 to 43, the total number of central government agencies cut from 100 to 61, and the number of provincial bureaucratic offices trimmed by 30 percent to 40 percent.[14]

But as in almost all the previous efforts at organizational streamlining in China, these efforts proved illusory at best, and transitory at worst. By 1986 it was acknowledged that the size and complexity of the bureaucracy was once again on the rise. By hiring "temporary" or "supplementary" staff on the pretext of the "pressure of work," bureaucratic agencies had rebuilt to their previous staff levels even though their authorized complement of officials had been formally reduced. China's bureaucracy remained caught in what one leading official sadly described as an "endless cycle of simplification, expansion, resimplification, and reexpansion."[15]

Institutionalizing the Process of Policymaking

For most of the history of the People's Republic, the Chinese policymaking process has centered on the drafting of lengthy, relatively systematic, and detailed national policy statements, known collectively as central documents. This process was severely disrupted by the intense factional struggle within the central Party leadership on the eve of Mao's death, and its resurrection was delayed by the conflict between Hua Guofeng and Deng Xiaoping in the late 1970s. It has only been since the removal of Hua Guofeng in 1982 that the process of drafting central documents has been fully revived.

In the late 1970s and early 1980s, the tensions between the reformers and the restorationists were still unresolved, and reform proposals were drafted piecemeal in a rather closed and secretive process. In industry, for example, the reformers began some experiments in 1978 to expand the authority of enterprise managers. The initiatives were launched without any extensive prior analysis by academic economists or government staffs and were not part of any comprehensive program of industrial reform. Nor were the experiments codified in any systematic document: the one outline produced was discussed by a small group of reformers but was never formally adopted by any central Party or state agency.[16]

Early changes in agricultural policy occurred in a similar fashion. A small group of younger intellectuals, many of them former Red Guards who had spent the early 1970s in the countryside, organized an ad hoc study group on agricultural issues, which formulated ideas and presented them to sympathetic senior leaders. Here, the policymaking process relied heavily on personal relationships: some of the members of the agricultural study group were the sons of high-ranking officials, while others were the classmates or friends of the assistants and secretaries to senior leaders. These young intellectuals helped design the experiments with the household responsibility system that began in 1979. But no systematic document on the subject was drafted or approved by the Party until late 1982.[17]

As the reformers consolidated their political position, however, the process of designing the reform program became more systematic, comprehensive, and consultative. Since 1982, the principal reforms have been discussed in lengthy policy documents, which introduce a broad range of measures, offer rationales for them, and explain the interconnections among them. These documents have included the Party decisions on urban economic reform in October 1984, the reform of science and technology in March 1985, educational reform in May 1985, building "spiritual civilization" in September 1986, and the Seventh Five-Year Plan in September 1985.

Moreover, the process of drafting these documents has become increasingly consultative. The proposal on educational reform, for example, went through eleven drafts that were discussed successively by forums of educational administrators and academic specialists, a central work conference on education, and by the Secretariat and Politburo. The entire process is said to have included consultations with more than ten thousand interested people.[18] Similarly, the guidelines for the Seventh Five-Year Plan went through eight drafts that were assembled by a writing group under Hu Yaobang and Zhao Ziyang. The first three drafts summarized and codified advice and suggestions from a group of specialists and scholars selected as an "outside brain trust." The next five were discussed by the Party Secretariat; considered at a forum of Party and government administrators, academic specialists, local officials, and enterprise managers; circulated for comments to all provincial Party committees, Central Committee members, and members of the central advisory and disciplinary commissions; debated at successive meetings of the Politburo and the Central Committee, and finally adopted by the National Conference of Party Delegates in September 1985.[19]

A key feature of the contemporary Chinese policymaking process has been the increasing opportunities for participation by scholars and specialists both inside and outside government, largely through the proliferation of policy staffs and "think tanks" throughout the Party and state bureaucracies. The State Council has created two research centers on domestic policy: one to examine macroeconomic policy and one to conduct feasibility studies of major investment projects. The Party Secretariat has a general policy research office and a second research center on agricultural policy. The State Commission on Reform of the Economic System, which is charged with designing and implementing the restructuring of the country's economic system, has its own research institute, largely composed of younger intellectuals. Most other ministries, from the Ministry of Foreign Economic Relations and Trade to the State Planning Commission, have established or expanded their own research institutes. And a growing number of provinces have created their own policy planning staffs.[20]

The staff members of these new think tanks and policy planning staffs, in turn, can call more readily on a quite lively research community outside the government bureaucracy. Scholars in the national and provincial academies of social science, and in many important universities, participate actively in the discussions of alternative reform proposals. Professional academic associations and scholarly journals have proliferated, providing forums for sharing ideas and communicating them to policy planners in the bureaucracy. Groups of young reform-minded intellectuals have organized their own salons, associations, and periodicals as a way of developing proposals for economic and political reform.

Increasingly, too, some aspects of the reform program have been drawn up in consultation with foreign specialists. A special work team was dispatched to the United States to discuss the draft decision on educational reform with groups of knowledgeable overseas Chinese. The guidelines for the Seventh Five-Year Plan were written at the same time as the World Bank was completing its second report on the Chinese economy, and some of the proposals presented in the World Bank's report correspond to some of the reform measures sketched out in the guidelines for the Five-Year Plan. Delegations of Chinese officials and scholars travel frequently to the United States, Japan, and Europe to gain ideas and information that might be useful to China's reform effort, and the Chinese welcome return visits by their foreign counterparts.

The aim of these organizational changes is to make the Chinese policymaking process more rational, systematic, and pragmatic. In a major speech in mid-1986, delivered as part of the consideration of the radical political reform in that year, Vice-Premier Wan Li called for the development of more scientific procedures for making policy. Wan described the Chinese policymaking process as one dominated by the past experience of individual leaders, the "personal likes and dislikes" of leading officials, and the invocation of non-representative examples of successful policy. The goal, in his words, was to replace this traditional method of reaching decisions utilizing a "comprehensive entity of knowledge" and "scientific theories, methods and means," as well as by greater consultation with those groups whose interests would be affected by policy change. Wan Li proposed that every policy initiative be based on objective analysis before it was adopted, and on careful monitoring and evaluation of results after it was implemented. At both stages, policy analysis and evaluation should be independent of the preferences of Party and state leaders. Otherwise, the vice-premier cautioned, we "would be better off without them," because the results would be "deceptive and dangerous."[21]

Although these measures have made the Chinese policymaking process more consultative and more scientific, policy research organizations remain small, understaffed, and undertrained, with a weak grounding in either theory or practice. Cost-benefit analyses and feasibility studies, although undertaken much more frequently than in the past, are still fairly primitive by the standards of advanced societies. But China has created the basis for a more systematic and knowledgeable consideration of significant economic and social policies.

Although intended to improve the ways in which central leaders reach decisions, some of the changes in the policymaking process that have occurred in the last decade have created problems. The more relaxed political environment, and the decentralization of the Chinese economy, have exacerbated many of the dysfunctions that originally stemmed from the traditional size and diffuseness of the Chinese bureaucracy. Studies of decisions in such areas as water policy and energy policy have revealed a lack of coherence and coordination in the formulation of policy, protracted debates among bureaucratic agencies with divergent interests and perspectives, lengthy delays in reaching decisions as disagreements are referred up the bureaucratic ladder, and gaps between the intentions of central leaders and how policies are implemented by administrative agencies.[22] Still, these problems are found in most complex bureaucratic systems. And they are arguably less serious than the "decisions at random" that previously characterized China's policymaking process.

REDEFINING ORGANIZATIONAL ROLES AND RELATIONSHIPS

Deng's strategy to institutionalize the post-Mao reforms also includes recasting the roles of China's three principal political institutions—the army, the Party, and the government—and redefining the relationships among them. The military has been returned to the barracks, and the officer corps has undergone a gradual process of rejuvenation and professionalization. The Party has been given less responsibility for administrative matters, and the criteria for recruiting new Party members have been revised. More tentatively, the state bureaucracy is being restructured to reduce the size and power of those government agencies responsible for the administration of state-owned enterprises. If these trends continue, the net result will be to reduce the power of the Party over the state, the influence of the military in civilian affairs, and the control of the government over the economy.

The Military

Deng Xiaoping believed that the inflated role assumed by the People's Liberation Army (PLA) in Chinese politics as a result of the Cultural Revolution posed a serious potential threat to the durability of his political and economic reforms. The military was commanded by men who were elderly, poorly educated, and relatively conservative. It had been one of the beneficiaries, and perhaps even one of the architects, of the priority on heavy industry and the emphasis on state planning that had been characteristic of most of the Maoist period. Like much of the Party apparatus, it seemed unconvinced of the need for a sweeping restructuring of the Chinese political or economic system. At a minimum, the military was a powerful interest group largely opposed to reform. And if a crisis over political succession occurred, the military was in a position to intervene in favor of leaders who might attempt to resurrect the policies and institutions of the pre-reform era.

Because of this potential, Deng Xiaoping has concentrated simultaneously on making the Chinese army a more professional organization while also ensuring civilian dominance in Chinese politics. In fact, Deng has given this aim the greatest personal attention since his rehabilitation toward the end of the Cultural Revolution in 1973. The importance that Deng has assigned to the subject is reflected in the many speeches and essays on military reform that appear in his *Selected Works*. To ensure his direct control over military reform, Deng has retained key positions in the military command almost continuously since 1973: as chief of staff in 1975–76 and again in 1977–80, as a vice-chairman of the Party's Military Affairs Commission from 1977 to 1981, and as chairman of the commission from 1981 onward.

From these positions, Deng restaffed the military high command by using many of the same principles, and employing many of the same strategies, as those applied in the reshaping of the civilian bureaucracy. Senior commanders have been gradually removed from office, first by assigning younger officers as their deputies, then by transferring them to new assignments outside the units where they had established their power bases, and finally by retiring them altogether. Promotions have been given to younger officers with more professional training, and special favor was shown to those who had graduated from one of the country's military academies or staff colleges.

Consequently, by the mid-1980s, about 70,000 to 80,000 officers had retired from the armed forces. The average age of the military high command had been reduced by about ten years, and most of the field officers were now even younger than their American counterparts. The percentage of field officers with a college education had increased to 60 percent—comparable to the ratio for civilian cadres at the provincial level. For general officers, the rising levels of education were equally impressive. In 1982 only 3 percent of commanders at this level had received even a senior middle school education. By 1986 that number had risen to 82 percent.[23]

Other aspects of the professionalization of the officer corps have come more slowly, however. Though the pace of retirement has been impressive overall, it has been difficult to remove officers at the highest echelons of the military chain of command. Preparations have been under way for several years to restore the system of formal personal ranks that was abolished on the eve of the Cultural Revolution, but the implementation of the decision has been delayed because of an absence of agreement on how the new grades should be allocated and a reluctance to assign formal ranks to superannuated officers whom the reformers want to retire. Although officers and soldiers were issued new uniforms in 1985, they still have been given no insignia of rank to pin on them.

A second aspect of military reform has been the restructuring and modernization of the armed forces. In 1985 Peking announced the demobilization of 1 million troops, from an army of about 4 million men and women. This decrease is to be achieved primarily by transferring some specialized branches of the military (such as the Armed Police and the Railway Corps) to their corresponding civilian ministries, and by reducing the size of the lightly armed and poorly trained local forces. Cuts may also be made in the political department of the PLA. In turn, the savings created by these reductions in force will make possible the modernization of the main forces and the development of the capability to engage in combined land-sea-air operations on a much larger scale than in the past. At the same time, China is making modest but steady progress in the development and production of new weapons, including tanks, artillery, antitank weapons, surface ships, submarines, interceptors, and ballistic missiles. Some of the technology for these new weapons systems is being imported from abroad, and some is being developed in China's own ordnance industry. The goal of the restructuring is not simply to build a more efficient and effective military force but to give the PLA a greater stake in, and more sympathy for, the process of technological modernization and economic reform.[24]

The restructuring of the armed forces is also designed to further the demilitarization of Chinese domestic politics. Reducing the size of the local forces will not only increase the military effectiveness of the PLA but will also shrink those sectors of the army that, in the past, have been most important in civilian politics at the local level. At higher levels of Chinese politics, Deng Xiaoping has been able to reduce the level of military representation in civilian politics to the lowest level in the history of the People's Republic. The PLA, which held 45 percent of the seats on the Central Committee elected at the height of the Cultural Revolution in 1969, gained only about 13 percent of those elected at the National Party Conference in 1985. Army officers, who held thirteen of twenty-five positions on the Politburo in 1969, occupied only three of twenty-two Politburo seats at the end of 1986. Military commanders no longer play a significant role in civilian politics at the local level.[25]

Despite the reduction in military representation in the highest levels of the Chinese Communist Party, the PLA remains a powerful force in national politics. The high command still enjoys close personal relations with China's top civilian leaders; and the military retains representation on the National People's Congress, the Central Committee, the Politburo, the Party Secretariat, and (assuming the minister of defense remains a military officer) on the State Council. Moreover, although the rate of turnover of high-ranking military officers has been high, the PLA is still a conservative organization, with interests in preserving a stable political order, ideological conformity, a controlled economy, and an emphasis on heavy industry.

The power of the military was strikingly revealed in the events surrounding the dismissal of Hu Yaobang as Party general secretary in early 1987. For years, Hu had sought the concurrent position as chairman of the Military Affairs Commission of the Party. But the military found him unacceptable and blocked his appointment. When the student protests swept across China in November and December 1986, the military joined with some conservative civilian leaders in demanding Hu's removal.

Over the longer term, it is not clear that the military has fully accepted a lesser role in Chinese political life. In the campaign against "bourgeois liberalization" in early 1987, for example, some military officers suggested that the military should be given more scope to combat the unorthodox and unacceptable ideas that had arisen in many quarters over the source of reform. The claim was reminiscent of the eve of the Cultural Revolution when, under Lin Biao, the PLA asserted its organizational and ideological superiority to the Party apparatus.

Still, the growing reform of Chinese politics, and the gradual transformation of the military into a more professional organization, should reduce the influence of the PLA in civilian affairs. So long as Chinese politics remains relatively stable, the PLA will be one interest group among many, although one that enjoys increasing influence over questions of military policy and national defense, and that retains a powerful voice on matters of civilian policy as well. But if there should be serious conflicts among the civilian leaders, and a collapse in the political norms that govern the resolution of those disputes, then the military retains the ability to intervene forcefully and possibly decisively in civilian affairs. Moreover, as the military becomes a more professional organization, the personal ties that have previously linked military commanders with their civilian counterparts will slowly erode. This development raises the possibility that, should the PLA again intervene in civilian affairs, it will do so at its own initiative and in pursuit of its own interests, rather than at the behest of any faction of the civilian leadership.[26]

The Party

Beginning in the mid-1950s, the Party became an ever greater force in the Chinese political process as the result of Mao's desire to place power in the hands of ideologically committed generalists instead of technically proficient specialists. The Party increasingly arrogated to itself the task of political administration that had originally been the responsibility of the state. The Party Secretariat and its functional departments superseded the State Council as the principal arena in which policy options were clarified and policy decisions translated into administrative guidelines. Party secretaries at all levels assumed responsibility for day-to-day decisionmaking, taking power away from government officials and enterprise managers. During the Cultural Revolution, the state apparatus was dismissed as a duplicative and redundant bureaucratic structure, and organizational reforms undertaken in the 1970s transformed the government bureaucracy into little more than the administrative arm of the Party.

The Cultural Revolution also saw a large increase in the size of the Party. Membership rose from about 20 million in 1965 to more than 35 million in 1977. By the time of Mao's death, about half of the Party had been recruited during the decade of the Cultural Revolution.[27] Although it would be incorrect to assume that all of these new Party members were devoted to Maoist values and programs, it is still true that they joined the organization when ideological commitment, as well as class background, were the principal criteria for recruitment. Many members recruited during this period could therefore be assumed to be skeptical about the post-Mao reforms, if not actively opposed to them.

These considerations have led to several serious changes in the Party since the early 1980s: the rectification of the Party organization to bolster support for reform; the recruitment of new Party members from different sectors of the Chinese population and with different political orientations than in the recent past; and, most important, the redefinition of the role of the Party to give other organizations somewhat greater autonomy.

After the fall of Hua Guofeng in 1981–82, as after earlier periods of leadership struggle in China, the Chinese Communist Party was the target of a rectification campaign, aimed at demoting the followers of discredited leaders, criticizing and discrediting their policies, and gaining greater understanding and support for the programs that the new Party leadership wanted to inaugurate. The rectification campaign following Hua's dismissal—which was also the first full-scale rectification movement after the purge of the Gang of Four—was announced at the Third Plenum in October 1983 and lasted for nearly four years. As in previous rectification movements, Party members were required to study compilations of documents that explained the goals of the campaign, examine their own performance according to those standards, and resolve to do better in the future. Rectification also provided the opportunity to reconstitute the leadership of the Party organization at all levels, from the provinces down to the grassroots.

Compared with the rectification movements of the late Maoist period, the rectification campaign of 1983–87 was orderly, moderate, and gradual. It unfolded slowly, from the central and provincial organs in 1983–84, to the middle levels in 1984–85, and finally to local branches in 1985–87. This step- by-step process avoided the disruption that might have been caused if the rectification had been conducted simultaneously at all levels of the Party. Moreover, the concept of "open-door rectification," so closely associated with Mao Zedong, was explicitly rejected in designing this first post-Mao rectification program. Here, the aim was to preclude the turmoil and conflict generated on previous occasions when people outside the Party had been authorized to criticize "unhealthy tendencies" or "erroneous policies" within the Party apparatus.[28]

One of the principal purposes of the Party rectification campaign was to expel from positions of leadership, and even from Party membership, the chief beneficiaries of the Cultural Revolution. According to the Central Committee resolution launching the campaign in 1983, the targets of the rectification fell into three categories: those who had been most active in the Red Guard and revolutionary mass organizations in the early phase of the Cultural Revolution, those who had gained power in the new government bodies and Party committee that were formed later in the Cultural Revolution, and those who had engaged in violence and disruption at any point between 1966 and 1976. As the rectification movement unfolded, it became evident that the turnover of high officials in the Party was substantial, but that the effect on the composition of the rank-and-file membership was much less serious. The final report on the campaign revealed that more than 200,000 members were expelled from the Party or denied the opportunity to renew their membership, and that more than 325,000 others received some lesser form of disciplinary action. Although the total number punished during rectification was large in absolute terms, and although the number expelled from the Party was more than five times as many as had originally been estimated, the victims of the movement still constituted little more than 1 percent of the Party's 47 million members.[29]

If the rectification was intended to increase the commitment of Party members to the post-Mao reform program, its success in doing so seems highly questionable. For one thing, the history of previous rectification campaigns demonstrates that they are better able to secure outward compliance than internal conversion. Through years of experience, Party members have learned how to pass through rectification programs passively, without having their political attitudes permanently remolded. Since accounts of the post-Mao rectification drive in the Chinese press—and even the official report on the movement presented to the Party—revealed that its implementation was often perfunctory, there is even more reason to believe that its impact was either minimal or transitory.

Furthermore, the aims of the rectification campaign were never clear or consistent. The focus of the movement was a subject of continuing controversy between the radical reformers and more conservative leaders: the radicals tried to use the campaign as a vehicle for promoting reform, whereas the skeptics attempted to direct it against the tendencies toward "bourgeois liberalization" that had allegedly arisen in the course of political relaxation and economic restructuring. In consequence, the themes of the rectification campaign changed constantly, as Chinese politics lurched from periods of retrenchment to periods of renewed reform throughout the mid-1980s.

Interestingly, neither group of leaders was completely satisfied with the results of the rectification. The radical reformers could take little pleasure in the fact that the rectification campaign was managed by Bo Yibo, a relatively conservative Party veteran, or that Deng Xiaoping was willing to compromise on the focus of the campaign as a way of preempting and coopting potential critics of the broader reform effort. Only on relatively brief and sporadic occasions, therefore, did the rectification campaign address the ideological and political obstacles to reform. Conversely, more conservative leaders have complained that they were prevented from dealing in a sustained or effective manner with the problems of "bourgeois liberalization" that arose in the early 1980s. In Bo Yibo's own words, "some leading comrades" (in other words, the radical reformers) had stressed "only the need to combat 'leftist' and not rightist ideas," thus allowing the development of a "widespread rightist ideological trend."[30]

If rectification is unlikely to have yielded a major transformation in the composition or attitudes of Party members, then a change in Party recruitment standards may produce somewhat greater results, at least over the longer run. During the Maoist period, the emphasis was placed on the class background and revolutionary commitment of potential Party members. Today, the reformers want to bestow Party membership on those groups that are believed to be among the strongest supporters of their program. To be sure, the Party—like mass communist parties anywhere—still seeks a fairly broad base of recruitment. A forum on Party recruitment conducted by the Party's organization department at the end of 1983, for example, continued to stress the desirability of drawing new members from workers, peasants, and military personnel. But for the first time since the mid-1950s, particular attention is being paid to recruiting intellectuals and college students. Of the 6.3 million new members admitted to the Party between 1980 and the middle of 1986, 22 percent were described as "technical professionals."[31] This figure corresponds with reports of Party recruitment at the provincial level, where about one-quarter of new Party members have been described as intellectuals.

These figures do not suggest that the Party is about to be dominated by intellectuals, but they do imply that those members with college education or technical training will gradually come to constitute a large and influential minority within the Party's ranks. Given the current emphasis on raising the educational qualifications for formal leadership positions, it is also very likely that the intellectuals now joining the Party will eventually occupy a disproportionate share of the administrative positions within the Party hierarchy.

Questions can properly be raised, however, about the feasibility of this new recruitment policy. In the past, the Party had little difficulty in attracting new members, if only because it was the most important channel of upward mobility in the country, and because it offered membership to those sectors of society whose low levels of education gave little hope of advancement through other channels. Today, in contrast, Party membership is no longer the sole source of social prestige or economic advancement. Individual and collective entrepreneurship now offers the opportunity for acquiring wealth, and the academic and managerial communities provide chances for gaining status and respect. Moreover, the demands of Party membership now conflict somewhat with the achievement of success through these alternative channels of upward mobility. Entrepreneurship implies the quest for profit, but Party members are still expected to pursue a life of frugality. Scholarship and invention imply freedom from ideological restraints, but Party members—much more than ordinary citizens—are still required to maintain a commitment to basic Marxist principles and premises.

Party membership may consequently now be much less appealing to many Chinese than was previously the case. It is true that the Party remains the most important route to political power at all levels of society, and membership in the Party will remain a prerequisite for those who wish to pursue political careers. But for those who are indifferent to politics, Party membership may now be seen as an unnecessary burden, rather than an attractive opportunity.[32]

Finally, the reform of the Party has included a reduction in its exercise of direct control over administrative matters, particularly at the middle and lower levels of Chinese society. According to the reformers, the growth of the Party's administrative power between the late 1950s and the late 1970s was undesirable for several reasons. The Party was neither large enough, nor skilled enough, to manage all the details of an increasingly complex economy. The concentration of political power in the hands of a closed, hierarchical organization contributed to the growing alienation of the Chinese people from their government and to the "crisis of confidence" of the early 1980s. Furthermore, if the Party was preoccupied with routine administrative work, it would be impossible for Party leaders to devote sufficient attention to more important concerns, such as setting long-term policy and educating the public in socialist values.[33] Indeed, if the Party were directly responsible for all administrative and political decisions, then the problems that Chinese society would inevitably encounter would be blamed on the Party's leadership. The Party should be monitoring and correcting the performance of other organizations, rather than directly assuming their responsibilities.[34]

The reformers say the Party should no longer be the "direct administrator, let alone the ruler," of the country.[35] This formula has implied a growing division of labor between the Party and the government, and between the Party and enterprise management, particularly at the grassroots. The jobs of first Party secretary and government chief executive at each level, held by the same person during most of the 1970s, have again been separated.[36] Party committees are not supposed to administer the day-to-day work of the government or give direct orders to government officials. And provincial governors, factory managers, and university presidents are gaining greater authority to make their own decisions and appoint their own subordinates, without first requiring the approval of the cognizant Party committee or Party secretary.

Nonetheless, if the Party is not supposed to be the "direct administrator" of the country, Chinese leaders still insist that it remain the "leader of national life." As one has put it, China's socialist system requires that "our Party exercise a planned and overall control over all national life, the development of the whole national economy and society, as well as the establishment of material and spiritual civilization." Deng Xiaoping made the same point even more directly in 1980, when he warned that if the principle of Party leadership were eliminated, "China will retrogress into divisions and chaos, and modernization would become impossible."[37]

Party leadership in post-Mao China is exercised through a variety of channels. Most important national policies are formulated by the central Party Secretariat, before being relayed to the state bureaucracy to be translated into detailed regulations and plans or to the national legislature to be set into law. At lower levels, too, Party committees still make decisions on all matters of basic policy and principle, even if they do not interfere in "routine work." In some places, when a county-level official wishes to convey a national or provincial decision downward to the grassroots for implementation, he will convene a meeting of township Party secretaries, rather than a conference of the heads of township governments.[38]

Second, the Party has maintained its web of cells and committees in all other important institutions: mass organizations, government agencies, and economic enterprises. It remains the responsibility of Party members and committees in those organizations to ensure that Party and state policies are effectively implemented. In January 1980, for example, Deng Xiaoping noted that the members of the Party committee in a factory should "always see to it that the production plans are met in terms of quantity, quality, and production costs, that their factory is technologically advanced and scientifically and democratically managed, that the managerial personnel have authority commensurate with their posts and can function efficiently and methodically, that the workers and office staff enjoy democratic rights and suitable working and living conditions." He also enumerated several other responsibilities that should still be borne by the Party committees. Deng denied that such a list of powers would give the Party a "finger in every pie," but subsequent discussions of factory autonomy have suggested, as already noted, that the Party retains a great deal of residual power over factory management.[39]

Finally, although the Party's control over personnel in other organizations has been reduced and decentralized, it retains the power to make all major appointments. Although there are now competitive elections for seats on people's congresses at the local level, all candidates are nominated in a process controlled by the Party. Managers and government officials may have the right to make a wider range of personnel appointments, but their decisions are still subject to review and approval by the organization departments of the Party. And enterprise managers are appointed by the Party personnel system, except in the case of a few smaller industrial enterprises where they are elected by the workers and staff. Despite a few proposals to end the Party's control over non-Party personnel altogether, the "cultivating, selecting, employing, and supervising" of government officials and enterprise managers is still regarded as one of the Party's most important functions.[40]

During the discussion of radical political reform in 1985–86, some radical reformers suggested further restrictions on the Party. Some argued that the autonomy of factories, universities, research institutions, and other basic-level enterprises could be guaranteed only if the Party committees in those units were completely disbanded. Others proposed that, given its dominance of the people's congresses, the Party could exercise policy guidance through legislative oversight rather than by giving directives to Party members working in the government bureaucracy. And as noted in chapter 7, some radical reformers wanted the Party to engage in direct electoral competition with other political parties and interest groups. These proposals reflected a common premise: limits on the power of the Party should not be grounded simply on the self-restraint of individual Party leaders and Party committees, but should be rooted in institutional procedures and safeguards that permanently limit the prerogatives of the Party.

These proposals did not receive a serious hearing in the the mid-1980s and are unlikely to gain one in the near future. Indeed, some of the radical reformers have criticized their own colleagues for wanting to go too far, too fast. Even so, despite the limits on the attenuation of the role of the Party, significant transformations are already under way. As noted in chapter 7, the Party no longer insists on obtaining active political commitment from all Chinese citizens, as it did during the Maoist era, but is content with more routinized programs of political education and with periodic efforts to eliminate "negative" or "deviant" attitudes. The Party no longer seeks to maintain direct control over all administrative details in China, but instead limits itself to formulating national policy and identifying and correcting the problems encountered in the course of modernization and reform. The Party no longer regards itself as mobilizing dispossessed and disenfranchised sectors of society, but seeks instead to identify and coopt China's emerging technical and intellectual elites. In short, the Party is now to act as a national manager, seeking to lead the system toward the goals the Party wants to pursue, but doing so after consultation with technical specialists and important interest groups.

The Government

If the PLA and the Party have lost some of their power and standing as the result of the post-Mao reforms, the government bureaucracy has been the principal beneficiary of many of these structural readjustments. Government officials are now much more influential in formulating economic policy than they were in the late Maoist period, and they have even acquired somewhat greater authority in some areas, such as culture and education, which had previously been the exclusive preserve of the Party.

The discussion of radical political reform in the middle of 1986, however, yielded some proposals that, if adopted, would seriously limit both the size of the government's economic bureaucracy and the extent of its control over the Chinese economy. As noted, the radical reformers believed that the autonomy of government agencies and basic-level units could not depend solely on the self-restraint of the Party, but would require the dismantling of many of the Party's grassroots organizations. Similarly, they were also convinced that the autonomy of state enterprises from bureaucratic interference could not rest completely on the self-discipline of government administrators. Instead, the reformers favored a big reduction in the size and power of the bureaucratic agencies responsible for the management of the economy.

Premier Zhao Ziyang explained the general concept behind this aspect of structural reform in his report on the Seventh Five-Year Plan, given at the National People's Congress in April 1986. Zhao said that the state should no longer be responsible for "assigning quotas, approving construction projects, and allotting funds and materials," which were its principal tasks under a system of mandatory planning. Instead, the government bureaucracy should conduct "overall planning, implement policies, organize coordination, provide services, use economic means of regulation, and exercise effective inspection and supervision." In short, as the economy was transformed from a centrally planned system into a regulated market, "the functions of the government departments concerned will have to change accordingly."[41]

Other Chinese officials and writers spelled out in greater detail some of the implications of this brief passage in the prime minister's report. One was that the government agencies responsible for the management of "products, industries, and trades" would be reduced in size or even abolished. In keeping with this premise, Peking announced in early 1987 that the Ministry of Machine Building and the Ministry of Ordnance Industry would be merged into a new State Commission of Machine Building, and there were hints that similar amalgamations might occur in commerce, foreign trade, culture, and education.[42] Some radical reformers spoke privately of eliminating most of the central industrial ministries, so that only a State Planning Commission and a Ministry of Industry and Trade, comparable to Japan's Ministry of International Trade and Industry, would survive.

Conversely, the state agencies responsible for economic regulation are to be strengthened. The chief beneficiaries of such a development would probably include the People's Bank of China, charged with managing the nation's monetary policy; the various specialized investment banks, responsible for the allocation of financial capital;

the State Statistical Bureau, the accuracy and relevance of whose data would be essential in the formulation of macroeconomic policy; the Ministry of Finance, charged with the setting of tax rates and the collection of state revenues; and the Ministry of Supervision and the Auditing Administration, responsible for ensuring the probity of state officials. The radical reformers have also shown an interest in creating or enlarging the government research institutes and commissions that design and implement the reform program, notably the Chinese Academy of Social Sciences, the State Commission for Restructuring the Economic System, and possibly a parallel state commission for political reform.

Third, the functions of the central planning agencies were also supposed to change. They would devote relatively less attention to formulating short-term production plans and place more stress on developing longer-range economic strategy, regulating the economy, and investigating and solving various social and economic problems.[43] Officials at the State Economic Commission, for example, suggested that they would focus less intensively on implementing the annual plan. Instead, they would be providing information to producers about the supply and demand of major products, evaluating and publicizing the quality of various capital goods and consumer products, and setting the ranges within which prices could float.

Finally, discussions of governmental reform have also suggested the desirability of a decentralization of administrative and legislative authority from the central government to the provinces and larger municipalities. Again, the details of the measures have not been announced, but it is likely that the reformers envision granting local governments greater power to enact their own regulations, adopt their own legislation, and adjust central policy to meet local conditions. Some of the responsibility for economic planning may also be transferred from the central planning agencies to their counterparts at the provincial and municipal levels. The problem is that, in practice, decentralization may run counter to the spirit of economic reform, in that it would give greater authority to local agencies that have both the desire and the capability to interfere directly in the operation of the marketplace.

Characteristically, experiments with some of these structural reforms were launched in several smaller cities in 1986. In Baoji, for example, functional Party departments that overlapped with government agencies were abolished, state bureaus that directly administered the economy were streamlined, and the departments responsible for policy research and information were enlarged.[44] But when Hu Yaobang fell from power in early 1987, this process of experimentation was only at a preliminary stage, and some radical reformers were discouraged at the lack of progress that had been achieved. It was not clear whether this aspect of political reform would be sustained, or abandoned, as China seemed to enter a more conservative period.

ARRANGING FOR THE SUCCESSION

As a final part of his effort to institutionalize the post-Mao reforms, Deng Xiaoping has also devoted much attention to creating a viable set of arrangements for political succession. His aim has been to forestall an intense conflict among contending leaders or a sudden change in national policy, similar to what occurred after the death of Mao Zedong in 1976.

Because Mao died in office as chairman both of the Party and of the Military Affairs Commission, his death created crucial political vacancies that had to be filled immediately. Mao had turned against those who had once been regarded as his heirs apparent—first Liu Shaoqi, then Lin Biao, and finally Deng Xiaoping— so that no leader was firmly established as Mao's successor. At the same time, there were deep cleavages between the beneficiaries and the victims of the Cultural Revolution, both of whom were well represented on the Politburo when Mao died. And, by launching the Cultural Revolution, Mao had seriously undermined the norms that might have regulated or moderated the waging of political conduct among these diametrically opposed groups.

Consequently, the succession arrangements that Mao left behind, a collective leadership built around Hua Guofeng, fell apart within weeks of Mao's death. Hua undertook a palace *coup* against the Gang of Four that was, in itself, a preemptive action against a similar coup that the Gang had allegedly been planning. Within six more years, Hua had been gently deposed, in favor of Deng Xiaoping, Hu Yaobang, and Zhao Ziyang.

Though Deng applauded the arrest and purge of the Gang of Four and personally masterminded the removal of Hua Guofeng, he has wanted to minimize the prospects of a similar episode occurring at the time of his own death. He has tried to design an institutionalized succession process so that the transition from one leader to another occurs as part of a regular circulation of elites rather than through occasional convulsive change. He has also sought to establish norms for moderating and resolving political conflict at the highest levels of the Party leadership.

Deng's succession arrangements seemed promising when they were first designed and implemented in the early 1980s. Gradually, however, the scheme decayed, as the leaders Deng tried to ease into retirement resisted their political demise, and as the successors that Deng tried to promote into higher office encountered objections and opposition from powerful groups and individuals. The sudden dismissal of Hu Yaobang as Party general secretary in January 1987 reflected the collapse of a major part of Deng's plan for the succession. It remains to be seen whether Deng can rebuild a viable succession arrangement in his few remaining years of active political life.

The Design of Deng's Succession Arrangements

As the first step in his succession strategy, Deng has sought the retirement of most senior members of the Politburo, so as to reduce the potential number of vacancies that the eventual demise of the most senior generation of Chinese leaders will produce. The task has been accomplished in three steps: in 1980 many elderly Party officials resigned from their concurrent positions on the State Council; in 1982, at the Twelfth Party Congress, a fairly small number of veteran leaders retired from the Politburo; and in 1985, at the National Party Conference, eight other senior Politburo members submitted their resignations. Several Politburo members have been transferred to the newly created Central Advisory Commission and Central Disciplinary Inspection Commission, easing their transition out of the first line of leadership. All told, the resignations and reassignments have reduced the number of senior leaders serving on the Politburo from eighteen (or two-thirds of the total membership) in 1982 to ten (or 45 percent) in 1985.

Nevertheless, as of early 1987 several powerful senior leaders well over the age of seventy, including Deng Xiaoping, Chen Yun, Li Xiannian, and Peng Zhen, remained on the Politburo and greatly influenced Party affairs. Other Party veterans who have been transferred to advisory positions, such as Wang Zhen, Bo Yibo, and Song Renqiong, still wielded power from the wings of the Chinese political stage. Because Deng still holds the position of chairman of the Military Affairs Commission, his death would create an important vacancy in a critical sector of the Party leadership. The deaths of the remaining veteran cadres will not be as fundamentally destabilizing as the deaths of Zhou Enlai and Mao Zedong in 1976. But they will not be as inconsequential for Chinese politics as the death of a former American president would be for the United States.

As the senior leaders have retired, Deng has sponsored the

selection of several generations of leaders to succeed them. As early as January 1980, Deng declared, "The primary task of veteran comrades is to select young and middle-aged cadres for promotion" into positions of leadership. "If we don't resolve it [this question] within three to five years," Deng warned his colleagues a year and a half later, "we shall be faced with catastrophe." The following year, Deng revealed that Chen Yun had proposed a program for training and promoting young and middle-aged cadres. In his address to the Twelfth Party Congress in 1982, Chen described the "smooth succession of younger cadres to older ones" as one of the most important challenges facing the Party.[45]

The successors that Deng sponsored between 1980 and 1985 fell into three echelons. At the top were the two men Deng had chosen to succeed him were he to die in the next few years: Hu Yaobang as general secretary of the Party and Zhao Ziyang as prime minister of the State Council. Below them was a second level of more junior leaders who were being groomed to succeed Hu and Zhao in due course: Hu Qili, Qiao Shi, Li Peng, and Tian Jiyun. By 1985 these four men had been placed on the Party Secretariat and each had received important administrative responsibilities. Hu Qili directed the day-to-day affairs of the Party; Qiao Shi was in charge of legal, political, and organizational matters in both the Party Secretariat and the State Council; Li Peng served as the vice-premier responsible for industry, science, and education; and Tian Jiyun was the vice-premier overseeing finance and economic reform.[46]

Below these leaders was a much larger group of even younger men and women who had been identified as potential leaders for both the Party and state organizations. In the early 1980s more than 100,000 cadres were selected as a "reserve force" of future officials. Drawn from the 2 million Chinese who had graduated from universities and polytechnical schools in the early 1960s, they were to obtain special training and receive promotions more rapidly than usual. By 1985, 1,000 of these young leaders had been placed at the ministerial and provincial levels, 20,000 in the central government bureaus and the prefectural governments, and another 100,000 at the county level. Moreover, a prominent member of that generation, Wang Zhaoguo (then aged forty-four), was appointed to the central Party Secretariat at the Twelfth Party Congress in 1985.[47]

By the mid-1980s, therefore, China seemed to be developing a regular system of promotion, rotation, and retirement. High-level service in government ministries, central Party departments, important mass organizations, or Party or state organizations at the provincial level constitute the key entry points to central leadership.

An individual's standing as a member of this pool of potential national leaders is confirmed by election to the Party's Central Committee. The most promising of the pool are appointed to the Party Secretariat, to positions as vice-premiers, or to both, with this ranking further certified by eventual election to the Party Politburo. Finally, one person emerges as general secretary of the Party and another as prime minister.

Retirements will also, under this scheme, be handled in routine fashion. Those ministers, vice-premiers, and Party secretaries who have not been selected for even higher positions will presumably retire at about age sixty-five. They may, however, retain a Politburo position, if they have achieved one, for a while longer. Those who are appointed as prime minister or Party general secretary will serve for one or two five-year terms. Then they may well be eased into partial retirement by election to a ceremonial position such as state president, head of the Chinese People's Political Consultative Conference, chairman of the National People's Congress, head of the Central Advisory Commission, or chairman of the Party's Central Discipline Inspection Commission. It originally appeared that the system of rotation would begin at the Thirteenth Party Congress in late 1987, and at the first session of the Seventh National People's Congress in early 1988, when Hu Yaobang and Zhao Ziyang would yield their positions as general secretary and prime minister to members of the second generation of successors.

Deng has sought to regulate and moderate conflict among the central political leaders by reinstating the norms of political competition that were seriously eroded during the decade of the Cultural Revolution. His goal has been to prevent political conflict from again becoming an all-out struggle for political survival and to develop mechanisms for deferring and resolving disagreements among the leadership.[48]

This aim has been achieved by reducing both the gains and the losses brought about through political competition. Many of Deng's organizational reforms reduce the power and privileges associated with political leadership. A more consultative style of politics, somewhat more stringent legal constraints on the exercise of political power, mandatory retirement ages and limited terms of office, and more meritocratic systems of recruitment and promotion are placing limits on political authority.

On the other side of the ledger, the costs of political defeat have also been reduced. Even those eased out of leading positions for political reasons, including both Hua Guofeng and Hu Yaobang, have not been denounced as "class enemies" or national traitors, as would have happened during the Cultural Revolution. Instead, they have been allowed a more graceful retirement into relative obscurity. The processes of organizational discipline have also been reformed so that the Party's disciplinary mechanisms can less readily be used as an instrument of factional conflict. And new norms have been created to restrain the mobilization of mass protest as a weapon in political struggle.

This aspect of political institutionalization can also be interpreted as an implicit bargain within the political leadership. Party leaders are expected to accept Party discipline, implement those decisions with which they disagree, and promote their preferred alternatives through orderly and peaceful procedures rather than through mass mobilization or factional maneuver. In return, they are guaranteed that national leadership will be exercised collectively, the power of individual leaders will be limited, affected interests will be consulted in the determination of national policy, and the rights of political minorities in the Party will be safeguarded.

The Collapse of Deng's Design for the Succession

Although they seemed to be carefully designed and well implemented, Deng's succession arrangements began almost immediately to encounter serious difficulties. Throughout the summer and fall of 1986, controversies surrounding the scheme became increasingly visible and intense, culminating in the premature dismissal of Hu Yaobang from his position as general secretary of the Party in January 1987. Although Hu's unacceptability to many powerful leaders and interest groups was critical in undermining the succession arrangements, other elements of the succession arrangement were also ill favored.[49]

Accusations of favoritism and nepotism plagued Deng's plans for the youngest generation of leaders. In 1981, when he called on the Party to find "one or two hundred thousand" younger leaders to be groomed as potential successors, Deng warned that the criteria used for selecting those leaders would have to be defined carefully. "To put it bluntly," Deng said, "the question of whether people are appointed on their merits or by favoritism has not been settled satisfactorily."[50] Nor was it effectively remedied later. Many Chinese believed that children of leading officials were being selected in large numbers as part of the "reserve force" of younger cadres. This so-called "princes' faction" received influential assignments in the Party, government, or armed forces in the mid-1980s and included the sons and daughters of former PLA marshals He Long, Ye Jianying,

Nie Rongzhen, and Chen Yi; of former Politburo members Li Weihan, Zhou Enlai, Ulanhu, and Liao Chengzhi; and of present Party leaders Wan Li, Xi Zhongxun, Yang Shangkun, and others.[51]

The rise of this favored group of cadre children caused opposition and resentment both inside and outside the Party. The Party's organization department tried to address these grievances, first by warning against favoritism and nepotism in the "reserve force" program and then by stipulating that promotions of the children of senior cadres should be specially reviewed by higher-level organization departments. Hu Yaobang apparently became personally interested in the controversy, launching an investigation of the economic crimes of the "princes' faction" in early 1986 and then proposing that the children of high-ranking officials be barred from membership on the Central Committee. By the end of August, it was announced that the "reserve force" program had become so unpopular that it had been canceled.[52]

A further shortcoming of the succession scheme was the lack of agreement among the Party veterans on the suitability of many of the members of the first and second echelons for positions of leadership. Within a few years after his appointment as the chief Party administrator in 1981, Hu Yaobang had acquired a reputation for making spontaneous statements that departed from established Party policy, tolerating those who expressed unorthodox views on ideological and political questions, and building a personal faction composed of former officials in the Communist Youth League, the organization that he had headed in the 1950s and 1960s. Hu Qili was seen by many more conservative leaders as predisposed to radical reform and was said to be too young to move directly into the post of general secretary of the Party. Tian Jiyun was held responsible for the inflation that had been connected with the price reform of early 1985; and Li Peng was considered in some quarters to be too sympathetic to the Soviet Union and to the Soviet model of economic planning. This failure to reach consensus about the details of the political succession reflected not only the shortcomings of particular candidates but also the remaining differences among the senior members of the Politburo and the Central Advisory Committee over the pace and scope of economic and political reform.[53]

Perhaps the most serious flaw in the succession arrangement was the reluctance of the most senior Party leadership to retire fully from political life. Some of those who had left the Politburo for advisory positions still wished to maintain an active role in Party leadership. Others who remained on the Politburo refused to retire until Deng Xiaoping agreed to join them. And Deng, who had apparently planned to retire fully at the Thirteenth Party Congress in 1987, began to hint that the political situation still would not permit him to do so.

By the middle of 1986, these developments began to wear away at Deng's original plan for a smooth political succession. Growing dissatisfaction with Hu Yaobang among senior Party leaders placed him under irresistible pressure to step down from the position of general secretary at the Thirteenth Party Congress in 1987. At the same time, however, it was increasingly clear that the military would not accept Hu as the chairman of the Military Affairs Commission, that Deng Xiaoping would not retire from an active role in Chinese political life, and that several of the other senior Party leaders might well try to cling to the honorific positions they held atop the Party and state bureaucracies. These prospects raised the possibility that when Hu retired from the Party Secretariat, there would be no prestigious advisory post into which he could gracefully move.

This stalemate apparently led to a confrontation between Deng and Hu at the Party work conference at Beidaihe in the summer of 1986 and at the subsequent Sixth Plenum in September. Given the fact that Hu had already lost the support of many senior Party leaders, this clash with the man who until then had been his principal political patron ensured that Hu Yaobang would be asked to retire as general secretary at the Thirteenth Party Congress. But the student demonstrations at the end of the year accelerated the process. The protests, and Hu's rather tolerant reaction to them, were seen as final evidence of Hu's laxity on political and ideological matters. In December, senior civilian and military leaders raised the demand for Hu's immediate resignation. In the end, Hu was forced to tender his resignation at an expanded meeting of the Politburo in the middle of January.

Officially, Hu Yaobang was charged with "errors," which were said to require his dismissal. He was accused of neglecting political work, tolerating the spread of liberal ideas in the Party, raising expectations for a rapid improvement in living standards, committing indiscretions in conversations with foreigners, and making decisions on domestic matters without consulting colleagues. Some accounts have suggested that the restructuring and restaffing of the Party were important in Hu's dismissal. Hu offended senior leaders by demands that one hundred more veterans be removed from the Central Committee at the Thirteenth Party Congress and by attempts to limit promotions for children of high-ranking cadres.

More generally, Hu's political travails could be said to reflect a "successor's dilemma," which is inherent in the succession arrangements in most personalistic, authoritarian political systems. On the one hand, Hu was well aware that Deng Xiaoping's active political life was nearing its end. If Hu were to succeed to Deng's position as China's preeminent political leader, he would have to build his own power base within the Party by staffing the Party bureauracy with trusted followers and by defining his own position on significant policy issues. In doing so, however, Hu ran the risk of alienating the senior generation of Party leaders, including Deng, whom he hoped to succeed. Hu's association with radical political reform, his persistent efforts to win the chairmanship of the Military Affairs Commission, and his attempts to promote the careers of men and women previously associated with him in the Communist Youth League were designed to strengthen his political position in the post-Deng era. But, in the end, these measures were Hu's undoing, as they turned influential Party veterans, and Deng Xiaoping, against him.

CONCLUSION

The dismissal of Hu Yaobang in early 1987 dramatized the limits to political institutionalization in post-Mao China. The confrontation between Hu and the Party veterans revealed the absence of clear and accepted norms defining the authority of the general secretary, specifying the power of senior Party cadres who had retired into advisory positions, establishing terms of office for high Party officials, or providing for the removal of a general secretary when he had lost the confidence of most of the Politburo. Indeed, the fact that Hu's resignation was accepted by an irregular session of the Politburo, attended by members of the Central Discipline Inspection Committee and the Central Advisory Committee, aroused heated debate among observers in both Hong Kong and the mainland over whether the action was in accordance with the provision of the Party constitution. At a minimum, Hu's ouster before the Thirteenth Party Congress violated the rudimentary norms on fixed terms of office for national leaders, and his replacement as acting general secretary by Premier Zhao Ziyang infringed the embryonic rule requiring the separation of Party positions from government offices.

The removal of Hu Yaobang also illustrated how much the Chinese political system centered around the personal authority of Deng

Xiaoping. Although Deng had withdrawn from active involvement in the details of policymaking in China, he remained the final source of authority in Chinese politics, the one who made or approved the most important decisions on policy and personnel. Moreover, although Deng had attempted to provide Chinese politics with more stability and predictability, he had nonetheless used highly personal and irregular measures on occasion to launch and sustain reform. Deng's endorsement of the principles of majority rule and Party discipline ran counter to his ruthless and effective efforts to undermine the authority of Hua Guofeng. Deng may have criticized Mao for attempting to name his own successor, but he also selected Hu Yaobang and Zhao Ziyang as his heirs apparent. And Hu's removal in early 1987 occurred primarily because he had lost the personal support and confidence of Deng Xiaoping.

Deng must act quickly and decisively if he is to rebuild the succession arrangements that were so seriously undermined by the events of late 1986 and early 1987. In the present Chinese context, the new general secretary will have to be more skillful, more collegial, and more respected than Hu Yaobang. It will be necessary to select a pool of talented second- and third-generation leaders from whom effective general secretaries and prime ministers can be drawn in the future. The norms concerning promotions, retirements, and rotations that were seriously weakened by the Hu Yaobang affair must be reestablished, and new principles governing the division of power between the general secretary and senior Party advisers must be created. Above all, a smooth succession will require the full retirement of the most senior generation of Party leaders so that their deaths will not create a destabilizing vacuum at the highest levels of the Chinese political system.

These important problems should not obscure, however, the accomplishments that Deng Xiaoping has achieved in his efforts to create a more stable and institutionalized political system. Deng has been able to retire large numbers of superannuated cadres from all levels of the Chinese bureaucracy. He has established new norms of political life that moderate the expression of differences and regulate the resolution of disputes. Although the succession to Deng may still be a difficult process, it is unlikely that it will be characterized by the violent struggles, mass mobilization, sweeping purges, and drastic changes in domestic and foreign policy that accompanied the death of Mao.

PART 3

The Future of Reform

CHAPTER 9

China and the International Community

FOR at least one hundred and fifty years, the world has awaited the modernization of China with both anticipation and apprehension. When compared with the advanced nations of Europe, and even with the Japan of the Meiji era, the China of the nineteenth and early twentieth centuries was technologically backward, economically stagnant, and politically divided. Nonetheless, Western strategists recognized early on that China's size, resources, and culture gave it enormous, and worrisome, potential. Napoleon is credited with the admonition that China should be allowed to sleep on, undisturbed. "When she wakes," he allegedly said, "she will shake the world." Franklin D. Roosevelt also foresaw the growing power of China, but he depicted it in more benevolent terms. Throughout World War II, Roosevelt insisted that China should eventually join the United States, Great Britain, and the Soviet Union as one of the four great powers that would guarantee the peace in a postwar world.

The awakening of China anticipated by Napoleon and Roosevelt does not date simply from the death of Mao Zedong in 1976. Ever since the Chinese Communist Revolution of 1949—some would say since the May Fourth movement of the late 1910s, or even since the self-strengthening movement of the late nineteenth century—China has been stirring. Even in the late Maoist period, before the reforms initiated by Deng Xiaoping, China was already widely considered an important force in international affairs. In the early 1970s, Henry Kissinger spoke of a five-sided international system, composed not only of the United States and the Soviet Union, but also of Japan, Europe, and China. Other analysts, in both the Soviet Union and the United States, talked about a "strategic triangle," in which Peking, Moscow, and Washington determined the balance of power in world politics. As they had for more than a century,

Western merchants saw China as perhaps the greatest untapped economic market in history, with a billion eager consumers and a nearly insatiable demand for modern technology.

These perceptions of China did not mean that the country, in any material sense, was the equal of the superpowers or even of Japan and Western Europe. China was, as it is today, a developing nation, whose aggregate wealth was a fraction of that of the Soviet Union, let alone that of the United States. During the later years of Mao's rule, China's gross national product per capita placed it in the ranks of some of the poorer nations of the third world. Its technology was obsolescent and was steadily falling behind world standards. Its military forces, although large in numbers, were deficient in equipment, training, and organization.

But China's size, strategic location, and independence from the two superpowers allowed it to occupy a "swing" role in international affairs that no other nation could match. No other major actor in global politics—not Japan, not Western Europe, and not Eastern Europe—could plausibly threaten to shift sides in the world strategic balance, moving from alignment with one superpower to tacit cooperation with another. No other large developing country—not Indonesia, not Nigeria, not Brazil—had its natural resources so magnified by a strategic location. And no other nation, not even India, could offer to Western commerce an untapped market of the scale of China's.

Furthermore, China had deployed limited material resources with special flair. In the mid-1950s, Peking started a surprisingly large and successful foreign aid program, sometimes providing technical and economic assistance to countries whose per capita income was larger than that of China. Through the clarity and self-assurance of its foreign policy doctrine, and through the skill and poise of its diplomats, China became a principal commentator on world developments. In its support of national liberation movements and communist insurgencies on three continents, Peking threatened the internal stability of those governments that had displeased it. And on numerous occasions, in Korea, in the Taiwan Strait, along the Sino-Indian and Sino-Soviet frontiers, as well as more recently in Vietnam, China showed a willingness to use its modest military resources in support of foreign policy objectives, even against more powerful adversaries.

In the post-Mao era, China's material resources are growing even more rapidly, enabling the country to realize even more of its potential. China's second revolution seems to have reversed the slow decline in economic growth rates that had plagued the late

Maoist period. The revival of scientific research, the development of academic exchange with foreign countries, and the import of foreign equipment are helping to raise China's technological level. China's economic and political reforms are again capturing the attention of much of the world, particularly in the socialist camp and among the developing nations, although those who are attracted by the Chinese model of today are often very different from those whose imagination was captured by the revolutionary Maoism of the late 1960s and early 1970s. China is committed to a long-term program of military modernization, with preliminary results already evident in better organization, improved training, updated tactics, and more sophisticated equipment.

Moreover, the arenas in which China is deploying resources are also expanding. China is now a member of almost all the major international organizations. It has vastly increased the level of foreign trade, broadened its range of trading partners, and expanded the scope of commodities that it buys and sells. It is not only welcoming foreigners to invest in China but is also beginning to make investments overseas. Its cultural, educational, scientific, and tourist exchanges have increased dramatically since the death of Mao Zedong little more than ten years ago. And although its influence remains limited, China's diplomatic reach now extends far beyond Asia, into Africa, Europe, the Middle East, and even Latin America.

From a broad historical perspective, these recent developments mean an unprecedented awakening for China on at least two dimensions. For the first time in history, the mainland of China is ruled by an effective government, with firm control over its territory, that is committed to sustained economic modernization as its highest priority. None of the previous regimes interested in reform and modernization, such as the government of the Kuang-hsü Emperor in 1898, or the government of Chiang Kai-shek in the late 1920s and early 1930s, were able to consolidate their power. Conversely, all the earlier Chinese governments that had established firm control over the country's vast population had been committed to other goals, be they the order and stability of the traditional imperial order or the continuing revolution of Mao Zedong. The combination of effective government and sustained modernization is unique to post-Mao China.

Second, for the first time since the late nineteenth century, China is seen as a powerful and legitimate force in international affairs. No longer is China viewed as the "sick man of Asia," or as a "derelict hulk" adrift in the seas of world politics. No longer is

China regarded as the satellite of a foreign power, as it was widely, if inaccurately, believed to be in the mid-1950s; or as a nation committed to the undermining and destruction of the international system, as it was generally, and perhaps somewhat more justly, considered in the mid-1960s. Today, China is seen as an important, independent, regional power, with growing global influence.

THE CURRENT IMPACT

If the first half of Napoleon's prophecy is rapidly being fulfilled, the second half is more problematic. Will the growth of China's political, economic, and military power shake the world, or shore it up? Thus far, China's emergence in the last decade has been a fairly positive and stabilizing development. Nonetheless, a few disturbing undertones give many of China's neighbors pause as they look toward the future.[1]

The positive features of Chinese foreign policy in the post-Mao era stem from the overriding priority of economic development. At a meeting of Chinese ambassadors in 1985, for example, Hu Yaobang and Zhao Ziyang emphasized the concept of "economic diplomacy," which they defined as the use of foreign relations to serve modernization. Commenting on the meeting, a communist newspaper in Hong Kong noted that "foreign policy is the extension of a country's domestic policy" and that Chinese foreign policy should therefore be placed in the service of China's "greatest national interest," which is now economic development.[2]

The emphasis placed on economics in China's contemporary foreign relations has had several manifestations and implications. Perhaps the most fundamental is Peking's desire for a peaceful and stable international environment so that China can devote as much energy as possible to the task of modernization and reform. As Deng Xiaoping put it in 1984, "China needs at least twenty years of peace to concentrate on our domestic development."[3] In keeping with this principle, China has adopted what can well be described as a policy of omnidirectional peaceful coexistence. With the exception of Vietnam, the People's Republic has tried to improve relations with its traditional rivals and adversaries, including India, Indonesia, and the Soviet Union. In contrast to the mid-1970s, when Peking encouraged the United States to undertake more forceful and effective resistance to Soviet expansion in the third world, and when it warned that arms control agreements between the two superpowers could only ratify and institutionalize the superior military position of the Soviet Union, China has more recently encouraged a reduction of tensions between Moscow and Washington and tentatively endorsed the arms control negotiations between them.

Peking's emphasis on economic development also implies China's acceptance of the legitimacy of the current international economic and political system. In the late Maoist period, China seemed bent on overthrowing the international order or at least making revolutionary changes in it. It called at various times for widespread "people's war" against the two superpowers, disparaged the United Nations and other international organizations, gave moral and material support to radical movements overseas, and proposed the creation of a "new international economic order." Today, such rhetoric has almost disappeared from Chinese commentary on international affairs. Peking has reduced, if not eliminated, even moral support for revolutionary movements in the third world. It has joined almost every significant international organization and has taken an active and constructive role in their work. Although China continues to advocate changes in the international economic system that would benefit the developing countries, its proposals for reform are less radical, less comprehensive, and less prominent than they were in the mid-1970s; and Peking advocates that they be adopted through negotiation and compromise, rather than through confrontation, between North and South.[4]

Finally, growing flexibility and pragmatism has characterized China's foreign relations in recent years. Although the repudiation of the doctrines of the past has not been as thoroughgoing in foreign affairs as in domestic matters, the Chinese have quietly abandoned the ideological framework that once provided both consistency and rigidity to its conduct of foreign affairs. Thus the "theory of the three worlds," announced by Mao Zedong and Deng Xiaoping in 1974, fully elaborated in 1977, and noted favorably in the resolution on Party history of 1981 as one of the few worthy theoretical innovations of the late Maoist period, is now rarely mentioned in discussions of the conceptual underpinnings of Chinese foreign policy.[5] Nor are analyses of international affairs constructed around the same ideological categories as in the past. Neither the United States nor the Soviet Union is frequently described as an imperialist power, although many of their policies are still called examples of superpower "hegemonism." China still claims that the attempts of Moscow and Washington to establish global and regional dominance are resisted by smaller countries, but it no longer depicts this process as an international "united front" or as a "people's war" on a global scale.

Instead, China now deals with international issues on a pragmatic, case-by-case basis, finding common ground with each superpower on some issues while opposing it on others. As Premier Zhao Ziyang said in 1986, Peking will determine its position on international questions "on the merits of each case" and will not base "closeness with or estrangement from other countries on the basis of their social systems and ideologies."[6] Thus China is usually supportive of American policy in Asia, particularly toward Indochina and Afghanistan, indicates its general approval of American military deployments in the region, and is more willing privately to acknowledge common interests with the United States even on sensitive issues like Korea and Taiwan. Peking remains, however, critical of American positions in the Middle East, South Africa, and Latin America. Similarly, China sharply opposes the Soviet military buildup in East Asia and its interventions in Afghanistan and Indochina. But Chinese views on some aspects of strategic arms control—for example, the Strategic Defense Initiative and nuclear free zones—parallel those of the Soviet Union.

China's new pragmatism has enabled Peking to be more flexible in dealing with sensitive issues than it was in the past, exemplified by Peking's acceptance of a range of economic relationships once regarded as ideologically proscribed. Similarly, in negotiations with Great Britain over the future of Hong Kong, Peking entered into a joint declaration that was more generous, more explicit, and more binding than most observers had believed would be possible. On other issues affecting the sensitive question of national sovereignty—from the nuclear cooperation agreement with the United States to the procedures for obtaining standby credit from the International Monetary Fund—Peking has also proved relatively supple and forthcoming. These developments reflect not only the openmindedness of China's current leadership but also a more professional and institutionalized process of foreign policymaking in Peking.

However, the rise of China's economic power and diplomatic clout in recent years has also been accompanied by a growing nationalism in Chinese foreign policy.[7] It is true that China denies any intention of becoming a superpower and insists that it remains a developing country sharing a common lot with the rest of the third world. As Deng Xiaoping assured a visiting foreign dignitary in May 1984, "China will always belong to the Third World . . . [and] will remain there even when it becomes prosperous and powerful, because China will never seek hegemony or bully others."[8] But Chinese leaders increasingly qualify this familiar assertion by adding that China, as a major power, occupies a status that sets it apart from other developing countries. One purpose of modernization and reform, officials say, is to build a successful and powerful China that will become more influential in international affairs. By the year 2000, Deng Xiaoping has pointed out, China could have an annual military budget of about $50 billion simply by allocating 5 percent of its gross national product to national defense. By the turn of the century, Deng continued, "China will be truly powerful, exerting a much greater influence in the world."[9]

Today, as in the past, Chinese nationalism has both official and popular components. The emergence of nationalistic elements in Chinese foreign policy is an integral part of the Party's increasing invocation of nationalistic appeals to bolster the legitimacy of a regime whose ideology provides a less powerful source of enthusiasm and support. Thus Chinese leaders at the highest level emphasize the need for reunifying the country under a single national government, stress China's growing wealth and power, and promise that, under their aegis, China will once again play a major role in the politics and economics of the Asian-Pacific region. That this appeal has struck a responsive cord among the Chinese people is suggested by the signs of mass nationalism that seem independent of official sponsorship and, frequently, outside central control. Spontaneous demonstrations have taken place after international sporting events, bearing a patriotic flavor when the Chinese team has won but possessing xenophobic undertones when China has lost. At the end of 1985, a wave of student protests occurred in several Chinese cities, protesting among other things the alleged revival of militarism in Japan and the growing Japanese economic presence in China.[10] A nationalistic mood is readily evident among younger Chinese intellectuals, one of whom told a gathering of Americans that his generation wants China to become the "benevolent leader of the whole world."

China's growing nationalism manifests itself in several ways. Strategically, it can be seen in the conviction that China should be an independent force in international geopolitics, with no formal alliance, or even an informal alignment, with either superpower. Nationalism is evident in territorial issues as well, as China stresses regaining sovereignty over Hong Kong and Macao, reunifying Taiwan with the mainland, and resolving border issues on favorable terms. Chinese leaders also insist that their economy not become dependent on, or unduly penetrated by, foreign interests or institutions; and they want China to be accorded equal, if not favorable, treatment in the international marketplace. And the desire to maintain a distinctively Chinese culture, uncontaminated by too much contact with Western ideas and values, can appropriately be described as a form of cultural nationalism.

Thus a blend of peaceful coexistence, economic interaction, and policy flexibility, combined with strategic, territorial, economic, and cultural nationalism, characterizes the post-Mao era. This combination of divergent tendencies helps explain the ambivalent attitudes about China that prevail in so much of Asia.

On the one hand, Peking's dedication to the tasks of economic development and reform seems to be producing an interest in a peaceful international environment, global economic prosperity, and conciliatory relations with its neighbors. Moreover, modernization also sharply reduces the possibility of two circumstances that, in the past, caused China to be a destabilizing force in Asia. No longer will China be a weak and disunified country that invites intervention and aggression by great powers, as was true in the first half of this century. And no longer is China a revolutionary force that supports insurgencies against neighboring governments or seeks to subvert international institutions, as was true during parts of the Maoist period. For these reasons, the rest of the region welcomes the present stage in Chinese foreign policy.

On the other hand, modernization means that Peking will have greater material resources with which to pursue goals in international affairs, and increasing Chinese nationalism raises the possibility that those goals may be defined in ways that compete or conflict with the interests of other Asian states. China's neighbors are acutely aware that, in the premodern period, China was the preeminent political and cultural force in East Asia, and they fear that a resurgent and modernizing China might attempt to reassert itself in an updated style. They recognize, too, that Peking still adopts the style of a *demandeur* in foreign relations, expressing moral indignation at any signs of being treated in ways that it considers unequal or unjust. They are understandably apprehensive, therefore, that the rise of Chinese power will, in the end, be a disruptive force in the Asian-Pacific region rather than a stabilizing factor.

Many Asians try to resolve this contradiction by hoping that, in the somewhat facetious words of a prominent Japanese sinologist, "China will continue to devote all of its energies to the tasks of modernization, but never succeed." In that circumstance, China would continue to be interested in a peaceful and stable international environment and in beneficial economic relations with its neighbors, but the People's Republic would never develop the power to pursue assertive foreign policy goals. This hope, while understandable, is unrealistic. Inevitably, China's commitment to a course of modernization will increase its national power and resources by the end of the century, enlarging its influence on the international economy, the global strategic balance, the Asian geopolitical environment, and the issues of territory and sovereignty along China's borders.

PROSPECTS

Before examining these four subjects in detail, two general observations are in order. A careful assessment of the impact of China's modernization on the international community warrants neither overly sanguine nor excessively apocalyptic scenarios. As the world's experience with Britain, France, Japan, Germany, the United States, and the Soviet Union has amply indicated, the rise of a great power is never a smooth or easy process. China's increasing military strength, economic activity, and political ambitions will inevitably cause tensions with certain countries, at certain times, over certain issues. Even so, it is difficult to conclude that China will be a fundamentally disruptive factor in either the strategic or the economic arenas. For one thing, since China is a large, continental nation, foreign markets and imported raw materials will always remain a secondary source of its economic growth. Moreover, China faces a far more stable and vital environment in Asia, and enjoys a much greater stake in the existing international order, than did Japan during the first half of this century. It is unlikely that China will seek or obtain regional hegemony through the exercise of raw military force.

Second, China's future involvement in international affairs will largely depend on the fate of domestic political and economic reform. Continued reform will increase China's competitiveness in the international economy, maintain China's incentives for a cooperative relationship with the United States, ease Hong Kong's reversion to Chinese sovereignty, and facilitate the resolution of the question of Taiwan. Conversely, retrogression toward a more administered economy and a more tightly controlled political system may restrict China's foreign economic interactions, encourage a further reconciliation with the Soviet Union, and complicate the reunification of Hong Kong and Taiwan with the Chinese mainland. Furthermore, if a retreat from reform were to be accompanied by a rise in an assertive or xenophobic form of Chinese nationalism, the development would almost certainly disrupt China's relations with many of its neighbors in the Asian-Pacific region.

As noted in the next chapter, although a retreat from reform is conceivable, the degree of retrogression is almost certain to be limited, and thus the impact on China's foreign relations will be moderate. Even if reform should falter, China is unlikely to return to the policies of economic autarky, strategic confrontation, and global revolution that characterized the most radical days of the Maoist period. Although the details of its policies would probably change, China would continue to maintain an interest in extensive interaction with the international economy, a stable environment in East Asia, and relative independence from both superpowers.

The International Economy

The fact that a country of China's size has become more interested in international commerce has led both to eager anticipation that the People's Republic will become a huge customer for other nations' exports and to grim apprehension that it will become a powerful competitor with other countries for capital and markets abroad. In reality, however, even though China's involvement in the international economy has increased markedly during the past ten years, the impact of that development has been less dramatic than extreme forecasts might have led one to expect. At the global level, China has not produced a fundamental change in the patterns of international trade and finance. The effect of China's policy of opening to the outside world becomes apparent only when one examines particular countries and particular commodities.

China's role in the world economy is still smaller than its vast territory and huge population might suggest. Despite the rapid growth in China's imports and exports, for example, two-way trade in 1985 still represented only about 1.98 percent of world totals, a small increase over the 1.95 percent share it enjoyed in 1959. Nor has China's entry into the world economy caused a great diversion of international capital flows. The commitments of $4.2 billion extended to China by the World Bank between 1981 and 1986 constitute only 4.8 percent of the bank's total lending during the same period. Despite its size, the financing that China has secured from the World Bank is only 68.4 percent of that extended to Indonesia, and 30.8 percent of that provided to India. China's net indebtedness at the end of 1985 was slightly more than 2.0 percent of the world total; and direct foreign investment in China in 1985 was a bit more than 4.0 percent of the global total.[11]

If one examines China's trade with certain geographic entities, however, then China's importance increases somewhat. The only major trading partner to which China is critically important is Hong Kong, about a quarter of whose trade in 1985 was conducted with the mainland. But both Japan and Singapore now have a big stake in their trade with China. In 1985 the People's Republic accounted for 7.1 percent of Japanese exports, a great increase over the 3.0 percent to 4.0 percent share that China had enjoyed earlier in the decade. Similarly, China supplied 8.2 percent of Singapore's imports—largely crude oil—also a rise over the 2.0 percent to 3.0 percent share that China had provided in the earlier years. Still, for all its other principal trading partners, including the United States and Western Europe, China constituted less than 5 percent of imports and exports, making it a relatively minor factor in their overall trading patterns.[12]

China has also gained a large share of the sales and purchases of some major trade commodities. Although China represents slightly less than 2.0 percent of total world trade, in 1985 it accounted for 8.5 percent of iron and steel imports, 7.9 percent of textile exports, and 7.6 percent of world clothing sales. In each case, this represented a doubling or trebling of China's share over 1975. For other major commodities, the China factor is smaller, but still significant. In 1985 China purchased 2.4 percent of world imports of machinery and equipment (up from 0.7 percent in 1975), and imported 3.7 percent of world sales of fabrics and fibers (up from 0.3 percent in 1975). In 1983 it accounted for 3.7 percent of cereals imports (higher than 1975, but lower than in the early 1980s), and 2.4 percent of world coal exports (up from 1.5 percent in 1975). In no case did China dominate world markets, but it had clearly become important in shaping them.[13]

China's greatest impact has been on certain industries in certain countries. Even in the United States, China has made a mark as both an importer and an exporter. China is a principal market for Washington State, for example, absorbing a large share of the state's exports of aircraft and lumber. China has also proved an effective competitor, sometimes devastatingly so, for American producers of such commodities as industrial cloth, clothespins, dinnerware, and mushrooms.[14]

For the rest of the century, China will probably continue to stress economic modernization and active participation in the international marketplace. In the aggregate, China's trade is likely to increase considerably between now and the year 2000, but with the rate of growth heavily dependent on how much domestic reforms increase the productivity and efficiency of Chinese industry. Independent forecasts by the World Bank and by Rock Creek Research, an independent American research firm specializing in the Chinese economy, suggest two broad possibilities. If China can sustain reform, and if those reforms gain further increases in economic efficiency, then China's two-way trade in the year 2000 will probably be in the range of $200 billion to $250 billion. If reform falters, or if for any reason productivity stays at present levels, then China's foreign trade will probably reach only $140 billion to $200 billion at the turn of the century.[15]

Even under the more optimistic of these two scenarios, however, China's foreign trade will increase more slowly in the next decade than in the early part of the post-Mao era. If China's two-way trade were to reach $225 billion in the year 2000, that would have meant an average growth rate of 8.1 percent each year over 1985, considerably less than the average of 19.7 percent that China enjoyed between 1978 and 1985. The more pessimistic scenario forecasts slower growth, perhaps 6.1 percent each year on the average. Accordingly, the ratio of trade to gross national product may well fall between now and the year 2000, from about 26.0 percent in 1985 to around 20.0 percent at the end of the century.

There are also two broad forecasts of China's need for foreign credit by the end of the century. If reforms continue, and the efficiency of China's export industry increases, then China's export earnings will grow more rapidly and its trade deficit would be limited. Conversely, should the reforms falter, then China's export potential would be lower, and the trade deficit would grow faster. The World Bank has projected total Chinese indebtedness at $128 billion to $158 billion current dollars in the year 2000, which would be equivalent to $57 billion to $70 billion in 1985 dollars.[16] The trade projections conducted by Rock Creek Research suggest comparable figures. The World Bank has pointed out that the service of this debt, at about 12 percent of exports, would be well within even the conservative ceiling of 15 percent that Peking has established for its debt service ratio.[17]

The impact of China's growing participation in the international economy between now and the year 2000 will depend on the growth of world trade during the same period. If China's trade should treble (rising from $70 billion in 1985 to $210 billion in the year 2000), and if world trade grows at an average annual rate of 5.0 percent, then China would represent about 2.5 percent of total world trade volume, somewhat more than it does today. If world trade were to grow at only 3.5 percent, however, then China would come to account for about 3.0 percent of the total. And if the growth of world trade were sluggish, increasing at an annual average of only 2.0 percent, then China might be responsible for 3.8 percent of total trade flows.

These forecasts do not warrant alarm over China's future in the international economy. Even under the most extreme projections, China's share of world trade at the turn of the century will not exceed 3.8 percent, less than that enjoyed by the Soviet Union in 1983 and only slightly greater than that of Italy. Exports will be constrained by the growing domestic demand for everything that China sells abroad—from energy to foodstuffs to manufactured goods—and by the inefficiencies and irrationalities of the Chinese industrial system. Nor, unlike Japan or the newly industrialized countries and regions, will China need to export in order to acquire large markets or to afford scarce raw materials. Imports will be restricted by the limits on the growth of exports and by China's cautious strategy toward international borrowing. The projections of China's capital requirements also suggest that China's demands on international financial markets will be fairly modest and acceptable. In a fundamental sense, the world economy has already accommodated the entry of China. In the future, therefore, the necessary adjustments to the growth of the Chinese economy should be more marginal in nature.

Nevertheless, although the growth of China's trade over the rest of the century should not unacceptably strain the international marketplace as a whole, it will certainly cause tensions for certain countries, in certain commodities, and at certain times. The impact will depend, above all, on the composition of Chinese trade. The principal issue is whether the trends already apparent in the composition of Chinese trade accelerate or whether the pace of change now begins to slow. Three trends will be especially important: how speedily China abandons the export of primary products (including foodstuffs, energy supplies, and raw materials) in favor of manufactures; the pace at which Chinese industry can shift from the export of labor-intensive items to the export of capital-intensive or even technology-intensive products; and the rate at which China replaces the import of machinery and equipment for its present imports of grain and industrial materials.

Most forecasts agree that the future composition of Chinese trade—like its total volume—will hinge on the fate of reform. If reform persists, then Chinese industry will have a greater ability to absorb foreign technology, increase domestic production of food and raw materials, produce goods that will be competitive on international export markets, and shift from labor-intensive manufactures to more capital-intensive or technology-intensive goods such as automobile parts or consumer electronics. Conversely, if the reforms slacken or reverse, the composition of China's trade will be more resistant to change: China will import more materials and foodstuffs from abroad and will export more primary goods and labor-intensive products. Forecasts by both Rock Creek Research and the World Bank show great differences in both the share and total volume of manufactured exports, depending on the development strategy China adopts.

These different scenarios will, of course, have important implications for China's trading partners and competitors. If the course of reform is sluggish, then China will continue to compete primarily with the other less developed countries, including those in South and Southeast Asia, which mostly export primary products and labor-intensive manufactures. All these countries will engage in extended competition to sell goods of fairly low export value on saturated markets in the developed nations. If, however, industrial reform enables China to become an efficient exporter of consumer electronics and industrial parts, then China may increasingly compete with the exports of the newly industrialized countries and regions elsewhere in Asia. Similarly, the more successful reform is, the more China will be able to turn to both the developed nations and the newly industrialized countries to supply it with more advanced technology and equipment than it can produce at home.

China's greater participation in the international economy is likely to generate four sets of issues that will require careful management in the years ahead. The first is the growth of Chinese exports. China's attempts to gain larger market shares for its exports, whether in labor-intensive manufactures or in more capital-intensive or technology-intensive products, will mean stiff competition for producers in other countries. Particularly if the growth in the world economy should slow, China's emergence as a significant exporter will intensify pressures for protectionism against China, expressed by limits and quotas on imports of Chinese goods and by restrictions on the export of technology to China. Protectionist pressures will intensify if China adopts a beggar-thy-neighbor policy, seeking through predatory pricing and marketing strategies to gain a larger market share while continuing to employ various regulatory procedures to close its markets to foreign imports.

The likely patterns in the direction of China's foreign trade will also produce tensions in its relations with trading partners. For the foreseeable future, China will engage in a form of triangular trade.

It will experience deficits in commercial relations with the developed countries and attempt to offset them with surpluses in trade with the developing nations. Both sides of this triangle are likely to become controversial. Chinese leaders still, to a large degree, seek balances in their trade with the developed countries. The structural deficits likely to occur in China's commercial relations with Japan, the European Community, and the United States will be, from the Chinese perspective, a constant irritant in Peking's political ties with those countries. Conversely, countries in Southeast Asia have begun to complain of the deficits that are emerging in their trade with the People's Republic and are pressuring China to open its markets to their exports of both primary commodities and manufactured goods.[18]

Third, China's involvement in international economic institutions raises issues of policy and equity that will require careful consideration. Both the World Bank and the Asian Development Bank must weigh China's needs against the demands and requirements of other large Asian borrowers, including both India and Indonesia. Members of the General Agreement on Tariffs and Trade (GATT) will have to determine the conditions under which China would be entitled to full membership in the organization. Despite the reforms of the last decade, Peking has not yet created an open trading system that meets the standards for membership in the GATT. Would promises to increase Chinese imports, similar to those made by Eastern European countries at the time of their admission to membership, warrant full Chinese participation in the GATT? Or should the GATT require more concessions from Peking, such as further progress toward relaxing administrative controls over imports, exports, and prices?[19]

Finally, the cycles that have characterized China's economic relations during the last decade, if they recur, will strain its relations with the international economy. Sudden surges in China's imports, fueled both by excessive domestic investment and by strong demand for foreign consumer goods, have periodically created crises in China's current accounts. On such occasions, and particularly in 1985–86, China has been forced to engage in draconian remedial measures, including drastic contraction of imports, tighter controls on foreign exchange, and larger borrowings from foreign banks. The sudden swings in China's foreign economic behavior pose great hardships on China's trading partners and investors, who find their contracts canceled or postponed, and their ventures in China starved of necessary foreign exchange. China will need to develop macroeconomic policies that can smooth out these cyclical fluctuations in its economy to minimize the disruption to foreign economic relationships.

Relations with the Superpowers

The interplay between interdependence and nationalism will characterize China's relationships with the Soviet Union and the United States for the foreseeable future.[20] Peking's continued emphasis on economic modernization will encourage it to maintain and develop economic ties with both superpowers. From the Soviet Union, and from Eastern Europe, China will seek information about experiments in the reform of Soviet-style economies. Peking will also be interested in the less advanced but less expensive technology that could serve as a useful complement to that imported in the 1950s. In turn, the Soviet Union could be a market for Chinese consumer goods, especially textiles, electronics, and footwear. From the United States, and from the West more broadly, China will seek more advanced technology, as well as information about capitalist management practices that might be incorporated into "socialism with Chinese characteristics." The growing economic interaction with the two superpowers, and China's stress on economic development and reform, will give Peking a lasting incentive to manage and moderate any geopolitical tensions in its relationships with Washington and Moscow.

Even so, Peking will continue to eschew any close strategic relationship with, or dependence on, either the United States or the Soviet Union. As Hu Yaobang put it in 1982, China does not want to "attach itself to any big power or group of powers."[21] Moreover, a sustained process of modernization will give China the resources needed to maintain a relatively independent posture toward the two superpowers and to avoid an alliance, or even a tight alignment, with either one of them. China's growing military power, greater internal stability, and conviction that the Soviet Union's expansionist momentum has slowed combine to give Peking a much greater sense of security than in the 1970s, when it felt obliged to form a "united front" with the United States against Soviet "social-imperialism."

This is not to say that China will refuse to forge a loose strategic relationship with the United States. Even under an independent foreign policy, limited forms of military and strategic cooperation will continue to exist between Peking and Washington, including sales of American arms and production technologies to China, sharing and joint collection of intelligence about Soviet military capabilities, and dialogues and exchanges between the national security establishments of the two countries. But these elements are unlikely to be translated into a close, comprehensive strategic relationship between China and the United States unless a drastic change occurs in the regional military balance in favor of the Soviet Union.

Conversely, China's increasing nationalism makes it unlikely that Peking will ever completely disregard the issues that it has identified as the "obstacles" to the improvement of relations with Washington and Moscow: the American commitment to a peaceful solution of the Taiwan question, Soviet military deployments in Siberia and Mongolia, Soviet support of Vietnam's invasion of Cambodia, and Soviet intervention in Afghanistan. China's interest in a peaceful environment and in economic relations with the two superpowers will encourage it to manage these issues flexibly and patiently, but Peking can also be expected to raise these questions from time to time, especially if it believes that new policy initiatives from Moscow or Washington are exacerbating the obstacles.

In short, China will continue to follow a policy of independence toward the two superpowers, avoiding confrontation or alignment with either the United States or the Soviet Union. China will maintain dialogue with both, object to some aspects of both countries' policies, and endorse, either tacitly or explicitly, the initiatives with which it agrees. Peking's economic ties with Washington and Moscow will help moderate the remaining differences over strategic and political issues, but could not be counted on to prevent serious strains in Sino-Soviet or Sino-American relations were Peking to perceive any substantial retrogression in either country's policy toward China.

Within these parameters, does it matter whether China sustains the current political and economic reforms? At the margin, the fate of reform could well make a difference. In the most general sense, reform increases the compatibility between China's economic system and that of the West, somewhat reduces the salience of human rights issues in American policy toward China, and facilitates the integration of China into the international economic order. Similarly, continued reform in China preserves an ideological contradiction in Sino-Soviet relations, at least insofar as the Chinese reforms have proceeded farther than those in the Soviet Union. This outlook would especially be true should China choose to adopt the measures described in this book as radical reform, or should Eastern European countries, inspired by China's example, seek their own independent course of political and economic development.

Conversely, the abandonment of some aspects of reform might contribute to an improvement of Sino-Soviet relations and would strain China's ties with the United States. The readoption of a modified Soviet model at home might be symbolized and reinforced by closer economic and political relations between Peking and Moscow, especially if China were willing to acknowledge its membership in an international communist system. In the same way, a retreat from reform would probably sour Sino-American economic and cultural exchanges, as China embarked on a more protectionist course. By widening the differences between the Chinese mainland and Taiwan, a retrogression from reform would reduce the prospects for a resolution of the Taiwan question. A tightening of political controls over Chinese society, and particularly over intellectuals, would raise questions in the United States about China's record on human rights. These developments could affect the political ties between the two countries.

In short, the fate of China's second revolution will impinge upon Peking's relations with the two superpowers, if only because Chinese conservatives feel more comfortable with the Soviet Union than with the United States, and because Americans feel more comfortable with China's radical reformers than with their more moderate counterparts. Still, the effect of the domestic factors on this aspect of Chinese foreign policy should not be exaggerated. China's economic order resembled that of the Soviet Union much more in the late Maoist period than it does today, and yet its relationship with Moscow has improved even as the differences between the two systems have widened. In the same way, Sino- American strategic relations were in some respects closer under Mao Zedong than under Deng Xiaoping.

Instead, the most important element in shaping China's posture toward the two superpowers will be the balance between the United States and the Soviet Union and the policies that each of them adopts toward China and East Asia. If Peking continues to tilt toward the United States, it will be because it perceives its geopolitical interests and perspectives to be more congruent with Washington's than with Moscow's. Conversely, if Peking decides to shift somewhat toward the Soviet Union, it will be because the Soviet Union has made genuine concessions in eliminating the three obstacles to Sino-Soviet relations or because China has concluded that the American policy and posture in Asia again pose a strategic threat to China. As of now, and particularly while Deng Xiaoping is alive, China will continue to find more points in common with the United States than with the Soviet Union, especially on issues involving Asia. Consequently, regardless of the fate of reform, the most likely scenario is for a continued tilt toward Washington, even as China tries to improve relations with Moscow.

The Asian Balance

The effects of China's current emphasis on economic modernization on the geopolitical balance in the Asian-Pacific region are, again, contradictory.[22] On the one hand, China's desire for a peaceful international environment, and for expanded trade and investment relations, has led it to improve relations with most of its neighbors. It has welcomed indirect trade with South Korea, and direct trade with Indonesia, even though it still lacks diplomatic relations with either country. It has somewhat improved relations with both Mongolia and India, although ties with neither country could properly be described as warm, and although China has a potentially serious border dispute with New Delhi. Peking has attenuated ties with insurgent communist parties throughout Southeast Asia, although it has not broken them off completely. It has slowed the rate of increase in its military spending to the point that, in real terms, Chinese military expenses have declined since the late 1970s. And it has cut overall troop strength by about 1 million soldiers, or 25 percent of the previous total.[23]

At the same time, however, recent years have seen a rise of nationalism in China, among both the leadership and the ordinary citizen alike. Moreover, China's modernization will greatly increase the resources that China brings to the conduct of its foreign affairs. Although China has decelerated military spending, Peking is clearly committed to the gradual development of its armed forces, including the creation of a more effective strategic missile corps, a blue water navy, and a more mobile ground force. China's growing economic strength will allow it to exercise economic leverage against its Asian-Pacific neighbors, rewarding those with whom it is pleased and punishing those with whom it is dissatisfied. Moreover, Peking's continuing ties with indigenous communist parties in Southeast Asia, and with local overseas Chinese communities, could be activated to serve Chinese interests if Peking so chose.

China's growing material resources raise the possibility that Peking may eventually expand the definition of its national interests and adopt a more assertive posture in their pursuit. Many Asian nations are concerned that China will seek to reestablish in some form the political and cultural hegemony that it enjoyed in Asia during the Ming and early Qing dynasties. Though such a possibility is remote, China probably will try to influence the resolution of important regional issues, perhaps acquiring enough power so that its consent or cooperation is needed before any solution can be effective.

Several issues could complicate Peking's relations with other Asian nations, in part by fanning the flames of nationalism in China. One involves territory. China has border disputes with most of the nations with which it shares a land frontier: North Korea, the Soviet Union, India, and Vietnam. There are potential conflicts over territorial seas and islands with Japan, South Korea, Vietnam, and, to a lesser degree, Indonesia and the Philippines. Should any Asian-Pacific country—and Japan is the most likely candidate— seek to support independence for Taiwan or even suggest an official relationship with the island, Peking's wrath would certainly be aroused.

Second, China's relations with Southeast Asia have an ethnic dimension. The large number of overseas Chinese in most of the region, and particularly in Indonesia and Malaysia, is an important potential irritant in China's relations with those countries. Overseas Chinese have played a disproportionate role in both the economic life and communist movements in much of Southeast Asia, and are frequently perceived, though often unfairly, as being more loyal to China than to their country of residence. In the past, Southeast Asian governments were concerned above all with the possibility of subversion by Chinese-inspired communist insurgencies, and those fears have not completely subsided. Increasingly, however, the tensions may revolve around economic issues. Overseas Chinese in Southeast Asia may be the target of pressure and criticism if they are believed to be monopolizing or controlling their country's trade with China, or if they are investing their financial capital in the People's Republic rather than in local projects. In turn, the maltreatment of overseas Chinese by Southeast Asian nations could, as happened in Vietnam in 1978, lead to a vigorous and angry Chinese response.

Tensions could also increase if any of Peking's smaller Asian neighbors were to act in ways that China believed shifted the regional balance of power in unfavorable directions. For the time being, Peking will be most concerned about the areas that it regards as central to national security: Mongolia, Indochina, Korea, and Southwest Asia. Peking's conflict with Vietnam since the late 1970s exemplifies the kinds of actions that might provoke a response by an increasingly assertive China. Peking perceived Vietnam's effort to establish domination over Indochina as an unacceptable change in the international balance in Southeast Asia, especially since it was undertaken with the support of the Soviet Union. China reacted to the Vietnamese intervention in Cambodia by invading northern Vietnam in 1979, increasing assistance to the Khmer Rouge and Thailand, and maintaining sustained political and military pressure on Hanoi. Similar efforts by India in South Asia, or by Indonesia in Southeast Asia, might well produce a comparable response. China might also react sharply to an accommodation between Vietnam and the Association of South East Asian Nations over the Cambodian issue, or between Pakistan and the Soviet Union over Afghanistan, particularly if it felt that China's security interests had not been given sufficient weight in the process of negotiation.

Japan's possible rise as a military power in Northeast Asia worries China, especially if accompanied by a deterioration of Japanese-American political relations. Although Chinese spokesmen have frequently acknowledged Japan's right to self-defense, they have also warned that its military capabilities "should be moderate and of a defense nature, and should not cause concern to its neighboring countries."[24] Peking has been alert to any signs of the rise of "militarism" or "chauvinism" in Japan or significant increases in Japan's military spending. Should Japan greatly accelerate its level of defense preparations, develop the ability to project force beyond its home islands, or assume security commitments outside its own territory, then it would almost certainly be subject to a harsh response from China.

Over time, too, China may begin to identify security concerns in areas beyond those that it now sees as critical to its defense. Peking has paid attention to developments in the South Pacific and has established a network of embassies and political relationships there that rival those of the superpowers. China's arms sales to participants in the Iran-Iraq conflict suggests a growing Chinese stake in the strategic balance in the gulf region of the Middle East. As China's resources grow, its interests may expand into areas that are now fairly peripheral to Chinese security calculations.

Finally, China's growing involvement in the international economy will introduce economic issues into Peking's relations with its Asian neighbors. With Japan, the tensions will focus on the large surplus that Japan enjoys in trade with China and the barriers obstructing the entry of Chinese goods to the Japanese market. Increasingly, too, China may come to criticize Japan's reluctance to transfer technology to China, the low level of Japanese investment in the People's Republic, and the low quality of some goods that have been exported to China by Japanese producers. With the developing countries of the region, economic issues will assume a somewhat different tone. Possibly, the competition with China for loans from the World Bank, access to the Japanese and American markets, and foreign investment will produce problems in the political relations between Peking and its smaller neighbors. As noted earlier, some Asian nations have already begun to complain of the deficits that have begun to emerge in their trade with China.

But more reassuring factors exist on the other side of the ledger. One is the dynamism of the Asian-Pacific region. Given the vitality of almost all Asian economies, and the growing political institutionalization in most of the region, there is little likelihood of a vacuum into which China could readily expand, as Japan thrust into Korea and China in the late nineteenth and early twentieth centuries. Furthermore, both superpowers, and several regional powers, are actively interested in the Asian strategic balance. If China were to begin to behave in an aggressive manner, it would be relatively easy to form a counterbalance against Peking at an early stage.

In addition, China today can be seen as a relatively satisfied power. It shows no signs of seeking any major changes in the national boundaries established in the last century and in the early 1900s, even though it regards many of the treaties that determined those borders to have been unequal and unjust. Thus Peking currently lays no claim to large parts of Siberia or to Mongolia, even though these territories were wrested from Chinese control by Russia between 1860 and 1920. Nor does China feel the need to avenge past affronts, as did Germany before World War II, or Peking itself during the Maoist period. Although China still lacks formal diplomatic relations with Indonesia, Singapore, and South Korea, it is widely accepted as an important regional power; and although it lags behind much of the region economically, almost every business community in Asia is eager to participate in China's development.

On balance, therefore, it would be naive to assume that China will be merely a passive and compliant force in Asian affairs, or that it will assume the role, as one New Zealand politician has put it, of the "friendly giant to the North." But it is unnecessarily alarmist to conclude that China's emergence as a regional power will pose as much threat to Asia as did the rise of Japan in the early twentieth century or the rise of the Soviet Union in the 1960s. Modernization will make China a more powerful force in Asia, and sporadic tensions will occur between Peking and its neighbors over economic, strategic, and territorial issues. But China's exercise of power will be constrained by an enduring interest in a peaceful environment, economic interdependence with the rest of the region, relative satisfaction with its standing in Asia, the vitality of the other East Asian societies, and the viability of the emerging regional balance of power. If China should act in an assertive fashion, it is more likely to be in response to a perceived challenge to its interests by other Asian countries than an opportunistic act of pure aggrandizement.

The fate of reform in China should have fairly little impact on this general forecast. A continued commitment to reform, of course, should make Peking more flexible and restrained in its regional policy, and, conversely, a retreat from reform might be connected with a rise in officially sponsored nationalism as a part of a tightening of political controls. But the correlation is likely to be loose and weak. Even a reform-minded China could encounter tensions with Asian nations over geopolitical or economic issues, as has already occurred in Peking's relations with Vietnam and Japan. Indeed, economic competition between China and the rest of Asia is likely to grow if reform in China succeeds. Conversely, a more orthodox China could easily be preoccupied with internal economic problems, interested in peaceful coexistence with neighbors, and committed to maintaining a reasonably wide range of economic relations with other Asian states.

China and Its Irredenta

The interaction of interdependence and nationalism is also evident in Peking's attitudes toward Hong Kong, Macao, and Taiwan.[25] On the one hand, the rise of Chinese nationalism is making this issue more salient for present-day Chinese leaders and, presumably, more difficult for future generations to ignore. Historically, strong and effective Chinese governments have considered it their duty to regain authority over those parts of the country that, in times of weakness, were removed from central control by foreigners or by rival regimes, and have seen success in this effort as proof of their power and prestige. Clearly, Deng Xiaoping has made the reunification of China one of the principal goals of his leadership—not necessarily one that will be accomplished in his lifetime, but one on which a good start should be made before he leaves the Chinese political stage. It would be very difficult for any Chinese government to ignore signs that political forces in either Taipei, Tokyo, or

Washington were attempting to promote an independent Taiwan, or that leaders in Hong Kong or London were planning to create a political system there that was unacceptable to Peking.[26]

Moreover, the growth of Chinese economic, political, and military resources gives Peking greater power to determine the future of the territories it claims. In the cases of Hong Kong and Macao, Peking has successfully compelled both Britain and Portugal to agree to restore sovereignty of the territories to China and is gaining greater economic influence over both places through a rapid expansion of trade and investment. China will gradually acquire the ability to exert military pressure against Taiwan, particularly through a naval blockade, and China's growing economic and strategic importance may also give it somewhat greater leverage over Taipei's supporters in Tokyo and Washington.

On the other hand, China's commitment to modernization also serves to moderate Peking's approach to the question of reunification. Peking's interest in maintaining and expanding Japanese, American, and European participation in China's development restrains its use of force against Taiwan. Its desire that Hong Kong serve as a bridge to the international community has similarly discouraged it from acting in heavy-handed ways against either Hong Kong or Macao. Moreover, at least until 1997, and probably for some time thereafter, Hong Kong and Taiwan each serve as political insurance for the other. China knows that mismanagement of the Hong Kong question would reduce, if not eliminate, the prospects for a peaceful resolution of the Taiwan question; and that, conversely, the use of force, concerted diplomatic pressure, or economic embargo against Taiwan would produce a destabilizing crisis of confidence inside Hong Kong as well.

The growing pragmatism characteristic of the foreign relations of post-Mao China has been especially apparent in the flexibility shown by Peking in its management of both the Hong Kong and Taiwan issues. Peking's agreement to maintain Hong Kong's current social, economic, and political systems for at least fifty years after its reversion to Chinese sovereignty in 1997, and its further willingness to specify the characteristics of those systems in great detail, were the key concessions that allowed an agreement between Britain and China in 1984, as well as the parallel compact with Portugal over Macao in 1987. Similarly, China's extension of the principle of "one country, two systems" to Taiwan, on even more generous terms than applied to Hong Kong, would have been inconceivable during the late Maoist period.[27]

The fate of reform will make a big difference in the prospects for all of China's irredenta. If the present reforms are sustained, and particularly if the radical reforms discussed since 1986 are adopted, the differences in economic system, social structure, and even political institutions between Hong Kong and Taiwan, on the one hand, and the rest of China, on the other, should be narrowed, although not eliminated. The standard of living and style of life in certain parts of China, particularly Shanghai and the southeast coast, should increasingly come to resemble those in Hong Kong and Taiwan. Under such circumstances, the citizens of Taiwan and Hong Kong would find greater appeal in extensive economic and cultural interaction with the mainland. And future generations of leaders in Peking would become even more flexible in their treatment of Taiwan and Hong Kong—more accommodating toward the former and less interventionist toward the latter. Together, all these developments would make the concept of "one country, two systems" more feasible, credible, and workable and would therefore increase the possibilities for a creative resolution of the Taiwan question at some point in the next century.

A retreat from reform, however, would greatly complicate Peking's relations with both Hong Kong and Taipei. At a minimum, it would perpetuate a wide gap between the social, economic, and political structures on the mainland and those in Hong Kong and Taiwan. It might be accompanied by a restructuring of the special economic zones in ways that reduced their ability to serve as buffers between Hong Kong, Macao, and Taiwan and the rest of China. A retreat from reform would probably reduce Peking's flexibility toward Taiwan, somewhat reduce Peking's interest in maintaining cooperative economic relations with the United States, and thus increase, if only marginally, the possibility that China would use diplomatic and economic pressure against Taiwan and its patrons. It might also make Chinese leaders less tolerant of political pluralism, rampant capitalism, and bourgeois culture in Hong Kong. In all these ways, retrogression in the course of domestic reform on the mainland would reduce the chances for a smooth transition of sovereignty in Hong Kong and for a peaceful solution to the Taiwan question.

IMPLICATIONS FOR THE UNITED STATES

China's second revolution has had, and will continue to have, important implications for each of the three principal dimensions of Sino-American relations: the geopolitical relationship between the two countries, economic ties between the United States and China, and the Taiwan issue. In each case, the post-Mao reforms have strengthened the underpinnings of the Sino-American relationship. But they have not eliminated the differences in perspective between the two countries and have sometimes introduced new tensions and problems.[28]

On the strategic dimension, for example, China's commitment to modernization should, for the foreseeable future, give Peking an interest in peace and stability in Asia, particularly on the Korean peninsula, that parallels the similar interests of the United States. At the same time, both countries are concerned about the expansion of Soviet military power in Siberia and the growth of Soviet political influence in Asia. And both nations acknowledge the mutual benefits that can be derived from American involvement in China's modernization. Such common interests make it unlikely that China and America will ever again become adversaries.

But the strategic relationship between China and the United States will continue to be constrained, both by the rise in Chinese nationalism and by the limits to economic and political reform in the People's Republic. Although China's commitment to modernization gives China and the United States a shared interest in peace and stability in Asia, it simultaneously reinforces Peking's desire to preserve strategic independence from Washington or from any other great power. An independent orientation in foreign affairs will be seen by Chinese leaders as the foreign policy that is most likely, in an age of increasing Chinese nationalism, to secure a firm domestic consensus and avoid unnecessary entanglement in the conflict between the two superpowers. Moreover, an independent strategic stance helps China to find markets and technology in both East and West. As a symbol of that independence, China will continue to criticize the American policies with which it disagrees and, to an extent that many Americans find objectionable, persist in describing the United States, as well as the Soviet Union, as a hegemonic power.

Furthermore, although the current reforms are liberalizing China's economic and political systems, they are unlikely ever to eliminate the structural and cultural differences between the two countries. Despite the fervent hopes of some Americans, and the naive predictions of others, China is not about to become a capitalist, pluralist, or laissez-faire society. And not even the most dogmatic Chinese would predict that the United States will experience a proletarian revolution or adopt a socialist economy. Nor has the attenuation of ideology in either country advanced to the point that differences in underlying institutions and values will become irrelevant to the relationship. Continued reform, and particularly the adoption of some features of radical political and economic reform, will narrow the gap between China and the United States but will not remove it altogether. Conversely, periods of political retrenchment, as during the movement against "bourgeois liberalization" in early 1987, may see intense criticism of American values and institutions in the Chinese press and arouse equally severe attacks on China's human rights record by American observers.

Thus the United States must accept a somewhat ambiguous strategic relationship with an independent but friendly China—a relationship in which China is neither ally nor adversary, and in which there are points of divergence, as well as convergence, in the policies of Peking and Washington. The relationship may well be difficult for Americans, who tend to feel more comfortable when the line between "friend" and "foe" is more clearly drawn. But as the world becomes more multipolar, dealing effectively with major independent powers will be a more critical task for the United States.

In the case of China, an effective and sustainable strategic relationship will require a mutual acknowledgment of the differences in ideology, social system, and national interest of the two countries. Both sides must accept that each will occasionally criticize the policies of the other. At the same time, constant dialogue and consultation must occur so that the issues arising from those differences can be managed in a mature and constructive manner and so that the two countries can act in tandem or in parallel in the areas in which they share common goals and perspectives. There is also room for a limited and cautious program of military cooperation between the two countries, featuring both the sale of weapons to China and technical exchanges between the military establishments on either side of the Pacific.

China's interest in rapid economic modernization, and especially its present commitment to economic reform, is promoting the development of economic and cultural ties with the United States. Indeed, as China adopts a more independent policy in the strategic arena, and as economic development assumes the highest priority in Peking's foreign relations, the relationship between China and the United States will become increasingly rooted in the economic bonds between the two countries.

Both nations can benefit from a cooperative economic relationship. For China, America is an important source of the technology, capital, and markets needed for the PRC's development effort. American universities and research institutions are a relatively accessible locus for training for Chinese students and scholars, and the American economy can offer China useful information about enterprise management, economic regulation, bureaucratic operations, and social welfare programs. For the United States, too, economic cooperation with China has much to offer. The United States has a comparative advantage in several sectors in which Chinese planners are especially interested, such as energy, transportation, advanced electronics, communications, and agricultural technology. All these areas offer the potential for American exports to China. In addition, as the investment climate in China improves, American firms will have more incentive to establish foreign ventures in China, with the output sold either on the Chinese domestic market or to consumers in third countries.

Although China and the United States can benefit from extensive economic and cultural interaction, the differences in economic structure, philosophy, and interest between the two societies will introduce problems into their relationship. The Chinese will object to the rise of protectionist sentiment in the United States and will criticize the remaining restrictions on the export of advanced technologies. Americans will protest the extent to which the Chinese market remains closed to foreign imports and will point out how the investment climate in China falls short of the ideal. Each side will be concerned about the business cycle in the other and complain about the decline of exports during periods of recession. The cultural contacts between the two societies will also create tensions, be they the alleged misconduct of foreign reporters and scholars in China, or the possible "brain drain" of Chinese students and scholars to the United States after the completion of their training and research programs in America.[29]

Indeed, China's outward-looking development strategy will probably increase its economic relations with the United States faster than the issues arising from the encounter can be resolved. A continued commitment to reform will ease the difficulties somewhat, and a retreat from reform will exacerbate them, but in either event economic issues will become increasingly prominent in U.S.-China relations, at a time when the strategic ties between the two countries will disappoint those who once anticipated a close Sino-American alignment against the Soviet Union. A continuing dialogue between the two societies, including the business and academic communities as well as the governments, will be necessary to identify these problems at an early stage and to develop workable and effective solutions.

The future of Taiwan is the third important dimension of con-

temporary Sino-American relations. China's interest in modernization and reform has helped moderate the impact of what remains
the most knotty and emotional issue in Sino- American relations.
China's desire for extensive economic interaction with the United
States, as well as its interest in discreet strategic ties with Washington, gives it a stake in preventing the Taiwan issue from
disrupting the broader Sino-American relationship. China's increasing pragmatism and professionalism has already promoted a more
flexible and restrained approach to the Taiwan question. Chinese
leaders, for example, now describe the future as "reunification"
rather than "liberation" and have a more subtle and sophisticated
interpretation of the internal political situation on the island. They
increasingly recognize a common interest with the United States
in the prudent management of the Taiwan issue. Their willingness
to grant Taiwan a large degree of autonomy after reunification, and
their implication that the use of force against the island would be
reserved only for the most dire circumstances, also signifies flexibility and restraint.

And yet, these positive developments should not obscure the fact
that fundamental differences of perspective remain between the
United States and China on the Taiwan question. To Peking, the
future of Taiwan is wholly a domestic issue in which no foreign
country has the right to interfere. Washington, in contrast, insists
that it has a legitimate historical and moral interest in a peaceful
future for Taiwan and its people. With the resolution of the Hong
Kong and Macao issues, Taiwan is the only part of China whose
reunification with the mainland is not yet ensured. This situation,
and rising Chinese nationalism, make it unlikely that the future of
Taiwan will ever lose its emotional salience to Chinese leaders.

The management of the Taiwan question, like the management
of the economic issues between China and the United States, will
require regular and candid dialogue between the two countries so
that misunderstandings can be clarified, differences narrowed, and
shared interests identified. The United States must take a prudent
approach to the sale of arms and military technology to Taiwan and
make clear that it would have no objection to the reunification of
Taiwan and the mainland if it occurred through a peaceful and
mutually acceptable process of convergence and dialogue. China
must realize that the resolution of the Taiwan question will require
more time than the settlement of the Hong Kong and Macao issues. Moreover, Peking must also learn that the key to that solution is not pressure or encouragement from the United States, but
rather developments in all three parts of China: continued stability,

prosperity, and reform on the mainland; further progress toward a
more representative government on Taiwan; and effective implementation of the Sino-British agreement on the future of Hong
Kong.

In the final analysis, China's second revolution poses a fundamental question for Americans. As already noted, China's emergence
as a great power offers both benefits and risks for the international
community. The benefit would be a prosperous and stable China,
engaged actively and constructively in the international economy
and contributing to the peace and security of the Asian-Pacific
region. The principal risk is that growing Chinese resources will be
harnessed to an assertive nationalism in ways that threaten the
national security of neighboring countries and the economic stability
of the entire region. The main challenge to the United States is to
devise a long-term policy toward China that will maximize the
benefits while limiting the risks.

The strategy might well include the following components. First,
and most basically, the United States should remain involved in
China's modernization, doing what it can to see that the process
succeeds. There is, admittedly, no guarantee that a successfully
modernizing China will use its growing economic and military
resources in ways fully congruent with American interests. Indeed,
as already suggested, differences will remain between China and
the United States on various diplomatic, strategic, and economic
issues. But a China whose program of economic development is
reasonably successful, and which has developed a stake in a mutually
beneficial relationship with the United States, is likely to continue
to promote stability and prosperity in Asia.

Moreover, were the United States to adopt a skeptical or aloof
attitude toward China's modernization, such a posture would do
little to prevent that process from occurring. China will, under
almost any circumstance, retain access to technology from Japan
and Western Europe. At most, therefore, American refusal to participate in China's modernization would only delay it slightly.
Moreover, such a posture would practically guarantee that Peking
would adopt a hostile position toward the United States and would
greatly increase the prospects of a close Sino-Soviet relationship. In
short, an American disengagement from China's modernization on
the grounds that Peking may turn into a powerful adversary of the
United States is almost certain to be a self-fulfilling prophecy.

The United States can still do more to assist in China's development. Once China is a member of the General Agreement on
Tariffs and Trade, the United States should make Chinese exports

eligible for preferential treatment under the Generalized System of Preferences, as all other developed nations in the West have already done. The controls on the export of advanced technology can be further streamlined. Chinese and American business executives can work together to improve the climate for foreign investment in China, and the academic communities of the two countries can improve the groundwork for sustained and productive scholarly cooperation. There is no reason why China should not receive appropriate developmental assistance from the United States, although the bulk of American concessional aid might well be channeled through the World Bank, the Asian Development Bank, and other international institutions. Indeed, some assistance by the United States would directly benefit American business. If the United States government were to provide trade financing on favorable terms, comparable to that offered by Japan, it would greatly facilitate the export of advanced American technology to China.

The United States has a further interest in the success of political and economic reform in China. Reform will improve the prospects for Hong Kong, facilitate a resolution of the Taiwan question, and improve the climate for American trade and investment in China. At the margin, it may slightly increase China's perception of common interests with the United States on global and regional issues. And further liberalization of China's economic and political systems would obviously be congruent with deeply held American values. These prospects offer a further incentive for Americans to cooperate with the process of modernization now under way in China. The more that process succeeds, the greater the chances that reform will continue and even accelerate.

Though the United States can and should support the process of reform in China, it would be unwise for Americans to imply that they favor one group of Chinese leaders over another or to channel resources disproportionately to those in China who declare themselves "pro-American" or "radical reformers." Such a stance is not likely to be effective, for the composition of China's leadership will depend principally on factors internal to China, rather than on the preferences of foreigners. Indeed, it might even be counterproductive because it might identify one group of Chinese leaders as the clients of the United States and suggest American interference in China's internal affairs. Thus the United States should be willing to work with all those in China who are attempting to build a more modern country that is engaged in the world economy and at peace with its neighbors. The United States should develop cooperative economic, academic, and cultural relationships with a full range of groups, regions, and institutions in China, and not just with those whom America believes sympathetic to the United States or supportive of thoroughgoing reform.

Managing the risks of China's modernization also has implications for American policy toward the rest of Asia. The emergence of a more assertive version of Chinese nationalism can be deterred if the other states in the region remain prosperous and viable and if there is an effective balance of power in the region. This suggests that America must remain actively involved in Asia, for the United States is a critical element in the multipolar system that is rapidly emerging in the region. The United States must also continue to promote the economic prosperity and political liberalization of the smaller countries in East Asia, especially the newly industrialized states and regions whose influence will increase in the years ahead. Moreover, in shaping policy toward China, the United States must be aware of the sensitivities of other Asian nations about the rapid development of Chinese military strength. The United States should avoid the appearance, or the reality, of a sinocentric Asian policy and should enlarge military cooperation with Peking in a prudent and gradual manner. Many of these policy imperatives require, in turn, a solution to the pressing problems currently confronting the American economy, notably the trade and budget deficits, and the imbalance between consumption and investment.

Ameliorating the tensions that will inevitably accompany China's emergence as an important force in world affairs will require constant dialogue and coordination between China and the United States, the United States and the rest of Asia, and China and its Asian neighbors. The United States, with its open society and wealth of foreign affairs institutions, is ideally qualified to sponsor much of this dialogue.

CHAPTER 10

The Future of the Second
Revolution

REFORM is one of the most challenging tasks in any political system. Like the revolutionary, the reformer seeks to make fundamental changes in political and economic institutions, many of which are supported by powerful interests and sustained by years of tradition. But the reformer, unlike the revolutionary, achieves change through peaceful means, rather than force, and by working through existing political institutions, rather than overthrowing them. The reformer and the revolutionary have equally ambitious aims, but the reformer must pursue them in a more circumscribed way.

The post-Mao era is not the first time in which modern China has attempted far-ranging political and economic reform. In 1898, during the Hundred Days reform, the young Kuang-hsü emperor and his advisers ordered sweeping changes in the nation's administrative bureaucracy, civil service examinations, and system of higher education. Between 1905 and 1911, at the end of the Manchu dynasty, the Empress Dowager Tz'u-hsi endorsed a national program of military and industrial modernization and took the first steps toward parliamentary government at both the provincial and national levels. And during the so-called Nanking Decade of 1928–37, the Nationalist government under Chiang Kai-shek resumed the military and industrial modernization that had been interrupted by the fall of the Manchu dynasty and the rise of the warlords in the 1910s and early 1920s.

Each of these movements fell victim to one of the typical pitfalls of reform. Unsuccessful at consolidating their power inside the imperial court, the reformers of 1898 were pushed aside by conservatives in their own government. Rather than satisfying the demands for political and social change from intellectuals, merchants, and local officials, the reforms of 1905–11 unleashed a revolutionary tide that, in the end, swept the Manchu dynasty away. Unable to subdue powerful local warlords, unwilling to confront China's landed rural gentry, and plagued by chronic corruption, the Nationalists under Chiang Kai-shek failed to establish an effective central government that could design and implement a program of national unity, land reform, and industrialization.

The history of reform in other communist countries presents a similarly checkered picture. The experiences of the Soviet Union and Eastern Europe since the onset of de-Stalinization in the mid-1950s suggest that the process of reform in communist systems can falter at any of three points. Reformers may prove unable to launch their program successfully, given the uncertainties and opposition that sweeping change always involves. They may therefore fall victim to what might be called the "Soviet disease," becoming trapped on a treadmill of partial adjustments, limiting them to a succession of small and relatively ineffective changes in policy, without developing the strength to undertake any more fundamental reforms.

Even if they are able to mobilize the political resources with which to launch a reform movement, reformers may be unable to sustain it over time. In this, the "Hungarian disease," the reforms create social and economic problems so severe that the support for reform collapses, and the reformers are obliged, at least temporarily, to tighten administrative controls over the economy, in an attempt to overcome the technical difficulties and social tensions that reform has encountered.[1]

Alternatively, reforms may generate popular pressures for further political liberalization that the Party is unable to accept. The situation in Poland in the late 1970s and early 1980s exemplifies the crisis that can be created when demands by intellectuals for greater freedom of expression combine with the desire of workers for higher standards of living and for independent trade unions. Indeed, of all these maladies to which reform can succumb, the "Polish disease" has been most worrisome to leaders in Peking.

The difficulties in sustaining reform in other commmunist countries, and memories of the dramatic changes that occurred in China after the death of Mao Zedong, have understandably raised pointed questions about the prospects for continued reform in post-Mao China. Will the reforms survive the death of Deng Xiaoping? Can the Chinese leaders cope effectively with the economic problems, political opposition, and social tensions that reform will inevitably produce? Will there be even further progress toward economic and political liberalization? Or did the dismissal of Hu Yaobang in early

1987 represent the high-water mark of reform, from which the tide of change will gradually recede?

Indeed, in the mid-1980s, there are grounds for genuine concern. Although the reforms have secured impressive economic and political benefits for the Chinese people, the easiest gains have already been won. From now on, economic progress may be slower, the problems connected with reform greater, and the measures required to overcome those problems more painful. In itself, such a development would gradually erode some of the popular support that reform now enjoys. Moreover, the differences within the Chinese leadership may also grow, as the consensus over the moderate package of reforms is replaced by controversy over the necessity and desirability of the more radical reform measures. Perhaps most important, within a few years, Deng Xiaoping will pass from the Chinese political scene. It is not yet clear whether the political institutions he has sought to create will be effective enough to resolve the controversies among the various schools of thought in the Party or whether Deng's successor will be skillful enough to maintain consensus within the national leadership.

THE BALANCE SHEET

One factor determining the future of China's reforms will be the balance of costs and benefits, risks and opportunities, that they provide to the nation as a whole and to various groups within it. As the reformers hoped, the reforms scored dramatic early successes—especially in boosting agricultural output, raising urban wages, promoting exports, and creating a more relaxed political climate—that enabled the reformers to build sizable reserves of grain, foreign exchange, and popular support. Nonetheless, the reforms have not been able to achieve all that their sponsors had intended, for the economy is still plagued by obstinate bottlenecks, the crisis of confidence in the Party's leadership has not yet been fully overcome, and the political process has been only partially institutionalized.

Moreover, since 1984–85 the reforms have encountered serious difficulties, including corruption, inflation, trade deficits, imbalanced budgets, shortfalls in grain production, and a growing perception of a decline in moral values. These problems forced the reformers to draw down their reserves of grain, foreign exchange, and popular support, in some cases to dangerously low levels. Even more serious problems, including economic inequality and political dissent, may lie ahead, the product of the contradictions that inhere in China's attempt to create a mixture of plan and market, and liberalization and control. Chinese leaders will be hard pressed to design and implement remedial measures that will be in keeping with the spirit of reform. Indeed, many of the most effective devices for coping with the shortcomings of reform may be nearly as painful as the problems they are intended to overcome.

Accomplishments and Disappointments

The post-Mao reforms have reversed the decline in economic growth rates that plagued the late Maoist period. The average annual rate of increase of rural output since 1979 has been 10.5 percent, well above the rates of 4.0 percent to 5.0 percent achieved in the 1950s, 1960s, and early 1970s. Even if these figures are adjusted to exclude rural industry, the sector of the rural economy that has enjoyed the most rapid rates of growth, agricultural output has increased at an average rate of nearly 7 percent a year. In industry, the figures are somewhat less impressive, if only because the post-Mao reforms were implemented later in the urban areas than they were in the countryside. The average rate of growth of industrial output between 1979 and 1982 was 6.8 percent, compared with 9.1 percent in the early 1970s and 11.7 percent in the late 1960s. Between 1983 and 1986, however, after the implementation of the urban industrial reforms had begun in earnest, industrial output rose at an average rate of 13.6 percent, substantially higher than at any time since the late 1950s.[2]

The increased pace of economic growth, in turn, reflects notable improvements in labor productivity in both industry and agriculture. When rural industry is excluded from the calculations, the average output of each agricultural laborer rose from 660 yuan in 1980 to 840 yuan in 1986, a nominal increase of 27 percent over six years. Labor productivity in industry remained stagnant in the early 1980s, but began to increase dramatically in 1983. By 1985 the annual output per worker had risen to 15,809 yuan, a nominal 31 percent increase over the average output of 12,080 yuan per worker in 1980.[3]

The acceleration of the rates of growth of industry and agriculture has allowed a large increase in nominal rural and urban incomes, as well as in patterns of consumption in both city and countryside. The average urban wage has more than doubled since 1978, rising from 614 yuan in 1978 to 1,329 yuan in 1986. Average peasant income over the same period has nearly tripled, from 134 yuan in 1978 to 424 yuan in 1986. Annual levels of consumption for peasants have increased from 132 yuan to 352 yuan, and have risen from 383 yuan to 865 yuan for non-peasants, over the same period. Consumption of grain has increased by almost a third, and that of pork has nearly doubled. Ownership of consumer durables, such as washing machines, television sets, refrigerators, and tape recorders has greatly increased in the cities; and ownership of bicycles, sewing machines, and radios has become commonplace in the countryside. Moreover, because the growth rates in the rural areas have been faster than those in the cities, the urban-rural gap has narrowed somewhat in the post-Mao era. The ratio of non-peasant consumption to peasant consumption, which was 2.9:1 in 1978, had fallen to 2.5:1 by 1986.[4]

China has also achieved dramatic gains in foreign economic relations. As noted in chapter 6, China's foreign trade in 1986, at more than $70 billion, was more than three times what it had been in 1978. The ratio of China's exports to its national output rose from 5.6 percent in 1978 to 13.9 percent in 1986, a more normal level for a country of China's size and at China's level of development. China absorbed $28.8 billion in foreign capital between 1979 and 1986, about one-quarter of it in direct foreign investment and the remainder in loans. Foreign capital was the equivalent of 12.3 percent of government expenditures on capital construction in 1985 and 7.1 percent of state revenues that same year—higher than the comparable ratios achieved at the height of Sino-Soviet cooperation under the First Five-Year Plan (1953–57). China has joined most of the principal international economic and financial institutions and is rapidly becoming familiar with the full range of mechanisms for the acquisition of foreign capital, technology, and information.[5]

In politics, too, achievements have been noteworthy since 1978. Despite the periodic tightening of controls on writers, artists, and intellectuals, daily life has become more relaxed, less arbitrary, and more predictable for the average Chinese citizen than it was in the late Maoist period. A rudimentary legal structure has been put in place and is being steadily elaborated and developed. More opportunities for political participation exist, particularly for intellectuals. A wider range of interests and institutions is consulted in the making of national decisions, especially on economic development strategy and on structural reform. Neither public policy, academic inquiry, nor artistic expression is as tightly constrained by doctrinal prescriptions as was true in the early 1970s.

Similarly, a good start has been made in institutionalizing the Chinese political process. Furthermore, a high rate of personnel turnover is bringing younger, better-educated officials into the Party and state bureaucracies. The role of the military in civilian politics has been reduced to more normal levels. The recruitment policies of the Party have been changed to assign greater priority to the admission of intellectuals to Party membership, and the basic-level Party committees now have less direct control over administrative matters in factories, offices, and other grassroots units than was true in the late Maoist period. The norms governing the resolution of political disputes have become stronger, and the stakes of political conflict have become much lower, than at the time of Mao's death.

Alongside these achievements, however, must also be set the goals that the post-Mao reforms have not yet achieved. Although rates of growth and levels of labor productivity have somewhat increased, other indicators of performance, especially in industry, have not been significantly improved. The productivity of capital, measured by output for each unit of fixed assets, has increased slightly since 1983, but remains slightly lower than it was in 1978, and far lower than in 1965.[6] The quality of industrial output has not improved greatly, nor has the proportion of industrial enterprises suffering losses been reduced. The improvement of labor productivity has been uneven. Some sectors, such as machinery, chemicals, and metallurgy, have enjoyed big increases in their output per worker. Food processing and textiles have seen more modest growth; and other sectors, such as coal, power, and petroleum, have witnessed almost no increases or have experienced a decline.[7] The share of state expenditures devoted to subsidizing the sale of staple commodities and underwriting the operation of insolvent state enterprises was virtually the same in 1986 as it was in 1981.[8]

Second, despite the priority that Chinese leaders have assigned to altering some of the basic sectoral relationships in the Chinese economy, they have achieved remarkably little progress. Although they want to lower the rate of investment, perhaps to about 25 percent of national output, it remains at more than 30 percent of national output and has fallen below that figure in only three years since 1978. Similarly, there has been little increase in the share of investment being channeled into energy and transportation, widely regarded as the two principal bottlenecks of the Chinese economy. In only one year, 1984, has the share of state investment allocated to these two sectors exceeded that in 1978. And despite the greater freedom for private and collective entrepreneurial activity in China's underdeveloped service sector, the share of GNP accounted for by services has risen only slightly, from 17 percent in 1981 to 20 percent in 1985. If services grow at the rate projected in the Seventh Five-Year Plan, they will provide 25 percent of China's GNP in

1990, which is still far below the ratio in the average low-income country.[9]

In the realm of domestic politics, the crisis of confidence that plagued a large part of the urban population in the late 1970s and early 1980s has not been completely resolved, despite the progress toward a more open and stable political system. To be sure, the acute alienation from the Party that seemed prevalent just after the death of Mao has largely been overcome. It has been replaced not so much by active support, as by passive acquiescence and apathy among large groups of the younger population. As one young Chinese intellectual has summarized the current attitudes of her generation toward the Party: "Party members aren't so bad. They're almost as good as us ordinary people." The Party has not been able to construct a compelling ideological justification for its programs, even though it has, particularly by Maoist standards, offered an unprecedentedly clear and comprehensive programmatic description of the reforms it wishes to undertake.

Finally, as noted in chapter 8, political institutionalization in post-Mao China remains incomplete. The division of labor among the Party, the state, the army, and enterprise managers is still sketchy and vague. The development of the legal system is still inadequate. The succession arrangements designed by Deng Xiaoping decayed and collapsed in the mid-1980s and must be rebuilt. The freedom offered to ordinary citizens in their daily lives is dependent on the continued restraint and indifference of the Party and state, rather than on any permanent grant of rights and immunities to the Chinese people. The ability of the political system to reach decisions and resolve disputes seems uncomfortably dependent on the personal authority of Deng and his relations with a handful of other senior leaders.

Problems

The fate of reform will also rest on the economic, political, and social difficulties it is likely to generate. Six sets of problems will be of particular import: shortages and imbalances in the economy, inflation and hyperinvestment, social and economic inequalities, corruption and crime, political dissent and cultural unconventionality, and the uncertainties inherent in a more open economy. Most of these difficulties are already apparent, but many of them could become more serious as the implementation of the reforms continues. If they become too severe, they could jeopardize the durability of the reform program. But, in each case, they can be remedied or ameliorated if the reformers have the will, skill, and power to do so.

One unhappy prospect would be the failure of various sectors of the Chinese economy to meet the expectations that have been established for them. In the domestic economy, shortages and imbalances are likely in several areas. Unless there are increases in investment in agriculture—by the state, the collective, or individual peasant households—it will be difficult to sustain the rates of growth in agricultural output that have been achieved since 1978. In particular, the possibility of chronic shortfalls in grain production remains because of the abandonment of mandatory quotas for grain and because of the relatively low purchase prices offered by the state under the procurement contract system. Unless state industry can sustain the initial increases in productivity registered in the mid-1980s, its output may stagnate, losses may mount, and its contribution to state revenues could fall short of requirements. Furthermore, various additional circumstances could also produce deficits in the state budget, including the necessity to increase subsidies for grain production or a loss of control over state capital construction expenditures.

In foreign economic relations, an acute imbalance in China's current accounts could easily recur. This outcome could result from import surges, such as those that occurred in the late 1970s and the mid-1980s, when a relaxation of restrictions on the use of foreign exchange allows the realization of the pervasive demands for imported capital equipment and consumer goods. Or a trade deficit could be the result of a weakness of the international market for Chinese exports, through the collapse of world prices (as in the case of petroleum) or the erection of import barriers (as in the case of textiles). A dearth of exports could also be produced by the preference of China's manufacturers to sell on their own domestic market rather than attempt to export overseas. Furthermore, unless the business climate improves, direct foreign investment in China could also fail to meet the expectations of Chinese leaders.

Popular support for the reforms would be especially endangered should increases in real incomes fall short of the pace attained in the late 1970s and early 1980s. Wages, incomes, and levels of consumption in both industry and agriculture have risen faster than labor productivity, suggesting that they are likely to slow down in the years ahead. If the gains of the past decade have produced expectations for rapid increases in living standards that cannot be fulfilled, the Party may face mounting dissatisfaction among both workers and peasants during the rest of the century. This problem may provide a partial explanation, in fact, for the campaign against "excessive consumption" and for the greater frugality and austerity that followed the dismissal of Hu Yaobang in early 1987.[10] Chinese leaders seem to be trying to limit popular expectations of the rate at which real incomes can be feasibly increased.

A second problem confronting China's post-Mao reforms is inflation. Inflation is almost inevitable when price controls are relaxed on goods that are in short supply or that have been underpriced or subsidized in the past. The problem has been made worse by characteristics of the economic situation in today's China, including a loss of control over the money supply, increases in wages that exceed the growth in labor productivity, and the devaluation of the renminbi to discourage imports. As noted in chapter 4, the retail price index rose to 6 percent in 1980, nearly 9 percent in 1985, and 6 percent in 1986, while hovering around 2 percent to 3 percent in the intervening years. The cost-of-living index for administrative staff and industrial workers, which may be a more accurate reflection of inflation for urban residents, was generally one percentage point higher in each year. Inflation is especially worrisome to Chinese leaders, and to older citizens, because it was the final cause of the collapse of the Kuomintang government in the late 1940s. The sporadic protests against price increases, and the tendency of the Chinese government to delay price reform during periods when the economy has been overheated, suggest that inflation remains a potentially serious political problem in contemporary China.

The chronic tendency of the Chinese economy toward high levels of investment, often in nonproductive projects or in undertakings unable to produce profits over the longer run, has also intensified inflationary pressures. These excessive levels of investment are inflationary because they strain supplies of construction materials and capital goods, often diverting them from projects that would ordinarily receive a higher priority. "Hyperinvestment" is a familiar problem in many socialist economies, where each locality has a stake in developing as wide a range of industrial enterprises and social facilities as possible. These tendencies have been exacerbated in post-Mao China as a consequence of granting enterprises and local governments greater autonomy over investment decisions without subjecting them to rational prices and strict financial discipline.

Controlling inflation will depend very much on the design and implementation of effective regulatory mechanisms for the Chinese economy. These include the development of control over the money supply and investment capital; the creation of measures to restrict the growth in wages and bonuses to the level of increases in productivity; the timing of price reform and the selection of the commodities whose prices will be decontrolled; and the imposition of more stringent financial discipline on industrial enterprise, to discourage managers from launching nonprofitable investment projects. None of these steps will be easy, but the large amount of surplus labor throughout the Chinese economy, and the low efficiency with which capital is used in Chinese industry, offer some hope that the level of inflation can be kept from becoming economically destabilizing or politically disruptive.[11]

Over the longer run, a further threat to economic reform is the emergence of socioeconomic inequality beyond levels that are politically acceptable. Some inequalities have already become apparent, particularly between those sectors of society that were the mainstay of the Maoist economic system (peasants engaged in grain production, workers in state-owned industry, and employees of the Party and state bureaucracies) and those sectors that have been created or enlarged by the post-Mao reforms (peasants who cultivate cash crops, private entrepreneurs, and workers in collectively owned service and industrial establishments in both city and countryside). The gaps in income between these two groups have already begun to generate protest and complaint, as reflected in the strikes by Peking bus drivers over the higher salaries received by the employees of collectively owned taxi companies and in the resentment of rural cadres and peasants at the "ten thousand yuan" households who have become wealthy by engaging in light manufacturing or rural services.

Other inequalities, although not yet widely apparent, are likely to emerge over time. Although the initial phase of the reforms has narrowed the gap between urban and rural incomes and consumption, differences between city and countryside are likely to widen again over the rest of the century, as increases in agricultural productivity lag behind those in industry. Indeed, the ratio of non-peasant consumption to peasant consumption reached a low of 2.2:1 in 1984 and has begun to increase slightly since then. Interregional inequality is also almost certain to increase, if only because some regions are better endowed than others with natural resources, transportation lines, and commercial centers, and because there are inadequate links between the dynamic coastal cities and the more backward areas in the interior. Social tensions may be produced by the development of a two-track educational system, with students divided between those who receive vocational training and those who are prepared for university.[12]

Thus far, the impact of growing inequality has been limited by the fact that almost all groups in Chinese society have experienced an improvement in their real standard of living, by the common perception that Maoist China was unjustly egalitarian, and by a consensus that some graduated material incentive is a necessary and desirable method for stimulating productivity and rewarding efficiency. But as the inequalities increase, they may become a social and political problem for the reformers, especially if they are no longer seen as the just product of greater effort but as the result of corruption, personal contacts, or structural inequities in the economy. Particularly worrisome would be the emergence of sizable groups at either end of the Chinese economic spectrum: an elite with high incomes earned through private economic activity or through investments, or an underclass of unskilled workers, poor peasants, or urban unemployed.

Still, the Chinese government is not without remedial measures to alleviate economic inequality. Taxation can place a ceiling over income and wealth, and welfare measures can provide a basic level of subsistence for families who encounter financial difficulties. Fiscal policy and state investment funds can also be used to transfer wealth from more advanced parts of the country to poorer regions. In all these ways, the state can intervene to prevent inequality from reaching levels that would be politically destabilizing.

In the political sphere, the most immediate problem to plague the reforms has been the rise of corruption. The development and manipulation of personal connections, or *guanxi*, has been an enduring aspect of life in China both before and after the Communist takeover, and both during the Maoist era and in the post-Mao years. Nepotism has also been commonplace, with its most recent manifestation the assignment of prized positions in the bureaucracy to the sons and daughters of ranking Party officials.

The form of corruption that has risen most rapidly during the post-Mao era has been graft and profiteering in the economy. Officials at every level of government have used their influence and positions for the economic betterment of themselves and their families. Unscrupulous factory managers and private citizens have bought merchandise from the state at subsidized prices and sold it on the marketplace for much more. Lively black markets have developed in foreign exchange, and small-scale "briefcase trading companies" have been established to acquire and distribute imported consumer goods that are in high demand.

These kinds of corruption have been produced by the loosening of administrative controls over the economy and society, without the development of sufficient legal restraints and auditing mechanisms to take their place. Over time, it may be possible to remedy them through the creation of clearer rules of administrative conduct, the creation of a more stringent and effective legal system, and the gradual professionalization of the bureaucracy. Meanwhile, however, Chinese politics will probably be convulsed from time to time by spectacular cases of corruption, such as that involving Hainan Island in 1985. Moreover, the rise in graft and malfeasance will be blamed on the reform of the domestic economy and on the growing interaction between China and the outside world.

Another problem is the emergence of unorthodox ideas and habits in Chinese society, whether in the form of political dissent or cultural experimentation. China already has witnessed the development of new life-styles that more conservative Chinese consider unacceptable. Longer hair, blue jeans, and T-shirts on young people are regarded by some older people as "spiritual pollution"; disco parties, rock concerts, videotapes of Hong Kong kung-fu movies, and semipornographic publications even more so. Some believe that a "lust for money" and for expensive consumer goods is corrupting their society, and that this development results from the opening of China to the West.[13]

Over the longer run, China may also be characterized by the rise of political dissent. Sporadic protests have been commonplace in post-Mao China, but have not yet crystallized into a systemic opposition movement, as exists in Taiwan, South Korea, or Poland. The student demonstrations of late 1986 raised the possibility, however, that sustained pressure for greater political and intellectual liberalization may soon become a feature of Chinese politics. Certainly improved levels of education, increased contacts with the outside world, and rising standards of living, especially in the cities, should push China in this direction. The issue facing future generations of Party leaders will be the blend of repression and accommodation with which they respond to the rise of political dissent. A more restrictive approach may suppress dissent temporarily, but may be more destabilizing in the end, whereas a more accommodative strategy would encourage some dissent, but would simultaneously direct it into institutionalized channels.

Finally, the reforms will have an impact on the level of uncertainty and risk that confronts individual workers, economic enterprises, and Chinese society as a whole. To be sure, some risks have been greatly reduced by the post-Mao reform program. The chances of foreign invasion are much lower now than at the height of the Cultural Revolution in the late 1960s; peasants face a sharply reduced risk of famine; urban residents enjoy greater guarantees against arbitrary actions by Party and state officials; and the society as a whole is less likely to encounter abrupt political change than during the Maoist era.

But other risks, particularly economic in nature, have risen because of the reforms. Chinese workers now face rising prices, more uncertain wage levels, and even the threat of unemployment. Enterprises face the risks inherent in changing market conditions, now to the point at which bankruptcy could be the cost of unwise managerial decisions. The country is now more vulnerable to the vagaries of the international economy than when its leaders adopted more autarkic foreign economic policies. A society that became accustomed to predictable stagnation during the Maoist period may find it difficult to adjust to a situation that is more dynamic, but also more uncertain.

General Explanations and Remedies

Each of the six problems just outlined has its own causes, but they are also attributable to the more general situation in which China now finds itself. As emphasized throughout this book, the post-Mao reforms are creating a mixed economic and political system, combining elements of both plan and market, and aspects of both political relaxation and authoritarianism. As a result, post-Mao China is suffering simultaneously from the difficulties and short-comings of all of the economic and political mechanisms it is trying to conjoin. The country has inherited the inefficiencies and rigidities of the plan: the tendencies toward local and national autarky, the chronic pressures toward hyperinvestment, and the inefficiencies and disincentives connected with an irrational system of prices. To those, it is now adding the instabilities and uncertainties of the marketplace, including inflation, inequality, and unemployment. China must continue to cope with the alienation, the factionalism, and the bureaucratism of its old political system. At the same time, however, it faces the newer challenges of political dissent, social deviance, and cultural heterodoxy that have resulted from the relaxation of political controls over Chinese society.

Furthermore, serious contradictions are certain to occur among the various elements that Chinese leaders are attempting to blend to form what they call a "planned commodity economy" and a "democratic dictatorship." The coexistence of a planned sector and a market sector in the Chinese economy, for example, exacerbates the problem of corruption. The fact that the same commodity is now available through two different channels and at two different prices—through state allocation agencies at a subsidized or controlled price, and through wholesale markets at a floating or market price—makes it possible to engage in highly profitable arbitrage for many industrial goods. The absence of an effective market for capital, labor, or land limits the ability of a Chinese enterprise to respond quickly and effectively to the signals sent by the markets that do exist for finished commodities and raw materials. The periodic crackdowns on political dissent and cultural heterodoxy make it difficult for Chinese intellectuals to respond enthusiastically to calls for scientific and artistic creativity, or for managers and entrepreneurs to fully exercise their autonomy in economic matters. Perhaps most basically, the substantial liberalization that has occurred in the Chinese economy makes the remaining restraints on political and intellectual life all the more glaring.

Finally, China is now—and is likely to remain for some time—in transition between the old regime and the new and can be expected to encounter serious difficulties along the way. The relaxation of administrative controls over the economy, in the absence of stringent financial discipline over enterprises, produces the periodic waves of investment and surges of imports that have been so damaging to the Chinese economy over the last several years. The deactivation of the totalitarian institutions that once constrained daily life in China, without the emergence of effective legal and judicial institutions in their place, is partly responsible for the rise of crime and corruption that has occurred under the post-Mao reforms. The deregulation of prices, when China is still characterized by a sellers' market for most commodities, is almost certain to produce serious levels of inflation. The discrediting of old values and doctrines, when Chinese intellectuals are still attempting to define a new "spiritual civilization" for their country, helps create a widespread sense of ideological uncertainty and cultural decay. And the uneven progress toward political liberalization also complicates matters: as one Chinese observer has put it, the Chinese people "now have the right to grumble about Party decisions, but not the power to influence them."

The problems engendered by reform, therefore, can be attributed in part to some common general causes, as well as to specific origins. In the same way, overcoming these shortcomings and difficulties will require not only specific curatives directed at each problem but also some remedial measures designed to increase the efficiency of the system as a whole. At least five measures fall into this category: vigorous competition among enterprises, the threat of bankruptcy for unprofitable producers, the emergence of markets for the factors of production, price reform, and managerial autonomy.

The essence of the economic reforms is to compel enterprises to pay greater attention to the profitability of their operations and to allow them to respond more rapidly and directly to the signals sent by the marketplace. Without the stimulus of vigorous competition and the threat of bankruptcy, enterprises will have relatively little incentive to avoid unprofitable or irrational decisions about investment, pricing, and product line. Without prices that accurately reflect relative scarcities, it will be extremely difficult for enterprises to perceive which commodities are in short supply and which are no longer in demand. Finally, without factor markets and managerial autonomy, enterprises will not be able to react to the signals being sent to them by the marketplace, for they will be unable to let go of surplus labor, or to acquire greater capital, labor, or raw materials, without the intermediacy of a cumbersome state bureaucracy.

Moreover, each of these five remedial measures is highly dependent on each of the others. Bankruptcy cannot be fairly imposed on enterprises if their managers do not enjoy autonomy from the state bureaucracy, if the cost of their inputs is set unreasonably high, or if the prices they can charge for their output are set unreasonably low. If price reform is undertaken in the absence of lively competition among enterprises, the result will be that prices are set at monopolistic or monopsonistic levels. And managerial autonomy is relatively meaningless in the absence of factor markets and is positively dangerous if there is no stringent financial discipline to guide the decisions that managers take concerning investments, pricing, and product lines. As one Chinese reformer has warned, giving factories greater autonomy in the absence of provisions for bankruptcy and competition would mean that Chinese industry would enter a "Bermuda triangle" of higher prices, higher subsidies, and therefore higher taxes.[14]

But though the five general remedies just mentioned are the keys to successful reform, they are also among the most sensitive political issues that the reformers currently face. Price reform runs the risk of inflation; bankruptcy threatens unemployment. Enterprise managers are reluctant to face effective competition from rival factories; local Party and government leaders are averse to grant enterprises full autonomy from their administrative control; and the national government hesitates to assign the allocation of labor, capital, and other factors of production to the workings of the marketplace.

Together, these key reforms conflict with many aspects of the socialist ethic in Chinese economic policy: stable prices, job security, a planned economy, and Party leadership.

The danger is that Chinese leaders may choose to deal with their economic difficulties by reimposing familiar administrative controls, rather than adopting further reforms that might prove unpopular. Faced with inflation, the decisionmakers might reimpose price controls rather than continue with price reform. Confronted with excessive investment, they might choose to allocate financial capital directly, rather than relying on a combination of competition, financial discipline, and higher interest rates to bring levels of investment under control. Or, concerned about growing inequalities within cities, Chinese leaders might reduce the opportunities for private and collective employment, rather than increase labor mobility by establishing a freer market for labor. These choices would be understandable, but each would move China away from reform and toward a more administered economy. Were these decisions ever to be taken, they would be convincing symptoms that China had contracted the Hungarian disease during the course of reform.

THE POLITICAL BASE FOR REFORM

What kind of political base does reform enjoy, and how will its evolution affect the future of reform? The attitudes of the officials at the top of the Party, state, and military bureaucracies, the preferences of important bureaucratic agencies, and the popular mood among workers, peasants, and intellectuals must all be considered. We will find that there is somewhat more consensus in favor of reform at the top of the Chinese political system than at lower levels; and that there seems to be growing acquiescence toward reform, if not active support for it, within the bureaucracy. Among ordinary Chinese citizens, the situation is more complex. Reform has engendered substantial support, but the difficulties that lie ahead, and the rise of new generations of Chinese into positions of authority, are grounds for suspecting that the popular base for reform may gradually erode unless effective measures can be taken to remedy the problems just outlined.

The Political Leadership

At the highest level of Chinese politics, support for reform has consolidated steadily since 1976. By 1982 almost all those leaders closely associated with the mass movements of the Cultural Revolution, and with the revolutionary Maoist strain in Chinese politics, had been removed from the leading bodies of the Party and government: the Gang of Four in 1976, the "little Gang of Four" in 1980, and the "model peasant" Chen Yonggui in 1982. During the same period, leaders who had been at the forefront of the restorationist programs of the late 1970s were also demoted or replaced. The "petroleum faction" was sharply criticized in 1980, and Hua Guofeng was removed from the Party chairmanship in 1981. In their place were put many veteran officials, exemplified by Deng Xiaoping, Peng Zhen, and Chen Yun, who had been purged during the Cultural Revolution and who were now ready for some degree of reform.

By the close of the Twelfth Party Congress in 1982, only three men who had joined the Politburo at the Ninth or Tenth Party Congresses in 1969 and 1973 (Li Desheng, Wei Guoqing, and Ni Zhifu) remained on that body. And with the convening of the Sixth National People's Congress the following year, only four members of the State Council appointed at the Fourth Congress in 1975 (Fang Yi, Kang Shien, Wan Li, and Zhang Jingfu) were reappointed to the cabinet. This step removed nearly all of those who had come to power at the height of the Cultural Revolution. Reformers now dominated both the Politburo and the State Council, as well as the Party Secretariat, which had been staffed with reformers when it was reestablished in 1980.

With the removal of the Maoists and the restorationists from the central Party and state leadership, however, the reform coalition began to divide into radical and moderate wings. Men like Hu Yaobang, Zhao Ziyang, Wan Li, and Deng Xiaoping favored rapid implementation of economic reform and, to a lesser degree, the further liberalization and restructuring of the political system. Other leaders, including Chen Yun, Peng Zhen, Hu Qiaomu, and Deng Liqun, seemed to support the more cautious and limited approach associated with moderate reform.

At first, the momentum seemed to be with the radical reformers. They were able to strengthen their position at the National Party Conference in the fall of 1985, when ten members of the Politburo and three members of the Secretariat, most of whom were in their late seventies or eighties, retired. On balance, the new appointments to these two key bodies gave the radical reformers an apparent majority on the Politburo and near dominance of the Party Secretariat.

But prominent representatives of the moderate reformers remained in key positions at the center and, presumably, in some of the provinces and ministries. None of the Politburo or Secretariat members who had expressed reservations about various aspects of reform over the previous several years—notably Chen Yun, Hu Qiaomu, Deng Liqun, or Li Xiannian—was removed or demoted at the National Party Conference in 1985. At least one of the new appointments to the Politburo and Secretariat, Vice-Premier Li Peng, seemed more sympathetic to the moderate reformers than to the radicals. Moreover, the radical reformers suffered a serious setback with the dismissal of Hu Yaobang in early 1987, raising the possibility that more conservative elements would make gains in representation on central Party and state bodies when the Thirteenth Party Congress convened in the fall of 1987 and when the Seventh National People's Congress met in the spring of 1988.

Although clear divisions remain at the highest levels of the Party, the range of views is substantially narrower than in the 1970s, and the center of gravity on the political spectrum has shifted markedly toward support for reform. In the 1970s deep and irreconcilable differences occurred between Maoists and pragmatists over whether to perpetuate or eradicate the changes in structure and policy made during the Cultural Revolution. The competition between the two groups had devolved into a struggle for political survival, with few limits on the strategies, rhetoric, or tactics that could be employed.

Today, the differences among the Party leaders are much narrower. Virtually no central Party or state leader seems to favor a return to the Soviet model of the 1950s, let alone to the Maoist policies and institutions of the 1960s and early 1970s. All accept the desirability of reform. They differ, however, on the pace of reform and, increasingly, on how far China should move toward a market economy, political liberalization, and alterations in the basic pattern of state ownership of the industrial economy.

Largely because the current differences between the moderate reformers and the radical reformers are not as wide as the differences between the moderates and the radicals of the 1970s, the cleavages among China's top leaders have not yet crystallized into contending factions engaged in the unprincipled pursuit of political power. The disagreements among them are more susceptible to compromise than was the case during the Cultural Revolution. Furthermore, today's leaders seem united by a conviction that, whatever their differences, policy debates must be conducted within the traditional norms of collective leadership, majority rule, and minority rights that were overturned, with such tragic results, during the Cultural Revolution. Deng Xiaoping has worked hard, and so far successfully, to establish rules of Chinese politics that restrict the strategies of political competition, limit the power gained by the winners, and reduce the political and physical consequences suffered by the losers.

Even so, the stability and institutionalization of top-level politics in China remain uncertain. For one thing, the differences between the moderate and radical wings of the reform coalition may deepen in the years ahead, as China completes the implementation of the earliest reforms on which they both could agree, and as more controversial issues begin to dominate the country's political agenda. Possibly, moderate and radical reformers will disagree more strenuously on the timing of wage and price reforms, the adoption of enterprise bankruptcy, and the degree to which mandatory planning should be abolished and managerial autonomy increased. They will certainly differ on the desirability of the even more radical economic and political reforms first introduced in 1986. The issue will be whether experiments with these controversial proposals will prove successful, and whether enough leaders now committed to undertake reform can be persuaded of the feasibility and necessity of more radical measures.

Moreover, there are strong tendencies in Chinese political culture to see politics in highly moralistic terms, to deny the possibility of a loyal political opposition, and to view political competition as a struggle for power among tightly organized personal factions. At the same time, when there is a strong authority atop the political system, cultural predispositions demand superficial expressions of harmony and prohibit the open expression of political differences. Thus a veneer of unity, which masks a cauldron of conflict underneath, often characterizes Chinese politics. In short, Chinese politics is usually less stable than it appears.

Should the facade of harmony begin to crack, Chinese politics could begin a rapid descent into intense factional conflict. A Gresham's law governs the political realm, as well as the economic: bad politics drives out good. Once one set of actors sees politics as a fight for political survival and acts accordingly, other groups and individuals have every incentive to act in similar fashion. For this reason, the apparent intensification of intraelite struggle in China before and after the dismissal of Hu Yaobang was grounds for concern.

While Deng Xiaoping is alive, he should be able to prevent the degradation of politics into an unprincipled conflict. After he passes from the political scene, however, there are no guarantees that a comparably strong leader will emerge, who can make key policy choices and enforce the norms of political competition. The degeneration of Chinese politics into factionalism in the post-Deng era therefore cannot be ruled out.

The Bureaucracy

The manageably narrow range of views on the Politburo, the State Council, and the Secretariat is not matched by similar consensus at lower levels in the Chinese system. Rather, the deeper one probes into the Chinese bureaucracy, and then into the Chinese society beneath it, the greater the opposition, either active or passive, one encounters.[15]

One common saying about the prospects for reform is that enthusiasm for the process is "hot at both ends but cold in the middle." This adage reflects the fact that reform has enjoyed the support of most of the leadership, and the backing of large sectors of the population, but it has had relatively few institutional con- stituencies. Though there was no strong support for radical Maoism in China's bureaucratic establishment, neither has there been much enthusiasm for reform. Instead, most of the bureaucracy has appeared initially to favor the conservative restorationism associated with Hua Guofeng.

Much of China's bureaucratic infrastructure was created or ex- panded during the mid-1950s, when the Soviet model was transferred to China. Consequently, many bureaucratic institutions have be- come interested in sustaining the Leninist-Stalinist model of eco- nomics and politics that prevailed before—and even during—the great Maoist campaigns such as the Great Leap Forward and the Cultural Revolution. These include four of the most important organizational networks that constitute the Chinese political order. One is the ministries of heavy industry, the principal beneficiaries of the priority assigned to that sector under the Stalinist model of development. These ministries see their resources threatened by the new stress on consumer goods, light industry, and services. A second is the state planning apparatus, which gained enormous power over the economy because of the adoption of a centrally planned economy in China, and whose influence would be drastically reduced by movement toward a market economy. The Party estab- lishment, especially the propaganda organs, has been a third source of bureaucratic resistance. The Party has a large stake in preserving the unitary organizational and ideological system of Chinese Len- inism, is concerned about the declining relevance of doctrine in post-Mao China, and resents the pressure from the reformers to transfer power over administrative matters from the Party to government bodies, enterprises, and other grassroots units. And finally, one must include important segments, although by no means the entirety, of the People's Liberation Army, which shares the Party's concern over the consequences of political liberalization and the worries of the heavy industrial ministries over the declining priority assigned to that sector of the economy.

To be sure, a few bureaucratic institutions seem to favor reform, if only its moderate versions. Compared with the bureaus charged with economic planning and heavy industry, the ministries responsible for agriculture, finance, commerce, light industry, and social services are more enthusiastic about the trends toward a market economy and consumerism. The finance agencies in China have always been opposed to the disequilibria created by the Stalinist and Maoist emphases on high speed and high accumulation, and the bureaus responsible for agriculture, consumer goods, housing, and other "nonproductive" investments have been disadvantaged by the neglect of these sectors in the Maoist period. Furthermore, some institutions—such as the Bank of China and the Ministry of Finance—benefit from a shift from administrative controls over the economy to regulatory mechanisms. And local authorities, especially at the provincial and municipal levels, gain from the decentralization of control over investment capital and foreign exchange.

For the most part, though, the Chinese bureaucracy is oriented more toward the perpetuation and "perfection" of the traditional model of state ownership and central planning than toward its fundamental restructuring. In addition, bureaucratic officials have some important personal interests that have been negatively affected by the reform program. There is widespread resentment at the mandatory retirement age that has been newly imposed on high- and middle-level cadres. And some veteran officials of worker or peasant background have complained about the youth and class background of their successors, claiming that China is being turned over to "immature intellectuals" rather than more experienced representatives of the working class.

This relatively pessimistic assessment of bureaucratic attitudes toward reform should be qualified in two ways, however. First, it is important to recognize that revolutionary Maoism has had little support within the principal institutions that govern contemporary China. At the time of Mao's death, the radicals had strong representation in only a few Party and government agencies, particularly those responsible for propaganda, culture, and education. They had also managed to gain control of leadership positions in a few provinces and municipalities. But the death of Mao removed their most important source of power, and since the purge of the Gang of Four and the reshuffling of the Party and state bureaucracies that followed, the support for revolutionary Maoism within the Chinese political establishment has been almost eliminated.

Further, there is reason to expect that, over time, the Chinese bureaucracy should become more acquiescent, if not enthusiastic, toward reform. The processes of restaffing, rectification, and recruitment, described in chapter 8, should bring younger leaders, more imbued with the spirit of reform, into positions of authority in the Party, the army, and the state. The reduction of staffs of bureaus responsible for administrative control over the economy will reduce the power of the guardians of the old economic system, and the expansion of the agencies responsible for reform and regulation will create new constituencies for the post-Mao reform program. Gradually, bureaucratic agencies should adjust to the new roles and missions assigned them in a restructured economic and political system, and even develop a vested interest in maintaining them. Even so, the bureaucracy will probably continue to be an obstacle to the adoption and smooth implementation of more radical reform measures.

Popular Constituencies

Since China remains, despite the post-Mao reforms, an authoritarian political system, the impact of public opinion on domestic policy is considerably less serious than in more pluralistic societies. Nonetheless, the subject does warrant a brief discussion. The growing consultativeness of the Chinese political system has given some sectors, particularly intellectuals, more influence over policy than was true in the Maoist period. Moreover, the rise of protest in a society that values order has also made Chinese leaders more sensitive to the attitudes of other urban groups, especially students and workers.

Assessing the political preferences of particular social groups in China is an even more difficult task than evaluating the preferences of the bureaucracy. There are almost no scientific surveys of the popular mood, and public opinion can shift over time in response to the vagaries of the economic climate and to the changing effects of the reforms on daily life. Nonetheless, a general outline of the attitudes of popular constituencies toward reform can be assembled from a careful reading of the Chinese press, interviews with knowledgeable Chinese, and informed speculation about the objective impact of reform on various sectors of Chinese society.

Peasants and workers presumably have a strong interest in greater prosperity and will support reforms that increase their income, provide more attractive consumer goods and more abundant social and cultural services, and offer better quality food and housing. They also will support reforms that increase their freedom to live their daily lives without intervention by the state, express opinions on political matters, and engage in individual or collective economic activity. In all these ways, the reforms have gained a considerable base of support among ordinary Chinese in both city and countryside.

Other aspects of reform may be less appealing. The rise of social and economic inequalities runs counter to strongly held egalitarian sentiment, rooted not only in revolutionary Maoism but also in the utopian traditions of the Chinese countryside. As noted earlier in this chapter, the emergence of a few wealthy families in both urban and rural areas—the individual entrepreneurs in the cities, and the so-called ten thousand yuan households in the countryside—is beginning to arouse dissatisfaction among those who earn less, particularly those in lower administrative positions in the bureaucracy and those who are retired on fixed pensions. These resentments will be intensified if the perception arises that the new economic elites have become wealthy through improper conduct: corruption, illicit relations with foreigners, or the exploitation of hired labor.

Inflation, particularly for goods and services that were previously heavily subsidized, could also erode support for reform. Increases in consumer prices would violate what many analysts have described as the implicit social contract between state and society in many communist systems: the denial of certain economic and political freedoms in exchange for the supply of the staples of life at low prices. The rapid rise in the price of food in 1985 was extremely unpopular, even though the regime attempted to provide wage supplements to compensate for it. Similarly, any increase in the price of housing or transportation in the cities, or of fertilizer and diesel fuel in the countryside, would also be controversial, possibly to the point of being politically explosive.

The interests of urban workers in stability and security may also be threatened by other aspects of reform. The new provisions for the bankruptcy of the state enterprises, the dismissal of unproductive workers, or the end to automatic promotions for state officials challenge the principle of secure lifetime employment. Proposed wage reforms that would link wages and bonuses more closely to the performance of enterprises could imply annual fluctuations in worker incomes. Workers may also fear that the emergence of political dissent among students would threaten the order and harmony of Chinese society. In all these areas, workers could well come to support, even demand, the restoration of tighter controls over the political system or the economy if the problems generated by reform became too severe.

The intellectuals present a different picture, for, while sharing some common interests with workers and peasants, they have some particular concerns of their own. Like the rest of Chinese society, intellectuals have gained a great deal from the economic achievements of the last decade: higher wages, better consumer goods, and increased social services. In addition, they have benefited from the greater freedom of scientific research and artistic creation that has characterized the post-Mao era, and from the end to the political persecution that they suffered during the Cultural Revolution.

Despite their satisfaction with most of what has occurred since 1978, many intellectuals share with workers and peasants a resentment toward the economic inequalities generated by reform. This is particularly since, as state employees on relatively fixed salaries, they have fewer opportunities for self-employment than peasants and fewer chances for obtaining bonuses for superior performance than workers. Moreover, as the sector of society responsible for the transmission of culture from one generation to the next, intellectuals are especially concerned about the decline of traditional values that can occur with rapid economic and social change. This often takes the form of an intense cultural nationalism that reinforces, but is still distinguishable from, the demand for ideological purity that permeates the Party apparatus. Some intellectuals have complained about the growth of a materialistic mentality, a decline of social consciousness, and a tendency to emulate the popular culture of Hong Kong and the rest of capitalist East Asia.

In the intellectual community, however, there are differences in attitudes among generations that are becoming of increasing interest both to foreign observers and to the Chinese themselves. (These may parallel generational cleavages within the working class, and even within the peasantry.) Four generations can be identified, even though there are no clear or firm boundaries among them.[16]

Older intellectuals, including those trained in the West (or in Western-style institutions in China) before 1949, are often sympathetic to more radical structural reform, ordered around markets, private ownership, political pluralism, and individual human rights. Moreover, as some of the most prominent victims of the Cultural Revolution, this generation has a particular distaste for revolutionary Maoism and may well wish to see China distance itself from that political tendency as far as possible.

Middle-aged intellectuals, consisting of those who received their higher education in the 1950s, seem more comfortable with a political system that retains significant elements of ideological orthodoxy and with an economic system that maintains a great deal of economic control. This generation's sympathy for the Soviet model, and its nostalgia for the China of the mid-1950s, is reinforced by the fact that its experiences during the Cultural Revolution were unlikely to have been as violent and disruptive as those experienced by either their elders or their juniors. Their academic training, acquired either in the Soviet Union or in China when the Soviet model was dominant, is the most narrow and, by present standards, the least adequate of all the generations under consideration here. They may therefore fear that a significant liberalization of the political and academic system would leave them unable to compete with their younger colleagues and would thus reduce their chances for upward mobility. Although relatively few would support a return to revolutionary Maoism, or even the revival of the restorationist policies of Hua Guofeng, this generation is much more inclined toward moderate reform than toward its radical variants.

Younger intellectuals, especially those directly involved in the Cultural Revolution, represent a third generation. Those who were in university or high school in the late 1960s had a particularly searing experience. Their forced transfer to the countryside in the late 1960s left them deeply disenchanted with revolutionary Maoism and disillusioned by the poverty and backwardness of rural China. Some of the most active members of this generation formed reading and study groups during their exile in the countryside and began to devise radical solutions to China's economic and political problems. These orientations were reinforced by the opportunities to study abroad after 1978, and by the freedom in the more liberal academic environment within China, to read Western economics, history, and political philosophy. This generation has been at the forefront of the radical reform movement, from the time of Democracy Wall onward.

Finally, as China entered the 1980s, a new generation of students mounted the political stage. In many respects they have carried on the traditions of their immediate elders, as reflected in the nation-wide protests in favor of political liberalization at the end of 1986. But Chinese draw distinctions between these two youngest generations of intellectuals. The generation of the 1980s is perhaps more theoretically sophisticated than that of the Cultural Revolutionary era, but has much less practical experience. There is also a strong strain of nationalism in the youngest generation of intellectuals, which has led some of its members to oppose any sign that the post-Mao reforms were leading to economic or political dependence on the West. This generation, therefore, has engaged in protests against some elements of China's "open door" to the outside world, including the 1985 demonstrations against Japan's "economic invasion" of China.

This analysis of the attitudes of workers, peasants, and intellectuals—when coupled with the earlier assessment of the likely political and economic problems facing reform—suggests the strong possibility that the popular political base for reform may well erode over the rest of the century. To be sure, not all the trends work in this direction. The reforms are creating their own beneficiaries, including younger technocrats, wealthy peasants, individual entrepreneurs, and workers in profitable industries. Over time, in fact, China will develop a socialist middle class, with a strong interest in both political stability and liberalization. The Cultural Revolution's generation of intellectuals—aggressive, ambitious, and open-minded—is growing in influence and prominence.

But three other trends concern those who favor the continuation and extension of reform. First, the emergence of any of the problems identified earlier in this chapter—inflation, inequality, corruption, dissent, or social deviance—will erode the political support for reform and raise demands for the reimposition of administrative controls over the economy and the political system. So, too, may serious fluctuations in economic performance, which give the impression of uncertainty and disorder.

Second, the reformers have already adopted and implemented those elements of their reform program that can produce rapid gains in the standard of living for the Chinese people. Henceforth, the rate of economic improvement is likely to be slower going and may not meet the expectations generated by the dramatic changes of the past decade. Moreover, many of the reforms that remain to be implemented, particularly price reform, wage reform, and enterprise bankruptcy, are almost certain to be extremely unpopular.

And finally, although the generation of the Cultural Revolution is rapidly increasing its influence, those trained in the 1950s will be the immediate beneficiaries of the retirements of China's senior officials and intellectuals. Now in their late forties and mid-fifties, the men and women trained under the influence of the Soviet model are directly in line to move into positions of authority as veteran leaders step aside. Many younger Chinese reformers believe that the installation of this generation in leading posts in the Party and state bureaucracy will inevitably cause the pace of reform to slow.

The possibility that the political support for reform may wither is illustrated by the fact that, in the mid-1980s, China has already witnessed rising resentment of inequalities in urban areas, heightened uncertainty about price reform in urban areas, and growing tensions over student protest and dissent, even among those who had previously been asssumed to be the main beneficiaries of reform. There is reason to believe that the radical reformers were dismayed, even shocked, by the outpouring of criticism of reform during the campaign against bourgeois liberalization following the fall of Hu Yaobang. The reformers will have to pay increasing attention to the maintenance of popular support for their programs and ensure that the perceived benefits of reform outweigh the costs. Otherwise, China may yet fall victim to the Hungarian disease, or even to the more virulent sort of political crisis experienced in Poland.

POSSIBLE SCENARIOS

As China approaches the last decade of the twentieth century, it is poised on a political spectrum running from radical reform to the restoration of revolutionary Maoism. The center of gravity on that spectrum has shifted dramatically in the last ten years, in favor of reform. But the fulcrum could shift again, either toward further liberalization or back to a more rigidly administered society. What factors will determine how far forward, or how far backward, China is likely to move?

Several contingencies will shape China's course between now and the end of the century. One is the evolution of the relative costs and benefits of the reform program. On the one hand, developments will depend on China's ability to sustain the benefits of reform: reasonably high rates of economic growth, steady improvements in the people's standard of living, and a secure and respected position in the international environment. On the other, the reforms must also minimize or avoid the problems of imbalance, inflation, inequality, corruption, and dissent, which would reduce their popular support.

To a degree, the composition of this balance sheet will depend on the skill of China's reformers in managing their economy, foreign relations, and domestic political constituencies. Reformers must find effective remedial mechanisms for coping with the shortcomings of reform and must conduct their foreign affairs with prudence and vision. They must also avoid any basic mistakes: appearing indifferent to the shortcomings that reform has created, sacrificing

China's interests in the international environment, or proposing new reform measures unacceptable to important sectors of the Chinese polity. Skillful management of these aspects of reform will require, in turn, either an effective collective leadership or a talented individual leader, after the death of Deng Xiaoping.

Unfortunately for the reformers, the relative costs and benefits engendered by the reforms will derive as much from their luck as their adroitness. Chinese agriculture, likely to become an increasingly vulnerable aspect of reform, is still highly vulnerable to the vagaries of the weather. Problems in China's relations with Hong Kong and Taiwan could well serve to discredit the reformers. And as the Chinese economy becomes more closely linked to the outside world, its health will be increasingly shaped by international factors outside Peking's control. China's ability to gain foreign markets, capital, and technology will rest on the vitality of the economies of the developed countries and the openness of foreign markets to Chinese exports.

The fate of reform will also depend on the ability of the skeptics and the critics to present a viable alternative: an attractive leader who can mobilize the dissatisfaction with reform and a set of policies that seem more effective than those that they would replace. Thus far, the critics have failed on both counts. They have not yet put forward an alternative leader, as Mao presented Lin Biao as an alternative to Liu Shaoqi in the mid-1960s, or as Deng Xiaoping presented himself as a possible replacement for Hua Guofeng in the late 1970s. Nor has their policy program yet attracted widespread support. The skeptics have been associated with campaigns or movements against "bourgeois liberalization" or "spiritual pollution," which are irrelevant to most workers and peasants and which alienate most of China's intellectuals. Only if the conservatives can develop a program that captures the imagination of those whose support for radical reform is wavering can they become a viable alternative for national leadership.

The attractiveness of a more conservative alternative will also be affected by the international environment, particularly the fate of reform in the Soviet Union and Eastern Europe. If Mikhail Gorbachev seems to be renouncing the Soviet model and adopting many elements of the Chinese experiment, then reformers in Peking can persuasively argue that there is no viable alternative to radical reform. But if reform in other socialist countries should falter, or if the Soviet Union and Eastern Europe can find ways of revitalizing their economies through more marginal changes in the Soviet model, then their example might be an attractive option for some in China as well. This connection between China and the Soviet Union explains why China's radical reformers profess optimism about the fate of Gorbachev's reforms: they have a strong interest in seeing the current Soviet experiment succeed.

Finally, as in all political life, timing will be critically important. The longer Deng Xiaoping lives, the more time he will have to rebuild the damage to the succession arrangements inflicted by the dismissal of Hu Yaobang, continue the restaffing and restructuring of the Party and state bureaucracies, and shepherd China through the difficulties of price reform and other politically sensitive reform measures. Equally important will be the timing of Deng's death relative to that of other senior Chinese leaders of the same generation. Reforms would be particularly vulnerable if Deng were survived by a man of comparable stature and prestige—a Chen Yun or a Peng Zhen—who could claim to be Deng's successor as China's paramount leader and who decided to sponsor a turn in a more conservative direction. And the timing of important Party and state meetings is also significant. If reform should falter on the eve of a National People's Congress or a National Party Congress, the conservatives would be in a much better position to gain representation on the State Council, Politburo, or Party Secretariat. In doing so, they might well be able to transform what would ordinarily be a temporary time of consolidation into a retrenchment of much longer duration.

It is possible to imagine some extreme scenarios in China, particularly after the death of Deng Xiaoping. There could be a severe deterioration of the economic situation, as a result of the coincidence of bad weather, an international recession, and the mismanagement of domestic economic policy. The Party leadership could split into competing factions, unable or unwilling to reconcile their differences. The country could face a level of chronic urban political dissent with which the leadership could not readily cope. In such a circumstance, one could conceive of a return to radical Maoism, as a way of mobilizing or deflecting dissent, or of a military coup, designed to restore order by seizing power from a divided and ineffective leadership.

Neither of these two extreme scenarios is likely, however. There are enough positive elements in the Chinese economy to make a total collapse highly implausible. The differences among the Party's highest officials have sufficiently narrowed to make a degeneration into intense factionalism improbable, although not unthinkable. Although dissent, as already noted, will gradually increase in the years ahead, it is not likely to assume proportions that the Party cannot control. Nor is there much lingering nostalgia for Maoism, or sympathy for military intervention in civilian politics.

The more plausible scenarios are therefore less dramatic. The most likely possibility is that China will move slowly, even haltingly, toward a more open, market-oriented economy and a more relaxed and consultative political system. Under this scenario, the regime would successfully develop the will and the ability to implement the critical elements of economic reform that so far remain incomplete. Prices would be made more rational and more flexible, the scope of mandatory planning reduced, and greater financial discipline imposed on enterprises. Chinese firms would be subject to greater competition from both domestic and foreign enterprises, and factory managers would wrest greater autonomy from both their Party committees and their cognizant government bureaus. Moreover, some aspects of radical economic reform—particularly the creation of labor and capital markets and changes in the system of state ownership of industry—would probably be introduced on a wider scale. In the political sphere, one can anticipate the gradual professionalization of the bureaucracy, the continued development of the legal system, a clearer division of labor between the Party and state, a decentralization of power from the central government to the provinces and municipalities, and a growing role for the people's congresses.

The most optimistic variant of this scenario would also see progress toward more radical political reform, such that the political system on the Chinese mainland might come more to resemble that on Taiwan in the 1970s. In such an event, there would be greater freedom of the press and of academic inquiry and fewer restrictions on experimentation in literature and art. Direct elections would gradually be instituted above county level and would involve more competition among candidates nominated by the Party. There might also be some contested elections within the Party, as a way of introducing a greater degree of democracy into the dominant Chinese political institution.

Still, even the most optimistic scenario would include limits on progress. It is unlikely that the present system of bureaucratic ownership of state industry would be abolished in favor of boards of directors or that mandatory planning and fixed prices would be eliminated. It is highly implausible that China will completely open its domestic market to imported products or to foreign ventures. Above all, it is not easy to conceive the Chinese Communist Party agreeing to dismantle its grassroots organizations in universities or factories, renounce Marxism as the guiding ideology of Chinese society, give up control over important personnel appointments in government agencies, or consent to the establishment of a multiparty system.

Moreover, even if reform should continue in the post-Deng era, there will be zigs and zags, advance and retreat, rather than smooth and steady progress. The course of reform will be characterized by fairly minor adjustments and modifications to reform programs, concerted but temporary attempts to use administrative controls to remedy particular economic problems, and even measures to set limits on the form and content of political expression. As in the past, these periods of retrenchment and consolidation will reflect both the difficulties encountered during the implementation of reform and the differences of opinion among Chinese leaders over the desirability of radical change. Given the moralistic tone of Chinese politics, the corrections may often seem excessive and may therefore encourage speculation that reform has permanently faltered. Chinese and foreign observers alike will find it difficult to distinguish between these temporary fluctuations and more enduring secular trends.

However, the possibility of a more pessimistic scenario remains, especially if the reforms encounter increasing technical difficulties, political obstacles, and popular dissatisfaction over time. There is the danger that inequalities, inflation, corruption, dissent, and crime will increase. China's post-Deng leadership may well be less unified, less skillful, and therefore less able to identify and agree on effective remedies for these problems. The economy may slow, as the initial stimulus of reform is exhausted and as later reform measures fail to increase agricultural and industrial productivity. Large parts of the population may become frustrated when living standards fail to rise as quickly as they expect. Above all, without Deng's personal authority, China's leaders may be unable to generate the requisite political, bureaucratic, and popular support for taking the difficult steps to make the economy more efficient. Consequently, the pessimistic scenario would envision a situation in which some reforms are rescinded, others modified, and still others indefinitely postponed.

Certain elements of both moderate and radical reform would be especially vulnerable to a period of retrogression. A more conservative leadership might well set limits on the size of individual enterprises and the sectors of the economy in which they could operate, the number of commodities subject to market prices or floating prices, the number of goods allocated by guidance planning or by market forces, the range of wages and bonuses provided in collective and private enterprises, and the array of incentives offered to potential foreign investors. In the political realm, conservative leadership would reassert the role of the Party in administrative matters at the grassroots, reaffirm the constraints on political and artistic expression, grant less power to legislative bodies, and tighten controls over the media, the universities, and the intellectual community in general.

Furthermore, a retreat from reform might also see the cancellation of several moderate reforms that have already proved controversial or problematic. Although it is unlikely that the household responsibility system would be abandoned, it is possible to imagine the reimposition of mandatory quotas for the production and delivery of important agricultural products and the compulsory formation of cooperatives for maintaining and expanding rural investment. Some of the special privileges now provided to the special economic zones and the open cities might be restricted or rescinded, including their authority to approve domestic investments and foreign contracts. The range of organizational formats offered to foreign investors might conceivably be narrowed, and the possibilities for wholly foreign-owned enterprises in China reduced. Academic exchanges with the West, particularly in the social sciences and humanities, might also be limited, and more Chinese students and scholars in these sensitive fields might be sent to other socialist countries.

Above all, this more pessimistic scenario would see a great reluctance to move forward with the unfinished agenda of reform in either the political or economic sphere. The most difficult aspects of moderate reform—price reform, competition among enterprises, bankruptcy, wage reform, and enterprise autonomy—would be implemented slowly, if at all. Experiments with markets for capital, land, and labor would be canceled or restricted, and there would be little interest in any basic change in the pattern of industrial ownership. Although the professionalization of the bureaucracy would probably continue, there would be little talk of further liberalization of either politics or ideology.

Nonetheless, just as there would be limits to progress under an optimistic scenario, so too would there be limits to retrogression even in this less favorable situation. Although they might be interpreted more conservatively and implemented more cautiously, the basic principles of moderate economic reform are likely to be retained: the household responsibility system in agriculture, expanded authority for industrial and commercial enterprises, a greater role for market forces in the determination of prices and the allocation of commodities, and tolerance of individual entrepreneurship in certain parts of the economy. Even under a pessimistic scenario, Chinese leaders would probably not isolate themselves from the international economy, halt the progress toward a more consultative political system, or reimpose arbitrary controls on the daily lives of ordinary Chinese. Above all, it is virtually inconceivable that post-Deng China would return to the revolutionary radicalism of the late Mao era or even to the restorationism of Hua Guofeng.

Moreover, even if the pessimistic scenario were to materialize in the years following the death of Deng Xiaoping, it is still possible for reform to regain momentum later on. A restoration of administrative controls over the economy, even if deemed necessary to cope with immediate problems, is unlikely to enable China to compete effectively with the dynamic economies elsewhere in Asia. Nor is a rigid political system likely to maintain support over the longer term, as China's level of education and standard of living continue to increase. A period of retrenchment and retrogression, therefore, might well give way once again to a period of renewed reform and liberalization. This pattern has been the experience of Eastern Europe, and it may well be the pattern in China too.

Despite the uncertainties that surround the processes of reform and succession in China, the range of possibilities for the future of China's second revolution is relatively bounded. Even under the more pessimistic contingencies, China is unlikely to return to the disorder and mobilization of revolutionary Maoism or even to the ossification and inefficiency of the Soviet model. Similarly, even under the most optimistic scenarios, China—at least in this century—is not likely to become a market economy, a capitalist system, or a pluralistic democracy. The issue is the blend of plan and market, political consultation and political control, individual entrepreneurship and state ownership, and international involvement and protectionism that Chinese leaders choose to adopt.

NOTES

CHAPTER I

1. Xinhua News Agency, March 28, 1985, in Foreign Broadcast Information Service, *Daily Report: China*, March 28, 1985, pp. D1–2, quotation on p. D1.

CHAPTER 2

1. The text of the official obituary is in "Message to the Whole Party, the Whole Army, and the People of All Nationalities throughout the Country," *Peking Review*, September 13, 1976, pp. 6–11. The description of the memorial services is ibid., September 24, 1976, pp. 7–11, 17–26, 39–42.
2. Descriptions of the popular mood in China following the death of Mao can be found in "Mao Tse-tung Dies in Peking at 82; Leader of Red China Revolution; Choice of Successor Is Uncertain," *New York Times*, September 10, 1976; Ross H. Munro, "Chinese Subdued Rather than Distraught over Mao," ibid., September 11, 1976; Jacques Leslie, "Carry On Mao Cause, Chinese Leaders Urge," *Los Angeles Times*, September 10, 1976; and Robert L. Bartley, "In China at Mao's Death," *Wall Street Journal*, September 10, 1976.
3. On the demographic consequences of the Great Leap Forward, see John S. Aird, "Recent Demographic Data from China: Problems and Prospects," in *China under the Four Modernizations*, Committee Print, Joint Economic Committee, 97 Cong. 2 sess. (Government Printing Office, 1982), pt. 1, pp. 171–223; and Ansley Coale, "Population Trends, Population Policy, and Population Studies in China," *Population and Development Review*, vol. 7 (March 1981), pp. 85–97. The estimate of the number of deaths in the Cultural Revolution is from Harry Harding, "The Chinese State in Crisis," in Roderick MacFarquhar and John K. Fairbank, eds., *The Cambridge History of China*, vol. 15: *Revolutions within the Chinese Revolution, 1966–1979* (Cambridge University Press, forthcoming).
4. This analysis of the economy of late traditional China is drawn from Mark Elvin, *The Pattern of the Chinese Past* (Stanford University Press, 1973); Dwight Perkins, *Agricultural Development in China, 1368–1968* (Aldine, 1969); and Albert Feuerwerker, *The Chinese Economy, 1870–1911*, Michigan Papers in Chinese Studies, no. 5 (University of Michigan, Center for Chinese Studies, 1969).
5. Valuable overviews of the structure of the Chinese economy include Nai-Ruenn Chen and Walter Galenson, *The Chinese Economy under*

Communism (Aldine, 1969); Audrey Donnithorne, *China's Economic System* (London: George Allen and Unwin, 1967); Christopher Howe, *China's Economy: A Basic Guide* (Basic Books, 1978); Nicholas R. Lardy, *Economic Growth and Distribution in China* (Cambridge University Press, 1978); and Dwight H. Perkins, *Market Control and Planning in Communist China* (Harvard University Press, 1966).

6. World Bank, *China: Socialist Economic Development*, vol. 1: *The Economy, Statistical System, and Basic Data* (Washington, D.C.: World Bank, 1983), p. 147; and Bruce L. Reynolds, "Reform in Chinese Industrial Management: An Empirical Report," in *China under the Four Modernizations*, pt. 1, pp. 119–37, cited on p. 123.

7. Liu Guoguang and Wang Ruisun, "Restructuring of the Economy," in Yu Guangyuan, ed., *China's Socialist Modernization* (Peking: Foreign Languages Press, 1984), pp. 89, 87.

8. Ibid. The level of inventory was estimated in 1980 as amounting to nearly half of a full year's industrial and agricultural output. See Audrey Donnithorne, "The Chinese Economy Today," *Journal of Northeast Asian Studies*, vol. 2 (September 1983), pp. 3–21, quotation on p. 3.

9. People's Republic of China, State Statistical Bureau, *Statistical Yearbook of China, 1984* (Hong Kong: Economic Information and Agency, 1984), p. 34. Throughout this book, the term *national output* refers to the net output of industry, agriculture, construction, transportation and communication, and commerce, but excludes other services. The term corresponds to the Western concept of *net material product* and to the Chinese concept of *national income*. For a definition of national income see World Bank, *China: Socialist Economic Development*, p. 244.

10. World Bank, *China: Socialist Economic Development*, pp. 33, 64; and Xue Muqiao, ed., *Almanac of China's Economy, 1984* (Hong Kong: Modern Cultural Company and Tai Dao Publishing, 1985), p. 63.

11. For Mao's own critique of the Soviet model, see "On the Ten Major Relationships," April 1956, in *Selected Works of Mao Tsetung*, vol. 5 (Peking: Foreign Languages Press, 1977), pp. 284–307; and "Critique of Stalin's Economic Problems of Socialism in the Soviet Union," 1959, in Joint Publications Research Service (JPRS), *Miscellany of Mao Tsetung Thought, 1949–1968*, pt. 1 (Arlington, Va.: JPRS, 1974), pp. 191–200.

12. Thus by the 1970s all but three provinces produced their own motor vehicles, often using the same design, but at extremely different rates of efficiency. A truck produced in a highly industrialized province might be produced in volume and sold at a profit; the same design manufactured in a more remote region would be, in effect, handmade, produced in small quantities, and sold at a loss. Liu and Wang, "Restructuring of the Economy," p. 94.

13. Ibid., p. 90.

14. This ideal is embodied in a directive issued on May 7, 1966, in Jerome

Ch'en, ed., *Mao Papers: Anthology and Bibliography* (Oxford University Press, 1970), pp. 103–05.

15. Mao's campaign style of planning is embodied in a directive drafted in February 1958 at the height of the Great Leap Forward: "Sixty Points on Working Methods," ibid., pp. 57–76. Even so, the decentralization that occurred during the Maoist period remained strictly limited in two ways: both the revenue available to local governments and the appointment of local leaders remained under tight central control. On available revenue, see Lardy, *Economic Growth and Distribution*, chap. 2; on local leadership, see Victor C. Falkenheim, "Continuing Central Predominance," *Problems of Communism*, vol. 21 (July-August 1972), pp. 75–83.

16. For the rate of investment, see State Statistical Bureau, *Statistical Yearbook of China, 1984*, p. 34. On the improvement of the terms of trade for agriculture in the Maoist period, see Terry Sicular, "Rural Marketing and Exchange in the Wake of Recent Reforms," in Elizabeth J. Perry and Christine Wong, *The Political Economy of Reform in Post-Mao China* (Harvard University, Council on East Asian Studies, 1985), pp. 83–110, quotation on p. 98.

17. Xue, *Almanac of China's Economy*, pp. 64, 63.

18. Jack Gray and Maisie Gray, "China's New Agricultural Revolution," in Stephan Feuchtwang and Athar Hussain, eds., *The Chinese Economic Reforms* (London: Croom Helm, 1983), pp. 151–84, quotation on p. 169.

19. The cosmopolitanism of some periods in Chinese history is emphasized by Michael Hunt, "Chinese Foreign Relations in Historical Perspective," in Harry Harding, ed., *China's Foreign Relations in the 1980s* (Yale University Press, 1984), pp. 1–42.

20. For a history of this aspect of China's foreign economic relations, see John King Fairbank, *Trade and Diplomacy on the China Coast: The Opening of the Treaty Ports, 1842–54* (Stanford University Press, 1969), chaps. 2, 3.

21. On this persistent ambivalence in Chinese politics, see Michel Oksenberg and Steven Goldstein, "The Chinese Political Spectrum," *Problems of Communism*, vol. 23 (March-April 1974), pp. 1–13.

22. On antiforeignism in modern Chinese history, see Kuang-Sheng Liao, *Antiforeignism and Modernization in China, 1860–1980: Linkage between Domestic Politics and Foreign Policy* (Hong Kong: Chinese University Press, 1984).

23. Christopher M. Clarke, "Soviet and U.S. Connections," *China Business Review*, vol. 14 (May-June 1987), pp. 25–26.

24. *Zhongguo duiwai jingji maoyi nianjian, 1984* (Yearbook of China's foreign economic relations and trade, 1984) (Peking: China's Foreign Economic Relations and Trade Publishing House, 1984), p. IV-68.

25. Ibid., p. IV-3. The data were then reconverted into *renminbi* according to the table of exchange rates in World Bank, *China: Socialist Economic Development*, p. 364. The estimates of national output, expressed in net material product, are drawn from ibid., p. 325.

26. See Alexander Eckstein, *Communist China's Economic Growth and Foreign Trade: Implications for U.S. Policy* (McGraw-Hill, 1966), pp. 220–21.

27. E. A. Kracke, Jr., "The Chinese and the Art of Government," in Raymond Dawson, ed., *The Legacy of China* (Oxford University Press, 1964), pp.309–39, quotation on p. 309.

28. On the traditional Chinese political system, see Etienne Balazs, *Chinese Civilization and Bureaucracy: Variations on a Theme*, trans. H. M. Wright (Yale University Press, 1964); T'ung-tsu Ch'u, *Local Government in China under the Ch'ing* (Stanford University Press, 1969); Kung-ch'uan Hsiao, *Rural China: Imperial Control in the Nineteenth Century* (University of Washington Press, 1960); Thomas A. Metzger, *The Internal Organization of Ch'ing Bureaucracy: Legal, Normative, and Communication Aspects* (Harvard University Press, 1973); Donald J. Munro, *The Concept of Man in Early China* (Stanford University Press, 1969); John R. Watt, *The District Magistrate in Late Imperial China* (Columbia University Press, 1972); and Silas H. L. Wu, *Communication and Imperial Control in China: Evolution of the Palace Memorial System, 1693–1735* (Harvard University Press, 1970).

29. Balazs, *Chinese Civilization and Bureaucracy*, p. 169.

30. For an overview of the Chinese political system, see A. Doak Barnett, *Cadres, Bureaucracy, and Political Power in Communist China* (Columbia University Press, 1967); Harry Harding, *Organizing China: The Problem of Bureaucracy, 1949–1976* (Stanford University Press, 1981); John Wilson Lewis, *Leadership in Communist China* (Cornell University Press, 1963); Franz Schurmann, *Ideology and Organization in Communist China*, 2d ed. (University of California Press, 1968); and James R. Townsend and Brantly Womack, *Politics in China*, 3d ed. (Little, Brown, 1986).

31. For discussions of the Maoist components of Chinese politics, see the essays in John Wilson Lewis, ed., *Party Leadership and Revolutionary Power in China* (Cambridge University Press, 1970); and Harding, *Organizing China*.

32. On the content of Maoist doctrine, see John Bryan Starr, *Continuing the Revolution: The Political Thought of Mao* (Princeton University Press, 1979); William A. Joseph, *The Critique of Ultra-Leftism in China, 1958–1981* (Stanford University Press, 1984); Maurice Meisner, *Marxism, Maoism, and Utopianism: Eight Essays* (University of Wisconsin Press, 1982); Chalmers Johnson, ed., *Ideology and Politics in Contemporary China* (University of Washington Press, 1973); Stuart R. Schram, "Mao Tse-tung and the Theory of the Permanent Revolution, 1958–69," *China Quarterly*, no. 46 (April-June 1971), pp. 221–44; Schram, "From the 'Great Union of the Popular Masses' to the 'Great Alliance'" *China Quarterly*, no. 49 (January-March 1972), pp. 88–105; and Schram, "Introduction: The Cultural Revolution in Historical Perspective," in his *Authority, Participation, and Cultural Change in China* (Cambridge University Press, 1973), pp. 1–108. On the role of

doctrine in Maoist politics, see Richard D. Baum, "Ideology Redivivus," *Problems of Communism*, vol. 16 (May-June 1967), pp. 1–11; and Harry Harding, Jr., "Maoist Theories of Policy-Making and Organization," in Thomas W. Robinson, ed., *The Cultural Revolution in China* (University of California Press, 1971), pp. 113–64.

33. Lin Biao, "Address to the Enlarged Session of the Politburo of the Central Committee," May 1966, in Michael Y. M. Kau, ed., *The Lin Piao Affair: Power Politics and Military Coup* (White Plains, N.Y.: International Arts and Sciences Press, 1975), pp. 326–45, quotations on pp. 341 and 345.

34. Zi Zhongyun, "The Relationship of Chinese Traditional Culture to the Modernization of China: An Introduction to the Current Discussion," *Asian Survey*, vol. 27 (April 1987), pp. 442–58, quotation on p. 454.

35. Chen Yun is quoted in *Ming Pao*, January 15, 1979, in Foreign Broadcast Information Service, *Daily Report: China*, January 18, 1979, pp. E1-9, quotation on p. E-2 (hereafter FBIS).

36. State Statistical Bureau, *Statistical Yearbook of China, 1984*, p. 24; and World Bank, *China: Socialist Economic Development*. These GNP values are derived from data on pp. 301, 321, expressed in 1979 dollars.

37. The analogy between China in the mid-1970s and Japan and the Soviet Union in the early 1960s is drawn from Dwight H. Perkins, "The International Consequences of China's Economic Development," in Richard H. Solomon, ed., *The China Factor: Sino-American Relations and the Global Scene* (Prentice-Hall, 1981), pp. 114–36.

38. The data on income distribution are drawn from World Bank, *China: Socialist Economic Development*, pp. 83–95; and World Bank, *China: Long-Term Development Issues and Options* (Johns Hopkins University Press, 1985), pp. 29–30. For further analyses of equality and inequality in China, see E. B. Vermeer, "Income Differentials in Rural China," *China Quarterly*, no. 89 (March 1982), pp. 1–33; Martin King Whyte, "Inequality and Stratification in China," *China Quarterly*, no. 64 (December 1975), pp. 684–711; Richard Curt Kraus, "The Limits of Maoist Egalitarianism," *Asian Survey*, vol. 16 (November 1976), pp. 1081–96; and William L. Parish, "Egalitarianism in Chinese Society," *Problems of Communism*, vol. 30 (January-February 1981), pp. 37–53.

39. World Bank, *China: Socialist Economic Development*, pp. 95–104. For another comparative analysis of the quality of life in China, see Nick Eberstadt, "Has China Failed?" *New York Review of Books*, April 5, 1979, pp. 33–40; April 19, 1979, pp. 41–45; and May 3, 1979, pp. 39–43.

40. For a description of life in one of China's poorest and most remote regions, see Steven W. Mosher, *Journey to the Forbidden China* (Free Press, 1985).

41. State Statistical Bureau, *Statistical Yearbook of China, 1984*, p. 34.

42. *Renmin Ribao*, March 30, 1981, cited in Robert F. Dernberger, "The Chinese Search for the Path of Self-Sustained Growth in the 1980's:

An Assessment," in *China under the Four Modernizations*, pt. 1, pp. 25–26.

43. On productivity, see Anthony M. Tang, "Agriculture in China: Problems and Prospects," in Norton Ginsburg and Bernard A. Lalor, eds., *China: The 80s Era* (Westview Press, 1984), pp. 145–72; and Robert Michael Field, "Slow Growth of Labour Productivity in Chinese Industry, 1952–81," *China Quarterly*, no. 96 (December 1983), pp. 641–64.

44. On consumption patterns and trends, see Nicholas R. Lardy, "Consumption and Living Standards in China, 1978–83," *China Quarterly*, no. 100 (December 1984), pp. 849–65; Nicholas R. Lardy, *Agriculture in China's Modern Economic Development* (Cambridge University Press, 1983), chap. 4; and W. Klatt, "The Staff of Life: Living Standards in China, 1977–1981," *China Quarterly*, no. 93 (March 1983), pp. 17–50.

45. World Bank, *China: Socialist Economic Development*, p. 321.

46. On population and employment problems, see K. C. Yeh, "Macroeconomic Changes in the Chinese Economy during the Readjustment," *China Quarterly*, no. 100 (December 1984), pp. 691–716; Tom Engle, "Reforming the Labor System: China's Leaders Struggle to Put the World's Largest Labor Force to Work," *China Business Review*, vol. 12 (March–April 1985), pp. 40–44; and World Bank, *China: Socialist Economic Development*, p. 174.

47. On availability of skilled manpower, see Yeh, "Macroeconomic Changes"; and World Bank, *China: Socialist Economic Development*, pp. 136–37.

48. On China's level of technology compared with other nations, see Jon Sigurdson, "Technology and Science—Some Issues in China's Modernization," in Joint Economic Committee, *Chinese Economy Post-Mao*, vol. 1: *Policy and Performance*, 95 Cong. 2 sess. (GPO, 1978), pp. 476–534; and A. Doak Barnett, *China's Economy in Global Perspective* (Brookings, 1981), p. 32. The estimate of the obsolescence of Chinese technology is drawn from Mary Lee, "The Curtain Goes Up: Peking Permits Foreign Investment All Along Its Coastline—Creating Different Rules and Added Confusion," *Far Eastern Economic Review*, January 31, 1985, pp. 50–51.

49. For an evaluation of the Chinese bureaucracy, see Harding, *Organizing China*, chap. 11; and Norman T. Uphoff and Milton J. Esman, *Local Organization for Rural Development: Analysis of Asian Experience*, Special Series on Rural Local Government, no. 19 (Cornell University, Rural Development Committee, 1974).

50. For educational levels of national leaders, see Premier Zhao Ziyang's report to the Standing Committee of the National People's Congress in March 1982 in FBIS, March 9, 1982, pp. K1–7, quotation on p. K3; for education of provincial leaders, see *Liaowang*, no. 21 (March 21, 1984), ibid., June 18, 1984, pp. K7–10, quotation on p. K8. For results of the sample census, see *Hongqi*, no. 11 (June, 1, 1980), ibid., June 17, 1980, pp. L6–10; and *Hongqi*, no. 7 (April, 1, 1985) in JPRS, *China Report*, June 17, 1985, pp. 28–31, quotation on p. 30.

51. On Mao's violation of traditional Party norms, see Frederick C. Teiwes, *Politics and Purges in China: Rectification and the Decline of Party Norms, 1950–1965* (M. E. Sharpe, 1979); and Teiwes, *Leadership, Legitimacy, and Conflict in China: From a Charismatic Mao to the Politics of Succession* (M. E. Sharpe, 1984).

52. *A Great Trial in Chinese History: The Trial of the Lin Biao and Jiang Qing Counter-Revolutionary Cliques, Nov. 1980–Jan. 1981* (Peking: New World Press, 1981), p. 21. I assume "personages in various circles" refers to intellectuals.

53. Anne F. Thurston, "Victims of China's Cultural Revolution: The Invisible Wounds," pt. 1, *Pacific Affairs*, vol. 57 (Winter 1984–85), pp. 599–620; and pt. 2, *Pacific Affairs*, vol. 58 (Spring 1985), pp. 5–27.

54. State Statistical Bureau, *Statistical Yearbook of China, 1984*, p. 459.

55. An especially insensitive editorial entitled "Deepen the Criticism of Teng Hsiao-ping in Anti-Quake and Relief Work," appeared in *Renmin Ribao* on August 11. See *Peking Review*, August 20, 1976, pp. 5–6.

56. Anita Chan, Stanley Rosen, and Jonathan Unger, *On Socialist Democracy and the Chinese Legal System: The Li Yizhe Debates* (M. E. Sharpe, 1985), p. 61. The wall poster was written by a collective authorship under the pen name of Li Yizhe.

57. *Asia-Pacific Report: Trends, Issues, Challenges* (Honolulu: East-West Center, 1986), p. 96.

CHAPTER 3

1. My analysis presents each political viewpoint in a pure and stylized form. It is not meant to imply that any particular Chinese leader or Chinese intellectual would necessarily endorse all of the values and policies associated with any of these abstract descriptions. For other analyses of the Chinese political spectrum in the late 1970s and early 1980s, see Carol Lee Hamrin, "Competing 'Policy Packages' in Post-Mao China," *Asian Survey*, vol. 24 (May 1984), pp. 487–518; Hamrin, "Competing Political-Economic Strategies," in *China's Economy Looks toward the Year 2000, vol. 1: The Four Modernizations*, Committee Print, Joint Economic Committee, 99 Cong. 2 sess. (Government Printing Office, 1986), pp. 72–89; and Dorothy J. Solinger, "The Fifth National People's Congress and the Process of Policy Making: Reform, Readjustment, and the Opposition," *Asian Survey*, vol. 22 (December 1982), pp. 1238–75.

2. "Production Goes Up after Wiping Out 'Four Pests,'" *Peking Review*, November 26, 1976, pp. 15–16, quotation on p. 16.

3. Yang Jung-kuo, "Confucius—A Thinker Who Stubbornly Upheld the Slave System," *Peking Review*, October 12, 1973, pp. 5–9, quotation on p. 7. For further analysis of the organizational program of the revolutionary Maoists, see Harry Harding, *Organizing China: The*

Problem of Bureaucracy, 1949–1976 (Stanford University Press, 1981), chap. 10.

4. "Speech at the Second National Conference on Learning from Tachai in Agriculture," December 1976, *Peking Review*, January 1, 1977, pp. 31–44, cited on p. 44.

5. Xinhua News Agency, December 2, 1982, in Foreign Broadcast Information Service, *Daily Report: China*, December 3, 1982, pp. K4–5, quotation on p. K5 (hereafter FBIS).

6. On the precedents for moderate reform in the mid-1950s and early 1960s, see David M. Bachman, *Chen Yun and the Chinese Political System*, China Research Monographs, no. 29 (University of California at Berkeley, Center for Chinese Studies, 1985); Nicholas R. Lardy and Kenneth Lieberthal, eds., *Chen Yun's Strategy for China's Development: A Non-Maoist Alternative* (M. E. Sharpe, 1983); and H. Franz Schurmann, "China's 'New Economic Policy'—Transition or Beginning?" *China Quarterly*, no. 17 (January-March 1964), pp. 65–91.

7. On the connection between the Hundred Flowers movement and contemporaneous events in the Soviet Union and Eastern Europe, see Harding, *Organizing China*, chap. 5. On Chinese interest in reform in Eastern Europe and the Soviet Union, see Nina P. Halpern, "Learning from Abroad: Chinese Views of the East European Economic Experience, January 1977–June 1981," *Modern China*, vol. 11 (January 1985), pp. 77–110; and Gilbert Rozman, *The Chinese Debate about Soviet Socialism, 1978–1985* (Princeton University Press, 1987).

8. For biographies of Hua Guofeng, see Ting Wang, *Chairman Hua: Leader of the Chinese Communists* (Montreal: McGill-Queen's University Press, 1980); and Michel Oksenberg and Sai-cheung Yeung, "Hua Kuo-feng's Pre-Cultural Revolution Hunan Years, 1949–66: The Making of a Political Generalist," *China Quarterly*, no. 69 (March 1977), pp. 3–53.

9. The best account of the events of 1975–76 leading to the fall of the Gang of Four is Ann Elizabeth Fenwick, "The Gang of Four and the Politics of Opposition: China, 1971–1976" (Ph.D. dissertation, Stanford University, 1983). See also Harry Harding, Jr., "China after Mao," *Problems of Communism*, vol. 26 (March-April 1977), pp. 1–18.

10. Ch'ih Heng, "From Bourgeois Democrats to Capitalist Roaders," *Hongqi*, no. 3 (March 1, 1976), in National Technical Information Service, *Selections from People's Republic of China Magazines*, March 1976, pp. 2–9, quotations from pp. 2, 4, 6.

11. "A Desperate Move before Destruction—Exposing Gang of Four's Sinister Plot to Forge Chairman Mao's 'Last Words,'" *Renmin Ribao*, December 17, 1976, cited in *Peking Review*, December 24, 1976, pp. 8–12, 32, quotations on pp. 8, 10.

12. Mao did hold the position of state president or its equivalent for most of the 1950s, but this position gave him less direct responsibility over the day-to-day work of the government than Hua enjoyed as prime

minister, a post that Mao never held. Moreover, Mao resigned the state chairmanship in 1959 and never reclaimed it.

13. On the bases of power in Chinese politics, see Lowell Dittmer, "Bases of Power in Chinese Politics: A Theory and an Analysis of the Fall of the 'Gang of Four,'" *World Politics*, vol. 31 (October 1978), pp. 26–60.

14. On Hua's struggle to maintain power, see Dorothy Grouse Fontana, "Background to the Fall of Hua Guofeng," *Asian Survey*, vol. 22 (March 1982), pp. 237–60; and Jürgen Domes, *The Government and Politics of the PRC: A Time of Transition* (Westview Press, 1985). Official contemporary summaries of Hua's line can be found in two major newspaper editorials of 1977: *Renmin Ribao*, April 11, 1977, and April 13, 1977, in *Peking Review*, April 15, 1977, pp. 8–10, 17, and April 22, 1977, pp. 38–40.

15. Hua Guofeng, *Continue the Revolution under the Dictatorship of the Proletariat to the End: A Study of Volume V of the 'Selected Works of Mao Tsetung'* (Peking: Foreign Languages Press, 1979), p. 1.

16. These quotations are drawn from Hua, *Continue the Revolution under the Dictatorship of the Proletariat*, pp. 3–5; Hua, "Political Report to the Eleventh National Congress of the Communist Party of China," August 1977, in *The Eleventh National Congress of the Communist Party of China (Documents)* (Peking: Foreign Languages Press, 1977), pp. 1–111, cited on pp. 51–52; Hua, "Speech at the Second National Conference on Learning from Tachai in Agriculture," p. 38, and "Carry Out in an All-Round Way the Strategic Policy Decision on Grasping the Key Link in Running the Country Well," an April 11, 1977, *Renmin Ribao* editorial cited in *Peking Review*, April 15, 1977, pp. 8–10, 17, quotation on p. 10.

17. On Hua's long-term development plan, see Hua Guofeng, "Unite and Strive to Build a Modern, Powerful Socialist Country," February 1978, in *Documents of the First Session of the Fifth National People's Congress of the People's Republic of China* (Peking: Foreign Languages Press, 1978), pp. 1–118. For analysis, see John L. Davie and Dean W. Carver, "China's International Trade and Finance," in *China under the Four Modernizations*, pt. 2, Committee Print, Joint Economic Committee, 97 Cong. 2 sess. (GPO, 1982), pp. 19–47, esp. pp. 23–26; Robert F. Dernberger and David Fasenfest, "China's Post-Mao Economic Future," in *Chinese Economy Post-Mao*, vol. 1: *Policy and Performance*, Compendium of papers submitted to the Joint Economic Committee, 95 Cong. 2 sess. (GPO, 1978), pp. 3–47; Nicholas R. Lardy, "Recent Chinese Economic Performance and Prospects for the Ten-Year Plan," ibid., pp. 48–62; Liu Guoguang and Wang Ruisun, "Restructuring of the Economy," in Yu Guangyuan, ed., *China's Socialist Modernization* (Peking: Foreign Languages Press, 1984), pp. 71–145, esp. pp. 102–04; Bruce L. Reynolds, "Reform in Chinese Industrial Management: An Empirical Report," in *China under the Four Modernizations*, pt. 1, pp. 119–37; and Dorothy J. Solinger, "Some Speculations on the Return of

the Regions: Parallels with the Past," *China Quarterly*, no. 75 (September 1978), pp. 623–38.

18. Guojia Tongjiju (State Statistical Bureau), *Zhongguo tongji zhaiyao, 1986* (Chinese statistical abstract, 1986) (Peking: Chinese Statistical Publishing House, 1986), p. 7.

19. "Carry Out in an All-Round Way the Strategic Policy Decision," *Peking Review*, April 15, 1977, pp. 9–10.

20. People's Republic of China, State Statistical Bureau, *Statistical Yearbook of China, 1984* (Hong Kong: Economic Information and Agency, 1984), pp. 26, 395.

21. The abandonment of the ten-year plan can be followed in an important Chinese chronology of economic policy: *Zhonghua renmin gongheguo jingji dashiji 1949–1980* (Economic chronology of the People's Republic of China, 1949–1980) (Peking: Chinese Social Sciences Publishing House, 1984), especially the entries for late 1978 and early 1979. See also Li Chengrui and Zhang Zhuoyuan, "An Outline of Economic Development, 1977–1980," in Yu Guangyuan, *China's Socialist Modernization*, pp. 3–69, esp. pp. 29–52.

22. The "two whatevers" were first contained in a joint editorial in *Renmin Ribao, Hongqi*, and *Jiefangjun Bao* on February 6, 1977, in FBIS, February 7, 1977, pp. E1–3; quotation on p. E3.

23. On Deng Xiaoping's career, see Howard L. Boorman, "Teng Hsiaop'ing: A Political Profile," *China Quarterly*, no. 21 (January-March 1965), pp. 108–25; Richard C. Bush, "Deng Xiaoping: China's Old Man in a Hurry," in Robert B. Oxnam and Richard C. Bush, eds., *China Briefing, 1980* (Westview Press, 1980), pp. 9–24; and Chi Hsin, *Teng Hsiao-p'ing: A Political Biography* (Hong Kong: Cosmos Books, 1978). See also the entries on Deng in Donald W. Klein and Anne B. Clark, *Biographical Dictionary of Chinese Communism, 1921–1965* (Harvard University Press, 1971); and Wolfgang Bartke, *Who's Who in the People's Republic of China*, 2d ed. (Munich, West Germany: K. G. Saur, 1987), pp. 51–53.

24. *Renmin Ribao*, August 22, 1984, in FBIS, August 23, 1984, pp. K1–6.

25. For Deng's views on economic and organizational issues in the 1950s and 1960s, see Byung-joon Ahn, *Chinese Politics and the Cultural Revolution: Dynamics of Policy Processes* (University of Washington Press, 1976); Parris H. Chang, *Power and Policy in China*, 2d ed. (Pennsylvania State University Press, 1978); Harding, *Organizing China*; Roderick MacFarquhar, *The Origins of the Cultural Revolution*, vol. 1: *Contradictions among the People, 1956–1957* (Columbia University Press, 1974); and MacFarquhar, *The Origins of the Cultural Revolution*, vol. 2: *The Great Leap Forward, 1958–1960* (Columbia University Press, 1983).

26. There are many general treatments of the struggle between Deng and Hua. Among the best by Western scholars are Parris H. Chang, "Chinese Politics: Deng's Turbulent Quest," *Problems of Communism*, vol. 30 (January-February 1981), pp. 1–21; Parris H. Chang, "The Last Stand of

Deng's Revolution," *Journal of Northeast Asian Studies*, vol. 1 (June 1982), pp. 3–20; Domes, *Government and Politics*, chaps. 9–11; Fontana, "Background to the Fall of Hua Guofeng"; John Gardner, *Chinese Politics and the Succession to Mao* (Holmes and Meier, 1982); H. Lyman Miller, "The Politics of Reform in China," *Current History*, vol. 80 (September 1981), pp. 258–62, 273; Peter R. Moody, Jr., *Chinese Politics after Mao: Development and Liberalization, 1976 to 1983* (Praeger, 1983); and Richard D. Nethercut, "Leadership in China: Rivalry, Reform, and Renewal," *Problems of Communism*, vol. 32 (March-April 1983), pp. 30–46. See also Stuart R. Schram, " 'Economics in Command?' Ideology and Policy since the Third Plenum, 1978–84," *China Quarterly*, no. 99 (September 1984), pp. 417–61; and Hung-mao Tien, *The Communist Party of China: Party Powers and Group Politics from the Third Plenum to the Twelfth Party Congress*, Occasional Papers in Contemporary Asian Studies, no. 2 (University of Maryland, School of Law, 1984). Hu Jiwei, then the chief editor of *Renmin Ribao*, reportedly provided the Central Party School with an official version of the struggle up to the middle of 1979. That report, entitled "Report on a Series of Struggles in the Top Echelons of the CCP," appeared in *Cheng Ming*, no. 34 (August 1, 1980), in FBIS, August 15, 1980, pp. U1–17.

27. The use of small bottles in this way is detailed in Domes, *Government and Politics*, p. 146; and Hu Jiwei, "Report on a Series of Struggles," in FBIS, August 15, 1980, p. U4.

28. The letter from Deng to Hua appears in *Issues and Studies*, vol. 20 (March 1984), pp. 95–96. For the communiqué of the Third Plenum of the Tenth Central Committee, see Xinhua News Agency, July 22, 1977, in FBIS, July 22, 1977, pp. E13–18.

29. On the debate over the characterization of the Gang of Four, see William A. Joseph, *The Critique of Ultra-Leftism in China, 1958–1981* (Stanford University Press, 1984), chaps. 5–7.

30. For Deng's critique of the "two whatevers," see "The 'Two Whatevers' Do Not Accord with Marxism," May 1977, in *Selected Works of Deng Xiaoping, 1975–1982* (Peking: Foreign Languages Press, 1984), pp. 51–52; and "Hold High the Banner of Mao Zedong Thought and Adhere to the Principle of Seeking Truth from Facts," September 1978, ibid., pp. 141–44. The quotations are from the latter article, cited on p. 141. "Seeking truth from facts," the principle that Deng counterposed to the "two whatevers," was first advocated publicly by Deng in his "Closing Address at the Eleventh National Congress of the Communist Party of China," August 1977, in *Eleventh National Congress*, pp. 189–95, quotation on p. 192. It was strongly endorsed the following month by Chen Yun, in his "Uphold the Revolutionary Work Style of Seeking Truth from Facts—In Commemoration of the First Anniversary of the Death of the Great Leader and Teacher Chairman Mao," *Renmin Ribao*, September 28, 1977, in FBIS, September 30, 1977, pp. E2–10.

31. It finally appeared in Xinhua News Agency, October 5, 1978, in FBIS, October 11, 1978, pp. E1–22.
32. For a valuable firsthand account of the Democracy Wall period of 1978–79, see Roger Garside, *Coming Alive: China after Mao* (McGraw-Hill, 1981). See also Kjeld Erik Brodsgaard, "The Democracy Movement in China, 1978–1979: Opposition Movements, Wall Poster Campaigns, and the Underground Journals," *Asian Survey*, vol. 21 (July 1981), pp. 747–74; David S. G. Goodman, *Beijing Street Voices: The Poetry and Politics of China's Democracy Movement* (London: Marion Boyars, 1981); Anne McLaren, "The Educated Youth Return: The Poster Campaign in Shanghai from November 1978 to March 1979," *Australian Journal of Chinese Affairs*, no. 2 (July 1979), pp. 1–20; Andrew J. Nathan, *Chinese Democracy* (Alfred A. Knopf, 1985), chaps. 1–2; and Jeremy T. Paltiel, "Recent Dissidence in China," *Studies in Comparative Communism*, vol. 16 (Spring-Summer 1983), pp. 121–37.
33. "The Communiqué of the Third Plenary Session of the Eleventh Central Committee of the Chinese Communist Party," *Peking Review*, December 29, 1978, pp. 6–16. The quotation on mass movements is from "Report to the Eleventh Congress of the Communist Party of China," p. 52. Hua's association with the Dazhai model is suggested by his convening of a national conference on the subject in December 1976, one of his first major acts after seizing power from the Gang of Four. See "Second National Conference on Learning from Tachai in Agriculture," *Peking Review*, December 17, 1976, pp. 10–12.
34. For the communiqué of the Fourth Plenum, see Xinhua News Agency, September 28, 1979, in FBIS, October 1, 1979, pp. L1–2. Ye Jianying's speech on the thirtieth anniversary of the founding of the People's Republic, which had been approved by the Fourth Plenum, was carried by Xinhua on September 29 and appeared in FBIS, October 1, 1979, pp. L8–34.
35. For a review of personnel changes during this period, see Christopher M. Clarke, "China's Revolution in Administrative Structure: Implementing Central Party and State Reforms in Post-Mao China," paper presented at the workshop on "Studies in Policy Implementation in the Post-Mao Era," sponsored by the Joint Committee on Chinese Studies of the American Council of Learned Societies and the Social Science Research Council, Columbus, Ohio, June 1983; David S. G. Goodman, "Changes in Leadership Personnel after September 1976," in Jürgen Domes, ed., *Chinese Politics after Mao* (Cardiff, Wales: University College Cardiff Press, 1979), pp. 37–69; Ting Wang, "Leadership Realignments," *Problems of Communism*, vol. 26 (July-August 1977), pp. 1–17; and Earl A. Wayne, "The Politics of Restaffing China's Provinces, 1976–1977," *Contemporary China*, vol. 2 (Spring 1978), pp. 116–65.
36. Tien, *The Communist Party of China: Party Powers and Group Politics*, pp. 42–43. The petroleum faction lost control of the State Planning

Commission in June 1980 and the State Economic Commission in March 1981.

37. "Resolution on Certain Questions in the History of Our Party since the Founding of the People's Republic of China," Xinhua News Agency, June 30, 1981, in FBIS, July 1, 1981, pp. K1–38, quotations are on pp. K35, K30, K22.

38. On the last stages in the struggle between Hua and Deng, see Gardner, *Chinese Politics and the Succession,* chaps. 5–7; Miller, "Politics of Reform"; Luo Bing, "Reorganization of the Nucleus of the Chinese Communist Party—The Truth of Hua Guofeng's Resignation and the New Troika," *Cheng Ming,* no. 40 (February 1, 1981), pp. 7–9, in FBIS, February 2, 1981, pp. U1–6; and Ying Ying, "The Great Inside Story on Hua Guofeng's Drop in Rank," *Cheng Ming Daily,* July 5, 6, 7, 9, 10, and 12, 1981, excerpted in British Broadcasting Service, *Summaries of World Broadcasts: Far East,* no. 6778 (July 18, 1981), pp. BII/1–4.

CHAPTER 4

1. Chen Yun, "Jingji xingshi yü jingyan jiaoxun" (Economic conditions and the lessons of experience), December 1980, in *Sanzhong quanhui yilai zhongyao wenxian xuanbian,* vol. 1 (Selection of important documents since the Third Plenum) (Jilin: People's Publishing House, 1982), pp. 601–07. This compendium was reprinted in Taiwan as *Zhonggong shiyijie sanzhong quanhui yilai zhongyang shouyao jianghua ji wenjian xuanbian* (Selection of important central speeches and documents since the Third Plenum of the Eleventh Central Committee of the Chinese Communist Party) (Taipei: Studies in Chinese Communism Magazine, 1983).

2. On urban reform, see "Decision of the Central Committee of the Communist Party of China on Reform of the Economic Structure," October 20, 1984, in Foreign Broadcast Information Service, *Daily Report: China,* October 22, 1984, pp. K1–19 (hereafter FBIS); on the Seventh Five-Year Plan, see "Proposal of the Central Committee of the Chinese Communist Party for the Seventh Five-Year Plan for National Economic and Social Development," in *Uphold Reform and Strive for the Realization of Socialist Modernization—Documents of the CPC National Conference* (Peking: Foreign Languages Press, 1985), pp. 11–62.

3. See table 5-1 in this volume; and Rock Creek Research, *1986 China Statistical Handbook* (Washington, D.C.: Rock Creek Research, 1986), p. 13.

4. This phrase is the principal theme in the report by Minister of Finance Wang Bingqian, "Report on the Implementation of the State Budget for 1985 and the Draft State Budget for 1986," March 26, 1986, in *The Fourth Session of the Sixth National People's Congress, April 1986*

(Peking: Foreign Languages Press, 1986), pp. 165–90, quotation on p. 174.

5. "Communiqué of the State Statistical Bureau of the People's Republic of China on the Statistics concerning National Economic and Social Development in 1986," in FBIS, February 25, 1987, pp. K25–36, cited on pp. K29, K33.

6. The quotation is from Xinhua News Agency, February 14, 1987, ibid., February 19, 1987, pp. K18–19, on p. K18. See also *Changjiang Ribao*, December 22, 1986, ibid., January 7, 1987, pp. K22–23; Xinhua News Agency, January 11, 1987, and January 15, 1987, ibid., February 5, 1987, pp. K19–25, and January 15, 1987, p. K21; and *Renmin Ribao*, February 12, 1987, ibid., February 19, 1987, pp. K27–29.

7. *Cheng Ming*, no. 86 (December 1, 1984), and no. 95 (September 1, 1985), ibid., December 3, 1984, pp. W2–7, and September 10, 1985, pp. W10–20, quotation on p. W12.

8. *Cheng Ming*, no. 99 (January 1, 1986), ibid., January 7, 1986, pp. W5–8.

9. For the standard definition of socialism in the early 1980s, see Ma Hong, ed., *Xiandai zhongguo jingji shidian* (Encyclopedia of the modern Chinese economy) (Peking: Chinese Social Science Publishing House, 1982), pp. 16–20. For Zhao's definition, see "Zhao Ziyang on Improving Economic Work," *Beijing Review*, November 23, 1979, p. 3; for Deng's view, see his speech to the National Party Conference in September 1985, in FBIS, September 23, 1985, pp. K8–13. For the reformulation of the nature of ownership under socialism, see *Jingji Ribao*, November 2, 1985, ibid., November 19, 1985, pp. K9–12, quotation on p. K8.

10. Zhongguo Xinwenshe, April 17, 1986, in FBIS, April 23, 1986, pp. K2–3.

11. See "Decision on Reform of the Economic Structure." For details of the negotiations over the content of the document, see *Cheng Ming*, no. 86 (December 1, 1984), in FBIS, December 3, 1984, pp. W2–7.

12. For the text of the resolution, see *Resolution of the Central Committee of the Communist Party of China on the Guiding Principles for Building a Socialist Society with an Advanced Culture and Ideology*, September 1986 (Peking: Foreign Languages Press, 1986), esp. pp. 12–13. On the process of drafting the resolution, and the controversies it entailed, see *Cheng Ming*, no. 109 (November 1, 1986), in FBIS, November 18, 1986, pp. K1–9.

13. Robert F. Dernberger, "Reflections of a 'China Specialist,'" in Janet A. Cady, ed., *Economic Reform in China: Report of the American Economists Study Team to the People's Republic of China, November 29– December 15, 1984* (New York: National Committee on U.S.–China Relations), pp. 1–5, quotation on pp. 2–3.

14. *On the Guiding Principles for Building a Socialist Society*, p. 13.

15. One intriguing comparison of China's reform program with that of the Soviet Union and Eastern Europe concluded that it would be necessary to plan for a comprehensive reform that would restructure all the chief

economic institutions and relationships. However, the plan would be implemented gradually. See *Shijie Jingji Daobao*, April 1, 1985, p. 3.

16. The debate in China closely paralleled the discussion of the advantages and disadvantages of "Fabian" and "blitzkrieg" strategies of reform in Samuel P. Huntington, *Political Order in Changing Societies* (Yale University Press, 1968), chap. 6.

17. *Guangming Ribao*, November 2, 1985, in FBIS, November 13, 1985, pp. K18–20.

18. Xinhua News Agency, September 14, 1986, ibid., September 16, 1986, pp. B1–3. Hu Qili has employed a hydraulic metaphor to make the same point: "We allow the little streams to flow. We simply watch in which direction the water flows. When the water flows in the right direction we build channels through which these streams can lead to the river of socialism." *L'Humanité* (Paris), June 13, 1986, in FBIS, June 23, 1986, pp. G16–17.

19. Peter Nan-shong Lee, "Enterprise Autonomy Policy in Post-Mao China: A Case Study of Policy-making, 1978–83," *China Quarterly*, no. 105 (March 1986), pp. 45–71; and Nina P. Halpern, "China's Industrial Economic Reforms: The Question of Strategy," *Asian Survey*, vol. 25 (October 1985), pp. 998–1012.

20. On the spiritual pollution campaign, see a *Renmin Ribao* article carried by Xinhua News Agency, November 15, 1983, in FBIS, November 17, 1983, pp. K1–5; and *Renmin Ribao*, November 17, 1983, ibid., November 21, 1983, pp. K1–2. For the limits on the drive against "bourgeois liberalization" in 1987, see Zhao Ziyang's speech on the occasion of the lunar new year, "On the Two Basics of the Party Line," *Beijing Review*, February 9, 1987, pp. 26–29; and also *Guangming Ribao*, January 29, 1987, in FBIS, February 11, 1987, pp. K12–14; *Renmin Ribao*, overseas edition, February 2, 1987, ibid., February 2, 1987, pp. K4–6; and *Liaowang*, no. 6 (February 9, 1987), ibid., February 20, 1987, pp. K1–3.

21. *Guangming Ribao*, December 17, 1983, in FBIS, December 23, 1984, pp. K1–2; *Cheng Ming*, no. 76 (February 1, 1984), ibid., February 7, 1984, pp. W1–5.

22. For Hu's remarks, see Chengdu radio, February 8, 1984, ibid., February 9, 1984, pp. K9–13, cited on p. K12; for commentary, see *Renmin Ribao*, February 20, 1984, and February 25, 1984, ibid., February 21, 1984, pp. K15–17, quotation on p. K16, and February 27, 1984, pp. K8–10. On the reorientation of the campaign against unhealthy tendencies, see Hu Qili's article in *Hongqi*, no. 8 (April 16, 1986), ibid., April 29, 1986, pp. K1–11.

23. Deng Xiaoping, "Uphold the Four Cardinal Principles," March 1979, in *Selected Works of Deng Xiaoping, 1975–1982* (Peking: Foreign Languages Press, 1984), pp. 166–91, quotation on p. 172.

24. Deng, "Implement the Policy of Readjustment, Ensure Stability and Unity," December 1980, ibid., pp. 335–55.

25. See, for example, Deng, "On Opposing Wrong Ideological Tendencies,"

March 1981, ibid., pp. 356–59; "Concerning Problems on the Ideological Front," July 1981, ibid., pp. 367–71; "Teng Hsiao-p'ing's 'Speech at the Second Plenary Session of the Twelfth Central Committee of the Chinese Communist Party,'" October 1983, *Issues and Studies*, vol. 20 (April 1984), pp. 99–111; and "Speech at the National Conference of the Communist Party of China," September 1985, in *Uphold Reform and Strive for the Realization of Socialist Modernization*, pp. 77–87.

26. Deng made this revelation in an address to a meeting of the Central Advisory Commission in October 1984. See Xinhua News Agency, December 31, 1984, in FBIS, January 2, 1985, pp. K1–6, cited on p. K1.

27. For more on this point, see Tang Tsou, "Political Change and Reform: The Middle Course," in Norton Ginsburg and Bernard A. Lalor, eds., *China: The 80s Era* (Westview Press, 1984), pp. 27–69.

CHAPTER 5

1. On the more limited economic adjustments considered in the immediate post-Mao period, see Liu Guoguang and Wang Ruisun, "Restructuring of the Economy," in Yu Guangyuan, ed., *China's Socialist Modernization* (Beijing: Foreign Languages Press, 1984), pp. 71–145, esp. pp. 102–04; and Bruce L. Reynolds, "Reform in Chinese Industrial Management: An Empirical Report," in *China under the Four Modernizations*, pt. 1, Committee Print, Joint Economic Committee, 97 Cong. 2 sess. (Government Printing Office, 1982), pp. 119–37.

2. For two speeches by Xue Muqiao criticizing the "new leap forward" of 1977–78, see *Jingji Yanjiu*, no. 2 (1981), in Foreign Broadcast Information Service, *Daily Report: China*, April 8, 1981, pp. K9–19 (hereafter FBIS); and *Gongren Ribao*, March 13, 1981, ibid., March 23, 1981, pp. L3–11.

3. For comprehensive overviews of rural reform, see Yak-Yeow Kuch, "China's New Agricultural-Policy Program: Major Economic Consequences, 1979–1983," *Journal of Comparative Economics*, vol. 8 (December 1984), pp. 353–75; Nicholas R. Lardy, "Agricultural Reforms in China," *Journal of International Affairs*, vol. 39 (Winter 1986), pp. 91–104; Vivienne Shue, "The New Course in Chinese Agriculture," *Annals*, vol. 476 (November 1984), pp. 74–89; and David Zweig and Steven Butler, *China's Agricultural Reform: Background and Prospects* (New York: China Council of the Asia Society, 1985).

4. On the adjustment of agricultural procurement prices, see Thomas B. Wiens, "Price Adjustment, the Responsibility System, and Agricultural Productivity," *American Economic Review*, vol. 73 (May 1983), pp. 319–24; Nicholas R. Lardy, *Agriculture in China's Modern Economic Development* (Cambridge University Press, 1983), esp. p. 108; and see Organization for Economic Cooperation and Development, *Agriculture in China: Prospects for Production and Trade* (Paris: OECD, 1985), p. 45.

5. On the renewed commercialization and diversification of agriculture,

see Richard Conroy, *"Laissez-faire* Socialism?: Prosperous Peasants and China's Current Development Strategy," *Australian Journal of Chinese Affairs,* no. 12 (July 1984), pp. 1–34; G. William Skinner, "Rural Marketing in China: Repression and Revival," *China Quarterly,* no. 103 (September 1985), pp. 393–413; and Terry Sicular, "Rural Marketing and Exchange in the Wake of Recent Reforms," in Elizabeth J. Perry and Christine Wong, eds., *The Political Economy of Reform in Post-Mao China,* Harvard Contemporary China Series, no. 2 (Harvard University, Council on East Asian Studies, 1985), pp. 83–110.

6. The figure 10 million to 15 million is based on the average rural household of 2.95 laborers in 1985. For the number of households, *Shijie Jingji Daobao,* September 16, 1985, in FBIS, October 1, 1985, pp. K8–9, cited on p. K9; for the number of laborers per household, Guojia Tongjiju (State Statistical Bureau), *Zhongguo tongji zhaiyao, 1986* (Chinese statistical abstract, 1986) (Peking: Chinese Statistical Publishing House, 1986), p. 110; on numbers employed in collective rural industry, Xinhua News Agency, September 26, 1985, in FBIS, October 2, 1985, pp. K8–9.

7. Tom Engle, "Reforming the Labor System: Leaders Hope Labor Reform Will Alleviate China's Unemployment Problem," *China Business Review,* vol. 12 (March-April 1985), pp. 40–44, cited on p. 43.

8. For excerpts of CPC Central Committee Document no. 1, "Some Questions concerning the Current Rural Economic Policies," January 1983, see Xinhua News Agency, April 10, 1983, in FBIS, April 13, 1983, pp. K1–13.

9. On the emergence and development of the responsibility system in agriculture, see Tang Tsou, Marc Blecher, and Mitch Meisner, "The Responsibility System in Agriculture: Its Implementation in Xiyang and Dazhai," *Modern China,* vol. 8 (January 1982), pp. 41–104; Graham E. Johnson, "The Production Responsibility System in Chinese Agriculture: Some Examples from Guangdong," *Pacific Affairs,* vol. 55 (Fall 1982), pp. 430–51; David Zweig, "Opposition to Change in Rural China: The System of Responsibility and People's Communes," *Asian Survey,* vol. 23 (July 1983), pp. 879–900; Zweig, "Context and Content in Policy Implementation: Household Contracts in China, 1977–1983," and Chung-min Chen and Owen Hagovsky, "Agricultural Responsibility System: An Irresponsible Retreat or a Responsible Adjustment?" both papers presented to the workshop, "Studies in Policy Implementation in the Post-Mao Era," sponsored by the Joint Committee on Chinese Studies of the American Council of Learned Societies and the Social Science Research Council, Columbus, Ohio, June 1983; and Thomas P. Bernstein, "Reforming China's Agriculture," paper presented to the conference, "To Reform the Chinese Political Order," sponsored by the Joint Committee on Chinese Studies of the American Council of Learned Societies and the Social Science Research Council, Harwichport, Mass., June 1984. On the problems created by the responsibility system, see Kathleen Hartford, "Socialist Agriculture Is Dead; Long Live Socialist Agriculture! Organizational Transformations in Rural

China," in Perry and Wong, eds., *The Political Economy of Reform*, pp. 31–62; Nicholas R. Lardy, "Prospects and Some Policy Problems of Agricultural Development in China," *American Journal of Agricultural Economics*, vol. 68 (May 1986), pp. 451–57; and Jan S. Prybyla, " *Pao-kan Tao-hu*: The Other Side," *Issues and Studies*, vol. 22 (January 1986), pp. 54–77.

10. On the separation of economics and government at the local level and the elimination of the commune, see Vivienne Shue, "The Fate of the Commune," *Modern China*, vol. 10 (July 1984), pp. 259–84. A Chinese overview is in Xinhua News Agency, June 4, 1985, in FBIS, June 5, 1985, p. K2.

11. Lardy, *Agriculture in China's Modern Economic Development*, pp. 194–95.

12. For the text of "Ten Policies of the CPC Central Committee and the State Council for Further Invigorating the Rural Economy," January 1985, see Xinhua News Agency, March 24, 1985, in FBIS, March 25, 1985, pp. K1–7. For the explanation of the new procurement system by Zhao Ziyang, see Xinhua News Agency, January 30, 1985, ibid., January 31, 1985, pp. K1–5. For official analyses, see "Reform the System of State Monopoly in the Purchase of Agricultural Products in Accordance with Economic Laws," *Hongqi*, no. 2 (January 16, 1985), in Joint Publications Research Service (JPRS), *China Report: Red Flag*, March 6, 1985, pp. 20–25; *Liaowang*, no. 4 (January 21, 1985), in FBIS, February 7, 1985, pp. K19–22; and *Banyuetan*, no. 3 (February 10, 1985), ibid., March 6, 1985, pp. K3–7.

13. A preliminary Western analysis of the termination of mandatory state procurement of agricultural products is Joseph Fewsmith, "Rural Reform in China: Stage Two," *Problems of Communism*, vol. 34 (July-August 1985), pp. 48–55.

14. See *Banyuetan*, no. 12 (June 25, 1986), in FBIS , July 16, 1986, pp. K21–22.

15. For Chen's remarks, see "Speech Delivered at the National Conference of the Communist Party of China," September 1985, Xinhua News Agency, September 23, 1985, in FBIS, September 23, 1985, K13–16, quotation on p. K14. The proposals for a revival of the system of mandatory procurement are reported in *Renmin Ribao*, November 2, 1985, ibid., November 13, 1985, pp. K15–16, cited on p. K16.

16. For the reformers' attempt to deal with the problem, see *Renmin Ribao*, November 4, 1985, ibid., November 22, 1985, pp. K13–14; and Tian Jiyun, "Issues concerning the Current Economic Situation and Reforms of [the] Economic Structure," Xinhua News Agency, January 11, 1986, ibid., January 13, 1986, pp. K5–22.

17. People's Republic of China, State Statistical Bureau, "Communiqué on the Statistics of 1986 Economic and Social Development," *Beijing Review*, March 2, 1987, pp. 20–26, cited on p. 20; Rock Creek Research, *1986 China Statistical Handbook* (Washington, D.C: Rock Creek Research, 1986), p. 7; and Ellen Salem, "Harvest of Doubt: Lagging

Grain Output Bolsters Chinese Conservatives' Fears," *Far Eastern Economic Review*, February 19, 1987, p. 92.

18. Guojia Tongjiju (State Statistical Bureau), *Zhongguo tongji zhaiyao, 1987* (Chinese statistical abstract, 1987) (Peking: Chinese Statistical Publishing House, 1987), p. 105. For rural growth rates in the earlier period see People's Republic of China, State Statistical Bureau, *Statistical Yearbook of China, 1984* (Hong Kong: Economic Information and Agency, 1984), p. 26. Brief surveys of the economic results of the rural reforms include Benedict Stavis, "Some Initial Results of China's New Agricultural Policies," *World Development*, vol. 13 (1985), pp. 1299–1305; and Thomas P. Bernstein, "Reforming Chinese Agriculture," *China Business Review*, vol. 12 (March-April 1985), pp. 45–49. On peasant incomes and consumption, see Lee Travers, "Post-1978 Rural Economic Policy and Peasant Income in China," *China Quarterly*, no. 98 (June 1984), pp. 241–59; Vaclav Smil, "Eating Better: Farming Reforms and Food in China," *Current History*, vol. 84 (September 1985), pp. 248–51, 273–74; "The Tremendous Successes Attained in the Reform of the Rural Economic Structure," *Hongqi*, no. 20 (October 21, 1984), in JPRS, *China Report: Red Flag*, December 10, 1984, pp. 77–80; and *Renmin Ribao*, August 15, 1984, in FBIS, August 17, 1984, pp. K11–12.

19. John McMillan, John Whalley, and Zhu Li Jing, "Incentive Effects of Price Rises and Payment System Changes on Chinese Agricultural Productivity Growth," Working Paper 2148 (Cambridge: National Bureau of Economic Research, 1987).

20. "The CPC Central Committee Circular on Rural Work in 1984," January 1984, Xinhua News Agency, June 11, 1984, in FBIS, June 13, 1984, pp. K1–11, cited on p. K1. For analysis, see the "Recent Developments" section in *China Quarterly*, no. 101 (March 1985), which includes Joyce Kallgren, "The Concept of Decentralization in Document No. 1, 1984," pp. 104–08; Kenneth Lieberthal, "The Political Implications of Document No. 1, 1984," pp. 109–13; Bruce Stone, "The Basis for Chinese Agricultural Growth in the 1980s and 1990s: A Comment on Document No. 1, 1984," pp. 114–21; and Y. Y. Kueh, "The Economics of the 'Second Land Reform' in China," pp. 122–31.

21. Minister of Agriculture He Kang has described the reduction of sown area and the diversion of agricultural land to other uses as a "great hidden peril in rural areas," cited in *Shijie Jingji Daobao*, April 1, 1985, in FBIS, April 12, 1985, pp. K20–21, quotation on p. K20.

22. On the effects of rural reforms on the provision of social services in the countryside, see Deborah Davis-Friedmann, "The Provision of Essential Services in Rural China," in Richard E. Londsdale and Gyorgy Enyedi, eds., *Rural Public Services: International Comparisons* (Westview Press, 1984), pp. 205–24.

23. On the revival of cooperatives in the countryside, see Du Runsheng, "Development of the Rural Economy: Several Social Objectives," *Hongqi*, no. 8 (April 16, 1985), pp. 14–19, in JPRS, *China Report: Red*

Flag, June 26, 1985, pp. 20–31; and *Jingji Yanjiu*, no. 4 (April 1985), in FBIS, June 13, 1985, pp. K6–19. Even before this new policy was announced Jack and Maisie Gray predicted that China would come to resemble the Danish rural economy, with "independent agricultural producers operating within a framework of co-operative supply, processing, marketing, credit, and research and development, and linked to these co-operatives by contract." See Jack Gray and Maisie Gray, "China's New Agricultural Revolution," in Stephan Feuchtwang and Athar Hussain, eds., *The Chinese Economic Reforms* (London: Croom Helm), p. 184.

24. Data on state investment in agriculture are from *Zhongguo tongji zhaiyao, 1986*, pp. 74–75; and ibid., *1987*, p. 64.
25. Ibid., *1986*, pp. 74–75; "The Seventh Five-Year Plan of the People's Republic of China for Economic and Social Development, 1986–1990," in *The Fourth Session of the Sixth National People's Congress, April 1986* (Peking: Foreign Languages Press, 1986), p. 125; see also Lardy, "Agricultural Reforms in China."
26. On reform of the planning and price system, see Christine Wong, "Material Allocation and Decentralization: Impact of the Local Sector on Industrial Reform," in Perry and Wong, eds., *Political Economy of Reform*, pp. 253–80.
27. *Guangming Ribao*, February 17, 1985, in FBIS, March 8, 1985, pp. K7–9, cited on p. K8.
28. Personal communication.
29. *China Daily*, October 9, 1984, in FBIS, October 9, 1984, p. K1.
30. "Decision of the Central Committee of the Communist Party of China on Reform of the Economic Structure," October 20, 1984, ibid., October 22, 1984, pp. K1–19, quotation on p. K8.
31. *Liaowang*, no. 19 (May 13, 1985), ibid., May 23, 1985, pp. K2–4. On the role of cities under China's urban reforms, see the articles by Dorothy Solinger: "Economic Reform," in Steven M. Goldstein, ed., *China Briefing, 1984* (Westview Press, 1985), pp. 87–108; "Wuhan: Inland City on the Move: Hubei's Capital Leads Other Inland Centers in Urban Reform Experiments," *China Business Review*, vol. 12 (March–April 1985), pp. 28–31; and "Reform of the Structure of the Economic System: A Spatial Interpretation," paper presented to the conference, "To Reform the Chinese Political Order," sponsored by the Joint Committee on Chinese Studies of the American Council of Learned Societies and the Social Science Research Council, Harwichport, Mass., June 1984.
32. Dong Fureng, "China's Price Reform," *Cambridge Journal of Economics*, vol. 10 (1986), pp. 291–300, cited on p. 297; and Xinhua News Agency, June 2, 1987, in FBIS, June 5, 1987, pp. K10–14.
33. *Renmin Ribao*, July 20, 1984, in FBIS, August 2, 1984, pp. K7–11.
34. Xinhua News Agency, March 30, 1985, ibid., April 2, 1985, pp. K5–6; and *Renmin Ribao*, May 24, 1985, ibid., June 4, 1985, pp. K3–7, cited on p. K6.

35. Rock Creek Research, *1986 China Statistical Handbook* (Washington, D.C.: Rock Creek Research, 1986), p. 18; and State Statistical Bureau, "Communiqué on the Statistics of 1986," p. 24.

36. On inflation, see Minoru Nambu, "Inflation in China," *JETRO China Newsletter*, no. 59 (November-December 1985), pp. 2–6, 22.

37. Luc De Wulf and David Goldsbrough, "The Evolving Role of Monetary Policy in China," *International Monetary Fund Staff Papers*, vol. 33 (June 1986), pp. 209–42, cited on pp. 224–230.

38. On reform of the enterprise, see Paul Hare, "China's System of Industrial Economic Planning," in Feuchtwang and Hussain, *The Chinese Economic Reforms* pp. 185–223; Sukhan Jackson, "Profit Sharing, State Revenue, and Enterprise Performance in the PRC," *Australian Journal of Chinese Affairs*, no. 12 (July 1984), pp. 97–112; Jackson, "Reform of State Enterprise Management in China," *China Quarterly*, no. 107 (September 1986) pp. 405–32; Peter Nan-shong Lee, "Enterprise Autonomy Policy in Post-Mao China: A Case Study of Policy-making, 1978–83," ibid., no. 105 (March 1986), pp. 45–71; Barry Naughton, "Finance and Planning Reforms in Industry," in *China's Economy Looks toward the Year 2000, vol. 1: The Four Modernizations*, Committee Print, Joint Economic Committee, 99 Cong. 2 sess. (GPO, 1986), pp. 604–29; Andrew G. Walder, "The Informal Dimension of Enterprise Financial Reforms," ibid., pp. 630–45; and Christine P. W. Wong, "Ownership and Control in Chinese Industry: The Maoist Legacy and Prospects for the 1980s," ibid., pp. 571–603.

39. The text of the May 1984 directive is in Xinhua News Agency, May 11, 1984, in FBIS, May 16, 1984, pp. K15–17. For analysis, see *China Daily*, August 9, 1984, ibid., August 10, 1984, pp. K3–4; *Jingji Ribao*, August 8, 1984, ibid., August 22, 1984, pp. K13–17; and Xinhua News Agency, August 20, 1984, ibid., August 22, 1984, pp. K12–13.

40. On bureaucratic resistance to enterprise autonomy, see Xinhua News Agency, October 30, 1984, ibid., November 2, 1984, p. K17; *Jingji Ribao*, December 13, 1984, ibid., December 26, 1984, pp. K16–18; *Renmin Ribao*, January 9, 1985, ibid., January 10, 1985, p. K1; and *Yangcheng Wanbao*, January 16, 1985, ibid., January 23, 1985, pp. P2–4.

41. The quotations are from Wo-Lap Lam, "Reform: The Manager vs. the Party Cadre," *Asiaweek*, March 22, 1985, pp. 41–44, cited on p. 42; "Enterprises Demand More Power," *Beijing Review*, June 16, 1986, pp. 6–7. See also *Renmin Ribao*, July 8, 1986, in FBIS, July 10, 1986, pp. K1–3; Xinhua News Agency, October 7, 1986, ibid., October 23, 1986, pp. K11–12.

42. On financial reform, see Audrey Donnithorne, "The Chinese Economy Today," *Journal of Northeast Asian Studies*, vol. 2 (September 1983), pp. 3–21; Martin Weil, "Capital Construction Reform: Economic Levers May Replace the Need for Austerity Measures in This Inefficient Sector," *China Business Review*, vol. 12 (March-April 1985), pp. 11–16; and Barry Naughton, "False Starts and Second Wind: Financial

Reforms in China's Industrial System," in Perry and Wong, eds., *Political Economy of Reform*, pp. 223–52.

43. On the shift from the submission of profits to the payment of taxes, see *Guangming Ribao*, January 29, 1984, in FBIS, February 17, 1984, pp. K21–25.

44. Xinhua News Agency, August 28, 1985, ibid., August 30, 1985, K5–11, cited on p. K6.

45. On the shift from grants to loans, see *Jingji Ribao*, January 29, 1985, ibid., February 7, 1985, pp. K5–6. On lack of strict budget constraints, see Daniel Brotman, "Reforming the Domestic Banking System: China's Banks Are Stronger, but Still Play Conflicting Roles," *China Business Review*, vol. 12 (March-April 1985), pp. 17–24.

46. Xinhua News Agency, June 2, 1987, in FBIS, June 5, 1987, pp. K10–14.

47. The data on extrabudgetary investment are from *Zhongguo tongji zhaiyao, 1986*, p. 73; and ibid., *1987*, p. 62. On hyperinvestment in China, see Katsuhiko Hama, "Systemic Reform and Financial Problems—The 'Investment Fever' Mechanism," *JETRO China Newsletter*, no. 47 (November- December 1983), pp. 7–14; and Hsin Chang, "The 1982–83 Overinvestment Crisis in China," *Asian Survey*, vol. 24 (December 1984), pp. 1275–1301. The difficulty in controlling extrabudgetary investments is discussed in Lin Fatang, "Key Projects during the Sixth Five-Year Plan," *Beijing Review*, January 9, 1984, pp. 22–27, cited on pp. 26–27; *Jingji Ribao*, June 14, 1985, and June 26, 1985, in FBIS, June 21, 1985, pp. K15–16; and July 5, 1985, pp. K16–18. According to Tian Jiyun, inability to control the scale of investment is the "core" of the problems China has encountered in the course of reform. Tian Jiyun, "Current Economic Situation," p. K11.

48. *Jingji Ribao*, August 2, 1986, in FBIS, August 11, 1986, pp. K18–19. For an example of one enterprise that went bankrupt see Xinhua News Agency, August 25, 1986, ibid., August 26, 1986, p. K6.

49. On the debate over the bankruptcy law in the National People's Congress, and its ultimate adoption, see *Liaowang*, overseas edition, no. 39 (September 29, 1986), in FBIS, October 7, 1986, pp. K1–3; and *Ta Kung Pao*, November 20–26, 1986, in FBIS, November 26, 1986, pp. K6–8.

50. The major statement of the goals and policies of educational reform is in "Decision of the CPC Central Committee on Reform of the Educational System," Xinhua News Agency, May 28, 1985, ibid., May 30, 1985, pp. K1–11. For analyses of educational reform in post-Mao China, see Marianne Bastid, "Chinese Educational Policies in the 1980s and Economic Development," *China Quarterly*, no. 98 (June 1984), pp. 189–219; Susan Shirk, "The Evolution of Chinese Education: Stratification and Meritocracy in the 1980s," in Norton Ginsburg and Bernard A. Lalor, eds., *China: The 80s Era* (Westview Press, 1984), pp. 245–72; and Stanley Rosen, "Recentralization, Decentralization, and Rationalization: Deng Xiaoping's Bifurcated Educational Policy," *Modern China*, vol. 11 (July 1985), pp. 301–46.

51. On the reform of the labor and wage systems, see Yue Guangzhao, "Employment, Wages, and Social Security in China," *International Labour Review*, vol. 124 (July-August 1985), pp. 411–22; Martin King Whyte, "Society," in Steven M. Goldstein, ed., *China Briefing, 1984* (Westview Press, 1985), pp. 39–60; and Tom Engle, "Reforming the Labor System: Leaders Hope Labor Reform Will Alleviate China's Unemployment Problem," *China Business Review*, vol. 12 (March-April 1985), pp. 40–44.

52. *Zhongguo tongji zhaiyao, 1987*, p. 22.

53. *China Daily*, July 2, 1986, in FBIS, July 29, 1986, pp. K29–30, cited on p. K29.

54. For the maximum period that workers are eligible to receive unemployment compensation, see Xinhua News Agency, September 9, 1986, ibid., September 12, 1986, pp. K23–24; for details of the full range of reforms in the system of employment, see *China Daily*, August 12, 1986, ibid., August 19, 1986, pp. K14–15; *Wen Wei Po*, August 15, 1986, ibid., August 26, 1986, pp. K8–10; *Liaowang*, overseas edition, no. 36 (September 8, 1986), ibid., September 18, 1986, pp. K6–10. The text of the new labor regulations can be found in Xinhua News Agency, September 9, 1986, ibid., September 25, 1986, pp. K1–7.

55. *Zhonghua renmin gongheguo jingji dashiji* (Economic chronology of the People's Republic of China) (Peking: China Social Science Publishing, 1984), pp. 585–86; "Decision of the Central Committee of the Communist Party of China on Reform of the Economic Structure," contained in a special insert in *Beijing Review*, October 29, 1984, quotation on p. XII; interviews in Peking, April 1985.

56. On egalitarianism, see Andrew J. Walder, "Wage Reform and the Web of Factory Interests," presented to the workshop, "Studies in Policy Implementation in the Post-Mao Era," sponsored by the Joint Committee on Chinese Studies of the American Council of Learned Societies and the Social Science Research Council, Columbus, Ohio, June 1983. For the critique of the new labor system, see *Banyuetan*, no. 18 (September 25, 1986), in FBIS, October 10, 1986, pp. K12–15.

57. *Liaowang*, overseas edition, no. 36 (September 1986), in FBIS, September 18, 1986, pp. K6–10, cited on p. K10.

58. For assessments of the effects of reform on industrial productivity, see William Byrd, "Enterprise-Level Reforms in Chinese State-Owned Industry," *American Economic Review*, vol. 73 (May 1983), pp. 329–32; and Thomas G. Rawski, "Productivity, Incentive, and Reform in China's Industrial Sector," paper presented to the annual meeting of the Association for Asian Studies, Washington, D.C., March 1984.

59. For background on the theoretical discussions about the role of the market in China, see Robert C. Hsu, "Conceptions of the Market in Post-Mao China: An Interpretive Essay," *Modern China*, vol. 11 (October 1985), pp. 436–60.

60. *Beijing Review*, October 11, 1982, pp. 21–27, cited on p. 22.

61. This formula is a slight variation of that which appears in Xinhua

News Agency, January 25, 1982, in FBIS, January 26, 1982, pp. K3–4, cited on p. K3.

62. A report on China in the year 2000 has said that, by that time, mandatory planning could become "basically non-existent," just as in Hungary and Yugoslavia. *Shijie Jingji Daobao*, January 6, 1986, in FBIS, January 27, 1986, pp. K13–14, quotation on p. K14.

63. Interview in Washington, D.C., July 1985.

64. *Beijing Jingji Kexue*, no. 5 (October 1983), in FBIS, January 11, 1984, pp. K7–14, quotation on p. K10; and *Guangming Ribao*, April 22, 1984, ibid., May 8, 1984, pp. K13–16. See also Fang Weizhong, vice-chairman of the State Planning Commission, "Develop a System of Planned Management with Chinese Characteristics and a Science of Planned Economy," *Hongqi*, no. 9 (May 1, 1984), in JPRS, *China Report: Red Flag*, June 27, 1984, pp. 44–51.

65. "Speech Delivered at the National Conference " (September 1, 1985), in FBIS, September 23, 1985, pp. K13–16, quotation on p. K14.

66. On the reform of the science and technology system, see "Decision on the Reform of the Science and Technology Management System," Xinhua News Agency, March 19, 1985, ibid., March 20, 1985, pp. K1–5. For analysis, see Denis Fred Simon, "Science and Technology Reforms: Lighting a Commercial Fire under China's Research Institutes," *China Business Review*, vol. 12 (March-April 1985), pp. 32–35. On technology as a commodity, see Fang Gongwen, "On Commercializing Technological Results," *Hongqi*, no. 16 (August 16, 1985), in JPRS, *China Report: Red Flag*, October 15, 1985, pp. 48–58.

67. Xinhua News Agency, August 23, 1986, in FBIS, August 25, 1986, pp. P2–3.

68. *Renmin Ribao*, August 22, 1986, and April 7, 1986, ibid., September 28, 1986, p. K17–22; and August 24, 1986, pp. K22–26.

69. Xinhua News Agency, September 17, 1986, ibid., September 18, 1986, p. R2.

70. *South China Morning Post*, September 8, 1986, ibid., September 10, 1986, pp. K6–7, cited on p. K6.

71. Xinhua News Agency, July 29, 1986, ibid., July 31, 1986, pp. K29–30; Robert Delfs, "China's Major Cities Join the Interbank Market," *Far Eastern Economic Review*, December 11, 1986, pp. 85–88; on the startup of the new Shanghai-based Bank of Communications see Vigor Fung, "Peking Loosens the Reins on a Multiservice Bank," *Asian Wall Street Journal Weekly*, November 24, 1986.

72. *Jingji Ribao*, September 19, 1985, in FBIS, October 2, 1985, pp. K4–6; *China Daily*, March 9, 1985, in FBIS, March 11, 1985, pp. O2–3; and *Jingji Ribao*, October 19, 1985, in FBIS, October 31, 1985, pp. K22–25, quotation on p. K24.

73. See *Beijing Review*, October 20, 1986, pp. 14–24. The phrase "Wenzhou miracle" is the running head of this article.

74. *Nongmin Ribao*, October 11, 1986, in FBIS, November 4, 1986, pp. K9–22, cited on pp. K17, 18; for a broader critique of individual industry,

see *Wenzhai Bao*, no. 299 (March 30, 1986), ibid., April 10, 1986, pp. K9–10.

75. "Gaige de jiben silu" (Basic thinking on reform), *Beijing Ribao*, May 19, 1986.

76. Xinhua News Agency, June 2, 1987, in FBIS, June 5, 1987, pp. K10–14.

77. The World Bank's second report on China reflects some recent Chinese thinking on the reform of the system of socialist ownership. See *China: Long-Term Development Issues and Options* (Washington, D.C.: World Bank, 1985), esp. pp. 164–66. See also Tom Engle, "Stocks: New Domestic Financial Tool," *China Business Review*, vol. 13 (January-February 1986), pp. 35–38.

78. *Renmin Ribao*, August 18, 1986, in *FBIS*, August 28, 1986, pp. K31–35, quotation on p. K33.

79. *Renmin Ribao*, September 26, 1986, ibid., October 22, 1986, pp. K5–11, cited on p. K7.

80. Ibid., p. K6.

81. See, for example, *Hongqi*, no. 5 (March 1, 1984), ibid., April 5, 1984, pp. K14–21; and *Guangming Ribao*, September 14, 1985, ibid., October 14, 1985, pp. K3–5.

82. *Jingji Yanjiu*, no. 1 (January 20, 1986), ibid., March 19, 1986, pp. K11–19, cited on p. K19. See also *Jingji Yanjiu*, no. 1 (January 20, 1986), ibid., March 21, 1986, pp. K13–22.

83. Many of these charges were summarized and refuted in a speech by Zhao Ziyang in May 1987. See Xinhua News Agency, July 9, 1987, in FBIS, July 10, 1987, pp. K1–8. For a survey of the criticisms of radical economic reform expressed in early 1987, see Ch'en Te-sheng, "The Impact of Mainland China's Political Changes on Its Economic Development," *Issues and Studies*, vol. 23 (June 1987), pp. 98–114.

84. William Safire, "Greatest Leap Forward," *New York Times*, December 10, 1984; and "Capitalism in China: Under Deng Xiaoping, It's Okay to Get Rich," *Business Week*, January 14, 1985, pp. 53–59.

85. Figures drawn from *Zhongguo tongji zhaiyao, 1986*, pp. 30, 70, and 89.

86. *Zhongguo tongji zhaiyao, 1987*, pp. 27, 30.

87. Ibid., p. 86.

CHAPTER 6

1. The trade data in this and the following paragraph are drawn from *Zhongguo duiwai jingji maoyi nianjian, 1984* (Yearbook of China's foreign economic relations and trade, 1984) (Peking: Chinese Foreign Economic Relations and Trade Publishing House, 1984) p. IV–3, where they are expressed in U.S. dollars. The data were then reconverted into renminbi according to the table of exchange rates in World Bank, *China: Socialist Economic Development*, vol. 1, *The Economy, Statistical System, and Basic Data* (Washington, D.C.: World Bank, 1983),

p. 364. The estimates of China's national output are drawn from ibid., p. 325.

2. On the controversies over foreign economic relations during this period, see Ann Fenwick, "Chinese Foreign Trade Policy and the Campaign against Deng Xiaoping," in Thomas Fingar and the Stanford Journal of International Studies, eds., *China's Quest for Independence: Policy Evolution in the 1970s* (Westview Press, 1980), pp. 199–224; and Kent Morrison, "Domestic Politics and Industrialization in China: The Foreign Trade Factor," *Asian Survey*, vol. 18 (July 1978), pp. 687–705.

3. See Peking radio, February 15, 1977, in Foreign Broadcast Information Service, *Daily Report: China*, March 9, 1977, pp. E9–14 (hereafter FBIS); and Kuo Chi, "Foreign Trade: Why the 'Gang of Four' Created Confusion," *Peking Review*, February 25, 1977, pp. 16–18.

4. The best available overview of the reforms in the foreign economic sphere, now somewhat outdated, is Samuel P. S. Ho and Ralph W. Huenemann, *China's Open Door Policy: The Quest for Foreign Technology and Capital* (Vancouver: University of British Columbia Press, 1984). See also Kevin B. Bucknall, "Implications of the Recent Changes in China's Foreign Trade Policies," *Australian Journal of Chinese Affairs*, no. 5 (1981), pp. 1–20; Friedrich W. Y. Wu, "From Self-Reliance to Interdependence? Developmental Strategy and Foreign Economic Policy in Post-Mao China," *Modern China*, vol. 7 (October 1981), pp. 445–82; and Huan Guocang, "China's Opening to the World," *Problems of Communism*, vol. 35 (November-December 1986), pp. 59–77.

5. An article coauthored by one of China's leading political economists, Huan Xiang, has suggested that the reform of China's foreign economic relationships constitutes a "change of quality rather than quantity." *Shijie Jingji*, no. 2 (February 10, 1984), in FBIS, April 5, 1984, pp. K5–14.

6. Chen Qiwei, "Why Is China Opening to the Outside?" *Beijing Review*, April 1, 1985, pp. 18–22.

7. The first quotation is from "Some Questions on Accelerating the Development of Industry," in Kenneth Lieberthal, *Central Documents and Politburo Politics in China*, Michigan Papers in Chinese Studies, no. 33 (University of Michigan, Center for Chinese Studies, 1978), app. 1, pp. 115–40, quotation on pp. 134–35. The second is from Xinhua News Agency, December 31, 1984, in FBIS, January 2, 1985, pp. K1–6, quotation on p. K4.

8. *Kaifang*, no. 12 (December 8, 1985), in FBIS, January 29, 1986, pp. K15–19, quotation on p. K15.

9. Xinhua News Agency, June 4, 1986, ibid., June 5, 1986, p. K16.

10. Examples of these allegorical arguments include *Guangming Ribao*, January 8, 1980, ibid., February 7, 1980, pp. L10–16; *Renmin Ribao*, March 12, 1981, and March 30, 1981, ibid., March 16, 1981, pp. L9–13, and April 3, 1981, pp. K8–10; *Guangming Ribao*, April 13, 1981, ibid., May 4, 1981, pp. K13–19; *Renmin Ribao*, April 30, 1981, ibid., May 7,

1981, pp. K5–7; and *Guangming Ribao*, November 23, 1981, ibid., December 10, 1981, pp. K9–14.

11. For evidence of these arguments, see *Renmin Ribao*, November 6, 1981, and November 24, 1981, ibid., November 17, 1981, pp. K3–6, and December 1, 1981, pp. K22–24.

12. This account is drawn from interviews in Peking in November 1985.

13. These arguments are drawn from *Guangzhou Yanjiu*, no. 1 (1985), in FBIS, April 17, 1985, pp. K8–14; *Renmin Ribao*, March 10, 1984, ibid., March 14, 1984, pp. K14–17; and *Shijie Jingji*, no. 5 (February 10, 1984), ibid., April 5, 1984, pp. K5–14.

14. On the concept of a "screen" to close out the "decadent and moribund things of the Western capitalist countries," see Gan Feng, "'Opening a Window' and 'Installing a Window Screen,'" *Hongqi*, no. 8 (April 16, 1985), in Joint Publications Research Service (JPRS), *China Report: Red Flag*, June 26, 1985, pp. 83–84.

15. For a representative criticism of China's foreign trade policy during the Maoist period, see Dong Fureng, "Some Problems concerning China's Strategy in Foreign Economic Relations," *International Social Science Journal*, vol. 35 (1983), pp. 455–67.

16. On the restructuring of the Chinese foreign trade apparatus, see John L. Davie and Dean W. Carver, "China's International Trade and Finance," in *China under the Four Modernizations*, pt. 2, Committee Print, Joint Economic Committee, 97 Cong. 2 sess. (Government Printing Office, 1982), pp. 19–47; Wang Linsheng and Chen Yujie, "Economic Relations with Foreign Countries," in Yu Guangyuan, ed., *China's Socialist Modernization* (Peking: Foreign Languages Press, 1984), pp. 673–718; and Arnold Chao, "Economic Readjustment and the Open-Door Policy," in Lin Wei and Arnold Chao, eds., *China's Economic Reforms* (University of Pennsylvania Press, 1982), pp. 205–19.

17. On the exceptions, see Vigor Fung, "China Weighing Measures to Narrow Trade Deficit," *Asian Wall Street Journal Weekly*, January 13, 1986.

18. Nicholas R. Lardy, *China's Entry into the World Economy: Implications for Northeast Asia and the United States* (New York and Lanham, Md.: Asia Society and University Press of America, 1987), p. 40.

19. On the 1984 reforms, see *Renmin Ribao*, September 20, 1984, in FBIS, September 24, 1984, pp. K13–14. For analysis, see Satoshi Imai, "Reform of China's Foreign Trade System," *JETRO China Newsletter*, no. 56 (May-June 1985), pp. 2–7, 22; and Robert Delfs, "Reverse for Full Ahead," *Far Eastern Economic Review*, October 11, 1984, pp. 84–86.

20. Interview in Peking, November 1985. Some estimates of the amount of foreign exchange transmitted to the central government are even lower. An economist in Hong Kong reportedly concluded in mid-1985 that the central government controlled only some 40 percent of the nation's foreign exchange. See Louise do Rosario, "Time to Pay the Piper: China's Spending Spree Comes to an Abrupt Halt," *Far Eastern*

Economic Review, August 22, 1985, pp. 100–101, cited on p. 101. Special economic zones and "open cities" often had higher retention rates, while factories producing export commodities under central control must often remit a higher share of foreign exchange to the central government. For an early discussion of the details of this reform, see Edith Terry, "Fujian Province: Decentralizing Foreign Trade," *China Business Review*, vol. 7 (September-October 1980), pp. 10–18, cited on p. 11.

21. See Vigor Fung, "China's Trading Companies Balk at Reforms," *Asian Wall Street Journal Weekly*, February 9, 1987.

22. Guojia Tongjiju (State Statistical Bureau), *Zhongguo tongji zhaiyao, 1987* (Chinese statistical abstract, 1987) (Peking: Chinese Statistical Publishing House), p. 90.

23. The share would have been even larger if goods that were classified as civilian exports but clearly intended for military uses, such as heavy trucks, were added to arms sales. See Clare Hollingworth, "Your Friendly Chinese Arms Merchant," *Asian Wall Street Journal*, June 10, 1985; and Gerald Segal and Anne Gilks, "China and the Arms Trade," *Arms Control*, vol. 6 (December 1985), pp. 256–81. China's rank among arms merchants to the third world is in Richard F. Grimmett, *Trends in Conventional Arms Transfer to the Third World by Major Supplier, 1979–1986*, Report 87–418F (Washington, D.C.: Congressional Research Service, 1987), p. 46, table 2F.

24. The data for 1986 in this paragraph are drawn from the People's Republic of China, State Statistical Bureau, "Communiqué on the Statistics of 1986 Economic and Social Development," *Beijing Review*, March 2, 1987, p. 25. For previous services accounts, see *Rock Creek Research China Economic Letter*, vol. 2 (December 15, 1986), p. 2.

25. *Zhongguo tongji zhaiyao, 1987*, p. 94.

26. Xue Muqiao, ed., *Almanac of China's Economy, 1984* (Hong Kong: Modern Cultural Company and Tai Dao Publishing, 1985), pp. 347–52; "Communiqué on the Statistics of 1986," pp. 24–25.

27. Nai-ruenn Chen and Jeffrey Lee, *China's Economy and Foreign Trade, 1981–85* (Washington, D.C.: International Trade Administration, Department of Commerce, 1984), p. 48, table 12; Nai-ruenn Chen, "U.S.-China Trade Patterns: The Outlook for Two Countries with a Lot to Share," *China Business Review*, vol. 13 (September-October 1986), pp. 16–20; and *China Business Review*, vol. 14 (May-June 1987), p. 32.

28. "Hong Kong and China's Trade Interdependence," *Asian Wall Street Journal Weekly*, December 22, 1986. Figures for exports and reexports are based on Government Information Services, *Hong Kong, 1987* (Hong Kong: Government Printer, 1987), p. 321.

29. Davie and Carver, "China's International Trade and Finance," pp. 24, 26, 30.

30. On these import surges, see Ryosei Kokubun, "The Politics of Foreign Economic Policy-making in China: The Case of Plant Cancellations with Japan," *China Quarterly*, no. 105 (March 1986), pp. 19–44.

31. See Xue Muqiao's speech in *Ming Pao*, October 4, 1986, in FBIS, October 6, 1986, p. K13.

32. In early 1985, Zheng Tuobin, the minister of foreign economic relations and trade, described imports as "chaotic" and attributed the situation to the "decentralized" pattern of foreign trade. *Ming Pao*, April 25, 1985, in FBIS, April 26, 1985, p. W2.

33. Official accounts of the scandal appear in Xinhua News Agency, July 31, 1985, ibid., August 1, 1985, pp. P1–2, and August 6, 1985, pp. P1–8. For a Hong Kong analysis sympathetic to Hainan's leaders, arguing that the island had little hope for development if it did not engage in this kind of grey market in foreign goods, see *Chiu-shih Nien-tai*, no. 187 (August 1, 1985), ibid., August 15, 1985, pp. W1–4.

34. William Feeney, "Chinese Policy in Multilateral Financial Institutions," in Samuel S. Kim, ed., *China and the World: Chinese Foreign Policy in the Post-Mao Era* (Westview Press, 1984), pp. 266–92; David Denny, "The Impact of Foreign Aid: Foreign Assistance Gains Acceptance in the Name of Modernization," *China Business Review*, vol. 13 (January-February 1986), pp. 22–24; Friedrich W. Wu, "External Borrowing and Foreign Aid in Post-Mao China's International Economic Policy: Data and Observations," *Columbia Journal of World Business*, vol. 14 (Fall 1984), pp. 53–61; and the section on China in "Focus on World Bank/IMF '86," in *Far Eastern Economic Review*, October 2, 1986, p. 92. The percentage of debt owed to international organizations is calculated from table 6-5 in this chapter.

35. For an overview of the efforts to remedy the trade imbalance, see Madelyn C. Ross, "Foreign Trade Offensives: A New Round of Changes to the Foreign Trade System Strengthens Central Planning, but also Allows Some Flexibility—for Those Who Play by the Rules," *China Business Review*, vol. 14 (July-August 1987), pp. 30–35. On licensing of imports, which began in 1982 but was intensified in 1985, see Martin Weil, "Tightening Up: Beijing Tries to Regain Control of a Splintered Economy," ibid., vol. 9 (May-June 1982), pp. 32–34; "Interview with Dai Jie," *JETRO China Newsletter*, no. 41 (November-December 1982), pp. 19–20; and Xinhua News Agency, June 24, 1985, in FBIS, June 26, 1985, p. K4. On import regulatory taxes, see Xinhua News Agency, July 14, 1985, ibid., July 19, 1985, p. K11; and Masaharu Hishida, "China's Import Adjustment Tax," *JETRO China Newsletter*, no. 59 (November-December 1985), pp. 23–24. On the reimposition of mandatory export quotas, see Zhongguo Xinwenshe, June 14, 1985, in FBIS, June 19, 1985, p. P1. On licensing of foreign trade companies, which included provisions that they must earn a certain amount of foreign exchange, have a clear business and geographic scope, and be owned by the state or by a collective, see *Guoji Shangbao*, January 16, 1986, ibid., February 7, 1986, pp. K16–21. On import controls, see *Wen Wei Po*, February 20, 1986, ibid., February 21, 1986, pp. W3–4; and Fair Trade Subcommittee of the American Chamber of Commerce in Hong Kong, "Import Controls in China: Protectionism with Chinese Char-

acteristics," *China Business Review,* vol. 14 (January- February 1987), pp. 42–45. For doubts about the efficacy of such measures, see Robert Delfs, "That Negative Feeling: China's Trade Is in Deficit: The Question Is by How Much?" *Far Eastern Economic Review,* February 6, 1986, p. 55.

36. These numbers are drawn from Xinhua News Agency, May 14, 1986, in FBIS, May 23, 1986, pp. K9–10. For further details of China's academic exchange programs, particularly with the United States, see various issues of *China Exchange News,* published by the Committee on Scholarly Communication with the People's Republic of China. See also David M. Lampton with Joyce A. Madancy and Kristen M. Williams, *A Relationship Restored: Trends in U.S.-China Educational Exchanges, 1978–1984* (Washington, D.C.: National Academy Press, 1986); and Leo A. Orleans, "Chinese Students and Technology Transfer," *Journal of Northeast Asian Studies,* vol. 4 (Winter 1985), pp. 3–25. For analysis of scientific and technological exchange, see Denis Fred Simon, "The Role of Science and Technology in China's Foreign Relations," in Kim, *China and the World,* pp. 293–318; Simon, "The Evolving Role of Technology Transfer in China's Modernization," in *China's Economy Looks toward the Year 2000,* vol. 2: *Economic Openness in Modernizing China,* Committee Print, Joint Economic Committee, 99 Cong. 2 sess. (GPO, 1986), pp. 254–86; and Liu Sheng-chi, "Communist China's Overseas Study Program since 1978," *Issues and Studies,* vol. 21 (August 1985), pp. 73–103.

37. Lampton with others, *A Relationship Restored,* p. 49, table 3- 16. Most Chinese students and scholars holding J-1 visas are sponsored by the PRC government.

38. Social sciences includes business management, education, and law. See Lampton with others, *A Relationship Restored,* p. 39, table 3-8.

39. One article in the leading newspaper for intellectuals, for example, warned that "foreign bourgeois elements" would try to "take advantage" of cultural exchanges to look for "so-called 'dissidents' and 'democratic individualists'" so as to "influence our country to get rid of socialist 'totalitarian' rule and adopt the road of 'liberalization.'" *Guangming Ribao,* September 24, 1983, in FBIS, October 7, 1983, pp. K5–9, quotation on p. K8.

40. Orleans, "Chinese Students," pp. 20–21.

41. The number of international exchange agreements is drawn from Kyna Rubin, "Recent S&T Reforms in China, Spring 1985," *China Exchange News,* vol. 13 (June 1985), p. 29. For the texts of those signed with the United States in one year, 1979, see Thomas Fingar and Victor H. Li, eds., "United States-China Relations in 1979: Agreements, Protocols, Accords, and Understandings," *Chinese Law and Government,* vol. 14 (Spring 1981), pp. 3–136. On training programs for Chinese managers, see Beth Keck, "China's Managers Look West: Enterprise Reforms Have Sparked New Interest in Western Management Techniques," and Richard W. H. Lee, "Training Ground for a New Breed of Professionals:

Chinese Managers Study American Ways at the U.S. Government's Training Center in Dalian," *China Business Review*, vol. 12 (May-June 1985), pp. 36–39, 39–41.

42. Xinhua News Agency, July 2, 1986, in FBIS, July 3, 1986, p. A1.

43. By 1986 China had become the third largest investor in manufacturing, after the United States and Japan. Xinhua News Agency, February 6, 1987, ibid., February 9, 1987, p. W3. Other sources estimate that China has invested more than $6 billion in all sectors of the Hong Kong economy, accounting for at least one-third of total foreign investment. See *The Economist*, November 9, 1985, p. 80.

44. For a summary of United Nations assistance programs in China, see Xue, *Almanac of China's Economy*, pp. 367–70.

45. *Hubei Ribao*, November 20, 1984, in FBIS, December 5, 1984, pp. G3–4.

46. On direct foreign investment in China, see David G. Brown, "Sino-Foreign Joint Ventures: Contemporary Developments and Historical Perspective," *Journal of Northeast Asian Studies*, vol. 1 (December 1982), pp. 25–56; Friedrich Wu, "Realities Confronting China's Foreign Investment Policy," *World Economy*, vol. 7 (September 1984), pp. 295–311; and Ann Fenwick, "Equity Joint Ventures in the People's Republic of China: An Assessment of the First Five Years," *Business Lawyer*, vol. 40 (May 1985), pp. 839–78.

47. For Deng's views on the possibility of compensation trade in 1975, see "Some Questions on Accelerating the Development of Industry," p. 134. On the description of joint ventures as a form of "state capitalism," see Xu Dixin, "Salient Feature: State Capitalism," *Beijing Review*, January 23, 1984, pp. 29–31.

48. A convenient summary of the various organizational mechanisms for the investment of foreign capital in China appears in *China Business Review*, vol. 10 (September-October 1983), p. 19.

49. Xue, *Almanac of China's Economy*, pp. 338–41.

50. For accounts of why foreigners have been hesitant to invest in China, see Jerome Alan Cohen, "Equity Joint Ventures: 20 Potential Pitfalls that Every Company Should Know About," *China Business Review*, vol. 9 (November-December 1982), pp. 23–30; James B. Stepanek, "Joint Ventures: Why U.S. Firms Are Cautious," ibid., vol. 7 (July-August 1980), pp. 32–33; and Stepanek, "Direct Investment in China: The Idea Was to Speed Up the Country's Development, but in Some Respects the Policy Is Having the Opposite Effect," ibid., vol. 9 (September-October 1982), pp. 20–27.

51. Winston Lord, "Sino-American Relations: No Time for Complacency," address to the National Council for U.S.-China Trade, May 28, 1986; James P. Sterba, "Great Wall: Firms Doing Business in China Are Stymied by Costs and Hassles," *Wall Street Journal*, July 17, 1986; and "Foreign Investment in China Posted a 20 Percent Drop in the First Half," *Asian Wall Street Journal Weekly*, August 4, 1986.

52. Some piecemeal improvements were announced in January. See Xinhua News Agency, January 24, 1986, in FBIS, January 27, 1986, pp. K5–6.

53. *Liaowang,* overseas edition, no. 34 (August 1986), ibid., September 4, 1986, pp. K3–6, cited on p. K4. On the September meeting, see *Wen Wei Po,* October 3, 1986, ibid., October 6, 1986, p. K8. For the text of the central regulations, see *Beijing Review,* October 27, 1986, pp. 26–28. For a brief summary of some of these local provisions, see Ellen Salem, "From the Top Down: The Provinces Join Peking in Investment Reforms," *Far Eastern Economic Review,* November 6, 1986, p. 84.

54. On the mechanisms for the repatriation of profit, see Vigor Fung, "China Seeks Ways for Joint Ventures to Convert Their Yuan Earnings into Foreign Exchange," *Asian Wall Street Journal Weekly,* January 6, 1986; Marcus W. Brauchli, "Peking Promotes Countertrade to Save on Hard Cash," ibid., January 13, 1986; "China to Ease Rules on Joint Ventures' Profit Repatriation," ibid., February 27, 1986; Mary Lee, "Making It All Legal: New Chinese Rules Mostly Codify Practice," *Far Eastern Economic Review,* February 6, 1986, p. 70; and Xinhua News Agency, January 24, 1986, in FBIS, January 27, 1986, pp. K5–6.

55. "China: Widening the Door?" *Asiaweek,* September 21, 1986, pp. 64–65.

56. On the origins of the special economic zones, see A. Doak Barnett, *The Making of Foreign Policy in China: Structure and Process* (Westview Press and Johns Hopkins University, School of Advanced International Studies, Foreign Policy Institute, 1985), pp. 20–21. For analysis, see Ai Wei, "The Special Economic Zones in Mainland China: An Analytical Study," *Issues and Studies,* vol. 21 (June 1985), pp. 117–35; Victor C. Falkenheim, "China's Special Economic Zones," in *China's Economy Looks toward the Year 2000,* pp. 348–70; Ann Fenwick, "Evaluating China's Special Economic Zones," *International Tax and Business Lawyer,* vol. 2 (Fall 1984), pp. 376–97; Joseph Fewsmith, "Special Economic Zones in the PRC," *Problems of Communism,* vol. 35 (November-December 1986), pp. 78–85; George Fitting, "Export Processing Zones in Taiwan and the People's Republic of China," *Asian Survey,* vol. 22 (August 1982), pp. 732–44; Guo-cang Huan, "The SEZs: Problems, Successes, Outlook," pt. 1, *East Asian Executive Reports,* vol. 7 (May 1985), pp. 11–16; pt. 2, ibid., vol. 7 (July 1985), pp. 15–18; Sonoko Nishitateno, "China's Special Economic Zones: Experimental Units for Economic Reform," *International and Comparative Law Quarterly,* vol. 32 (January 1983), pp. 175–85; Michael West Oborne, "China's Early Windows on the World: The Special Economic Zones," *OECD Observer,* no. 133 (March 1985), pp. 11–12, 21–22; Jan S. Prybyla, "Mainland China's Special Economic Zones," *Issues and Studies,* vol. 20 (September 1984), pp. 31–50; and Clyde D. Stoltenberg, "China's Special Economic Zones: Their Development and Prospects," *Asian Survey,* vol. 24 (June 1984), pp. 637–54. Early Chinese descriptions of the zones can be found in *Jingji Yanjiu,* no. 6 (June 20, 1981), in JPRS, *China Report: Economic Affairs,* August 13, 1981, pp. 1–12; and *Jingji Yanjiu,* no. 8 (August 20, 1981), ibid., September 30, 1981, pp. 34–42.

57. Zhongguo Xinwenshe, December 7, 1986, in FBIS, December 19, 1986, p. K15.
58. Liang Xiang in *Jingji Ribao*, December 11, 1985, ibid., January 24, 1986, pp. P1–12, cited on p. P3; and Falkenheim, "China's Special Economic Zones," p. 356, table 1.
59. Falkenheim, "China's Special Economic Zones," p. 356, table 1, and p. 358, table 2.
60. See Xue, *Almanac of China's Economy*, pp. 338–41; and see Zhang Peiji, "China's Strategy and Policy on Utilizing Foreign Capital," paper presented to the conference, "The Role of Foreign Investment in National Development with Special Reference to China," sponsored by the Institute of World Economics and Politics of the Chinese Academy of Social Sciences and the Sloan School of Management of the Massachusetts Institute of Technology, Hangzhou, March 1985, p. 24.
61. Falkenheim, "China's Special Economic Zones," pp. 366–67.
62. *Hsin Wan Pao*, June 27, 1985, in FBIS, July 11, 1985, pp. W11–12, quotation on p. W11.
63. For an article arguing that inland provinces, too, should be allowed to set up special economic zones, see *Jingji Ribao*, June 3, 1985, ibid., June 12, 1985, pp. K5–6. Gu Mu, the most senior Party leader responsible for foreign economic policy, has acknowledged that this is a frequently asked question. See *Jingji Guanli*, no. 4 (April 5, 1985), ibid., June 20, 1985, pp. K15–18. For an analysis of these controversies, see Susan Shirk, "The Domestic Political Dimensions of China's Foreign Economic Relations," in Kim, *China and the World*, pp. 57–81.
64. Edith Terry, "Doing Business with China's Three Great Cities: Beijing, Tianjin, and Shanghai," *China Business Review*, vol. 7 (March-April 1980), pp. 14–25; Terry, "Fujian Province: Decentralizing Foreign Trade"; Christopher M. Clarke, "Decentralization," *China Business Review*, vol. 11 (March-April 1984), pp. 8–10; and Victor Falkenheim, "Fujian's Open Door Experiment: Innovative Province Learns the Pros and Cons of Success," ibid., vol. 13 (May-June 1986), pp. 38–42. On the special authority given to Shanghai, see Carolyn L. Brehm, "Shanghai Unleashed," ibid., vol. 10 (September-October 1983), pp. 12–14.
65. These quantitative limits are drawn from Imai, "Reform of China's Foreign Trade System," p. 4; and *Renmin Ribao*, overseas edition, August 25, 1985, in FBIS, August 30, 1985, pp. A1–4.
66. *Nanfang Ribao*, June 11, 1984, ibid., June 18, 1984, pp. K1–7.
67. On the open cities, see Zhang Peiji, "China's Strategy," and Louise do Rosario, "Bumpy Capitalist Road: Hong Kong's Business Partners in China Find That the Going Is Not Always Smooth for Private Enterprise," *Far Eastern Economic Review*, January 31, 1985, pp. 72–74. Convenient summaries of the plans for each open city and comparisons of the tax treatment for foreign investment in the open cities and in the special economic zones can be found in "China's 'Open' Coastal

Cities at a Glance" and "Rules concerning Income Taxes and the Unified Industrial and Commercial Tax in China's Special Economic Zones, Economic and Technical Development Zones, and 14 'Open' Coastal Cities," *JETRO China Newsletter*, no. 53 (November-December 1984), pp. 15–17, 19–20. On the results of the open city policy, see Zhongguo Xinwenshe, September 2, 1985, in FBIS, September 5, 1985, pp. A4–5.

68. For a comprehensive summary of the bewildering array of local tax provisions, see "Overview of Investment Incentives," *China Business Review*, vol. 13 (May-June 1986), pp. 20–23.

69. *Banyuetan*, no. 4 (February 25, 1985), in FBIS, March 13, 1985, pp. K21–23, quotation on p. K22.

70. See Du Runsheng, "Development of the Rural Economy: Several Social Objectives," *Hongqi*, no. 8 (April 16, 1985), in JPRS, *China Report: Red Flag*, June 26, 1985, pp. 20–31. Interestingly, in this article Du substitutes a Peking-Tianjin-Tangshan triangle for the Min River delta around Fuzhou.

71. Interviews in Peking, November 1985.

72. For an overview of this debate, see *Cheng Ming*, no. 94 (August 1, 1985), in FBIS, August 7, 1985, pp. W1–8.

73. The quotation from the press appeared in *Renmin Ribao*, December 10, 1984, ibid., December 14, 1984, pp. K1–4, cited on p. K1. The second anecdote was obtained in an interview in Shenzhen, April 1985. These comments echo an earlier slogan, allegedly raised by some Party leaders in 1984: "Give Shenzhen back to us!" *Cheng Ming*, no. 84 (October 1, 1984), ibid., October 5, 1984, pp. W2–5, quotation on p. W4.

74. *Zhongguo Fazhi Bao*, June 28, 1985, ibid., July 8, 1985, pp. K18–19.

75. *Liaowang*, no. 34 (August 20, 1984), ibid., September 11, 1984, pp. K1–3, cited on p. K2. For a representative defense of the present open door policy against analogies with the past, see Li Mingsan, "What Are the Basic Differences between Opening to the Outside World and Old China's 'Open Door'?" *Hongqi*, no. 4 (February 16, 1985), in JPRS, *China Report: Red Flag*, April 12, 1985, pp. 79–81.

76. *Chiu-shih Nien-tai*, no. 186 (July 1, 1985), in FBIS, July 11, 1985, pp. W2–8.

77. *Jingji Ribao*, February 22, 1986, ibid., March 5, 1986, pp. P1–8, quotation on pp. P7–8.

78. Perhaps the most authoritative defense was that given by Zou Erkang, a leading Shenzhen official, to the Hong Kong newspaper *Ta Kung Pao*, July 26, 1985, ibid., August 1, 1985, pp. W1–7. See also *Renmin Ribao*, May 17, 1985, ibid., May 24, 1985, pp. K5–7; *Kaifang*, no. 5 (May 8, 1985), ibid., May 31, 1985, pp. K9–11; and *Jingji Ribao*, September 16, 1985, ibid., October 3, 1985, pp. P1–4. Shenzhen's defenders have also quibbled with the statistical data presented by their critics, arguing that only a small part of the Chinese capital invested in Shenzhen

came from the central government. See *Renmin Ribao,* October 7, 1985, ibid., October 18, 1985, pp. K5–9.

79. *Jingji Ribao,* January 25, 1986, ibid., January 31, 1986, pp. K7–10.
80. Xinhua News Agency, August 1, 1985, ibid., August 2, 1985, p. D1.
81. *Kuan Chiao Ching,* no. 160 (January 16, 1986), ibid., January 30, 1986, pp. W4–11, cited on p. W7.
82. *Asia-Pacific Report: Trends, Issues, Challenges* (Honolulu: East-West Center, 1986), p. 98.
83. The job-creating potential of exports is from *Lilun Yuekan,* vol. 9 (September 25, 1985), in FBIS, November 6, 1985, pp. K13–24, cited on p. K17. The value of industrial exports and the size of the state industrial labor force are from *1986 China Statistical Handbook,* p. 24; and *Zhongguo tongji zhaiyao, 1986,* p. 28.
84. Dong, "Some Problems concerning China's Strategy," cited on p. 458. For a representative defense of import-substitution strategies, see Teng Weixao, "Socialist Modernization and the Pattern of Foreign Trade," in Xu Dixin and others, *China's Search for Economic Growth: The Chinese Economy since 1949* (Peking: New World Press, 1982), pp. 167–92.
85. *Guangming Ribao,* July 4, 1985. I am grateful to Denis Fred Simon for bringing this article to my attention.

CHAPTER 7

1. On the "crisis of faith" in the late 1970s and early 1980s, see the article by Deng Liqun in *Gongren Ribao,* March 27, 1981, in Foreign Broadcast Information Service, *Daily Report: China,* March 30, 1981, pp. L10–12 (hereafter FBIS). On the danger of a Polish crisis in China, see Liao Gailong, "The '1980 Reform' Program of China," *Ch'i-shih Nien-tai,* no. 134 (March 1981), ibid., March 16, 1981, pp. U1–19, cited on p. U11.
2. For comprehensive Chinese descriptions of the moderate political reforms, see Deng Xiaoping, "On the Reform of the System of State and Party Leadership," August 1980, in *Selected Works of Deng Xiaoping, 1975–1982* (Peking: Foreign Languages Press, 1984), pp. 302–25; Liao Gailong, "The '1980 Reform' Program"; and Feng Wenbin, "On the Question of Socialist Democracy," *Renmin Ribao,* November 25, 1980, in FBIS, December 2, 1980, pp. L9–15. For Western analyses, see Thomas P. Bernstein, "Domestic Politics," in Steven M. Goldstein, ed., *China Briefing, 1984* (Westview Press, 1985), pp. 1–20; Victor C. Falkenheim, "Institutionalization and Reform in China's Party-State Structure," in *Mainland China's Modernization: Its Prospects and Problems* (Taipei and Berkeley: Institute of International Relations, and University of California at Berkeley, Institute of East Asian Studies, 1981), pp. 50–61; David S. G. Goodman, "Modernization and the Search for Political Order in the PRC," *Issues and Studies,* vol. 21 (April 1985),

pp. 23–43; William H. Joseph, "The Dilemmas of Political Reform in China," *Current History*, vol. 84 (September 1985), pp. 252–55, 279–80; Hong Yung Lee, "Ideology, State, and Society in China," *Journal of International Affairs*, vol. 39 (Winter 1986), pp. 77–89; and Tang Tsou, "Reflections on the Formation and Foundations of the Communist Party-State in China," in his *The Cultural Revolution and Post-Mao Reforms: A Historical Perspective* (University of Chicago Press, 1986), pp. 259–334.

3. On religion, see excerpts of the important article by Zhao Fusan that appear in *Renmin Ribao*, November 7, 1985, in FBIS, November 21, 1985, pp. K16–17. For analysis of the state of religion in post-Mao China, see Richard Bohr, "Religion in the People's Republic of China: The Limits of Reform" (New York: China Council of the Asia Society, 1982); and Richard Bohr, "State and Religion in the PRC Today: The Christian Experience," paper presented to the Fifteenth Sino-American Conference on Mainland China, sponsored by the Institute of International Relations, Taipei, June 1986.

4. On the degree of intellectual freedom in China, see Merle Goldman, "Culture," in Goldstein, *China Briefing, 1984*, pp. 21–38; Liang Heng and Judith Shapiro, *Intellectual Freedom in China after Mao: With A Focus on 1983* (New York: Fund for Free Expression, 1984); Perry Link, "Intellectuals and Cultural Policy after Mao," in A. Doak Barnett and Ralph N. Clough, eds., *Modernizing China: Post-Mao Reform and Development* (Westview Press, 1986), pp. 81–102; and Judith Shapiro and Liang Heng, "China: How Much Freedom?" *New York Review of Books*, October 24, 1985, pp. 14–16.

5. "Constitution of the People's Republic of China," December 1982, in *Fifth Session of the Fifth National People's Congress, November–December 1982* (Peking: Foreign Languages Press, 1983), Article 1 (on p. 9). In Chinese Communist terminology, the proletariat included peasants as well as the industrial labor force. On the rehabilitation of former pariah groups, see Hong Yung Lee, "Changing Patterns of Political Participation in China: A Historical Perspective," paper presented to the workshop on "Studies in Policy Implementation in the Post-Mao Era," sponsored by the Joint Committee on Chinese Studies of the American Council of Learned Societies and the Social Science Research Council, Columbus, Ohio, June 1983.

6. "Constitution of the People's Republic of China," Article 5 (on p. 11) and Article 33 (on p. 22). On the post-Mao legal order, see Richard Baum, "China's Post-Mao Legal Reforms in Historical and Comparative Perspective," paper presented to the conference, "To Reform the Chinese Political Order," sponsored by the Joint Committee on Chinese Studies of the American Council of Learned Societies and the Social Science Research Council, Harwichport, Mass., June 1984; Frances Hoar Foster, "Codification in Post-Mao China," *American Journal of Comparative Law*, vol. 30 (Summer 1982), pp. 395–428; Masanobu Kato, "Civil and Economic Law in the People's Republic of China,"

ibid., vol. 30 (Summer 1982), pp. 429–57; Shao-chuan Leng, "Criminal Justice in Post-Mao China," *China Quarterly*, no. 87 (September 1981), pp. 440–69; Shao-chuan Leng and Hung-dah Chiu, *Criminal Justice in Post-Mao China: Analysis and Documents* (Albany, N.Y.: State University of New York Press, 1985); and Byron Weng, "Some Key Aspects of the 1982 Draft Constitution of the People's Republic of China," *China Quarterly*, no. 91 (September 1982), pp. 492–506.

7. "Constitution of the People's Republic of China," Article 24 (on pp. 18–19), Articles 51–52 (on p. 28); and "Constitution of the Communist Party of China," September 1982, in *The Twelfth National Congress of the CPC*, September 1982 (Peking: Foreign Languages Press, 1982), pp. 89–130, cited on p. 14. The quotations on the responsibilities of writers are from Wang Meng, later appointed minister of culture. See Xinhua News Agency, November 5, 1985, in FBIS, November 6, 1985, pp. K3–5, cited on p. K3.

8. John S. Aird, "Coercion in Family Planning: Causes, Methods, and Consequences, in *China's Economy Looks toward the Year 2000*, vol. 1: *The Four Modernizations*, Committee Print, Joint Economic Committee, 99 Cong. 2 sess. (Government Printing Office, 1986), pp. 184–221, quotation on p. 185.

9. In 1986, for example, Vice-Premier Qiao Shi warned lawyers that, while they should defend the "legitimate rights and interests of the citizens," they should never "violate the interests of the state and the collective ... for the sake of their clients." *Renmin Ribao*, July 8, 1986, in FBIS, July 14, 1986, pp. K26–28, quotation on p. K27.

10. For discussions on the limits to the development of the legal system, see Amnesty International, *China: Violations of Human Rights: Prisoners of Conscience and the Death Penalty in the People's Republic of China* (London: Amnesty International Publications, 1984); John F. Copper, Franz Michael, and Yuan-li Wu, *Human Rights in Post-Mao China* (Westview Press, 1985); and Amnesty International, *Amnesty International Report, 1986* (London: Amnesty International, 1986), pp. 215–19.

11. For further discussions of the expansion of political participation in post-Mao China, see Andrew J. Nathan, *Chinese Democracy* (Alfred A. Knopf, 1985); David G. Strand, "Reform of Political Participation," paper presented to the conference, "To Reform the Chinese Political Order," sponsored by the Joint Committee on Chinese Studies of the American Council of Learned Societies and the Social Science Research Council, Harwichport, Mass., June 1984; and Brantly Womack, "Modernization and Political Reform in China," *Journal of Asian Studies*, vol. 43 (May 1984), pp. 417–40.

12. On elections, see Nathan, *Chinese Democracy*, chap. 10; Brantly Womack, "The 1980 County-Level Elections in China: Experiment in Democratic Modernization," *Asian Survey*, vol. 22 (March 1982), pp. 261–77; and John P. Burns, "The Implementation of Sub-Village Elections in South China, 1979– 1982," and Barrett L. McCormick, "Re-

forming the People's Congress System: A Case Study of the Implementation of 'Strengthening Socialist Law and Socialist Democracy' in Post-Mao China,'' both papers presented to the workshop, "Studies in Policy Implementation in the Post-Mao Era," sponsored by the Joint Committee on Chinese Studies of the American Council of Learned Societies and the Social Science Research Council, Columbus, Ohio, June 1983.

13. Significantly, however, this fact was reported in a Hong Kong newspaper, and not in the Chinese press. *South China Morning Post,* April 13, 1986, in FBIS, April 21, 1986, pp. W4–5. For earlier discussions of the expansion of the role of the people's congresses, see *Renmin Ribao,* September 10, 1980, ibid., September 17, 1980, pp. L2–9, cited on pp. L5–7; and Xinhua News Agency, September 8, 1980, ibid., September 10, 1980, pp. L13–14.

14. On modification of draft legislation at the national level, see Xinhua News Agency, August 26, 1985, ibid., August 27, 1985, pp. K1–2; on modification of the budget at the county level, see Tian Sansong, "Tongxiang County: Two Years after the People's Deputy Elections," *Beijing Review,* February 1, 1982, pp. 13–19, 21, cited on p. 15. For the failure of the National People's Congress to pass a resolution in support of the movement against "spiritual pollution," see Xinhua News Agency, December 8, 1983, in FBIS, December 9, 1983, pp. K10–11. On the debates over the national bankruptcy law, see Xinhua News Agency, August 29, 1986, and September 5, 1986, ibid., September 2, 1986, p. K12, and September 8, 1986, p. K1; *Liaowang,* overseas edition, no. 39 (September 29, 1986), ibid., October 7, 1986, pp. K1–3; and *China Daily,* November 17, 1986, ibid., November 17, 1986, pp. K3–4.

15. On the role of trade unions, see Richard Morris, "Trade Unions in Contemporary China," *Australian Journal of Chinese Affairs,* no. 13 (January 1985), pp. 51–68; and *Gongren Ribao,* February 27, 1986, in FBIS, April 1, 1986, pp. K10–12.

16. One democratic party, the Jiusan Society, played a big role in questioning the feasibility of the mammoth Three Gorges dam on the Yangtze River. On the democratic parties in general, see James D. Seymour, "China's Satellite Parties Today," *Asian Survey,* vol. 26 (September 1986), pp. 991–1004. On the role of the Jiusan Society, see Seymour, "Satellite Parties," p. 998; and Kenneth Lieberthal and Michel Oksenberg, *Bureaucratic Politics and Chinese Energy Development* (Washington, D.C.: U.S. Department of Commerce, International Trade Administration, 1986), pp. 309–10.

17. See, for example, Zhongguo Xinwenshe, January 3, 1986, in FBIS, January 8, 1986, pp. P2–3.

18. The student protests of late 1986 will be discussed later in this chapter. For other examples of protest in recent years, see Agence France Presse, July 27, 1985, in FBIS, July 31, 1985, p. K11; Xinhua News Agency, April 29, 1985, and May 4, 1985, ibid., April 30, 1985, pp. K1–2, and May 6, 1985, pp. K1–2; Agence France Presse, June 20, 1985, ibid., June

21, 1985, p. R5; and *Cheng Ming*, no. 97 (November 1, 1985), ibid., November 6, 1985, pp. W1–8.

19. Xinhua News Agency, September 11, 1981, ibid., September 14, 1981, pp. K2–10, cited on p. K9.

20. For analysis of the restrictions placed on electoral activity, see Nathan, *Chinese Democracy*, chap. 10.

21. Press accounts describe delegates to the National People's Congress as presenting "suggestions, criticisms, and opinions," which are then forwarded to "relevant departments" to be "handled." Xinhua News Agency, February 27, 1987, in FBIS, March 3, 1987, pp. K18–20.

22. Changsha radio, November 12, 1986, and Xinhua News Agency, November 15, 1986, ibid., November 17, 1986, pp. P3–5.

23. For such proposals, see *Guangming Ribao*, April 14, 1981, ibid., April 29, 1981, pp. K2–4.

24. See, for example, *Renmin Ribao*, November 13, 1984, ibid., November 14, 1984, pp. K7–9.

25. Liao, "The '1980 Reform' Program," pp. U14–15.

26. On workers' congresses, see *Gongren Ribao*, February 18, 1981, in FBIS, March 4, 1981, pp. L13–16; Xinhua News Agency, February 24, 1981, ibid., February 24, 1981, pp. L11–12; and Agence France Presse, March 20, 1981, ibid., March 20, 1981, pp. L1–2. For analysis, see Martin Lockett, "Enterprise Management—Moves towards Democracy?" in Stephan Feuchtwang and Athar Hussain, eds., *The Chinese Economic Reforms* (London: Croom Helm, 1983), pp. 224–56.

27. On the role of the democratic parties, see "Central Committee Notice on Issuing 'Minutes of the National United Front Work Conference,'" February 1982, *Issues and Studies*, vol. 19 (September 1983), pp. 95–105; and Seymour, "Satellite Parties."

28. On the restrictions on independent organization, see Agence France Presse, February 20, 1981, in FBIS, February 20, 1981, p. H1; and Xinhua News Agency, December 11, 1984, ibid., December 12, 1984, pp. K1–2. On the suppression of secret societies, see *Nongmin Ribao*, June 27, 1986, ibid., July 16, 1986, pp. K1–4.

29. On controls over illegal publication, see *Guangming Ribao*, December 20, 1985, ibid., January 6, 1986, pp. K8–10; and Zhongguo Xinwenshe, March 31, 1986, ibid., April 4, 1986, pp. K19–20.

30. *Renmin Ribao*, April 14, 1985, in FBIS, April 15, 1985, pp. K1–15, cited on p. K5; and "Document of the Central Committee of the Chinese Communist Party: Decisions on Current Guidelines for Propaganda in Newspapers, Periodicals, News Reporting, and Broadcasts," February 1981, *Issues and Studies*, vol. 18 (July 1982), pp. 110–17.

31. See for example, Hangzhou radio, January 1, 1987, in FBIS, January 2, 1987, p. O6; Zhengzhou radio, December 31, 1986, ibid., January 5, 1987, pp. P6–7; and Peking television, December 26, 1986, ibid., December 29, 1986, pp. R1–2.

32. *Selected Works of Mao Tsetung*, vol. 5 (Peking: Foreign Languages Press, 1977); and Hua Kuo-feng, *Continue the Revolution under the*

Dictatorship of the Proletariat to the End (Peking: Foreign Languages Press, 1977).

33. "Communiqué of the Third Plenary Session of the Central Committee of the Communist Party of China," December 1978, in *Peking Review*, December 29, 1978, pp. 6–16, cited on p. 16; *Guangming Ribao*, February 11, 1979, in FBIS, March 14, 1979, pp. E1–9; and Xinhua News Agency, September 9, 1980, ibid., September 11, 1980, pp. L10–11.

34. *Renmin Ribao*, January 9, 1981, ibid., January 23, 1981, pp. C1–3.

35. On the transformation of ideology in post-Mao China, see Bill Brugger, ed., *Chinese Marxism in Flux, 1978–84* (M. E. Sharpe, 1985); William A. Joseph, *The Critique of Ultra-Leftism in China, 1959–1981* (Stanford University Press, 1984); Helmut Martin, *Cult and Canon: The Origins and Development of State Maoism* (M. E. Sharpe, 1982); and Stuart R. Schram, "'Economics in Command?' Ideology and Policy since the Third Plenum, 1978–84," *China Quarterly*, no. 99 (September 1984), pp. 417–61.

36. See Bill Brugger, "Alienation Revisited," *Australian Journal of Chinese Affairs*, no. 12 (July 1984), pp. 143–52.

37. Perhaps the most notorious article presenting this point of view contained the sentence, "We cannot expect the writings of Marx and Lenin of that time to provide solutions to our current problems." The sentence was later corrected to read: "provide solutions to *all* our current problems" (emphasis added). *Renmin Ribao*, December 7, 1984, and December 8, 1984, in FBIS, December 7, 1984, pp. K1–2, quotation on p. K1; and December 10, 1984, p. K21.

38. Chengdu radio, February 8, 1984, ibid., February 9, 1984, pp. K9–13, quotation on p. K11; and *Renmin Ribao*, March 29, 1984, ibid., April 2, 1984, pp. K3–5.

39. Zhongguo Xinwenshe, October 1, 1984, ibid., October 1, 1984, pp. K22–23, cited on K23.

40. Deng Xiaoping, "Speech at the Third Plenary Session of the Central Advisory Commission of the Communist Party of China," October 1984, in Deng Xiaoping, *Build Socialism with Chinese Characteristics* (Peking: Foreign Languages Press, 1984) pp. 54–64, quotation on pp. 59–60.

41. Two typical Western assessments that reached this conclusion were William Safire, "Greatest Leap Forward," *New York Times*, December 10, 1984; and the editorial, "Burying Marx," *Wall Street Journal*, December 11, 1984.

42. Nanning radio, December 25, 1983, in FBIS, December 28, 1983, pp. P3–5, quotation on p. P4.

43. Thomas B. Gold, "'Just in Time!' China Battles Spiritual Pollution on the Eve of 1984," *Asian Survey*, vol. 24 (September 1984), pp. 947–74, quotation on p. 965.

44. For general assessments of these campaigns, see Perry Link, "Introduction: On the Mechanics of the Control of Literature in China," in Perry Link, ed., *Stubborn Weeds: Popular and Controversial Chinese Liter-*

ature after the Cultural Revolution (Indiana University Press, 1983), pp. 1–28; and Judith Shapiro and Liang Heng, *Cold Winds, Warm Winds: Intellectual Life in China Today* (Wesleyan University Press, 1986).

45. See Kjeld Erik Brodsgaard, "The Democracy Movement in China, 1978–1979: Opposition Movements, Wall Poster Campaigns, and Underground Journals," *Asian Survey*, vol. 21 (July 1981), pp. 747–74.

46. Anthony J. Kane, "Literary Politics in Post-Mao China," *Asian Survey*, vol. 21 (July 1981), pp. 775–94.

47. Gold, "Just In Time!"

48. Thus each campaign has featured a major article or editorial on the necessity of upholding the four cardinal principles. See, for example, *Renmin Ribao*, April 19, 1979, in *Beijing Review*, May 11, 1979, pp. 11–14; *Renmin Ribao*, April 24, 1981, pp. 1, 4, in FBIS, April 27, 1981, pp. K8–16; and *Guangming Ribao*, November 15, 1985, in FBIS, November 20, 1985, pp. K1–8.

49. On Deng Liqun's role, see *Ming Pao*, October 21, 1983, ibid., October 24, 1983, pp. W2–3; and *Cheng Ming*, no. 76 (1984), ibid., February 7, 1984, pp. W1–11. On Wang Zhen, see Xinhua News Agency, October 24, 1983, ibid., October 26, 1983, pp. K1–3, quotation on p. K2; and Xinhua News Agency, October 23, 1983, ibid, October 25, 1983, pp. K5–6.

50. Xinhua News Agency, September 23, 1985, and September 26, 1985, ibid., September 23, 1985, pp. K13–16, and September 26, 1985, pp. K33–35, quotation on p. K34.

51. Deng, "Uphold the Four Cardinal Principles," March 1979, in *Selected Works*, pp. 166–191; "Concerning Problems on the Ideological Front," July 1981, ibid., pp. 367–71, quotation on pp. 367, 368; and "Teng Hsiao-p'ing's Speech at the Second Plenary Session of the Twelfth Central Committee of the Chinese Communist Party," October 1983, *Issues and Studies*, vol. 20 (April 1984), pp. 100–11, definition on pp. 104–05.

52. Xinhua News Agency, December 8, 1983, in FBIS, December 12, 1983, pp. K5–6, cited on p. K6; quotation in *Guangming Ribao*, December 17, 1983, ibid., December 23, 1983, pp. K1–2.

53. Hu Qili's May Day speech is in Xinhua News Agency, April 30, 1986, ibid., May 2, 1986, pp. K2–10. On the significance of the speech, see Zhongguo Xinwenshe, May 3, 1986, ibid., May 5, 1986, pp. K3–4; and *China Daily*, June 9, 1986, ibid., June 11, 1986, p. K11–13. For Deng Xiaoping's comments on political reform, see *Wen Wei Po*, July 21, 1986, ibid., July 24, 1986, pp. W1–3, quotation on p. W1; and *Ta Kung Pao*, July 16, 1986, ibid., July 21, 1986, pp. W4–7. On the Party's working group on political reform, see *South China Morning Post*, August 13, 1986, ibid., August 13, 1986, pp. W5–6; and "A Superagency for Political Reform," *Asiaweek*, November 9, 1986, p. 30.

54. For Wang Zhaoguo, see Xinhua News Agency, July 16, 1986, in FBIS, July 21, 1986, pp. K21–22; and *Hongqi*, no. 17 (September 1, 1986),

ibid., September 22, 1986, pp. K8–21. For Yan Jiaqi, see Zhongguo Xinwenshe, June 17, 1986, ibid., June 18, 1986, pp. K5–7; *Guangming Ribao*, June 30, 1986, ibid., July 16, 1986, pp. K9–13; and Zhongguo Xinwenshe, September 11, 1986, ibid., September 19, 1986, p. K25.

55. *Shijie Jingji Daobao*, April 21, 1986, ibid., May 14, 1986, pp. K4–5, quotation on p. K4.

56. Hu Qili's May Day speech, p. K4; *Renmin Ribao*, March 14, 1986, ibid., March 25, 1986, pp. K27–29, quotation on p. K29; and *Shijie Jingji Daobao*, April 21, 1986, ibid., May 14, 1986, pp. K4–5.

57. *Gongren Ribao*, November 2, 1985, ibid., May 22, 1986, pp. K3–10, quotation on p. K6; *Shijie Jingji Daobao*, April 21, 1986, ibid., May 13, 1986, pp. K11–13, quotation on p. K12; *Hongqi*, no. 9 (May 1, 1986), ibid., May 28, 1986, pp. K11–22, cited on p. K19.

58. The senior economist was Yu Guangyuan: see *Renmin Ribao*, May 16, 1986, ibid., June 2, 1986, pp. K1–8, cited on pp. K6– 7, K2; for a similar view, see *Guangming Ribao*, April 30, 1986, ibid., May 19, 1986, pp. K4–12. On the calls for an end to censorship, see *Yangcheng Wanbao*, December 4, 1986, ibid., December 19, 1986, pp. K4–8. On the reduction of political education, see "Tightening the Screws," *Asiaweek*, February 1, 1987, pp. 8–17, cited on p. 13.

59. For Zhu Houze's views, see *Wenzhai Bao*, no. 325 (June 29, 1986), in FBIS, July 14, 1986, pp. K23–24; and Xinhua News Agency, July 16, 1986, ibid., July 17, 1986, pp. K3–4. For those of Wang Meng, see *Renmin Ribao*, July 13, 1986, ibid., July 17, 1986, pp. K4–6.

60. On Shekou, see *Hongqi*, no. 19 (October 1, 1986), in Joint Publications Research Service (JPRS), *China Report: Red Flag*, November 26, 1986, pp. 35–42. On Tianjin, see "Democracy in One Zone," *Asiaweek*, September 7, 1986, p. 19. On Wenzhou, see "A Superagency."

61. *Renmin Ribao*, May 30, 1986, in FBIS, June 2, 1986, pp. K8–12, quotation on p. K10.

62. On Fei Xiaotong, see Zhongguo Xinwenshe, July 30, 1986, ibid., July 31, 1986, pp. K2–3; for the earlier version of this proposal, introduced in the 1950s, see Harry Harding, *Organizing China: The Problem of Bureaucracy, 1949–1976* (Stanford University Press, 1981), pp. 147–48. On proposals for a press law, see *Ching Pao*, no. 91 (February 10, 1985), pp. 20, 22, in FBIS, February 21, 1985, pp. W1–4; and *Wen Hui Pao*, August 30, 1986, ibid., September 12, 1986, pp. K1–6. Debate over the suitability of a multiparty system was stimulated by a newspaper interview with a Swiss sinologist who claimed that China's level of economic development was not sufficiently advanced to warrant democratic pluralism. Many younger Chinese intellectuals felt that such a view was too pessimistic and argued that China should make more rapid progress toward a competitive electoral system. See "Full Speed Ahead," *Asiaweek*, October 5, 1986, pp. 58–65; and *Cheng Ming*, no. 110 (December 1, 1986), in FBIS, December 12, 1986, pp. K11–18.

63. Fang Lizhi, "A Chinese Tom Paine Speaks Out on Democracy," *Washington Post*, January 18, 1987. Yan Jiaqi had also spoken about

human rights, noting, "The realm that government's power should particularly not violate is 'human rights.'" *Guangming Ribao*, June 30, 1986, in FBIS, July 16, 1986, pp. K9–13, quotation on p. K12.

64. *Hongqi*, no. 3 (February 1987), pp. 22–26, in FBIS, February 19, 1987, pp. K5–10, quotation on p. K7; and see also "Fear and Loathing," *Asiaweek*, February 1, 1987, pp. 12–13.

65. *Yangcheng Wanbao*, December 6, 1986, in FBIS, December 12, 1986, pp. K9–11, quotation on p. K10; and *Yangcheng Wanbao*, December 2, 1986, ibid., pp. K8–9, quotation on p. K8.

66. "Resolution of the Central Committee of the Communist Party of China on the Guiding Principles for Building a Socialist Society with an Advanced Culture and Ideology," September 1986, Xinhua News Agency, September 28, 1986, in FBIS, September 29, 1986, pp. K2–12, quotations from pp. K10, K8. For information on the debates surrounding the drafting of the document, see *Cheng Ming*, no. 109 (November 1986), in FBIS, November 18, 1986, pp. K1–9.

67. On the revision of the election law, see *China Daily*, November 17, 1986, ibid., November 17, 1986, pp. K9–10. On the role of local elections in sparking the student demonstrations, see, for example, Agence France Presse, December 10, 1986, ibid., December 11, 1986, pp. O1–2; *Hong Kong Standard*, December 11, 1986, and December 15, 1986, in FBIS, December 11, 1986, pp. O2–3; and December 15, 1986, p. O1; Agence France Presse, December 17, 1986, ibid., December 17, 1986, p. O1; and *South China Morning Post*, December 11, 1986, ibid., December 11, 1986, pp. O1–2.

68. On the influence of contemporaneous events elsewhere in Asia, see Agence France Presse, December 10, 1986, in FBIS, December 11, 1986, pp. D1–2; and Agence France Presse, December 25, 1986, ibid., December 29, 1986, p. R6.

69. For a map of the student protests, see Robert Delfs, "Conservatives Blame Reforms for Continued Demonstrations: Now the Right's Turn," *Far Eastern Economic Review*, January 8, 1987, pp. 8–9, appearing on p. 9.

70. See, for example, James K. Schiffman, "'Exploring for Ideas': Chinese Student Protestors Speak Out on Country's Rigid One Party Sytem," *Asian Wall Street Journal Weekly*, January 12, 1987.

71. Xinhua News Agency, December 28, 1986, in FBIS, December 30, 1986, pp. K6–8, cited on p. K7.

72. The term is from H. Gordon Skilling, "Group Conflict and Political Change," in Chalmers Johnson, ed., *Change in Communist Systems* (Stanford University Press, 1970), pp. 215–34.

73. Zhao Ziyang, "Report on the Work of the Government," March 25, 1987, in FBIS, March 26, 1987, pp. K1–26, quotation on p. K23.

74. On the historical and cultural basis for this viewpoint, see Nathan, *Chinese Democracy*; and Donald J. Munro, *The Concept of Man in Contemporary China* (University of Michigan Press, 1977).

75. *Jingji Ribao*, May 9, 1985, in FBIS, May 21, 1985, pp. K2–5.

CHAPTER 8

1. Xinhua News Agency, March 28, 1981, in Foreign Broadcast Information Service, *Daily Report: China*, March 30, 1981, pp. L2–9, quotation on p. L7 (hereafter FBIS); Deng Xiaoping, "Streamlining Organizations Constitutes a Revolution," January 1982, in *Selected Works of Deng Xiaoping, 1975–1982* (Peking: Foreign Languages Press, 1984), pp. 374–79, quotation on p. 374; and *Renmin Ribao*, September 20, 1983, in FBIS, September 27, 1983, pp. K10–12, quotation on p. K11.

2. On the restaffing of the bureaucracy, see John P. Burns, "Reforming China's Bureaucracy, 1979–82," *Asian Survey*, vol. 23 (June 1983), pp. 692–722; Jean-Pierre Cabestan, "Comment devient-on ministre en Chine Populaire?" (How does one become a minister in People's China?), *Revue d'Etudes Comparatives Est-Ouest*, vol. 16 (December 1985), pp. 47–86; Christopher M. Clarke, "China's Reform Program," *Current History*, vol. 83 (September 1984), pp. 254–56, 273; Clarke, "Rejuvenation, Reorganization, and the Dilemmas of Modernization in Post-Deng China," *Journal of International Affairs*, vol. 39 (Winter 1986), pp. 119–32; Hong Yung Lee, "China's Twelfth Central Committee: Rehabilitated Cadres and Technocrats," *Asian Survey*, vol. 23 (June 1983), pp. 673–91; William deB. Mills, "Generational Change in China," *Problems of Communism*, vol. 32 (November-December 1983), pp. 16–35; and Mills, "Leadership Change in China's Provinces," ibid., vol. 34 (May-June 1985), pp. 24–60.

3. On the retirement of elderly officials, see Xinhua News Agency, February 10, 1985, in FBIS, February 11, 1985, pp. K1–7; *Hsin Wan Pao*, April 9, 1985, ibid., April 9, 1985, pp. W1–2; and *Hong Kong Standard*, February 6, 1987, ibid., February 9, 1987, pp. K2–3.

4. *Wenzhai Bao*, no. 327 (July 6, 1986), ibid., July 17, 1986, p. K30.

5. See Deng Xiaoping, "The Primary Task of Veteran Cadres Is to Select Young and Middle-Aged Cadres for Promotion," July 1981, in *Selected Works*, pp. 361–66; and "Advisory Commissions Will Be a Transitional Measure for the Abolition of Life Tenure in Leading Posts," July 1982, ibid., pp. 391–93.

6. Statistics for members of the Central Committee and State Council are from Clarke, "Rejuvenation, Reorganization, and the Dilemmas of Modernization" pp. 128, 123. Statistics on provincial leaders are from Xinhua News Agency, January 23, 1984, in FBIS, January 23, 1984, pp. K1–2.

7. Peking radio, February 3, 1985, in FBIS, February 5, 1985, pp. K1–8, cited on pp. K6, K1.

8. Data in this paragraph are drawn from Xinhua News Agency, January 5, 1984, January 22, 1984, and January 23, 1984, ibid., January 5, 1984, p. K8, January 23, 1984, pp. K1–2, and January 25, 1984, pp. K21–24; *Liaowang*, no. 21 (May 21, 1984), ibid., June 18, 1984, pp. K7–10, cited on p. K8; Xinhua News Agency, October 17, 1984, and September 8,

1985, ibid., October 24, 1984, pp. K9–13, cited on pp. K9–10, and September 9, 1985, pp. K1–2.

9. Hua Guofeng, "Report on the Work of the Government," June 1979, *Beijing Review*, July 6, 1979, pp. 5–31, quotation on p. 24. The communiqué of the Third Plenum the previous December had also proposed the development of mechanisms for the "examination, reward and punishment, promotion and demotion" of cadres. See "Communiqué of the Third Plenary Session of the Eleventh Central Committee of the Communist Party of China," December 1978, *Peking Review*, December 29, 1978, pp. 6–16, quotation on p. 12.

10. For reports on some of these experiments, see Wuhan radio, November 15, 1986, in FBIS, November 17, 1986, p. P3; Xinhua News Agency, November 14, 1986, ibid., November 17, 1986, p. Q1; and *Renmin Ribao*, November 17, 1986, ibid., November 25, 1986, p. R1.

11. *Ta Kung Pao*, September 30, 1986, ibid., October 1, 1986, p. K2.

12. For discussions of the possibility of a civil service law and civil service examinations, see *Shijie Jingji Daobao*, February 11, 1985, ibid., March 5, 1985, pp. K1–4; *Renmin Ribao*, May 28, 1985, and June 14, 1985, ibid., June 4, 1985, pp. K7–9, and June 21, 1985, pp. K2–3.

13. Deng, "Streamlining Organizations," p. 376.

14. Statistics on vice-ministers, directors, and deputy directors are derived from Burns, "Reforming China's Bureaucracy," p. 713, table 11. The statistics on central Party staff are from Clarke, "Rejuvenation, Reorganization, and the Dilemmas of Modernization," p. 128. The statistics on central ministries and central government agencies are from You Chunmei, "Woguo dangqian xingzheng gaige de lilun he shijian" (The administrative reforms facing our country in theory and practice), *Xinhua Wenzhai*, no. 88 (April 1986), pp. 4–8, cited on p. 7. Statistics on provincial bureaucratic offices are from Xinhua News Agency, January 5, 1984, in FBIS, January 5, 1984, p. K8.

15. You, "Xingzheng gaige"; and *Hongqi*, no. 17 (September 1986), in FBIS, September 22, 1986, pp. K8–21, cited on p. K13.

16. Nina P. Halpern, "China's Industrial Economic Reforms: The Question of Strategy," *Asian Survey*, vol. 25 (October 1985), pp. 998–1012.

17. Thomas P. Bernstein, "Reforming China's Agriculture," paper presented to the conference, "To Reform the Chinese Political Order," sponsored by the Joint Committee on Chinese Studies of the American Council of Learned Societies and the Social Science Research Council, Harwichport, Mass., June 1984.

18. *Liaowang*, no. 23 (June 10, 1985), in FBIS, June 26, 1985, pp. K11–17, cited on p. K12.

19. *Liaowang*, no. 39 (September 30, 1985), ibid., October 21, 1985, pp. K9–14.

20. Nina Halpern, "Making Economic Policy: The Influence of Economists," in *China's Economy Looks toward the Year 2000*, vol. 1: *The Four Modernizations*, Committee Print, Joint Economic Committee, 99 Cong. 2 sess. (Government Printing Office, 1986), pp. 132–46. On

"policy consultation organizations" in the provinces, see Xinhua News Agency, November 22, 1986, ibid., November 26, 1986, p. K8.

21. Xinhua News Agency, August 14, 1986, ibid., August 19, 1986, pp. K22–33, cited on pp. K28, K25. For a defense of more traditional leadership methods, see Xiong Fu, "Discussing Methodology for the Study of the Science of Leadership— Preface to 'The Science of Leadership,'" *Hongqi*, no. 9 (May 1, 1986) in Joint Publications Research Service (JPRS), *China Report: Red Flag*, June 10, 1986, pp. 35–40.

22. See David M. Lampton, "Chinese Politics: The Bargaining Treadmill," paper presented to the Fifteenth Sino-American Conference on Mainland China, sponsored by the Institute of International Relations, Taipei, June 1986; and Kenneth Lieberthal and Michel Oksenberg, *Bureaucratic Politics and Chinese Energy Development* (Washington, D.C.: U.S. Department of Commerce, International Trade Administration, 1986), esp. chaps. 4 and 8.

23. See Paul H. B. Godwin, "The Chinese Defense Establishment in Transition: The Passing of a Revolutionary Army?" in A. Doak Barnett and Ralph N. Clough, eds., *Modernizing China: Post-Mao Reform and Development* (Westview Press, 1986), pp. 63–80; and Xinhua News Agency, December 21, 1986, in FBIS, December 22, 1986, p. K10.

24. See John Frankenstein, "Military Cuts in China," *Problems of Communism*, vol. 34 (July-August 1985), pp. 56–60.

25. On the changing role of the People's Liberation Army in Chinese civilian affairs, see Monte R. Bullard and Edward C. O'Dowd, "Defining the Role of the PLA in the Post-Mao Era," *Asian Survey*, vol. 26 (June 1986), pp. 706–20; Ellis Joffe, "Party and Military in China: Professionalism in Command?" *Problems of Communism*, vol. 32 (September-October 1983), pp. 48–63; Alastair I. Johnston, "Changing Party-Army Relations in China, 1979–1984," *Asian Survey*, vol. 24 (October 1984), pp. 1012–39; and Richard D. Nethercut, "Deng and the Gun: Party-Military Relations in the People's Republic of China," ibid., vol. 22 (August 1982), pp. 691–704.

26. For an elaboration of the argument in this paragraph, see Harry Harding, "The Role of the Military in Chinese Politics," in Victor Falkenheim, ed., *Citizens and Groups in Contemporary China*, Michigan Monographs in Chinese Studies, no. 56 (University of Michigan, Center for Chinese Studies, 1987), pp. 213–56.

27. For data on the recruitment of Communist Party members, see James R. Townsend and Brantly Womack, *Politics in China*, 3d ed. (Little, Brown and Company, 1986), pp. 282–300.

28. The official guidelines for the rectification campaign are in "The Decision of the Central Committee of the Communist Party of China on Party Consolidation," October 1983, *Beijing Review*, October 17, 1983, pp. I–XII. For analysis, see Lowell Dittmer, "Party Rectification in Post-Mao China," paper presented to the Thirteenth Sino-American Conference on Mainland China, sponsored by the Institute of International Relations, Taipei, June 1984; and Jeremy T. Paltiel, "The

Interaction of Party Rectification and Economic Reform in the CCP—
1984," paper presented to the annual meeting of the Association for
Asian Studies, Philadelphia, Pa., March 1985.

29. For the final report on the rectification campaign, issued by Bo Yibo,
see Xinhua News Agency, May 31, 1987, in FBIS, June 2, 1987, pp. K3–
18. Initially, it was estimated that only 40,000 people would be required
to resign from the Party in the course of the movement. See *Pai Hsing*
no. 97 (June 1, 1985), ibid., June 3, 1985, pp. W1–35. On the question
of quotas, see *Renmin Ribao*, January 3, 1984, in FBIS, January 10,
1984, pp. K2–4; and *Pai Hsing*, no. 97 (June 1, 1985), ibid., June 3, 1985,
cited on p. W21.

30. Xinhua News Agency, May 31, 1987, ibid., June 2, 1987, pp. K3–18.

31. Xinhua News Agency, December 13, 1983, and September 25, 1986,
ibid., December 19, 1983, pp. K7–8, and September 26, 1986, p. K14–
15, cited on p. K14.

32. The liberalization of post-Mao China has even made it possible for
some Chinese to pursue political careers outside the Party. Some
younger Chinese intellectuals interested in politics have chosen to join
the small "democratic parties." They explain that, even though they
understand that they will not be eligible for the highest political
positions, they will be eligible to participate in a wide range of political
activities, join the Chinese People's Political Consultative Conference
at either the national or provincial levels, and exercise some influence
in the consideration of national policies. At the same time, they will
not be subject to the internal discipline or have to cope with the
internal politics of the Chinese Communist Party.

33. Major discussions of the role of the Party include Liao Gailong, "The
'1980 Reform' Program"; and Xiong Fu, "A Probing Discussion of the
Party's Position and Role in National Life," *Hongqi*, no. 9 (May 1,
1981), in JPRS, *China Report: Red Flag*, July 1, 1981, pp. 1–12.

34. For a candid statement of the last argument, see *Shijie Jingji Daobao*,
September 5, 1986, in FBIS, October 3, 1986, pp. K5–7.

35. Xiong, "A Probing Discussion."

36. The appointment of Zhao Ziyang to serve concurrently as acting general
secretary and as prime minister in January 1987 was an important
violation of this general principle.

37. Xiong, "A Probing Discussion"; and Deng Xiaoping, "The Present
Situation," in *Selected Works*, pp. 224–58, quotation on p. 253.

38. Xinhua News Agency, January 22, 1985, in FBIS, January 24, 1985, pp.
K20–21.

39. Deng, "The Present Situation," p. 256. On the supervisory role of the
Party, see also Hu Yaobang, "Create a New Situation in All Fields of
Socialist Modernization," September 1982, in *The Twelfth National
Congress of the CPC, September 1982* (Peking: Foreign Languages Press,
1982), pp. 7–85, cited on pp. 70–71. On the resulting ambiguities in
the division of labor between Party secretaries and factory managers,
see Cao Zhi, "Improve and Strengthen the Party's Leadeship in Enter-

prises," *Hongqi,* no. 14 (July 16, 1985), in JPRS, *China Report: Red Flag,* September 11, 1985, pp. 21–29.

40. Jia Chunfeng and Teng Wensheng, "Women dang dui zhizhengdang jiahshe lilunde gongxian" (The contributions of our party to the theory of building the ruling party), *Hongqi,* no. 7 (April 1, 1983), pp. 14–18, 30. For a description of the present *nomenklatura* system, see Melanie Manion, "The Cadre Management System, Post-Mao: The Appointment, Promotion, Transfer, and Removal of Party and State Leaders," *China Quarterly,* no. 102 (June 1985), pp. 203–333.

41. Zhao Ziyang, "Report on the Seventh Five-Year Plan," March 1986, in *The Fourth Session of the Sixth National People's Congress, April 1986* (Peking: Foreign Languages Press, 1986), pp. 1–61, quotation on p. 48.

42. See Wu Suchi, "Fully Realize the Importance of Government Institutions Changing Their Management Functions and Improving Their Work Style," *Hongqi,* no. 13 (July 1986), in JPRS, *China Report: Red Flag,* August 21, 1986, pp. 71–77; and You, "Xingzheng gaige," pp. 4–8.

43. These proposals were intriguingly similar to earlier measures introduced at the height of the Great Leap Forward. At that time, however, the powers taken away from the central government ministries would have been transferred to the provinces, not assigned to the marketplace. See Harry Harding, *Organizing China: The Problem of Bureaucracy, 1949–1976* (Stanford University Press, 1981), p. 176.

44. *Shaanxi Ribao,* December 5, 1986, in FBIS, December 19, 1986, pp. T2–3, cited on p. T3.

45. Deng, "The Present Situation," pp. 250–51; Deng, "The Primary Task," p. 361; and "Speech by Chen Yun at the Congress," in *Twelfth National Congress,* pp. 135–39, quotation on p. 135.

46. For biographies of some of the important leaders in these two generations, see Shu-shin Wang, "Hu Yaobang: New Chairman of the Chinese Communist Party," *Asian Survey,* vol. 22 (September 1982), pp. 801–22; David L. Shambaugh, *The Making of a Premier: Zhao Ziyang's Provincial Career* (Westview Press, 1984); "Hu Ch'i-li—New Mayor of Tientsin," *Issues and Studies,* vol. 16 (August 1980), pp. 86–89; Li P'eng—Vice Premier of the State Council," ibid., vol. 21 (September 1985), pp. 158–63; Yü Yü-lin, "Ch'iao Shih's Appointment as a Vice Premier," ibid., vol. 22 (May 1986), pp. 1–3; and Christopher M. Clarke, "China's Third Generation: Today's Key Technocrats Are Being Groomed as Leaders of Tomorrow," *China Business Review,* vol. 11 (March-April 1984), pp. 36–38. For discussion and analysis of the concept of "generations" in the Chinese succession, see Ting Wang, "An Analysis of the P.R.C.'s Future Elite: The Third Echelon," *Journal of Northeast Asian Studies,* vol. 4 (Summer 1985), pp. 19–37.

47. On this "reserve force" of young cadres, see *Renmin Ribao,* March 23, 1984, in FBIS, April 4, 1984, pp. K5–10, cited on p. K6; *Hongqi,* no. 16 (August 16, 1983), ibid., September 16, 1983, pp. K2–10; *Liaowang,* no. 37 (September 10, 1984), ibid., October 4, 1984, pp. K18–22, cited on

pp. K18, 20–21; Xinhua News Agency, September 7, 1985, and February 10, 1985, ibid., September 9, 1985, p. K2, and February 11, 1985, pp. K1–7. For biographies of new members of the Politburo and Secretariat, including Wang Zhaoguo, see Xinhua News Agency, September 24, 1985, ibid., September 24, 1985, pp. K7–11.

48. The norms of Chinese politics are thoroughly and perceptively analyzed in Frederick C. Teiwes, *Leadership, Legitimacy, and Conflict in China: From a Charismatic Mao to the Politics of Succession* (M. E. Sharpe, 1984). The fullest official statement of the political norms of the post-Mao era is the Central Committee resolution, "Guiding Principles for Inner-Party Political Life," February 1980, *Beijing Review*, April 7, 1980, pp. 11–20.

49. For an early account of the decay of the succession arrangements, see *Cheng Ming*, no. 108 (October 1, 1986), in FBIS, October 10, 1986, pp. K1–5.

50. Deng, "The Primary Task," p. 361.

51. On the emergence of the "princes' faction," see *Cheng Ming*, no. 94 (August 1, 1985), in FBIS, August 6, 1985, pp. W1–5. For a response, insisting that the children of leading cadres represented only a fraction of newly appointed officials and members of the Central Committee, and that all of them were experienced and well qualified, see *Ming Pao*, December 30, 1985, ibid., December 31, 1985, pp. W1–2.

52. Xinhua News Agency, February 1, 1986, ibid., February 3, 1986, pp. K3–7; Zhongguo Xinwenshe, August 29, 1986, ibid., September 4, 1986, p. K17; *Cheng Ming*, no. 108 (October 1, 1986), ibid., October 10, 1986, pp. K1–5; and "Elders in Charge," *Asiaweek*, March 15, 1987, pp. 23–24.

53. See *Chiu-shih Nien-tai*, no. 195 (April 1, 1986), in FBIS, April 4, 1986, pp. W9–10; *Cheng Ming*, no. 102 (April 1, 1986), pp. 64–65, ibid., April 8, 1986, pp. W2–6; and *South China Morning Post*, July 14, 1986, ibid., July 16, 1986, pp. W8–10.

CHAPTER 9

1. General overviews of China's post-Mao foreign policy include Harry Harding, ed., *China's Foreign Relations in the 1980s* (Yale University Press, 1984); Samuel S. Kim, ed., *China and the World: Chinese Foreign Policy in the Post-Mao Era* (Westview Press, 1984); and Robert G. Sutter, *Chinese Foreign Policy: Developments after Mao* (Praeger, 1986).

2. *Wen Wei Po*, December 20, 1985, in Foreign Broadcast Information Service, *Daily Report: China*, December 20, 1985, pp. W1–2, cited on p. W1 (hereafter FBIS). On the importance of economics in contemporary Chinese foreign policy, see Allen S. Whiting, "China and the World: Independence vs. Dependence," forty-sixth George Ernest Morrison Lecture in Ethnology (Canberra: Australian National University, 1985).

3. Deng Xiaoping, "A New Approach towards Stabilizing the World

Situation," February 1984, in Deng Xiaoping, *Build Socialism with Chinese Characteristics* (Peking: Foreign Languages Press, 1985), pp. 23–24, quotation on p. 24.

4. Samuel S. Kim, "Chinese World Policy in Transition," *World Policy Journal* (Spring 1984), pp. 603–33; and Kim, "China and the Third World: In Search of a Neorealist Foreign Policy," in Kim, *China and the World*, pp. 178–211. A typically moderate analysis of China's position on demands for a "new international economic order" can be found in Zhang Shie, "Viewpoints on a New World Economic Order," *Beijing Review*, January 16, 1984, pp. 23–26.

5. The theory of the three worlds posited that international affairs was characterized by the resistance of the developing countries (the third world), supported at times by the developed nations of Europe and Japan (the second world), against the economic and political hegemonism of the United States and the Soviet Union (the first world). See "Third World Awakening and Growing Strong in United Struggle," *Peking Review*, March 22, 1974, pp. 6–8; Editorial Department of *Renmin Ribao*, "Chairman Mao's Theory of the Differentiation of the Three Worlds Is a Major Contribution to Marxism-Leninism," *Peking Review*, November 4, 1977, pp. 10–43; and "Resolution on Certain Questions in the History of Our Party since the Founding of the People's Republic of China," June 1981, in FBIS, July 1, 1981, pp. K1–38, cited on p. K19.

6. Zhao Ziyang, "Report on the Seventh Five-Year Plan," March 25, 1986, *Beijing Review*, April 21, 1986, pp. I–XX, quotation on pp. XVII, XVIII.

7. On nationalism in Chinese foreign policy since the death of Mao Zedong, see Allen S. Whiting, "Assertive Nationalism in Chinese Foreign Policy," *Asian Survey*, vol. 23 (August 1983), pp. 913–33; and Michel Oksenberg, "China's Confident Nationalism," *Foreign Affairs*, vol. 65 (1986), pp. 501–23.

8. Deng Xiaoping, "Safeguard World Peace and Ensure Domestic Development," May 1984, in *Build Socialism*, pp. 28–29, quotation on p. 28.

9. Deng Xiaoping, "Speech at the Third Plenary Session of the Central Advisory Commission of the Communist Party of China," October 1984, ibid., pp. 54–64, quotations on pp. 58 and 60. See also Deng's "We Should Follow Our Own Road Both in Revolution and in Economic Development," October 1984, ibid., pp. 65–66.

10. On the anti-Japanese protests of late 1985, see Agence France Presse, October 30, 1985, in FBIS, October 31, 1985, pp. D1–2; Daniel Southerland, "China Cracks Down on Students: Posters Criticizing Japan, Calling for Freedoms Removed from University," *Washington Post*, October 10, 1985; Kyodo, October 30, 1985, in FBIS, October 31, 1985, p. D1; John F. Burns, "China Fights Student Protest against 'Open Door,'" *New York Times*, November 27, 1985; and Mary Lee, "Winter of Discontent: Peking Tries Hard to Neutralize Student Protest," *Far Eastern Economic Review*, December 5, 1985, p. 16.

11. China's share of world trade is calculated from data in chap. 6, table 6–3 in this book; and International Monetary Fund, *International*

Financial Statistics, vol. 40 (February 1987), pp. 74, 75. China's share of World Bank loan commitments is based on World Bank, *Annual Report,* various years. Figures on China's net indebtedness and direct foreign investment in China are drawn from chap. 6, tables 6-7 and 6-8, in this book. The figures have been compared with the world totals in Organization for Economic Cooperation and Development and Bank for International Settlements, *Statistics on External Indebtedness: Bank and Trade-Related Non-Bank External Claims on Individual Borrowing Countries and Territories at End-June 1986* (Paris and Basle: OECD and BIS, 1987), pp. 9–12, table II.

12. Central Intelligence Agency, *China: International Trade* (Washington, D.C.: CIA, various years); and International Monetary Fund, *Directions of Trade* (Washington, D.C.: IMF, various years).

13. The data on energy exports are calculated from United Nations, *Energy Statistics Yearbook, 1982,* and *Energy Statistics Yearbook, 1983* (New York: United Nations, 1984 and 1985), table 14 in both volumes. Data on the other commodities are calculated from CIA, *China: International Trade,* various years; General Agreement on Tariffs and Trade, *International Trade* (Geneva: GATT, various years); and United Nations Conference on Trade and Development, *Yearbook of International Commodity Statistics, 1985* (New York: United Nations, 1985), p. 147, table 2.4.1.

14. On the competitive effect of Chinese exports for American industries, see Martin Weil, "The Textiles Deadlock: Negotiators Are Playing Beat the Clock in the Toughest Round of Talks to Date," *China Business Review,* vol. 9 (November- December 1982), pp. 31–35; Robert Delfs, "Rapid Growth to a Small Role: Promise of a Vast Market Is Only Partly Fulfilled after Earlier Euphoria Wanes," *Far Eastern Economic Review,* February 28, 1985, pp. 94–95; Andrew Heyden, "The Modern Ceramics Trade: Quality Problems Still Limit China's Exports to Low Value Markets," and J. M. Richards, "Protectionism and the ITC: China's Non-market Economy, Low Wages, and Lack of Cost Accounting Make It Particularly Vulnerable to Charges of Unfair Trade Practices," both in *China Business Review,* vol. 9 (September-October 1982), pp. 13–17 and 28–31; Phillip D. Fletcher, "The Issue of Imports: How U.S. Industry Spells Relief," and Jerome Turtola, "Textile Trade Tensions: Protectionist Threat Looms over Sino-U.S. Textile Trade," both ibid., vol. 13 (September-October 1986), pp. 22–25 and 26–30.

15. For the World Bank estimates, see World Bank, *China: Long-Term Development Issues and Options* (Johns Hopkins University Press, 1985), p. 107, table 6.6. There they were expressed in current dollars in the year 2000; they have been reconverted into 1985 dollars assuming, as does the World Bank, an average annual inflation rate of 5.6 percent. For the Rock Creek Research estimates, see Albert Keidel, Robert Bruce, Nicole Carter, and Rosemary Draper, *The Role of Technology Transfer for China's Economic Future,* prepared for the Office of Technology Assessment, U.S. Congress (Washington, D.C.: Rock Creek

Research, May 1986), chaps. 2 and 9. A U.S. government forecast, reported to me privately, concludes that China may enjoy a trade volume of $220 billion (in 1986 dollars) in the year 2000.

16. World Bank, *China: Long-Term Development Issues and Options*, p. 107, table 6.6. Again, the figures presented in that table have been recalculated into 1985 dollars assuming an average annual inflation rate of 5.6 percent.

17. This is based on the World Bank formula that a 15 percent ratio of debt service to exports is equivalent to a 75 percent ratio of net indebtedness to exports. This formula, in turn, is founded on the assumption of an average interest rate of 10 percent and an average repayment period of 10 years. See World Bank, *China: Long-Term Development Issues and Options*, p. 107, n. 10.

18. Vigor Fung, "Asian Nations Tackling China on Trade," *Asian Wall Street Journal*, May 16, 1986.

19. Discussions of the issues raised by China's application for full membership in the GATT can be found in Penelope Hartland-Thunberg, "China's Modernization: A Challenge for the GATT," *Washington Quarterly*, vol. 10 (Spring 1987), pp. 81–97; and Robert E. Herzstein, "China and the GATT: Legal and Policy Issues Raised by China's Participation in the General Agreement on Tariffs and Trade," *Law and Policy in International Business*, vol. 18, no. 2 (1986), pp. 371–415.

20. On China's relations with the two superpowers, see Carol Lee Hamrin, "Emergence of an 'Independent' Chinese Foreign Policy and Shifts in Sino-U.S. Relations," in James C. Hsiung, ed., *U.S.-Asian Relations: The National Security Paradox* (Praeger, 1983), pp. 63–84; Hamrin, "China Reassesses the Superpowers," *Pacific Affairs*, vol. 56 (Summer 1983), pp. 209–31; Edmund Lee (Huan Guocang), "Beijing's Balancing Act," *Foreign Policy*, no. 51 (Summer 1983), pp. 27–46; Thomas W. Robinson, "China's Dynamism in the Strategic Triangle," *Current History*, vol. 82 (September 1983), pp. 241–44, 276, 280–81; Jonathan D. Pollack, "China and the Global Strategic Balance," in Harding, *China's Foreign Relations in the 1980s*, pp. 146–76; Robert G. Sutter, "Realities of International Power and China's 'Independence' in Foreign Affairs, 1981–1984," *Journal of Northeast Asian Studies*, vol. 3 (Winter 1984), pp. 3–28; and Thomas W. Robinson, "The United States and China in the New Balance of Power," *Current History*, vol. 84 (September 1985), pp. 241–44 and 281.

21. Hu Yaobang, "Create a New Situation in All Fields of Socialist Modernization," September 1982, in *The Twelfth National Congress of the Communist Party of China, September 1982* (Peking: Foreign Languages Press, 1982), pp. 7–85, quotation on p. 55.

22. Although there are many studies of China's relations with particular countries in Asia, and with the principal subregions that compose modern Asia, there are few comprehensive overviews of Peking's policies toward the region as a whole. The best of those include Steven

I. Levine, "China in Asia: The PRC as a Regional Power," in Harding, *China's Foreign Relations in the 1980s*, pp. 107–45; Jonathan D. Pollack, "China's Changing Perceptions of East Asian Security and Development," *Orbis*, vol. 29 (Winter 1986), pp. 771–94; and Robert S. Ross, "China's Strategic Role in Asia," in James W. Morley, ed., *The Pacific Basin: New Challenges for the United States*, Proceedings of the Academy of Political Science, vol. 36 (New York: Academy of Political Science, 1986), pp. 116–28.

23. For military expenditures see *Stockholm International Peace Research Institute Yearbook, 1986* (Oxford: Oxford University Press, 1986), p. 231, app. 11A, table 1. For analysis of this cut in manpower, see John Frankenstein, "Military Cuts in China," *Problems of Communism*, vol. 34 (July-August 1985), pp. 56–60.

24. Agence France Presse, August 12, 1986, in FBIS, August 12, 1986, p. D1.

25. On Taiwan, see Hungdah Chiu, "Prospects for the Unification of China: An Analysis of the Views of the Republic of China on Taiwan," and John Quansheng Zhao, "An Analysis of Unification: The PRC Perspective," both in *Asian Survey*, vol. 23 (October 1983), pp. 1081–94 and 1095–1114; Guo-cang Huan, "The Future of Taiwan: A View from Beijing," and Yu-ming Shaw, "The Future of Taiwan: A View from Taipei," both in *Foreign Affairs*, vol. 63 (Summer 1985), pp. 1064–80 and 1050–63; and C. L. Chiou, "Dilemmas in China's Reunification Policy toward Taiwan," *Asian Survey*, vol. 26 (April 1986), pp. 467–82. On Hong Kong, see Frank Ching, *Hong Kong and China: For Better or for Worse* (New York: China Council of the Asia Society and the Foreign Policy Association, 1985); and Harry Harding, "The Future of Hong Kong: Making the Joint Declaration Work," *China Business Review*, vol. 12 (September-October 1985), pp. 30–37.

26. Deng described the reunification of China, along with socialist modernization and opposition to hegemonism, as one of the "three major tasks of our people in the 1980s." The following year, he said that the "reunification of the motherland" is the "most important issue" facing the country, and he depicted it as an "unfinished task left to us by our predecessors." See Deng, "Opening Speech at the Twelfth National Congress of the Communist Party of China," September 1982, in *Build Socialism*, pp. 1–5, quotation on p. 4; and "A Concept for the Peaceful Reunification of the Chinese Mainland and Taiwan," June 1983, ibid., pp. 18–20.

27. On the application of the "one country, two systems" formula to Taiwan, see Deng, "Concept for the Peaceful Reunification," pp. 18–20. For details of the Hong Kong agreement see *Sino-British Joint Declaration on the Question of Hong Kong* (Peking: Foreign Languages Press, 1984).

28. For general overviews of Sino-American relations and the policy options confronting the United States on major issues, see A. Doak Barnett, *China Policy* (Brookings, 1977); U. Alexis Johnson, George R. Packard,

and Alfred D. Wilhelm, Jr., eds., *China Policy for the Next Decade* (Oelgeschlager, Gunn and Hain, 1984); and Steven I. Levine, "China and the United States: The Limits of Interaction," in Kim, *China and the World*, pp. 113–34.

29. There have been several dramatic cases of scholars and reporters who were thrown out of China for alleged misconduct. The most well-known scholar is Stanford graduate student Steven Mosher, who was expelled from Stanford's doctoral program in 1983 because of controversial actions he took while conducting fieldwork in southern China. Several foreign journalists have also incurred the wrath of the Chinese authorities, most notably New York Times Peking bureau chief John Burns, who was expelled from China in July 1986; and Lawrence MacDonald, a U.S. citizen working for Agence France Presse who was expelled in January 1987.

CHAPTER 10

1. On the Soviet disease, see Gertrude E. Schroeder, "The Soviet Economy on a Treadmill of 'Reforms,' " in *The Soviet Economy in a Time of Change*, Committee Print, Joint Economic Committee, 96 Cong. 1 sess. (Government Printing Office, 1979), pp. 312–40. On the Hungarian disease, and the retreat from reform in Eastern Europe, see Morris Bornstein, "Economic Reform in Eastern Europe," in *East European Economies Post-Helsinki*, Committee Print, Joint Economic Committee, 95 Cong. 1 sess. (GPO, 1977), pp. 102–34; and Wlodzimierz Brus, "The East European Reforms: What Happened to Them?" *Soviet Studies*, vol. 31 (April 1979), pp. 257–67.

2. These data for the 1980s are based on table 5-1 in chap. 5 in this book.

3. Data on labor productivity in agriculture are calculated from data on agricultural output and the rural labor force in Guojia Tongjiju (State Statistical Bureau), *Zhongguo tongji zhaiyao, 1987* (Chinese statistical abstract, 1987) (Peking: Chinese Statistical Publishing House, 1987), pp. 17, 24, and 37. For figures on labor productivity in industry see ibid., p. 62.

4. *Zhongguo tongji zhaiyao, 1987*, pp. 100, 105, 98, and 99. By 1986, nearly 60 percent of urban families owned washing machines, 93 percent owned a television set, 50 percent owned tape recorders, and 13 percent owned a refrigerator. In the countryside, more than 90 percent of all families owned bicycles, more than 50 percent owned radios, and more than 40 percent owned a sewing machine. Ibid., *1987*, pp. 104 and 107. The increase in industrial output in 1984–85, however, did produce a slight widening of the urban-rural gap. The ratio of peasant consumption to non-peasant consumption reached its narrowest point in 1984, at 2.2:1, and widened somewhat to 2.46:1 in 1986. Ibid., p. 98.

5. Data on trade and the absorption of foreign capital are from tables 6-1

and 6-8, chap. 6 in this book. Foreign capital was then converted into renminbi at the rate of Y2.94 to US$1.00, given in Rock Creek Research, *1986 China Statistical Handbook* (Washington, D.C.: Rock Creek Research, 1986), p. 22, and compared with the levels of state expenditures on capital construction and government revenues given ibid., pp. 13 and 4. The comparable ratios for the 1950s can be found in Robert F. Dernberger, "Mainland China's Development Strategy: Investment Financing Needs and Sources," *Issues and Studies,* vol. 22 (December 1986), pp. 74–103, cited on pp. 81, 78.

6. Each yuan in fixed assets in state-owned industry produced 1.13 yuan of output in 1985, compared with 1.08 yuan in 1984, 1.06 yuan in 1983, 1.14 yuan in 1978, 1.31 yuan in 1965, and 1.33 yuan in 1952. These figures are calculated from the data in *Zhongguo tongji zhaiyao, 1986,* pp. 12 and 49. For a more optimistic assessment, based on a comparison of increases in national output to new investment in productive projects, see *Rock Creek Research China Economic Letter,* vol. 3 (March 23, 1987), pp. 41–42.

7. *Zhongguo tongji zhaiyao, 1986,* p. 62.

8. The level of subsidy in 1981 can be found in Luc De Wulf and David Goldsborough, "The Evolving Role of Monetary Policy in China," *International Monetary Fund Staff Papers,* vol. 33 (June 1986), pp. 209–42. For the 1986 subsidy see *Rock Creek Research China Economic Letter,* vol. 3 (April 6, 1987), p. 51.

9. For rates of investment, see *Zhongguo tongji zhaiyao, 1987,* p. 7. For the share of state investment channeled into energy and transportation, see ibid., p. 66. On the size of the service sector in China in 1981, and for its share of GNP in other low-income countries, see World Bank, *China: Long-Term Development Issues and Options* (Johns Hopkins University Press, 1985), p. 23. The share of GNP accounted for by services in 1985, and the share projected for 1990, are calculated from data in "The Seventh Five-Year Plan of the People's Republic of China for Economic and Social Development, 1986–1990," in *The Fourth Session of the Sixth National People's Congress, April 1986* (Peking: Foreign Languages Press, 1986), pp. 63–141, cited on p. 73.

10. On calls for restraints on consumption see, for example, Xinhua News Agency, February 14, 1987, in FBIS, February 19, 1987, pp. K18–19; and *Renmin Ribao,* February 12, 1987, ibid., February 19, 1987, pp. K27–29.

11. Chinese economists usually argue that an overall rate of inflation of about 2 percent to 3 percent is tolerable from both a political and an economic perspective. See *Guangming Ribao,* January 31, 1987, in FBIS, February 19, 1987, pp. K19– 20, cited on p. K19.

12. On the expansion of the rural-urban gap, see World Bank, *China: Issues and Options,* p. 19. On interregional inequality, see H. Kevin Mc-Neelege, "China's Emerging Spatial Strategy," paper presented to the Conference on the Role of Transnational Corporations in the World Economy, sponsored by Nankai University, Tianjin, October 1986.

13. For a brief but pointed condemnation of the "fetish of materialism," "premature consumerism," "cultural decadence," and "commercialized and sensualized arts" that allegedly characterize post-Mao China, see Duan Liancheng, *Sunshine and Shadows—A Veteran Journalist's Reflections on China in Transition* (Peking: Beijing Review Publications, 1986), pp. 22–24. A similar view has been expressed by at least one American observer. See Orville Schell, *To Get Rich Is Glorious: China in the 80's* (Pantheon Books, 1984).
14. *Zhongguo Qingnian Bao*, July 15, 1986, in FBIS, July 25, 1986, pp. H1–3.
15. This discussion of bureaucratic attitudes toward reform draws on Susan L. Shirk, *The Politics of Chinese Industrial Reform*, Research Papers in Political Science, no. 1 (University of California at San Diego, Department of Political Science, 1987); and on two unpublished papers by David M. Bachman of Princeton University: "State Structure and Recurring Patterns of Change in China" (November 1982) and "Leaps and Retreats in the Chinese Political Economy" (February 1984).
16. On the generational differences in the intellectual community, the seminal work is Li Zehou and Vera Schwarcz, "Six Generations of Modern Chinese Intellectuals," *Chinese Studies in History*, vol. 17 (Winter 1983–84), pp. 42–56. For a broader generational analysis of Chinese politics, see Michael Yahuda, "Political Generations in China," *China Quarterly*, no. 80 (December 1979), pp. 793–805.